Welcome to iPad for Beginners

Four years after the very first iPad was released, they have become part of our everyday lives. You would therefore be forgiven for forgetting what a masterful invention it is and the power it has to transform and enhance how we live, work and play. If you have just purchased your first iPad, prepare for it to be part of your every activity as a personal assistant and entertainment centre combined. This newly revised edition of iPad for Beginners will get you started and help you realise the potential of your gadget, afforded by their versatility, portability and functionality. You can create documents and spreadsheets, send emails, take and share photographs, edit movies, download media and so much more – all from one lightweight, handheld device. Let this comprehensive guide get you rolling and you will soon wonder what you did without it!

iPad for Beginners

Imagine Publishing Ltd
Richmond House
33 Richmond Hill
Bournemouth
Dorset BH2 6EZ
☎ +44 (0) 1202 586200
Website: www.imagine-publishing.co.uk
Twitter: @Books_Imagine
Facebook: www.facebook.com/ImagineBookazines

Publishing Director
Aaron Asadi

Head of Design
Ross Andrews

Production Editor
Jen Neal

Senior Art Editor
Greg Whitaker

Assistant Designer
Alexander Phoenix

Photographer
James Sheppard

Printed by
William Gibbons, 26 Planetary Road, Willenhall, West Midlands, WV13 3XT

Distributed in the UK, Eire & the Rest of the World by
Marketforce, Blue Fin Building, 110 Southwark Street, London, SE1 0SU
Tel 0203 148 3300, www.marketforce.co.uk

Distributed in Australia by
Network Services (a division of Bauer Media Group), Level 21 Civic Tower, 66-68 Goulburn Street, Sydney, New South Wales 2000, Australia, Tel +61 2 8667 5288

Part of the
iCreate™
bookazine series

IMAGINE
PUBLISHING

Contents

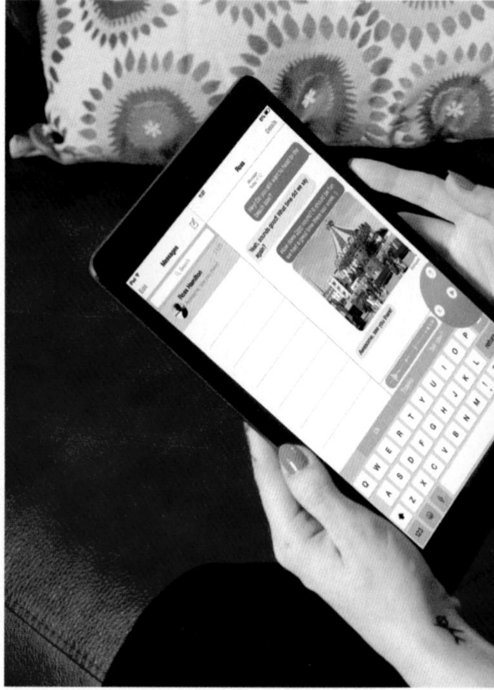

Essential guide

Setting up

Getting started

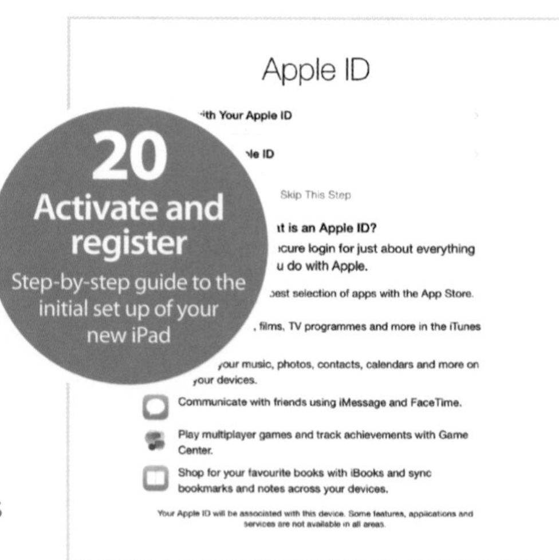

The next step

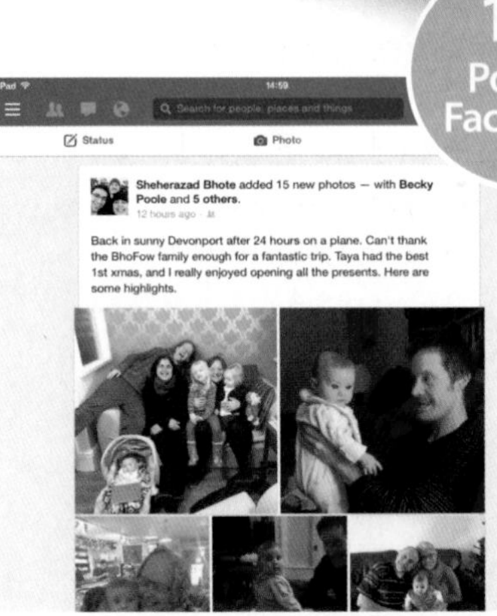

Essential apps

Glossary

The iPad essential guide

Everything you need to know to navigate and use your tablet like a pro

Now that you have finally got your hands on a new iPad you'll no doubt be highly curious about how to use it. In truth though, it couldn't be simpler. The operating system (iOS) is simple and intuitive to use and all of the key apps come pre-installed and will be visible as app icons on your Home screen. Before you get to experience those things though you will need to go through an initial set-up process when firing up your device for the first time. This takes the form of several steps that explain the features that need to be set-up and guide you through the process of activating them. The first step is creating an Apple ID (or signing in if you have an Apple ID already). This is linked to all aspects of your iPad, from buying apps and items from the iTunes Store to utilising Apple's excellent iCloud service and all that is required is a valid email address and a secure password.

A lot of the services and features on your iPad that are set up during this process are optional and can be tweaked later if you prefer, or when you discover what suits you best. For such matters the Settings app is your best friend because all of the different facets of your iPad are presented in a simple list – just tap on a category and begin exploring the many options associated with it.

Once you are set up, take time to explore the many core apps that come pre-installed on your device, such as Safari (for web browsing), Mail (for checking your emails), Calendar (your personal organiser) and Maps (for exploring the world). Before too long you'll probably be chomping at the bit to download other apps and games, in which case you need to launch the App Store app from your Home screen. This online store is brimming with apps of all descriptions, some of which require payment (this is linked to your Apple ID) and others, which are totally free – such as Facebook and Twitter. Both of these services are integrated in iOS, so once you download and log into the services through the Settings app you will be able to update your status or tweet while in any of the core apps.

> "Take time to explore the core apps that come pre-installed on your device"

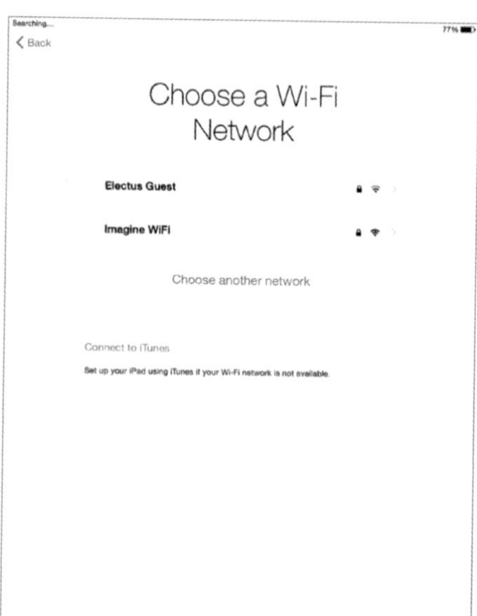

Fig: To get started, connect to a Wi-Fi network and start shopping for new apps and content

Explore the iPad's hardware

Learn how to find your way around your device

Power button
This button on the side of your device can be tapped to put your device to sleep or a long-press will power the phone down completely

Wi-Fi icon
If you are connected to a Wi-Fi network then the signal strength will be displayed by this icon

Volume buttons
The volume buttons on the side of your device are used to control sound output and you can also assign functionality to the Camera app

Apps
The main home screen displays most of the pre-installed apps in a grid system. Tap on an app to launch it

Battery icon
This icon shows the current battery level of your device. Go to Settings>General>Usage to view it as a percentage figure

Camera
Your iPad comes with a front and rear-facing camera. Look here and say 'cheese' to your perfect selfie!

Dock connecter
The port on the bottom of your iPad is used by the lightning cable to connect your device to a power source or computer

Home button
Pressing this button can wake your device up and close apps to return to the main Home screen

First steps

Take the time to learn the basics of your iPad which we highlight here

Turn on/off

How to power-up your device or shut it down completely using the power button

01 To turn on your iPad, hold down the power button at the right until the logo is displayed.

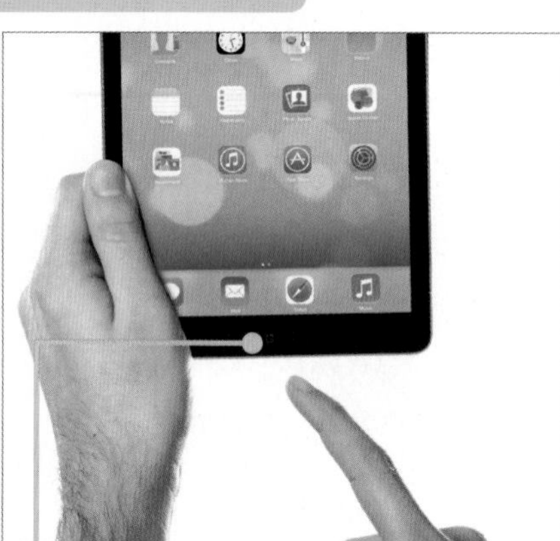

02 If your iPad is in sleep mode, press the power button to wake it up or press the Home button.

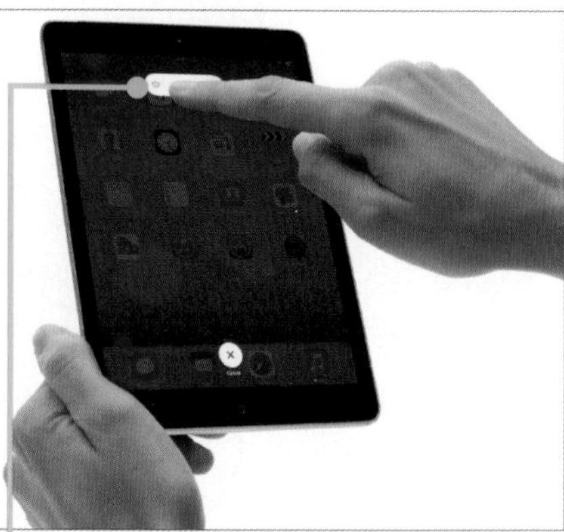

03 To turn your iPad off, hold the power button until the screen dims and move the slider right.

Sleep mode

Conserve your iPad's battery power when the device is not in use

Go to Settings>General and then tap Auto-Lock to set how soon your iPad will automatically lock and go to sleep when idle.

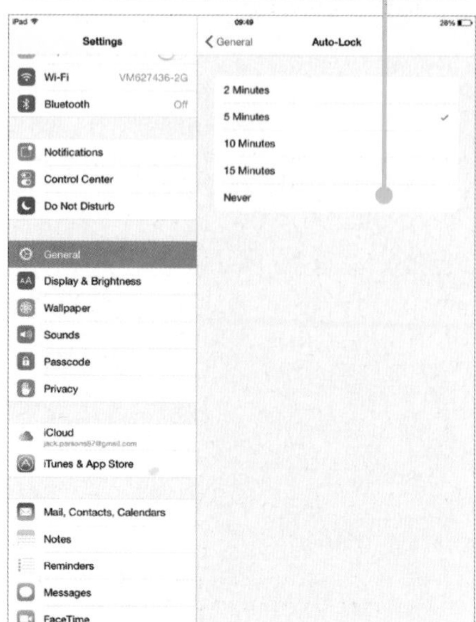

Unlock

Determine how your iPad is unlocked ready for use

Go to Settings>Passcode and turn Passcode on. Set a simple passcode or disable the 'Simple Passcode' feature to use something more complex.

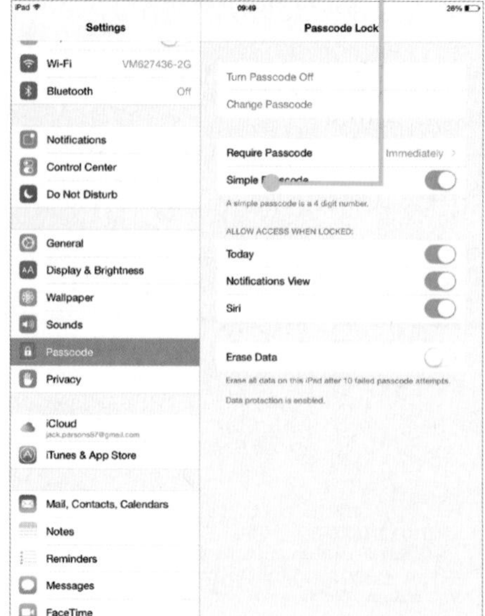

Charging

All you need to know about powering-up your iPad

To charge your iPad, use the lightning cable to connect to a plug socket or computer and it will be indicated by the icon next to the battery.

Change volume

Discover how to adjust the sound output of your iPad for all kinds of purposes

01 On your home screen, use the volume buttons on the side of the iPad to adjust the ringer volume. Do the same in an app to adjust the volume.

02 You can also swipe up from the bottom of the screen while in any app to access the Control Centre and you will see the volume option there also.

Rotation lock

Learn how to lock your iPhone's screen orientation to keep it in landscape or portrait mode

01 Position your device in the orientation you wish to lock it in and then swipe up from the bottom of the screen to access your Control Centre.

02 Now tap the top-right icon (with the padlock on) to lock the current orientation. Repeat the process to unlock it again.

Brightness

Learn how to adjust the brightness of your iPad screen to suit any conditions

01 Adjusting screen brightness can be done by going to the Settings app and tapping on Display & Brightness or swiping up to access Control Centre.

Apps

How to organise your apps neatly on your home screen

01 Apps can be moved by pressing and holding on the icons until they all shake and then dragging them into new positions.

Mute

Learn how to cut all sound on your device instantly

To mute the ringer instantly, flick the switch above the volume buttons on your iPad. Repeat to unmute.

Syncing

iCloud ensures all of your info and files stay up to date

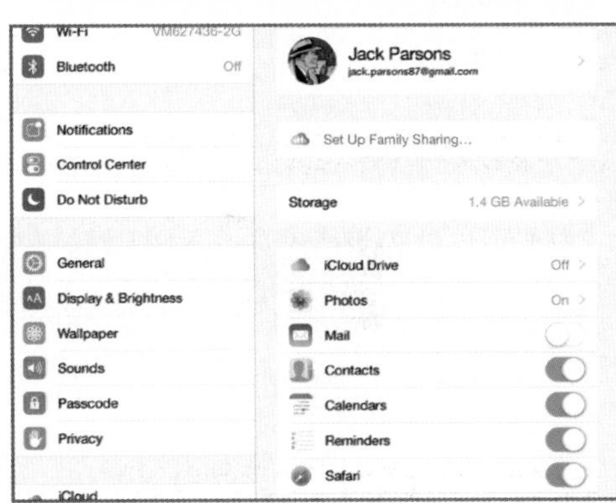

Sign in using your Apple ID and then move the sliders to enable the service for various apps.

Folders

Folders are a great way to help keep apps organised

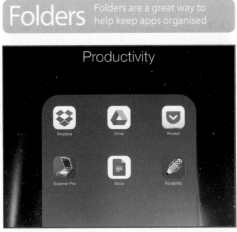

Press and hold on an app icon until they all shake and then drag an icon on top of another icon to create a folder.

Safari

Safari is your iPad's default web browsing app and it comes packed with features to make web trawling an intuitive experience. The URL field at the top of the interface doubles up as a search field (just type in keywords to perform searches) and the list icon to the left of the field initiates Reader mode, which presents web pages in a stripped-down, easier to read format. The icons at the top of the interface allow you to share web content and view your open tabs, but it is the book icon that is most intriguing as this provides access to your bookmarks, items added to your Reading List (for offline reading) and links that have been shared with people whom you follow on Twitter. By tapping on the tabs icon you can view and close open tabs, open a private tab and scroll down to see web pages open on other iOS and Mac OS X devices that you can access

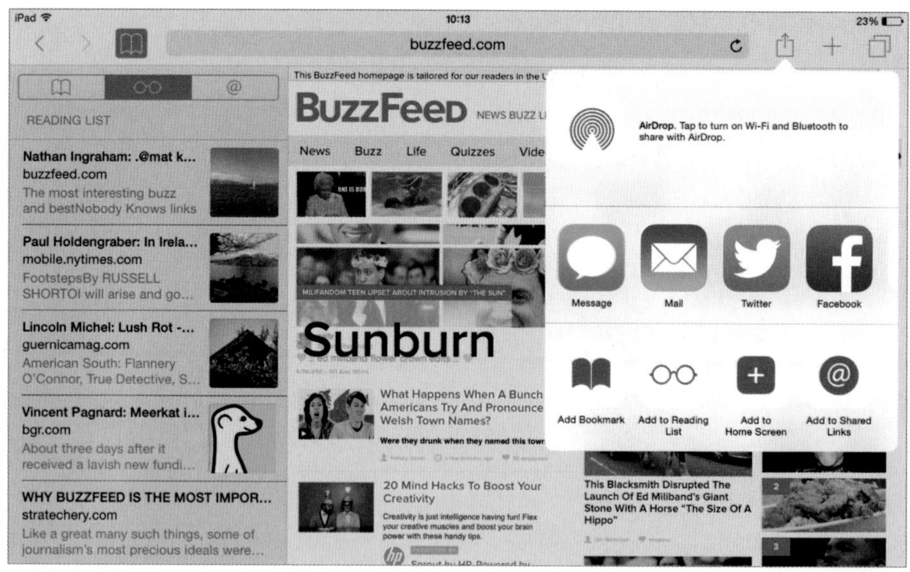

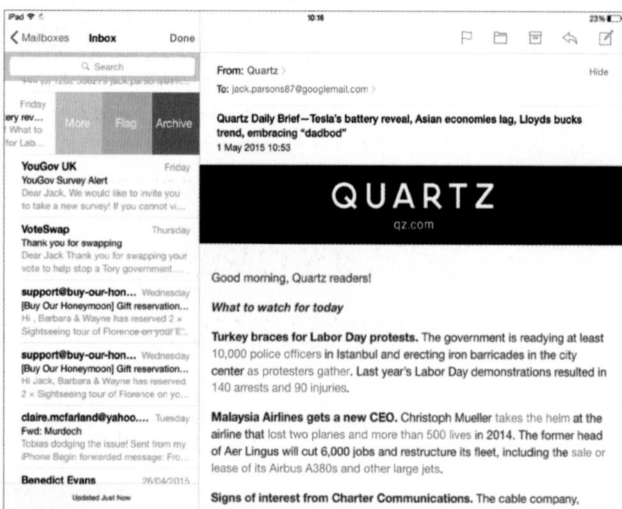

Mail

For all of your emailing needs, the Mail app is your iPad's default email app and is feature-rich for all of your email management needs. When launching the Mail app for the first time you will need to go through an initial set-up process – but this involves little more than entering a valid email address and password. Once done, you can start sending emails almost instantly by tapping on the pen and paper icon in the top-right corner of the interface. Simply enter the recipient(s), add a subject and then enter your body text. If you wish to send media attachments then you can do this by tapping the share icon while in other apps (such as Photos) and then choosing the email option. All of your emails can be organised into neat little folders to make viewing and managing them easier and you can also mark people as VIPs so that their mails go into a special priority inbox. While in your mailbox, swipe left on an email to see options to Flag, Archive and more.

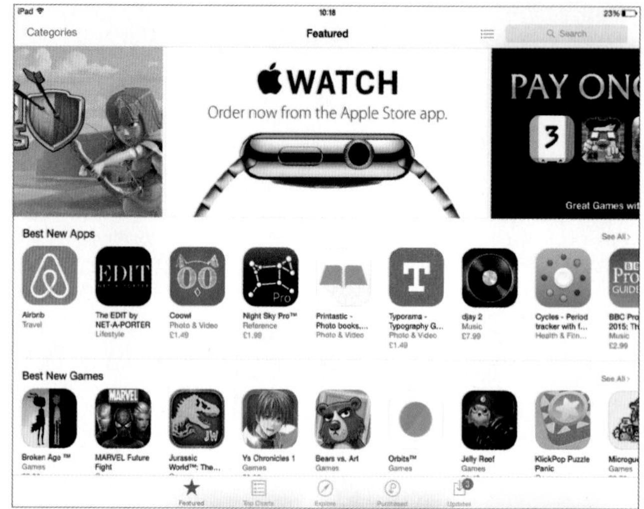

App Store

The App Store is your first port of call for purchasing and downloading new apps. When you launch the app for the first time you will be dumped on the Featured page, which flags up the newest and most exciting apps as well as providing options to redeem iTunes vouchers, send apps as gifts to other people and sign in or out of your Apple ID. To start exploring in more detail, there are icons at the bottom of the interface for Top Charts, Explore, Search and Updates. Top Charts lets you view the current best sellers. Tapping on 'Categories' in the top-left corner also lets you view apps by category, such as Games, Music and Entertainment. The Explore option is a relatively new feature that lets you see which apps are popular in your current area and Search lets you enter keywords to find specific apps. The Updates section lists all possible updates for the apps that you own (that you can download for free) and you can also view apps you have purchased in the past and re-download them to your current device.

Tuesday

10 Calendar

Stay organised in your professional and personal life

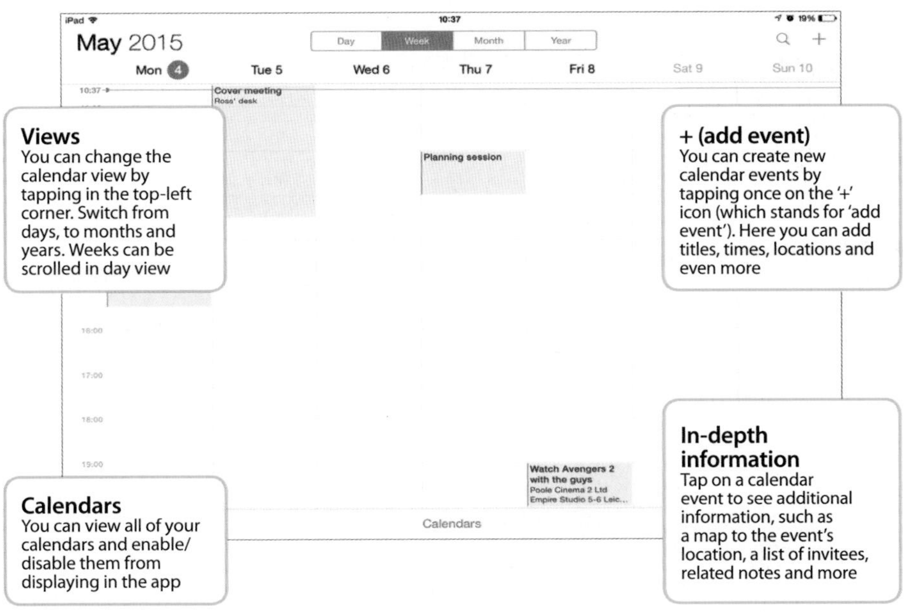

May 2015
Day Week Month Year
Mon 4 Tue 5 Wed 6 Thu 7 Fri 8 Sat 9 Sun 10
Cover meeting
Ross' desk
Planning session
Watch Avengers 2 with the guys
Calendars
Views
You can change the calendar view by tapping in the top-left corner. Switch from days, to months and years. Weeks can be scrolled in day view
+ (add event)
You can create new calendar events by tapping once on the '+' icon (which stands for 'add event'). Here you can add titles, times, locations and even more
Calendars
You can view all of your calendars and enable/ disable them from displaying in the app
In-depth information
Tap on a calendar event to see additional information, such as a map to the event's location, a list of invitees, related notes and more

Reminders

Get acquainted with the app that never lets you forget…

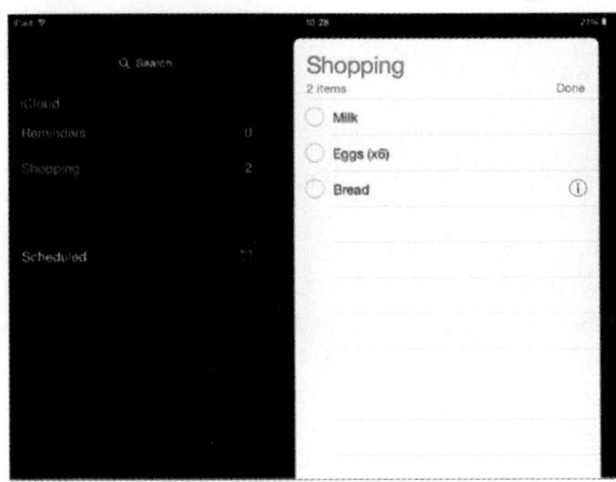

01 You can create a new list by tapping on 'Add List' in the bottom-left of the screeb. Give your new list a name to make it easy to track and then colour-code it for further easy reference. Tap 'Done' when finished.

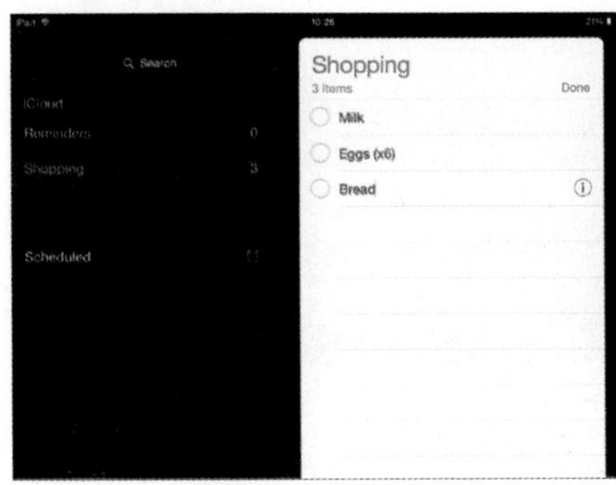

02 Tap on a line in a list to add a new reminder item. Tap the small 'i' icon next to an entry to add more details, so as a time to be reminded and a location that triggers a reminder when you are in range.

Read a book on your iPad

iBooks

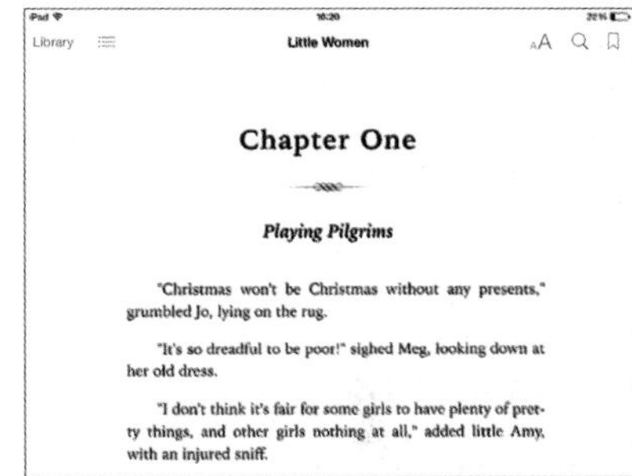
Little Women

Chapter One

Playing Pilgrims

"Christmas won't be Christmas without any presents," grumbled Jo, lying on the rug.

"It's so dreadful to be poor!" sighed Meg, looking down at her old dress.

"I don't think it's fair for some girls to have plenty of pretty things, and other girls nothing at all," added little Amy, with an injured sniff.

The brilliant iBooks app now comes pre-installed on your device. From within this app you can use the Featured, Top Charts and Search icons at the bottom of the interface to browse the store for fresh content and see all of your books displayed on shelves. Tap to open it and see a range of options to tailor the experience and add notes and bookmarks.

Get mags delivered

Newsstand

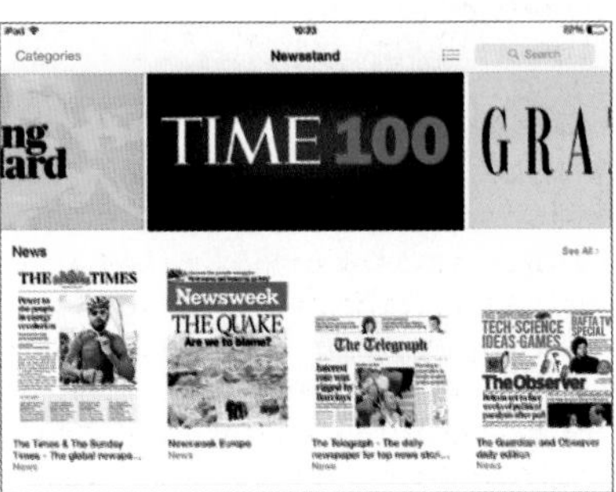

Like iBooks, Newsstand allows you to read on your iPad, but the key difference being that the reading material consists of newspapers and magazines. Most print publications are going digital now and you can subscribe to mags and dailies in the store and get new issues delivered without having to lift a finger.

Maps

Explore the world with your iPad's built-in navigation system

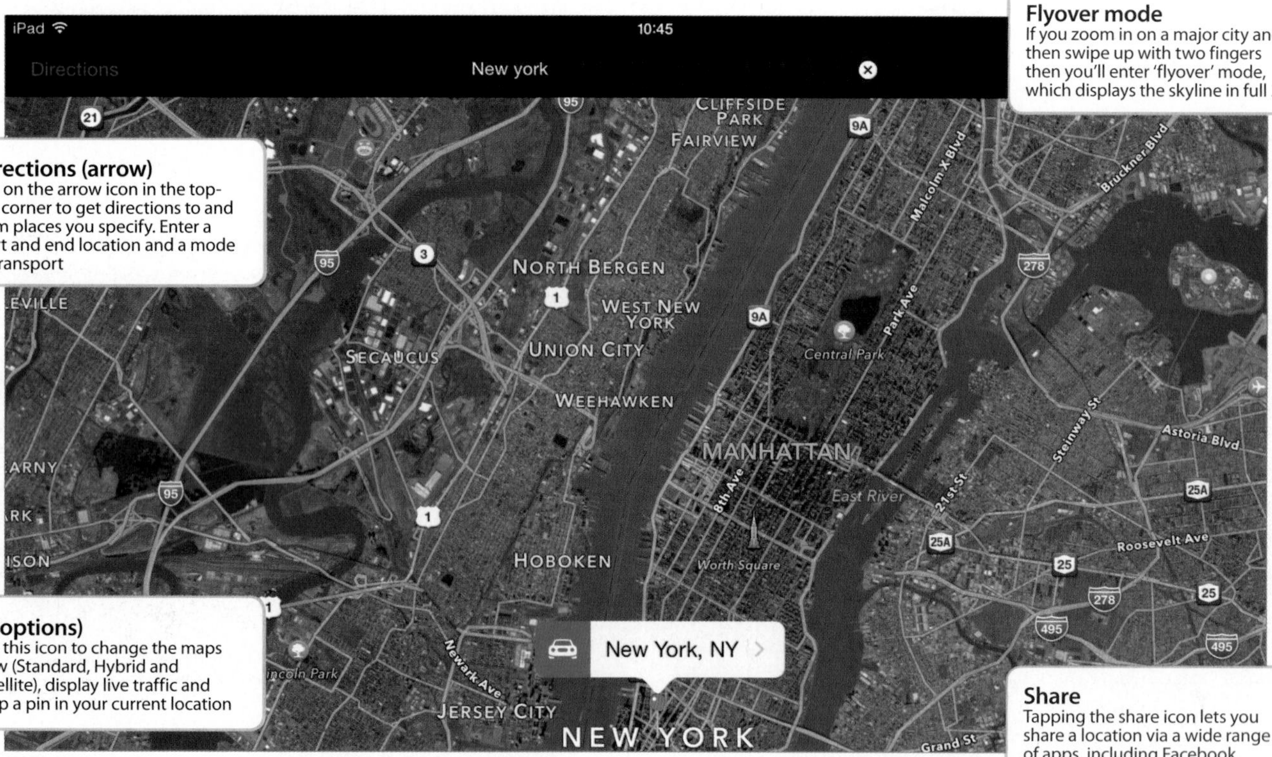

Flyover mode
If you zoom in on a major city and then swipe up with two fingers then you'll enter 'flyover' mode, which displays the skyline in full 3D

Directions (arrow)
Tap on the arrow icon in the top-left corner to get directions to and from places you specify. Enter a start and end location and a mode of transport

'i' (options)
Tap this icon to change the maps view (Standard, Hybrid and Satellite), display live traffic and drop a pin in your current location

Share
Tapping the share icon lets you share a location via a wide range of apps, including Facebook and Twitter. You can also add to favourites here

Camera & Photos

Your iPad's Camera and Photos apps have been intrinsically linked to make capturing and editing images as simple as possible. The Camera app features a dynamic set of shooting modes and live filters (as well as new features such as a shutter delay timer) and the Photos app groups your captured images together into time frames and locations. You can also perform a surprisingly versatile sequence of edits and share them with friends and family. You can jump straight to your iPad's Photos app from within the Camera app by tapping on the thumbnail of the last image you took and the Camera app itself can be launched via your Home screen, Control Centre or by swiping up on the camera icon on the Lock screen to ensure that you never miss a moment.

01 While in your iPad's Camera app, swipe through the various modes displayed just above the shutter button. You can also apply live filter effects to your photos by tapping on the filter icon in the lower-right corner. There is a whole range of filters and effects to choose from. You will also discover the options to enable or disable the iPad's flash, enable HDR (high dynamic range) mode and set a timer at the top.

02 The Photos app on your iPad lets you view your captured images, share them with other people, mark them as favourites, delete them or perform some incredible edits. Tapping on the Edit option provides options to crop your image, change the filter, adjust the colour levels and more. You can also auto-enhance the images to save you time. Once you have applied your edits, just tap Done.

Facebook & Twitter

The Facebook and Twitter services have been integrated into your iPad's operating system so that you can update your status and compose tweets from within all of Apple's other pre-installed apps. To get started though you must still download the free apps from the App Store and then launch your Settings app. Tap on the Facebook and Twitter settings options respectively and then ensure that you are logged into your accounts. Once done, you'll be able to tap the share icon from within other apps such as Photos and Maps and then share content from your current app through the now-integrated social networks. You can, of course, still launch the Facebook and Twitter apps from your Home screen and enjoy all of the features that they provide. As previously mentioned, Twitter is also cleverly integrated into the Safari app – just tap on the book icon followed by the '@' tab and all of the links that the people you follow share in Twitter will be listed for you to tap on.

"Download the free apps from the App Store"

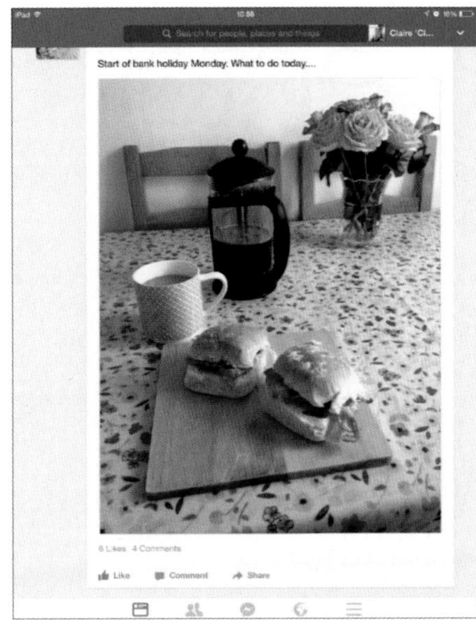

01 The Facebook is app integrated into the operating system to make it easier for you to share content. Through the app you can post content, stay up to date in your social loops and more. There are also apps for Facebook Groups and Messenger. Messenger lets you send unlimited messages to friends.

02 The Twitter app's integration with your iPad makes it easy to tweet from whatever app you're in. The app makes staying on top of your social life a breeze. You can scroll through your timeline to see what the folk you follow are tweeting and then reply, retweet or mark a tweet as a favourite via the icons underneath each one.

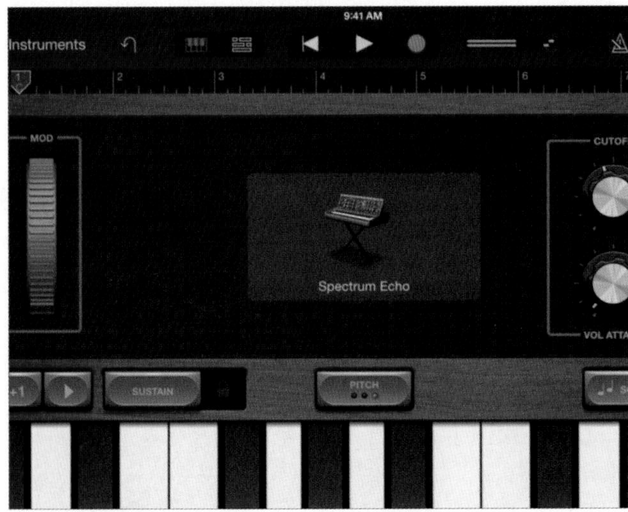

iLife

iLife refers to a collection of apps designed to help you embrace life and the creative possibilities it presents. It includes iMovie and GarageBand – free to download from the App Store. To transform videos captured through the Camera app into professionally-edited blockbusters then iMovie provides all of the tools, including themes and effects. GarageBand is an all-in-one music making and recording app. With the right connectors you can plug your instruments into your phone to lay down a track or there is a wide range of 'Smart' instruments included to play on screen.

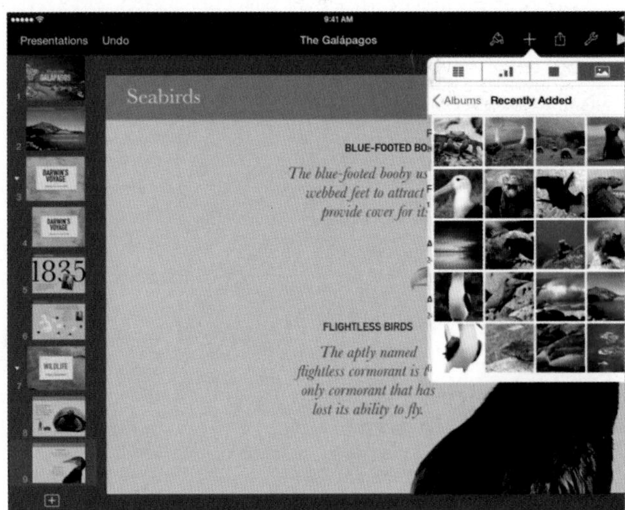

iWork

iWork is also a collective term for a series of apps. These apps include Pages, Numbers and Keynote, which focus on documents, spreadsheets and presentations. In Pages you can create professional-looking documents, posters and leaflets, whereas Numbers lets you apply all kinds of formulas to your charts to make your figures tally up. Everything you create can be presented through Keynote, or you can use this app to construct eye-catching presentations. All of these apps are free to download from the App Store and everything is synced between devices via iCloud.

Game Center

Discover the many features that your iPad gaming portal has to offer

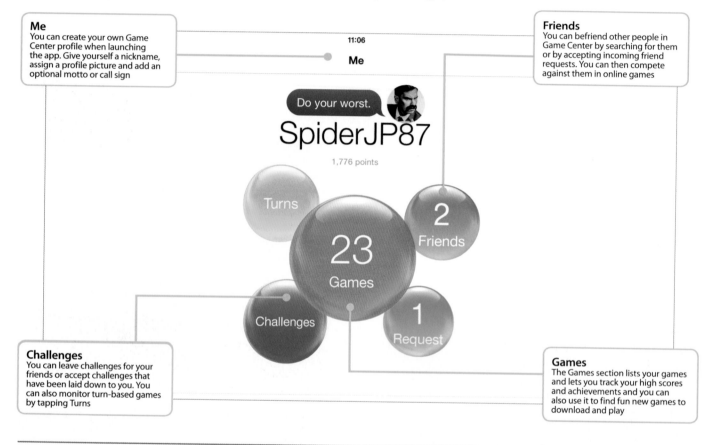

Me
You can create your own Game Center profile when launching the app. Give yourself a nickname, assign a profile picture and add an optional motto or call sign

Friends
You can befriend other people in Game Center by searching for them or by accepting incoming friend requests. You can then compete against them in online games

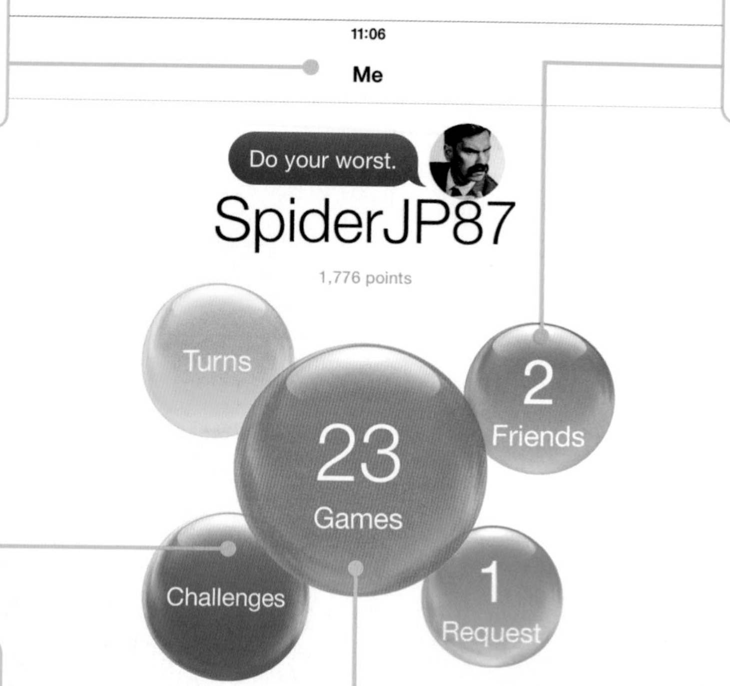

Challenges
You can leave challenges for your friends or accept challenges that have been laid down to you. You can also monitor turn-based games by tapping Turns

Games
The Games section lists your games and lets you track your high scores and achievements and you can also use it to find fun new games to download and play

iTunes & Music

The iTunes store, accessible from its own app on your iPad's home screen, is a sprawling online shop for music and visual entertainment. You can buy or rent movies or TV shows to view in your Videos app or shop and download tracks or albums to listen to in your Music app. New content is well flagged up and the comprehensive search engine means that you're never far away from what you want to watch or listen to. Any music you buy will be automatically downloaded to your Music app and here you will be able to create playlists. All of your purchased music is also synced to iCloud Drive. This means that if you put your iPad down and switch to your iPhone, you can open the iTunes app and tap the cloud icon to re-download it onto your current device.

01 The iTunes app is where you go to shop for new music, movies and TV shows to download and enjoy on your iPad (or any other iDevice you may own, such as an iPad). iTunes is a constantly changing environment as new content arrives on the iTunes store to purchase all the time. Use the icons at the bottom of the app interface to jump to the various sections and begin browsing content.

02 All of the music that you purchase and download through the iTunes app will be made playable through your iPad's Music app. Tap to open up the Music app and view your downloaded music. Then just tap on individual tracks to begin playing them. You can create your own original playlists to suit any occasion or mood. Genius Mixes are preselected compilations of songs from your music library.

Accessories

You can also connect other devices to your iPad, such as keyboards and speakers. Here we explore some of the possibilities

Stylus
Controlling objects with your fingers undoubtedly feels more natural, but a stylus can be great for adding precision to your work. A few companies have created such devices that work very well with the iPad's capacitive screen

QDOS case
Your iPad is an expensive bit of kit so you will no doubt want to take good care of it to ensure that your investment lasts. Cases like this QDOS Libris one is perfect for protecting your iPad as not only does it protect against scratches, it also adds functionality as it can be folded into a stand

Protective film
Even if you prefer your iPad to be without a case, you should consider a film to protect its most important part: the screen. Some high-quality ones not only protect it from scratches, they actually make it easier to clean as fingerprints don't stick as easily as they would on a bare piece of glass

Headphones
The sound quality of the external speakers is limited, especially when playing music or games, so a decent set of headphones can really enhance your experience. It also protects other people from your sonic preferences!

Bookarc stand
This is the perfect accessory if you want to go hands free with your device. The Bookarc stand can hold your iPad in four different positions for displaying, storing, charging and hands free use

Setting up

"Once you start using your iPad, you'll wonder how you managed previously"

36 Change the wallpaper

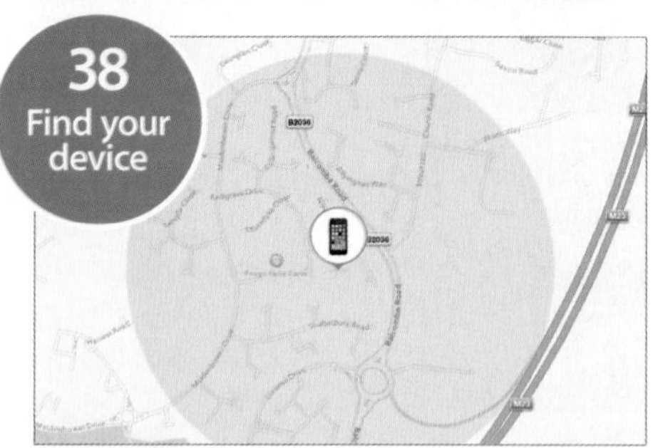

38 Find your device

48 Get to know iTunes

Bring your iPad to life with these easy-to-follow tips

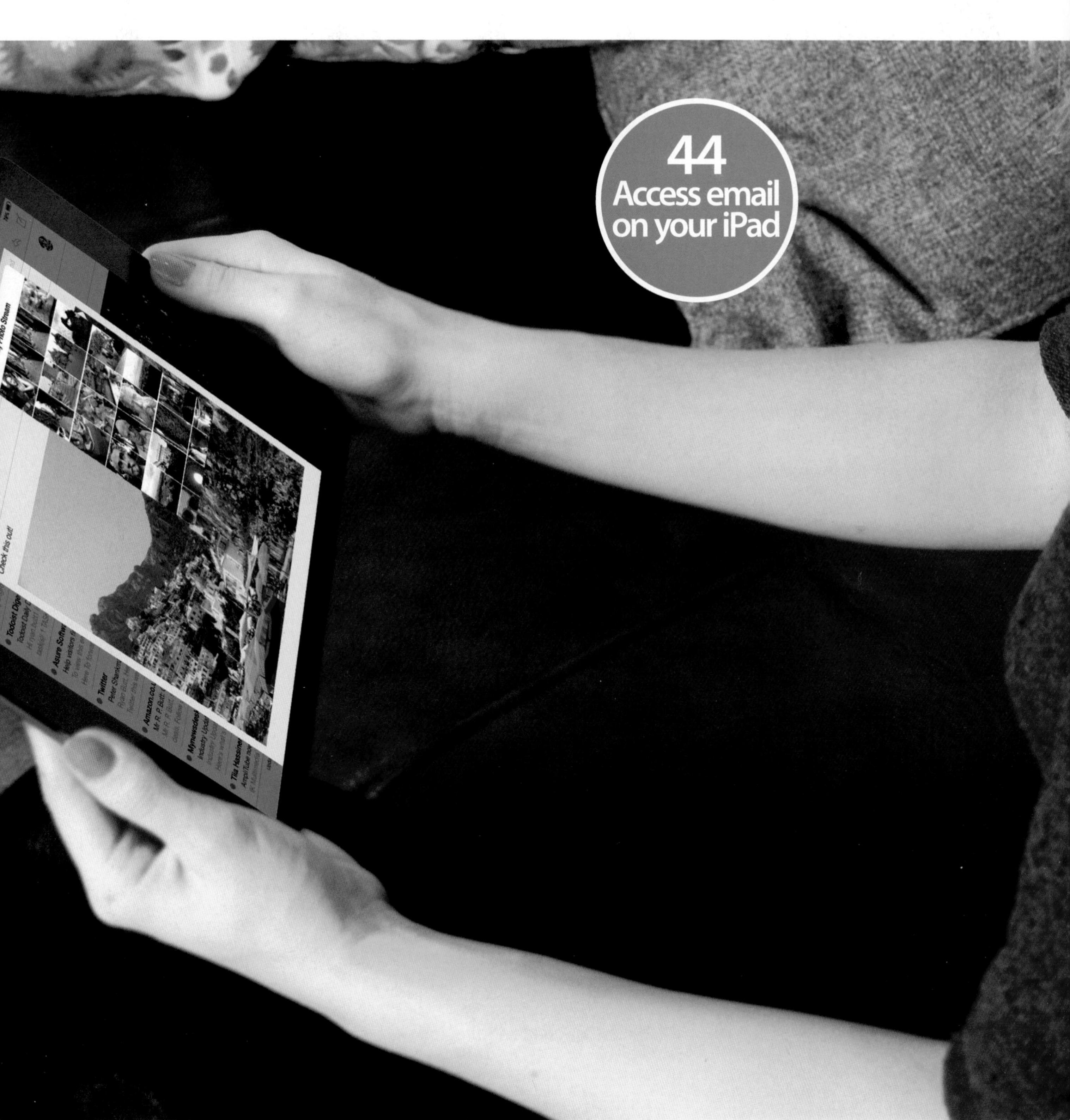

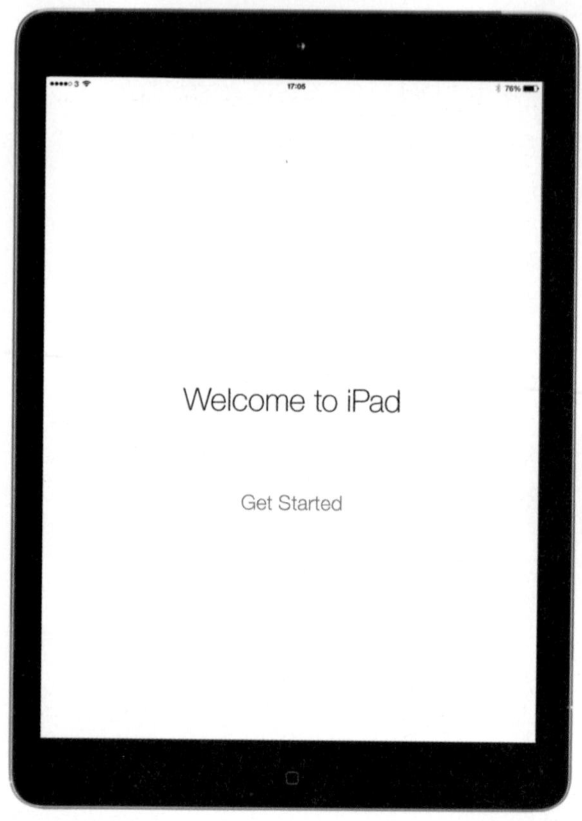

Activate and register your new iPad

Just got an iPad? We'll guide you through the process of setting up your device and registering it to your Apple ID

With a keen sense of excitement and anticipation, you unpack your brand-new iPad from its box and are ready to activate it and start using it to enhance your life. But whereas previously you would have to have had a computer to plug your iPad into to start the setup process, ever since iOS 5 you are no longer required to tether your device to a computer. This means the entire setup can be carried out independently, which makes it a quick and easy process.

All you have to do to activate your iPad is connect your new device to a power source and then press the Sleep/Wake button, which is situated on the top of your iPad. This will bring up a generic iPad lock screen with a slider at the bottom. Tap and hold on the slider with your index finger and swipe it to the right to unlock the device and gain access to its beautiful interface, adorned with all the apps you might possibly need to begin with.

The next series of screens will guide you through the setup process. In this tutorial we will take you through each stage of the process and explain the requirements at every screen in order to help get you up and running as quickly as possible.

"All you have to do is connect your device to a power source and press a button"

Activation Prepare your iPad

01 Unlock your device

When you first switch on your iPad you will be presented with a plain-looking lock screen with a slider at the bottom. Tap and hold the slider and swipe it to the right to unlock the iPad.

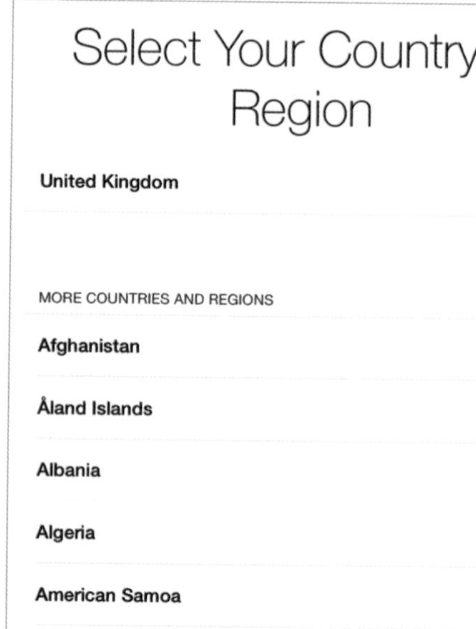

02 Choose language and region

On the first two set-up screens you will need to choose a native language for your device and your region so that the content of the iTunes and App Stores can be set accordingly.

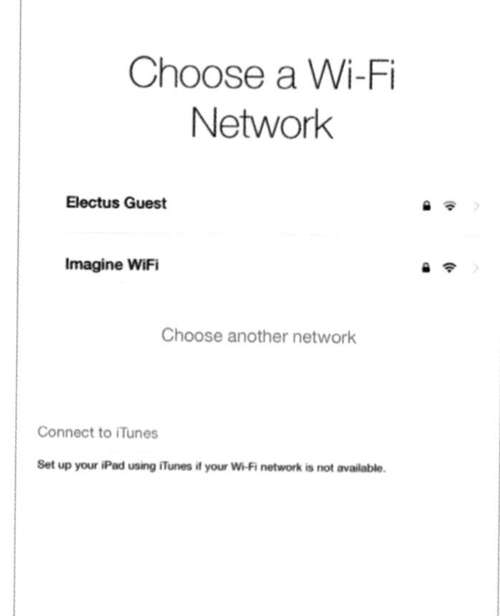

03 Connect to a network

Your iPad chiefly relies on a Wi-Fi network to be able to connect to the internet and fuel a wealth of different services. If you are within range of a Wi-Fi network then it will be detected.

Exploring your Home screen

Once your iPad has been set up, you can start exploring

Your Settings
Your first port of call should be the Settings app. Tap on this to start modifying and customising certain aspects of your device

Your Dock
The Dock is a row of app icons at the bottom of the screen. This Dock is present no matter which of your screens you're on. It is best if it holds your most-used apps for easy access

Your apps
A selection of Apple apps are built in to the operating system and will appear on your Home screen as standard. Tap on an icon to launch the app

Adding apps
The Dock contains four apps as standard but you can add an extra one by tapping and holding on an icon until it starts to shake. You can then drag apps into the desired position with your finger

Tweaking options
If you couldn't decide whether to activate certain services such as Find My iPad and iCloud during the initial setup process, you can do it later. Just tap on your Settings app and you will find the relevant options to activate and start using these features.

Location Services

Enable Location Services

Disable Location Services

What is Location Services?

Location Services allows apps like Maps and services like Spotlight Suggestions to gather and use data indicating your approximate location.

About Location Services

Set Up iPad

Set Up as New iPad

Restore from iCloud Backup

Restore from iTunes Backup

What does restoring do?

Your personal data and purchased content will appear on your device automatically.

Apple ID

Sign In with Your Apple ID

Create a Free Apple ID

Skip This Step

What is an Apple ID?

An Apple ID is your secure login for just about everything you do with Apple.

Get access to the best selection of apps with the App Store.

Shop for music, films, TV programmes and more in the iTunes Store.

Access your music, photos, contacts, calendars and more on all your devices.

Communicate with friends using iMessage and FaceTime.

Play multiplayer games and track achievements with Game Center.

Shop for your favourite books with iBooks and sync bookmarks and notes across your devices.

Your Apple ID will be associated with this device. Some features, applications and services are not available in all areas.

04 Location Services

Location Services allows apps to gather and use data indicating your approximate location, which can be very useful. Enable or disable it here. If unsure, you can reactivate it later in Settings.

05 Set up iPad

The next screen presents you with three options. You can either set up the device as a new iPad, which is what we'll be doing, or restore it from previous settings backed up to iCloud or iTunes.

06 Sign in

You'll need your own Apple ID to enjoy the main features of your iPad, such as being able to download apps, music and videos and back up and sync your data and settings with iCloud.

Setting up

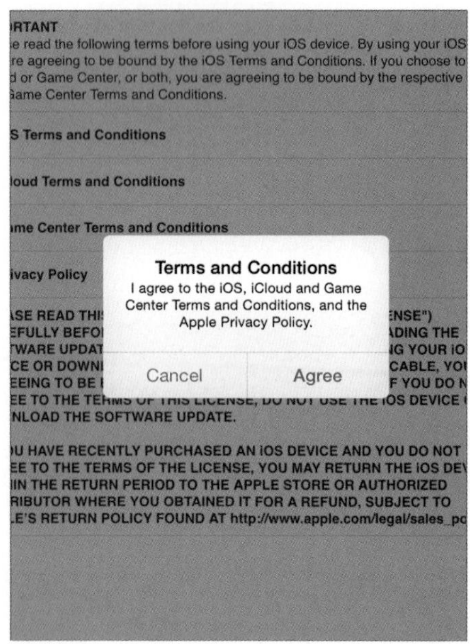

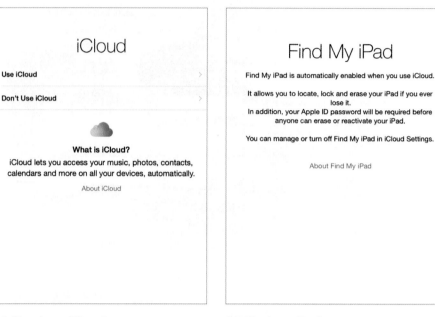

07 Read the T&Cs

After signing in you will be presented with a screen containing the Terms and Conditions relating to all aspects of your iPad, including the Apple services that you will be using such as iCloud, Game Center and so on.

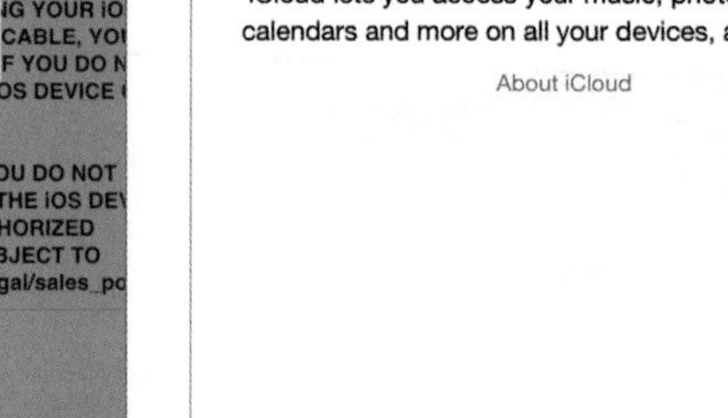

08 Sign in to iCloud

If you wish to use iCloud to back up your data and purchases, use your Apple ID to sign into your free account. iCloud lets you access music, photos, contacts and more on all of your devices automatically and is well worth using.

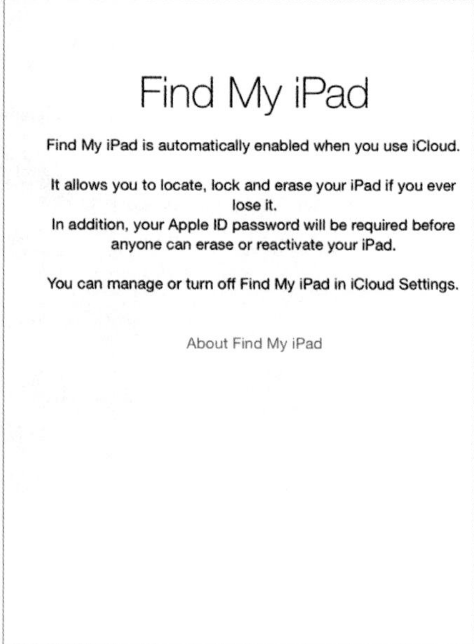

Find My iPad
Find My iPad is automatically enabled when you use iCloud.
It allows you to locate, lock and erase your iPad if you ever lose it.
In addition, your Apple ID password will be required before anyone can erase or reactivate your iPad.
You can manage or turn off Find My iPad in iCloud Settings.
About Find My iPad

09 Find my iPad

If you misplace your iPad, the Find My iPad service will help you locate it on a map, and even play a sound or display a message. You can even activate this service to sync the location of your device with your iCloud.

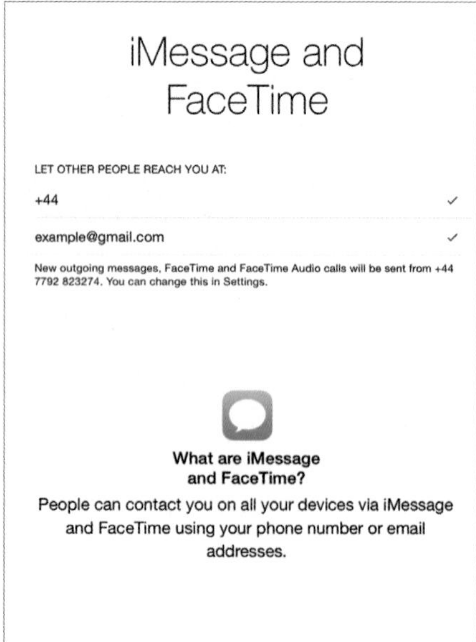

10 FaceTime and iMessage

FaceTime lets you speak face-to-face with people from a distance using your iPad's built-in camera, while iMessage provides a free messaging service with other iMessage users. To get started, enter your email address or phone number.

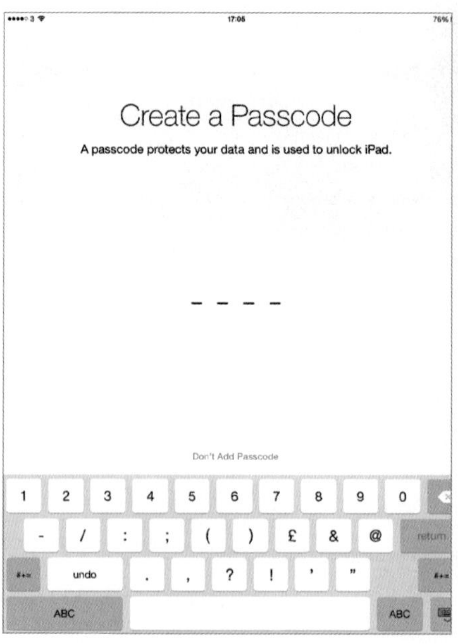

11 Create a passcode

At this point you can enter a four-digit passcode that will be used to secure your iPad. The code will need to be entered every time you unlock your device. It is a valuable safety function that prevents others from gaining access to your data.

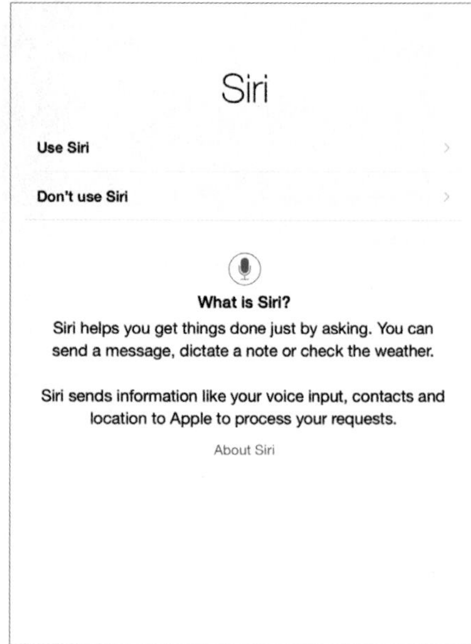

12 Siri

At this stage you can choose to enable Siri, your iOS-based personal assistant. Once activated, you will be able to ask Siri questions or give commands in plain English to access apps, make calls, find information and more.

Exploring your Settings

Start personalising your iPad through Settings

Settings
Airplane Mode
Wi-Fi Imagine WiFi
Bluetooth On
Mobile Data
Personal Hotspot Off
Carrier 3
Notifications
Control Centre
Do Not Disturb
General
Display & Brightness
Wallpaper
Sounds
Passcode
Privacy
iCloud
iTunes & App Store
Mail, Contacts, Calendars

General
About
Software Update
Siri
Spotlight Search
Handoff & Suggested Apps
Accessibility
Multitasking Gestures
Use four or five fingers to:
• Pinch to the Home Screen
• Swipe up to multitasking
• Swipe left or right between apps
USE SIDE SWITCH TO:
Lock Rotation
Mute
Rotation Lock is available in Control Centre.
Usage
Background App Refresh
Auto-Lock 2 Minutes
Restrictions Off

The categories

All of the categories to which the Settings apply will be presented in a list on the left-hand side of the screen. Tap an option to bring up its individual screen of settings

Side Switch

The switch on the side of your device can be used for muting sound or locking your screen rotation. The latter is very useful and you can assign it from the General section

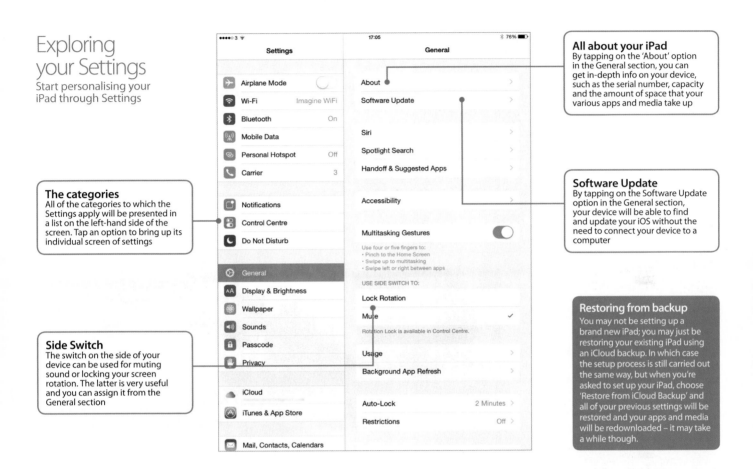

All about your iPad

By tapping on the 'About' option in the General section, you can get in-depth info on your device, such as the serial number, capacity and the amount of space that your various apps and media take up

Software Update

By tapping on the Software Update option in the General section, your device will be able to find and update your iOS without the need to connect your device to a computer

Restoring from backup

You may not be setting up a brand new iPad; you may just be restoring your existing iPad using an iCloud backup. In which case the setup process is still carried out the same way, but when you're asked to set up your iPad, choose 'Restore from iCloud Backup' and all of your previous settings will be restored and your apps and media will be redownloaded – it may take a while though.

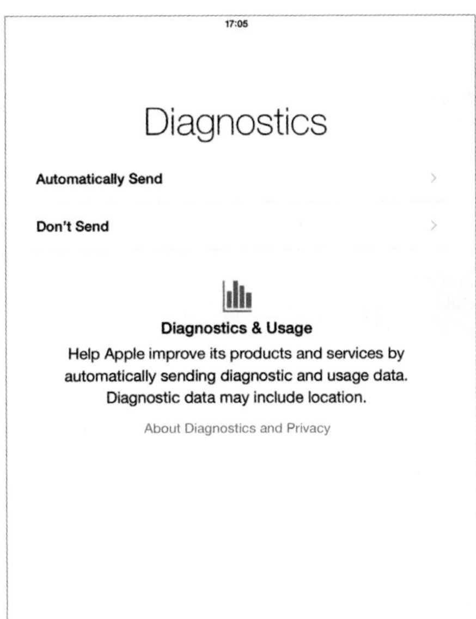

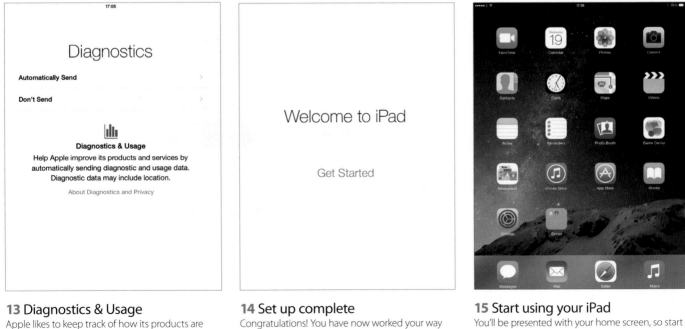

13 Diagnostics & Usage

Apple likes to keep track of how its products are performing, so this screen allows you to send diagnostic data straight to Apple. Opt for 'Don't Send' to keep your information private.

Welcome to iPad

Get Started

14 Set up complete

Congratulations! You have now worked your way through the entire set-up process. A screen will confirm the process is complete, so what are you waiting for? Tap on the 'Get Started' button!

15 Start using your iPad

You'll be presented with your home screen, so start tapping on icons to launch apps and find your way around, experimenting with the gestures needed to operate your new device.

Change Settings to suit your needs

The Settings app is the epicentre of your iPad. Here you can customise everything from how apps work to the look and feel of the display

On the first page of the iPad screen you will see an application called Settings with an icon that looks like a cog in a machine. And this is an apt metaphor for the application and its role in helping you design your user experience. This controls how your iPad works, allows individual apps to be configured, and sets the look and feel of the screens. This is essentially where you can make all the simple touches that will personalise your device and make it truly 'yours'. With it, you can also enforce security facilities, log on to Wi-Fi networks, save battery power, add signatures to emails, configure the web browser Safari to use specific search engines and much, much more. It is perhaps the most important app on your iPad. Learn what it has to offer and how you can change or configure things, and you will be able to take control of the iPad to make it work the way you want it to.

In this tutorial we are going to help you navigate the app and introduce you to some of the key features within Settings – the ones that you may want to check out straight away to get yourself acquainted to the system. More specific tutorials will follow to show you functions in more depth, but for now, let's delve into the nerve centre of this incredible piece of kit.

"Learn what the Settings have to offer and make the iPad work the way you want it to"

Settings Work your way around the iPad control system

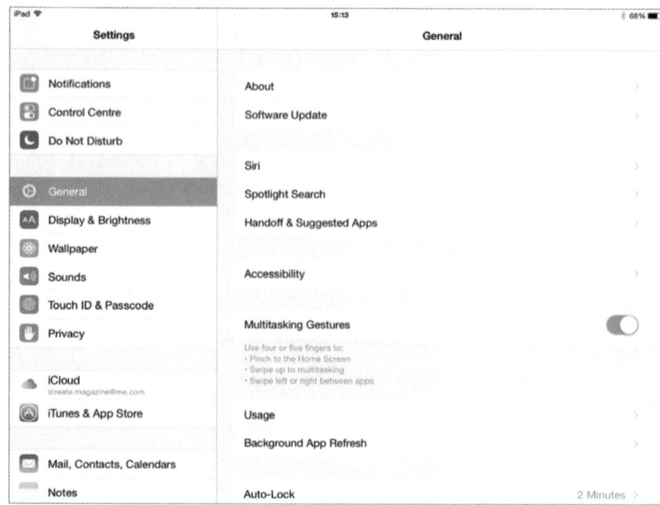

01 Go to Settings

Turn your iPad on and slide the bar across to unlock it. On the very first screen is the Settings app. Tap once on it to launch. There are a great number of parameters but you'll find a lot of useful things to tweak in the 'General' section. If this isn't automatically selected, tap on it now.

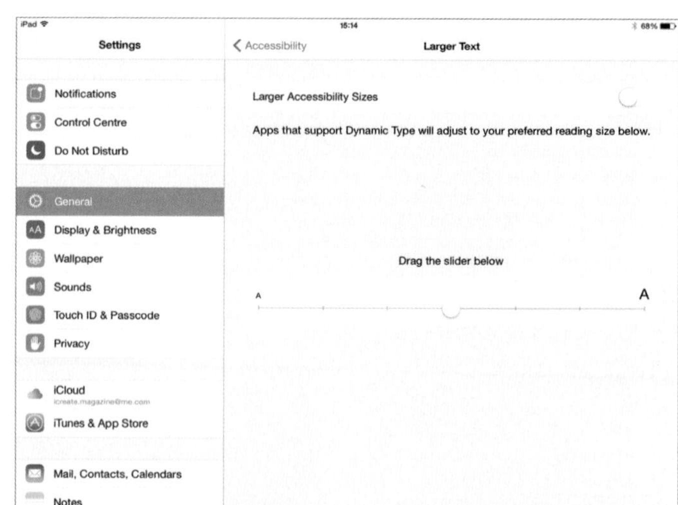

02 Tweak general settings

Within the General settings you can set up Siri, adjust the text size, make your device easier to use if you have an impairment, determine the function of the side switch and set a passcode lock on your device (if you didn't do it during the initial setup process).

The Settings menu laid out in full

Work your way around this user-friendly settings menu

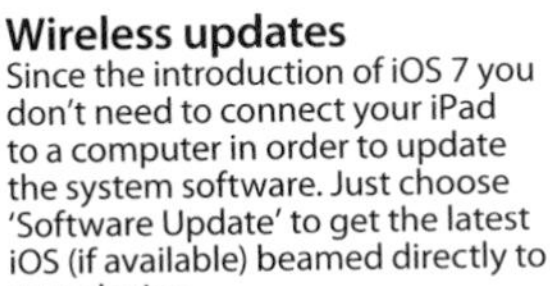

Wireless updates
Since the introduction of iOS 7 you don't need to connect your iPad to a computer in order to update the system software. Just choose 'Software Update' to get the latest iOS (if available) beamed directly to your device

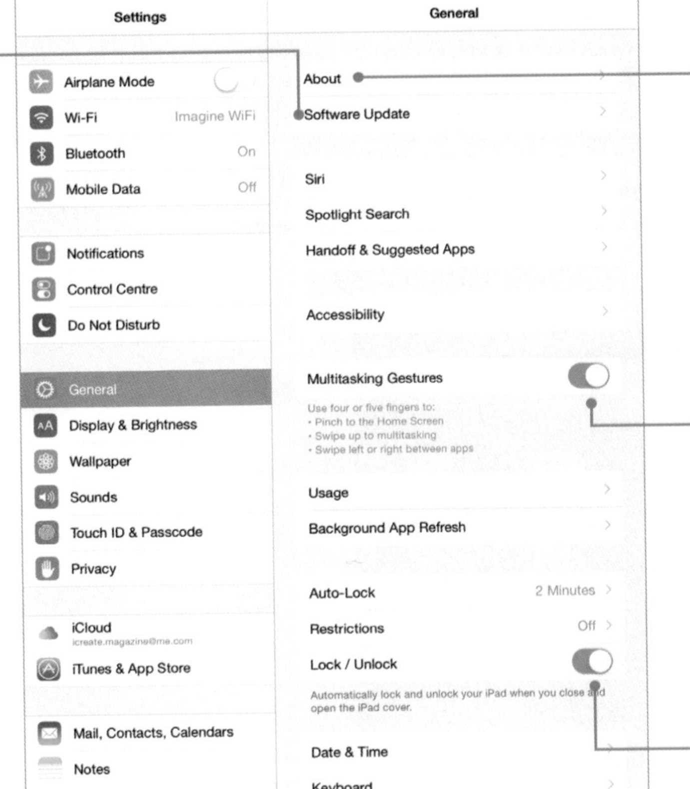

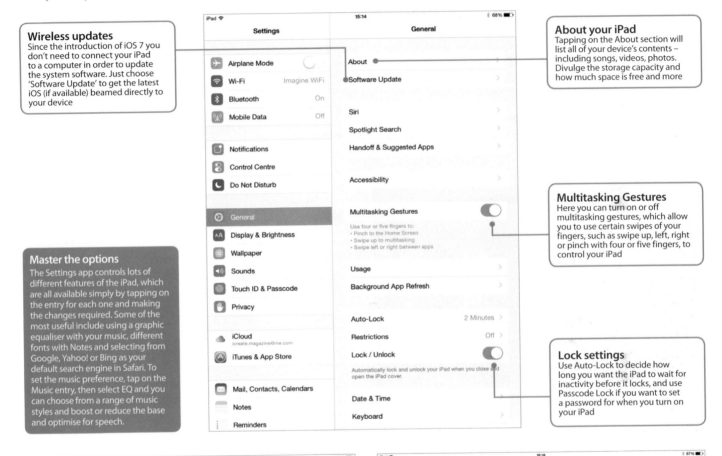

About your iPad
Tapping on the About section will list all of your device's contents – including songs, videos, photos. Divulge the storage capacity and how much space is free and more

Multitasking Gestures
Here you can turn on or off multitasking gestures, which allow you to use certain swipes of your fingers, such as swipe up, left, right or pinch with four or five fingers, to control your iPad

Master the options
The Settings app controls lots of different features of the iPad, which are all available simply by tapping on the entry for each one and making the changes required. Some of the most useful include using a graphic equaliser with your music, different fonts with Notes and selecting from Google, Yahoo! or Bing as your default search engine in Safari. To set the music preference, tap on the Music entry, then select EQ and you can choose from a range of music styles and boost or reduce the base and optimise for speech.

Lock settings
Use Auto-Lock to decide how long you want the iPad to wait for inactivity before it locks, and use Passcode Lock if you want to set a password for when you turn on your iPad

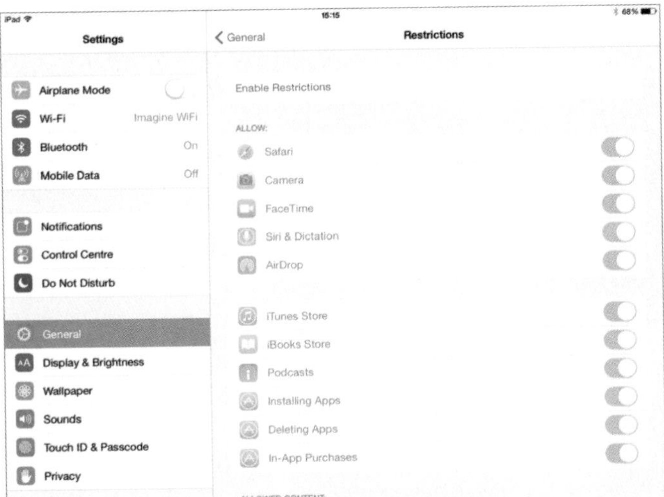

03 Enable Restrictions
The 'General' section also has one of the most important settings options, especially if you let your kids play with the iPad. Here you can turn off in-app purchases, access to iTunes and much more. Just tap Enable Restrictions and you are prompted to set a passcode. Make it memorable.

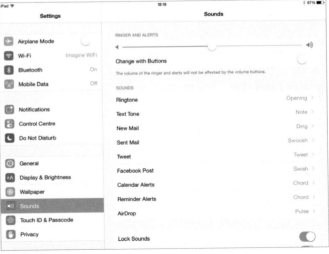

04 Explore the Settings
The layout of the Settings screen has been changed slightly in recent updates. As such some settings, such as Sound, which were once part of other sections now have their own standout section that's accessible from the list on the left. Explore this list to fully get to grips with your device and what it can do.

Set up a Wi-Fi connection

To make the most of your iPad, you'll want to connect to Wi-Fi and get online. Here's how to do it…

For all the iPad's uses and versatility, it doesn't really come into its own until you have Wi-Fi access. Sure you can play games, write documents and take photos, but you can't do the really big stuff if you don't have wireless internet access.

Internet access turns your iPad from an impressive piece of expensive kit into something that opens up worlds. This is in part due to the magnificence that is the App Store, a virtual store that gives you access to literally thousands of different applications, ranging from popular games like *Angry Birds* and *Real Racing* to GPS devices, interactive encyclopaedias, word processing apps and much, much more.

Your iPad is a portal to a host of fantastic services, but first you need to give it access to the Internet – only then do your options become plentiful. Follow our simple instructions in this easy-to-follow tutorial and unleash the potential of Apple's powerful device. You won't regret it.

Settings Switch on Wi-Fi

01 Getting started

Take a look through the various home screens on your iPad and find the Settings icon – it's silver in colour with some cog illustrations.

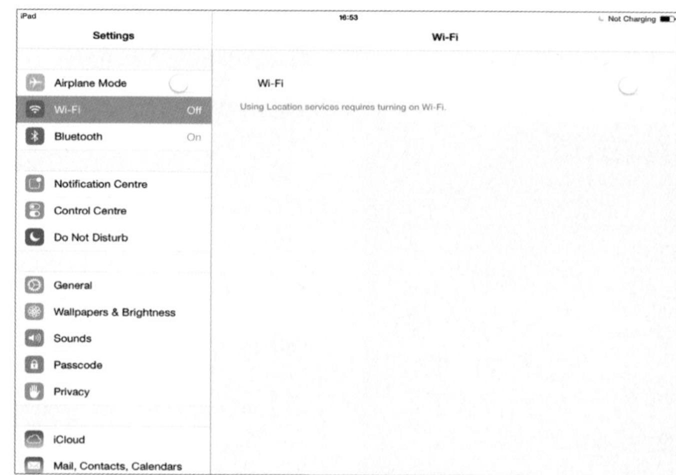

02 Locate Wi-Fi

After entering Settings, the second option down is Wi-Fi. Tap on it and then turn Wi-Fi on by sliding the button.

03 Find your connection

Your iPad will now start looking for available connection points. Ignore 'Ask to Join Networks' at the bottom and simply tap on your connection.

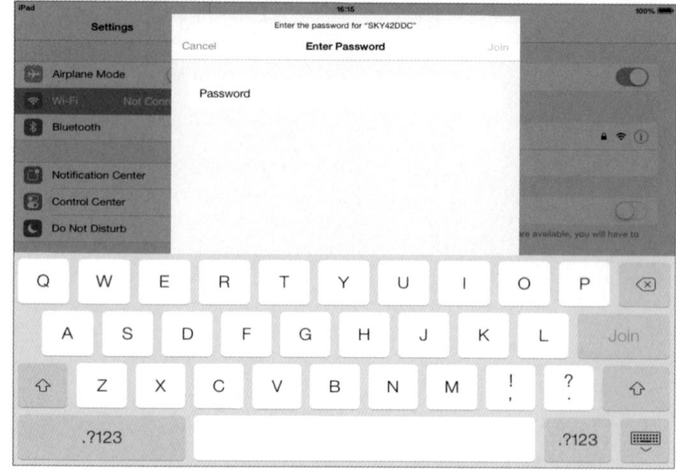

04 The final hurdle

You are now ready to enter your Wi-Fi password. Fill in your details on the keyboard. Once filled in, select Join and you're done.

Connect to a Bluetooth device

Manage your iPad Bluetooth connectivity in just a few taps

If you've ever wanted to hook up a wireless speaker, keyboard or even remote control to your iPad, it's probably connecting via Bluetooth. Bluetooth is an incredibly universal technology that allows different devices to connect to each other wirelessly. It might've started off as a bit of a battery-hog with a low range but, over the years, each Bluetooth standard has brought with it a larger distance over which devices can be connected and far better power efficiency.

Managing Bluetooth connections on your iPad is easy as they're all contained within a single settings menu. What's more, the process for setting and up and disconnecting Bluetooth devices is exactly the same, no matter what you're working with. The only difference you might come across is when some devices request a passcode to connect. This keeps them secure and stops unauthorised access. Generally speaking, these passcodes are contained within the device's instruction manual and, once you've cracked that, you'll be connected.

Settings Manage your iPad Bluetooth connections

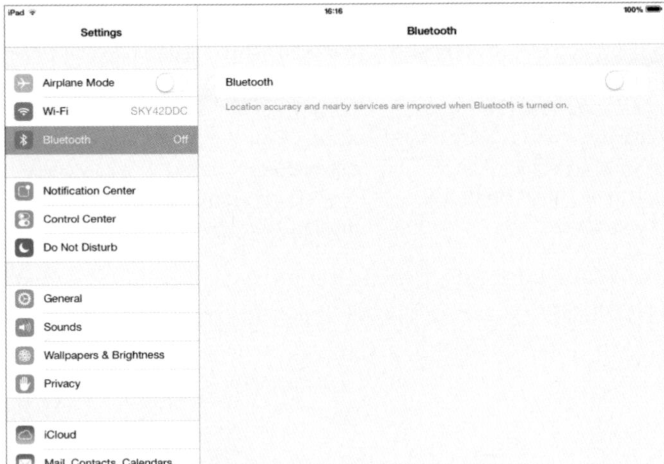

01 Find your settings

In your iPad's Settings app, tap on the Bluetooth tab in the sidebar to view the available Bluetooth devices nearby. Turn your Bluetooth on.

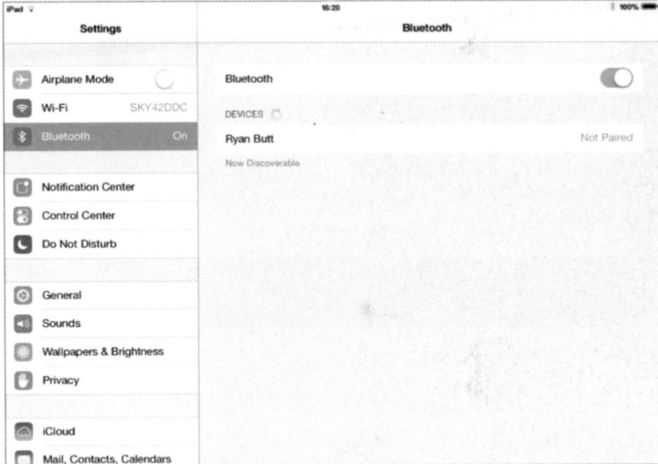

02 Select to connect

Once you've decided on the device you want to connect to, tap on its name as it appears on your iPad's screen. Your iPad will then start connecting.

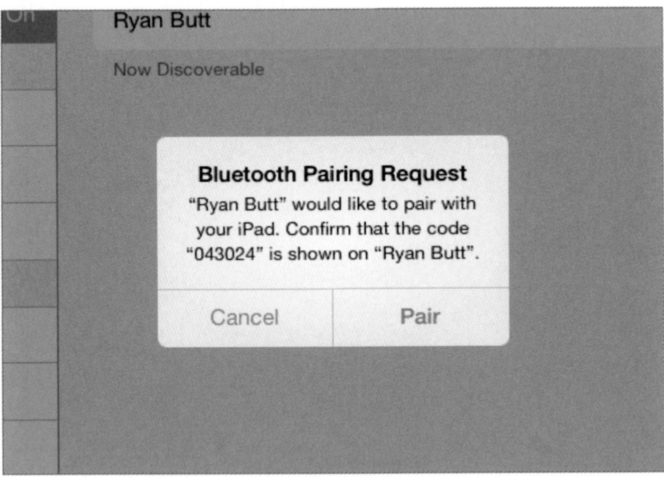

03 Pairing codes

As a security measure, you may be asked to confirm that a numerical code is correct on each device. Once you've done this tap Pair to continue.

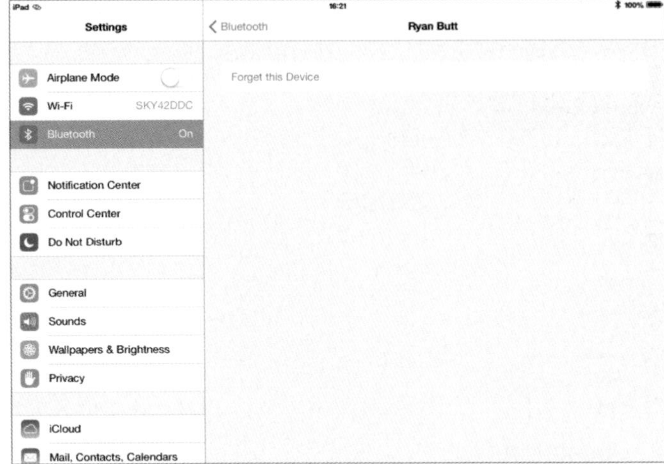

04 Forget it

To stop a Bluetooth device from pairing when it's in the vicinity of your iPad, tap the triangle next to its name then hit the 'Forget this Device' button.

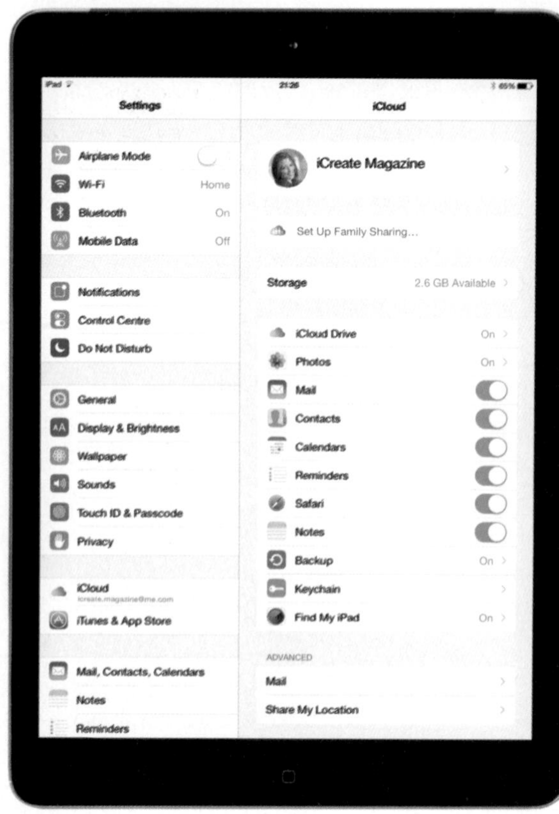

Set up iCloud and start syncing

All of your documents can be moved wirelessly from device to device without you having to lift a finger

With iOS 5 came iCloud, a service from Apple that is so much more than just a hard drive in the sky and has transformed how our remote devices can be integrated into our lives. Free to all iOS users, iCloud automatically and securely stores your content so that it's always available on your iPad, iPhone, Mac… whatever Apple device you're using. Through iCloud you can get full access to your music, apps, photos and documents, and it also wirelessly syncs all your emails, contacts and calendars to keep them up-to-date across all of your devices.

When you sign up for iCloud you get 5GB of free storage, which is more than enough for personal use because all your apps, books and movies that are pushed to all your devices don't count against your free storage. And seeing as your mail, documents, account info, settings and other app data don't use up much space, you'll find that your free quota actually goes quite a long way.

With your iPad, you can set up an iCloud account for free and start syncing data between all your devices instantly. These easy steps will show you how to get up an running right away.

"When you sign up for iCloud you automatically get 5GB of free storage"

iCloud Setting up your personal iCloud

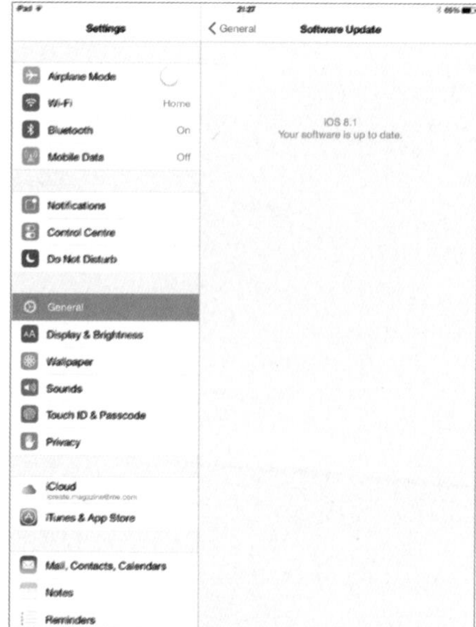

01 Update your iOS

iCloud comes as part of iOS 8, so either connect your iPad to your computer or open Settings> General>Software Update and ensure you're running the latest iOS software.

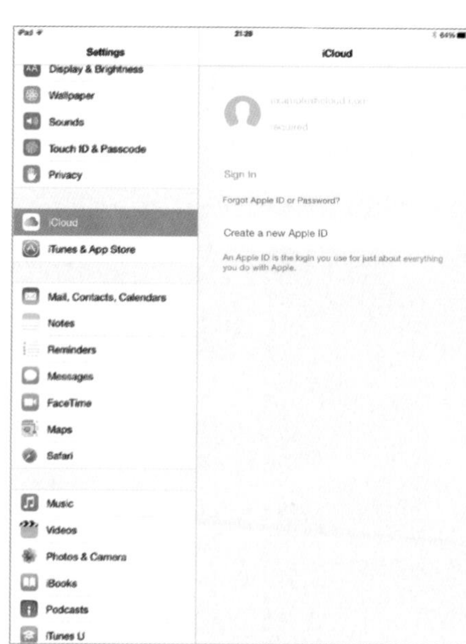

02 Find iCloud

There is very little tinkering to do to set up your iCloud. Still in the Settings app, tap the iCloud icon in the left-hand sidebar to access the options that you need.

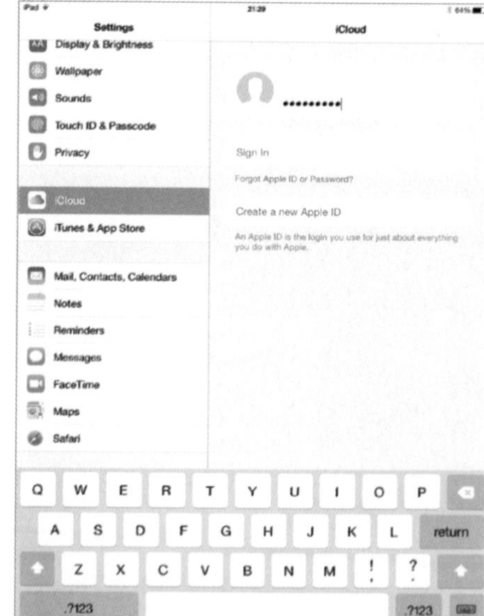

03 Sign in

To activate your iCloud account you will need to log in using your Apple ID, which uses the same email address and password that you use for your other services, such as iTunes and the App Store.

Your iCloud Settings

Activating your free iCloud account is simple and easy to manage

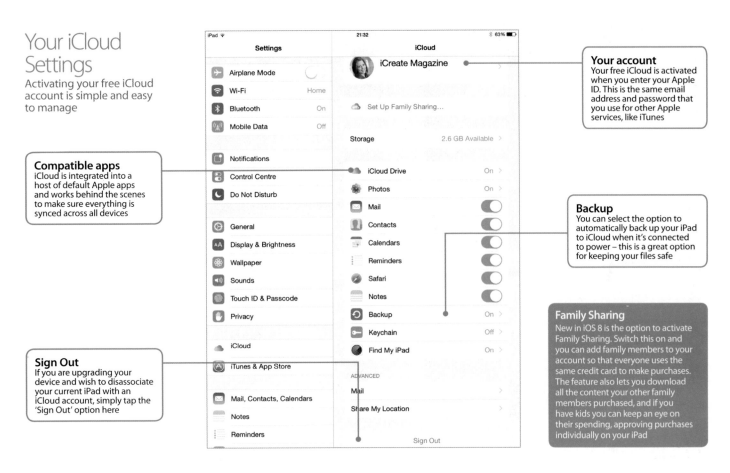

Your account
Your free iCloud is activated when you enter your Apple ID. This is the same email address and password that you use for other Apple services, like iTunes

Compatible apps
iCloud is integrated into a host of default Apple apps and works behind the scenes to make sure everything is synced across all devices

Backup
You can select the option to automatically back up your iPad to iCloud when it's connected to power – this is a great option for keeping your files safe

Sign Out
If you are upgrading your device and wish to disassociate your current iPad with an iCloud account, simply tap the 'Sign Out' option here

Family Sharing
New in iOS 8 is the option to activate Family Sharing. Switch this on and you can add family members to your account so that everyone uses the same credit card to make purchases. The feature also lets you download all the content your other family members purchased, and if you have kids you can keep an eye on their spending, approving purchases individually on your iPad

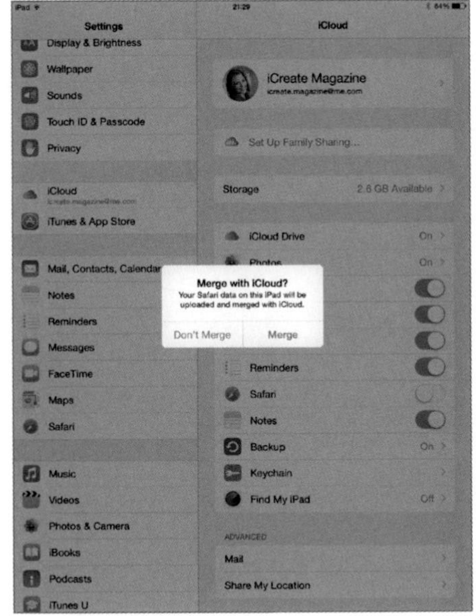

04 Merge data

If you've already set up an iCloud account on another device, you will be asked if you'd like to merge data, such as calendars, with the data that exists on the iCloud.

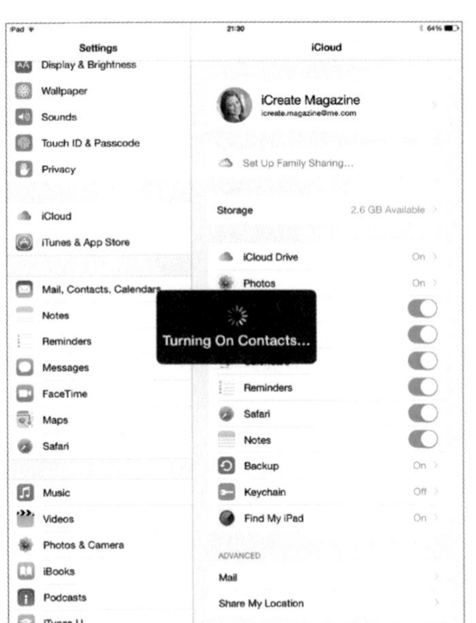

05 Start syncing

Select which of the apps utilise the service, such as Mail, Contacts, Calendar, Reminders, Safari Bookmarks, Notes, Photo Stream and Documents & Data. Move the sliders to activate the apps.

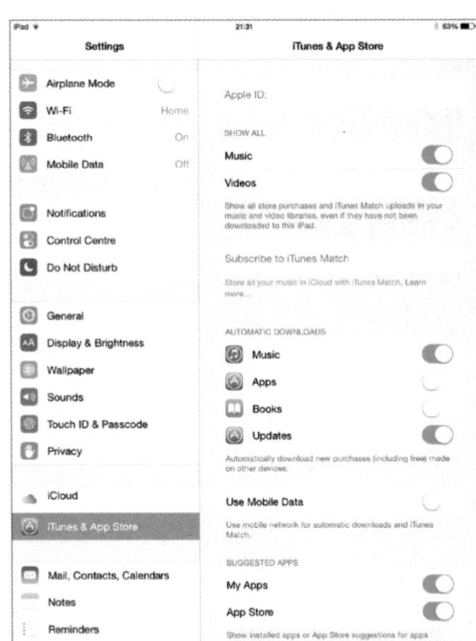

06 Automatic downloads

To get more from iCloud, click on the iTunes & App Store section in Settings and then turn on Automatic Downloads for all the options to download new purchases from other devices.

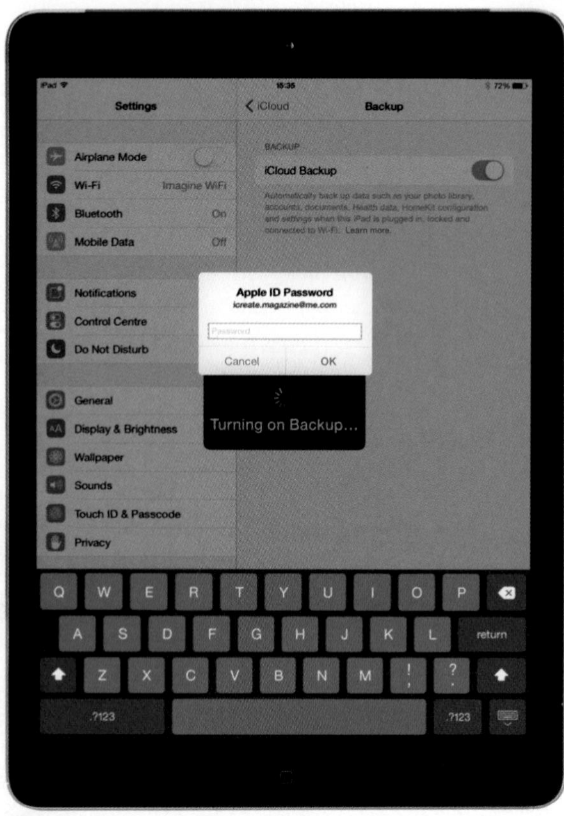

Back up your iPad using iCloud

With iCloud you can back up all of your important iPad data to your own virtual hard drive

Your iPad is like a bank vault where all kinds of important stuff is stored. So what happens if it gets lost or goes awry? Nothing, that's what. Thanks to iCloud, all of your data is automatically backed up and kept safely in your own cloud storage space so it will never be lost. What this means is that when your iPad is connected to a power source and a Wi-Fi network, all of your media, photos, videos, settings, app data and messages are backed up.

When you set up a new iOS device or need to restore the information on the one you already have, iCloud Backup does all the heavy lifting. All you have to do is ensure that your device is connected to Wi-Fi, enter your Apple ID and all of your important data will sync between your other Apple devices so that it appears instantly on them all without you having to worry about a thing.

As you will have read elsewhere in this book, the benefits of using iCloud are vast, and the way in which it goes about its business in the background without you having to conduct any manual processes is just another prime example of how Apple is striving to make your life easier. Here we show you how to do your first back up.

"Another prime example of how Apple is striving to make your life easier"

iCloud Activate iCloud and back up your data

01 Update your iOS

If you don't have the latest version of iOS, connect your device to your computer through iTunes and check to ensure you have the latest free software update installed on your device.

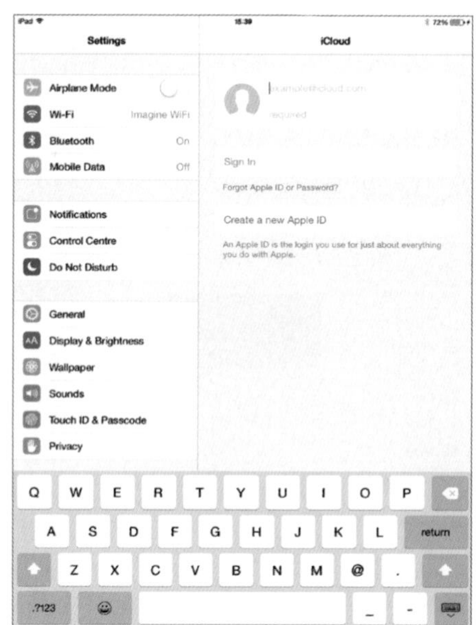

02 Launch Settings

From your iPad's home screen, launch your Settings app and, in the left-hand column, you will see a new category called iCloud. Tap on this and then enter your Apple ID and password.

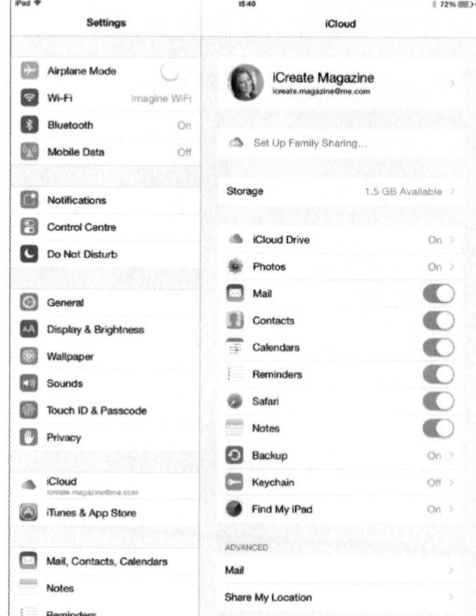

03 Set up

Once your personal iCloud account has been set up and you have selected which of your apps you would like to sync, tap on Backup at the bottom of the list to initiate the process.

Backing up with iCloud

Once activated, your iCloud will begin backing up your stuff automatically

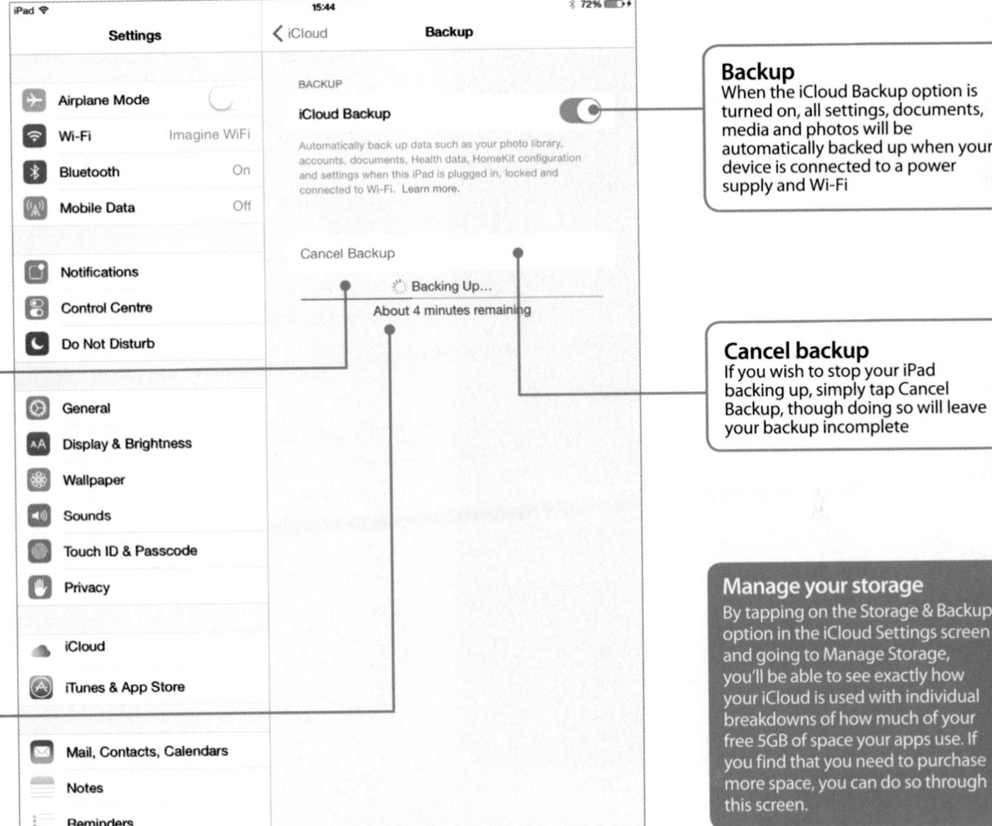

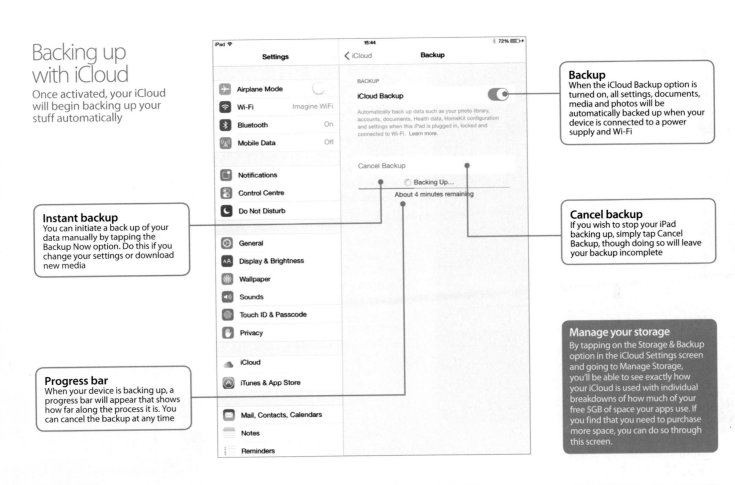

Backup
When the iCloud Backup option is turned on, all settings, documents, media and photos will be automatically backed up when your device is connected to a power supply and Wi-Fi

Instant backup
You can initiate a back up of your data manually by tapping the Backup Now option. Do this if you change your settings or download new media

Cancel backup
If you wish to stop your iPad backing up, simply tap Cancel Backup, though doing so will leave your backup incomplete

Progress bar
When your device is backing up, a progress bar will appear that shows how far along the process it is. You can cancel the backup at any time

Manage your storage
By tapping on the Storage & Backup option in the iCloud Settings screen and going to Manage Storage, you'll be able to see exactly how your iCloud is used with individual breakdowns of how much of your free 5GB of space your apps use. If you find that you need to purchase more space, you can do so through this screen.

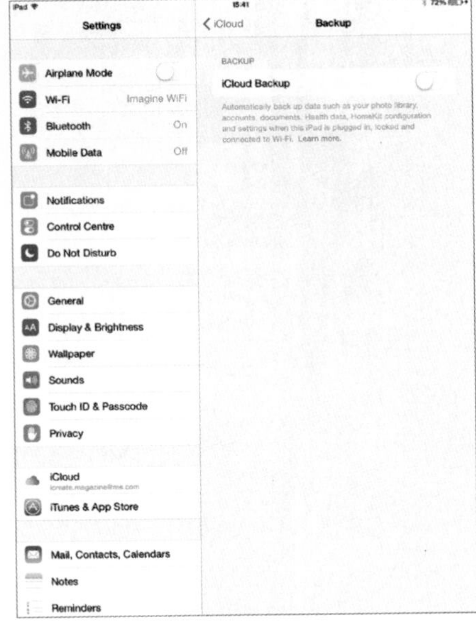

04 Turn on Backup

On this screen you will be able to monitor and manage your iCloud storage space, but more importantly you will see an option called iCloud Backup. Ensure that the slider is moved to 'On'.

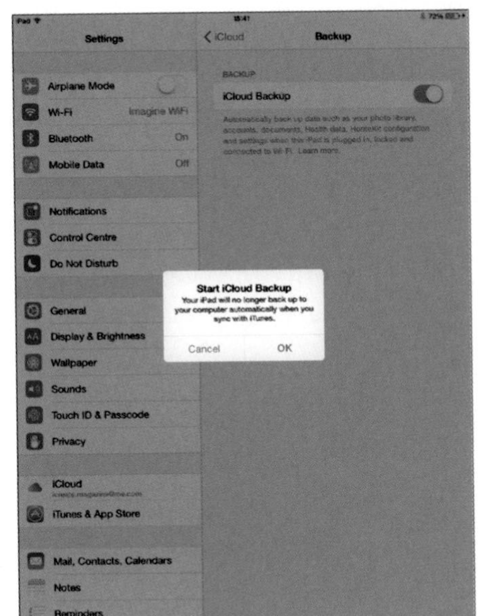

05 Wait for the activation

You'll be presented with a message saying that your iPad will no longer sync to iTunes when connected to your computer. Tap OK and wait for a minute while the Backup feature is activated.

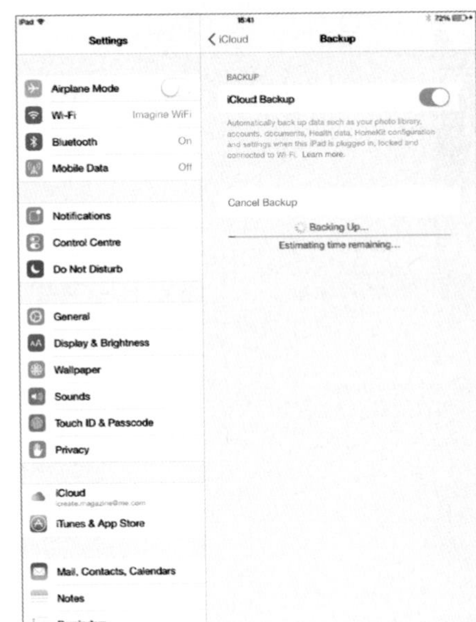

06 Start backing up

Your iPad will now back up when connected to a power source and a Wi-Fi network, but you can perform the backup whenever you want by accessing this screen and tapping Backup Now.

Set a passcode lock

Protect your iPad from prying eyes by setting a passcode that will ensure only you have access to everything

These days, people can store a lot of sensitive data on their tablets, whether it's log-in details for online accounts, private messages, or documents that only you are meant to see. If someone could gain access to your iPad, there may be a lot that you wouldn't want anyone to see.

Of course, this applies on a more basic level, too. You may have friends who think it's funny to send messages to people from your iPad when you leave it unattended for a few minutes. Thankfully, Apple's iOS offers a very simple way for you to keep your device secure. By setting a passcode, you can ensure there is at least some of protection for the contents of your iPad.

Working just like a PIN, you can set a passcode that only you know, and every time you turn your iPad on or unlock it, you'll have to enter this code before gaining access to everything within it.

Choosing a code that you'll remember is imperative, but there are a range of settings that will allow you to personalise your security to the level you desire. From selecting the option to use a more complex password, to erasing data upon a number of incorrect entries, you can tailor how you want the Passcode Lock to work for you. No longer will you need to worry about your iPad's data falling into the wrong hands, or friends updating your Facebook status to something untoward…

"Thankfully, Apple's iOS offers a very simple way for you to keep your device secure"

Settings Turn on Passcode Lock

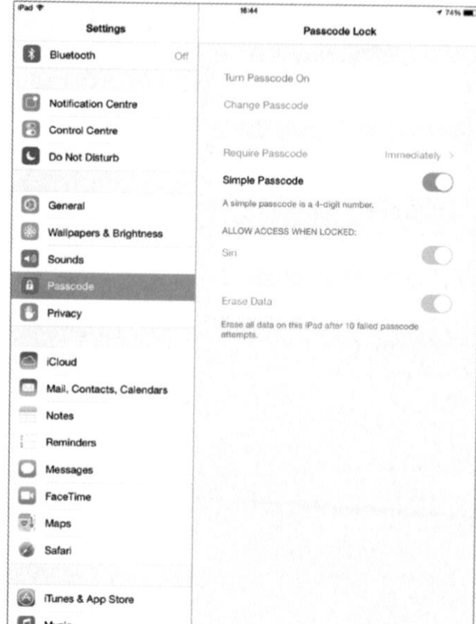

01 Through Settings

From the home screen, select the Settings icon. On the left-hand menu in the latest version of iOS you'll find a Passcode option. Tap here to reveal the settings options.

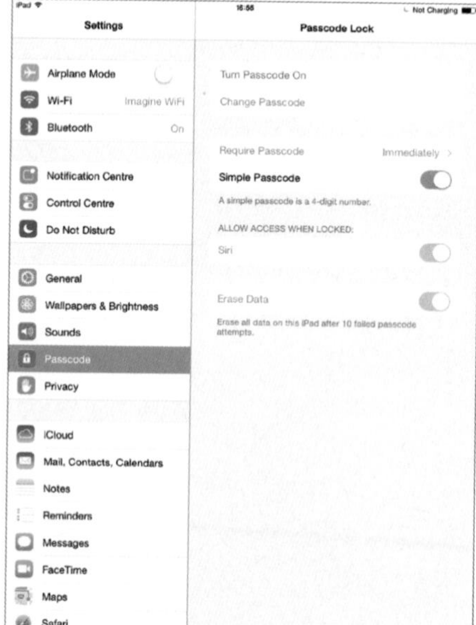

02 Passcode Lock

Within the Passcode setting, you'll see this display of options. Currently there is no passcode set on this iPad. In order to change this, tap the Turn Passcode On option.

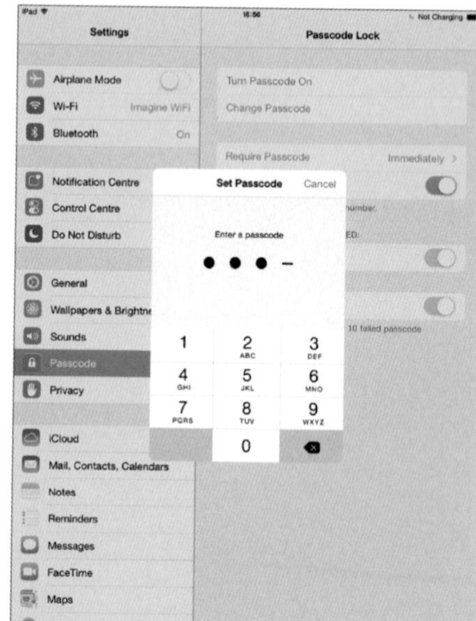

03 Enter a code

You will be asked to enter a four-digit passcode. Make sure to choose something you'll remember, but nothing too obvious that people will guess. Re-enter the code to confirm when asked.

Added iPad security

Your passcode options

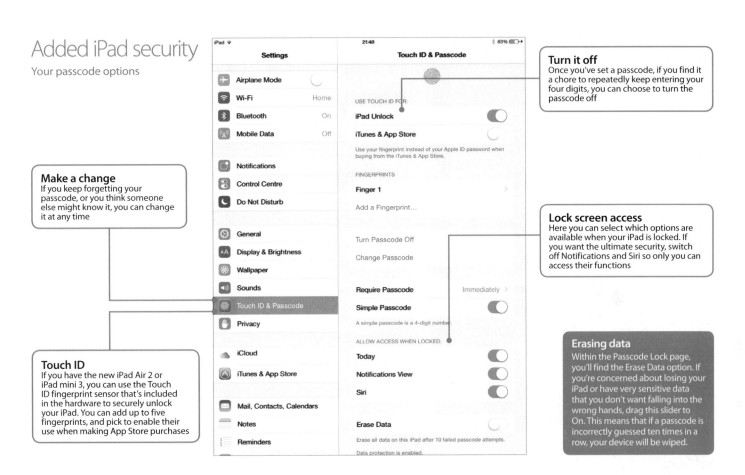

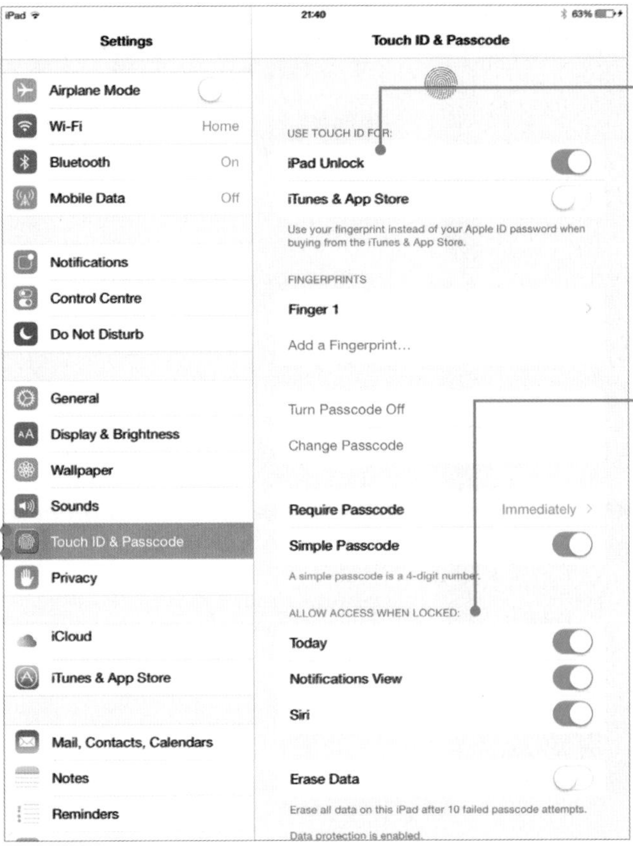

Make a change
If you keep forgetting your passcode, or you think someone else might know it, you can change it at any time

Touch ID
If you have the new iPad Air 2 or iPad mini 3, you can use the Touch ID fingerprint sensor that's included in the hardware to securely unlock your iPad. You can add up to five fingerprints, and pick to enable their use when making App Store purchases

Turn it off
Once you've set a passcode, if you find it a chore to repeatedly keep entering your four digits, you can choose to turn the passcode off

Lock screen access
Here you can select which options are available when your iPad is locked. If you want the ultimate security, switch off Notifications and Siri so only you can access their functions

Erasing data
Within the Passcode Lock page, you'll find the Erase Data option. If you're concerned about losing your iPad or have very sensitive data that you don't want falling into the wrong hands, drag this slider to On. This means that if a passcode is incorrectly guessed ten times in a row, your device will be wiped.

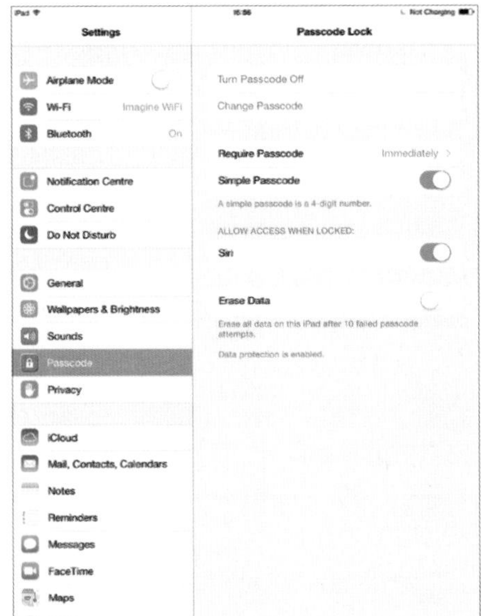

04 Extra options

Once you've set your passcode, you'll notice that a number of extra options are now available. You can turn the passcode off or change the numbers if you so wish.

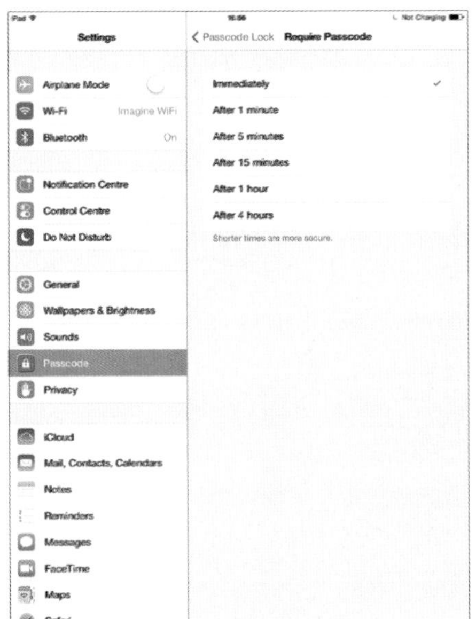

05 Set the requirement

By tapping the Require Passcode option you can determine how long after you lock your iPad that you need to enter the passcode. Shorter periods of time are safer.

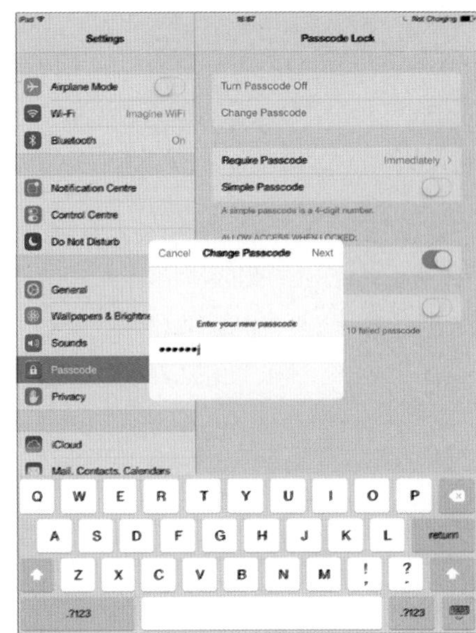

06 More complex

If you're not happy with a four-digit passcode, move the slider on the Simple Passcode option to off. You can then set a longer passcode made up of letters, numbers and special characters.

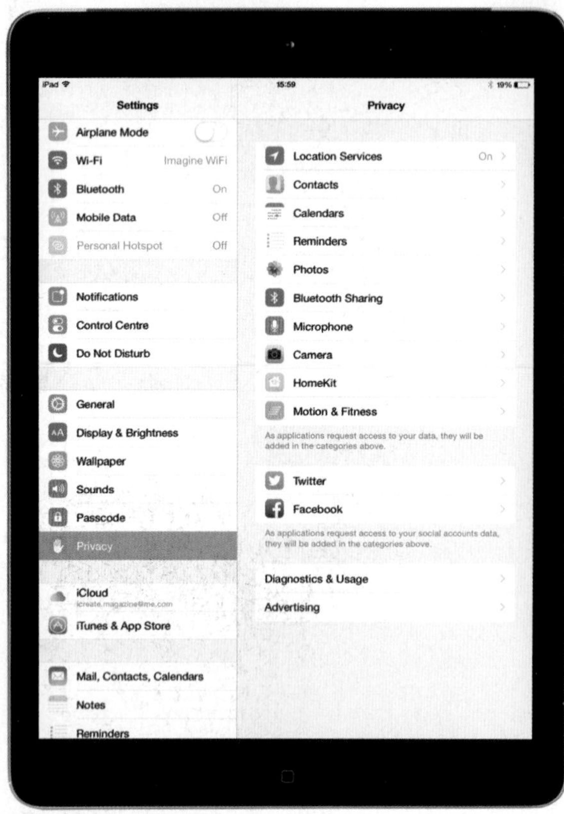

Take control of your privacy settings

Keep control of your privacy by monitoring what actions your iPad apps can and cannot perform

In today's age of digital information, personal details are often moved around at a moment's notice. Think about it: your iPad contains a gamut of personal information. What addresses do you have on your tablet? Do you use your iPad for personal banking online?

In general terms, you should always be sure to set up the Find My iPad app, which is supplied by Apple for free and knows what to do if your iPad is lost or stolen. But thanks to new features that were introduced recently, there are other ways to monitor and control the privacy of the data contained on your iPad. Apple now allows users to control which apps are able to gain access to specific data on their tablets, adding a new level of security and peace of mind. This is especially beneficial for all those times when you're not exactly sure whether an app is using sensitive information or not.

While you might find it hard to believe your iPad will fall into the wrong hands, do take the time to configure these settings.

> "Thanks to new features introduced recently, there are other ways to control the privacy of your data"

Settings Secure your iPad's privacy

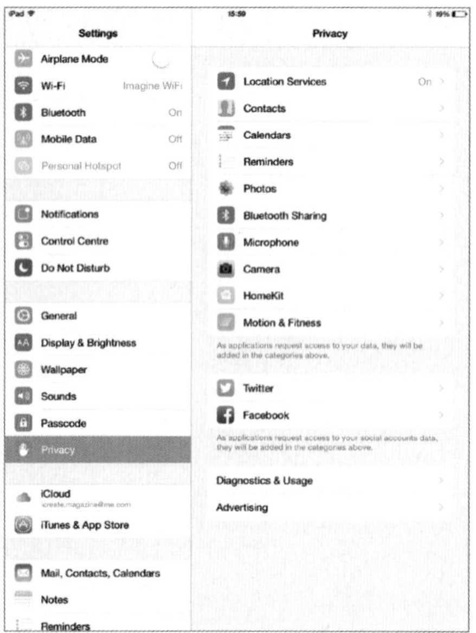

01 Locate Settings

The Privacy settings can be found in Settings. Under this header are options for Location Services, Contacts, Calendars, Reminders, Photos, Bluetooth Sharing, Twitter and Facebook.

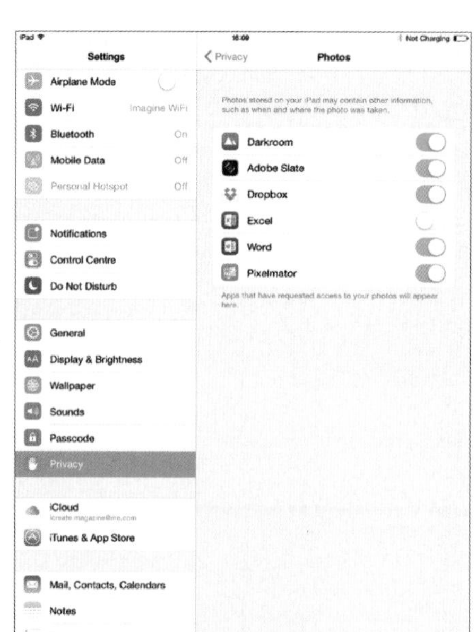

02 Seeking permission

Navigating to each of the sections gives you a suitable list of apps that have requested access to various information on your device. You can enable or disable access via the toggle.

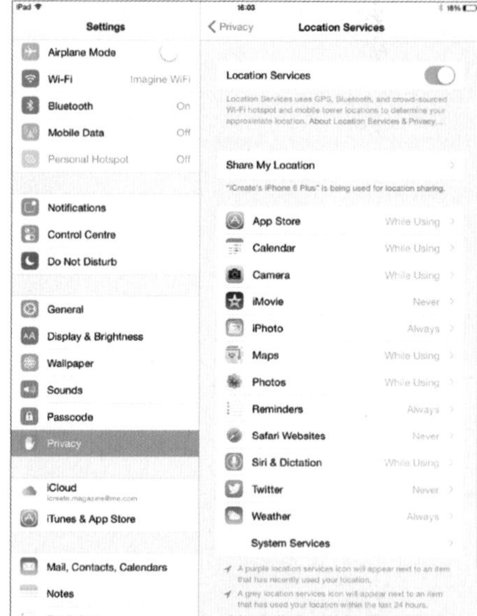

03 Location Services

When you enter this area, you will be told which apps have requested your location. More than that, however, you will also be able to see which app has used location services recently.

Finding yourself on the iPad

Keep an eye on the apps tracking your location and make sure only trusted sources know where you are

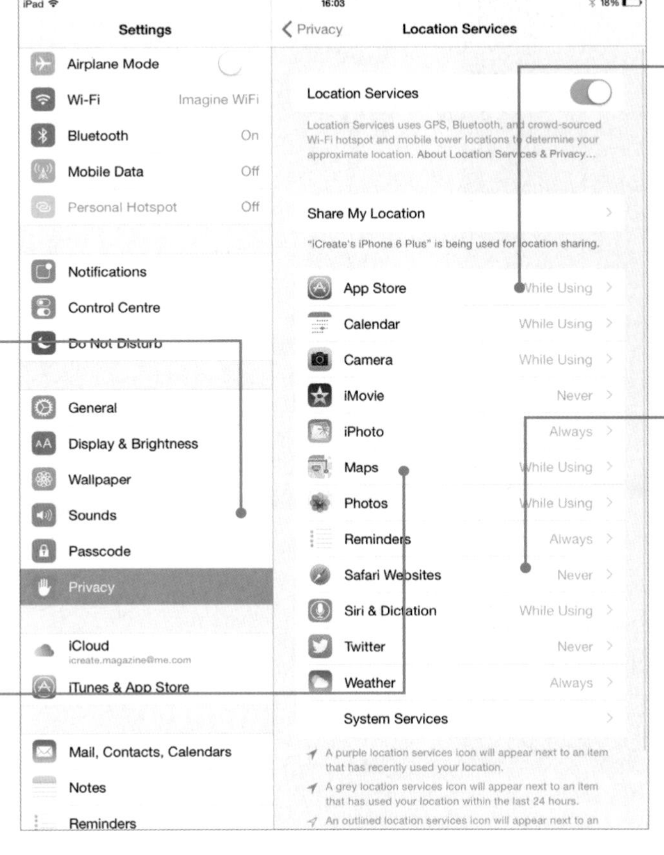

Your location
When an app has recently looked up your location, an arrow will show up next to its name. Grey arrows denote that an app has looked up your location in the last 24 hours

Privacy section
All of the issues relating to privacy on the iPad are stored within this section, which is accessible from your main Settings screen

System Services
This area contains options like compass calibration, time zone settings and location-based iAds. None are vital, unless you regularly use compass-based directions

System apps
System apps like Camera, Maps and Siri will all need to know your location to function properly. These apps can be trusted, so don't worry about switching them on

Battery life
It may be a good idea to disable Location Services for apps and system services that can be used without tracking your location in order to conserve battery life. Go to Settings and then Privacy, tap on Location Services and System Services.

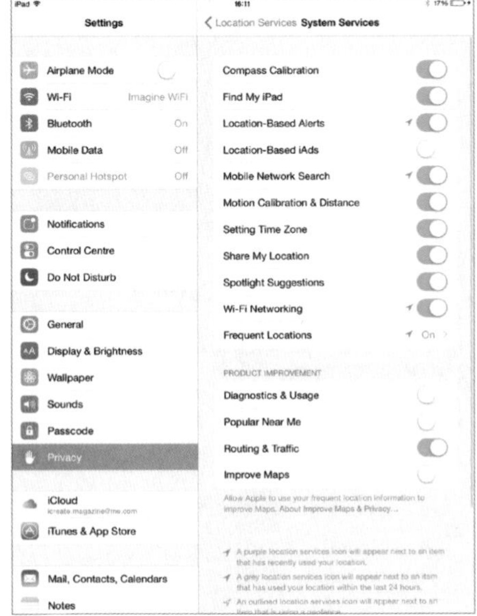

04 System Services
In Location Services, you will find that you can enable or disable location services for System Services such as Diagnostics & Usage, Compass Calibration and much more.

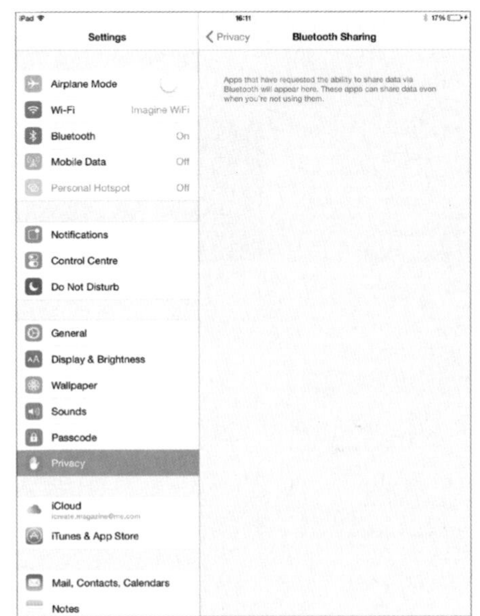

05 Bluetooth privacy
Apps that want to share information via Bluetooth will appear here. These apps can share data even when you're not using them, so be careful to monitor this section occasionally.

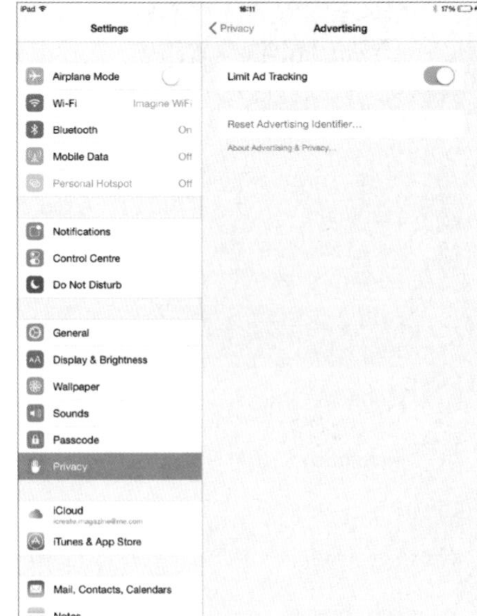

06 Advertising
At the bottom of the main Privacy page is a section called Advertising. The new advertising identifier can be used to give you more control over advertisers' ability to use tracking methods.

Change your iPad's wallpaper

Find out how to quickly customise the background of your iPad's home and lock screens

With the iPad, Apple enables users to change the image used as the background for the home screen and lock screen. This may seem like a trivial addition to the software set, but for Apple it's pretty big. It is a company that deals in absolutes and employs a closed system to prevent people from making the iOS environment look bad. So we're glad that we get to add a little individuality to distinguish between iPads. We're also pretty pleased that it's possible to have two different images set for the lock screen and home screen at the same time.

Making changes to the system is very simple; it works in a very similar way to the iPhone, only you can see much more of the action path that you take to get to a change in settings. This makes the system clearer and easier to use. Proficiency at this simple task should give you the courage to explore the settings further to get even more use from your iPad and make improvements to the way it works for you.

Whether it's an image from the iPad's supplied Wallpaper set or a photo from your album, follow this step-by-step tutorial to instantly customise your iPad and have it looking the way you want it to.

"We're glad that we get to add a little individuality to distinguish between iPads"

Settings Change the wallpaper

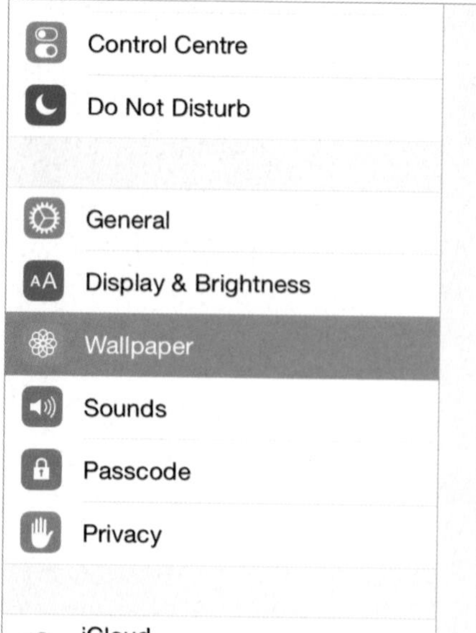

01 Cog tapper

Load the Settings by tapping its icon on your iPad's home screen. You will then be taken to the screen above. Tap on Wallpapers on the left-hand side, in the third block down.

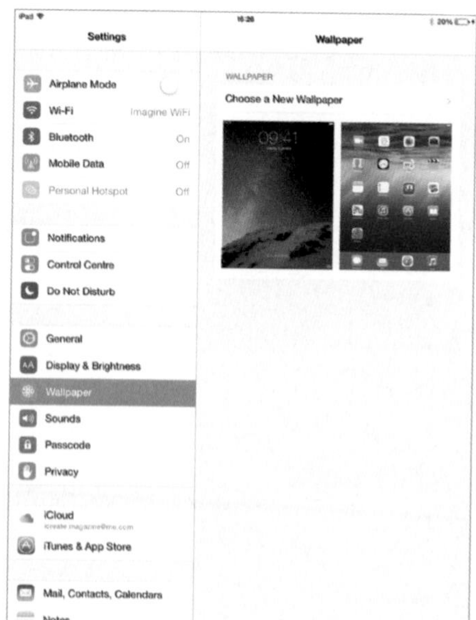

02 Wallpaper

The screen will show you what you currently have selected. To change your background, simply tap on the Choose a New Wallpaper option. This will take you through to a new menu.

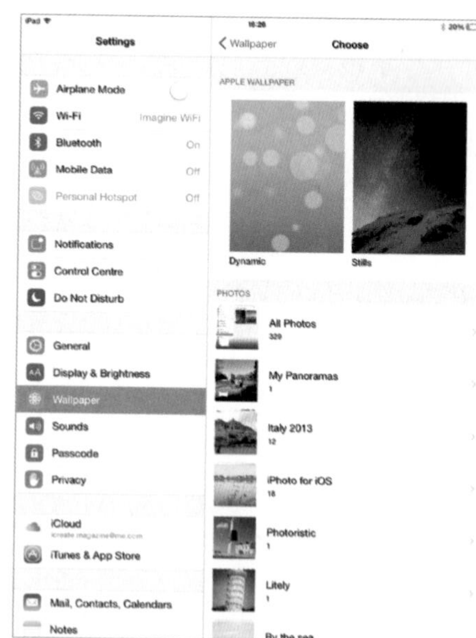

03 Options

You now have several options from which choose in order to get a suitable picture. Choose the album that you wish to pick from. Tap on that album to then bring up the contents.

Customising your home screen

Making the most of all that screen real estate

Wallpaper Preview

16:27

Friday 12 June

✓ Setting Wallpaper...

Cancel | Set Lock Screen | Set Home Screen | Set Both | Perspective Zoom: Off

Move around

While positioning your picture you will be able to see just how responsive the iPad touch screen is. It's a testament to hardware and software unity

Simplicity

Apple always makes interfaces easy to use. There's no mass of dialogue and only really a couple of major options here, so it is easy to make changes

Great resolution

The iPad screen has a fantastic 2048 x 1536 display at 264 pixels per inch (ppi) resolution, so having a cool image on your home and lock screen is a must

Undo changes

Apple also makes it easy for you to change your mind and go back to the last action. In this case just hit the Cancel button

Settings

The settings system on the iPad follows the same pathways as those on the iPhone, only instead of shunting the view to the left or right as options are chosen, you can see the result of your choice to the right of the static options list.

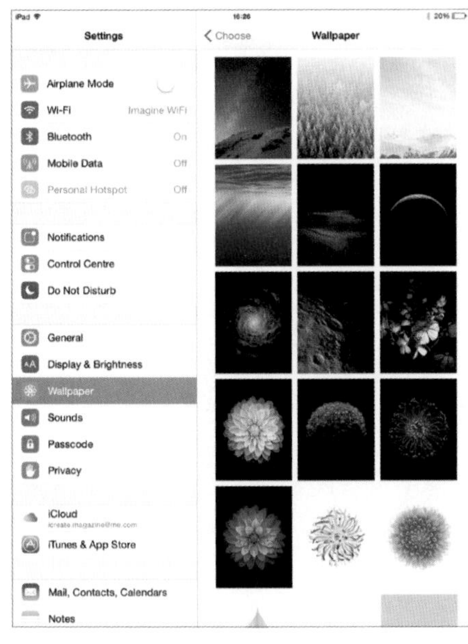

04 Preview

Once in the album of your choice, make your final selection and simply tap on that picture. You'll then be taken directly to a preview screen to see your selected image in full.

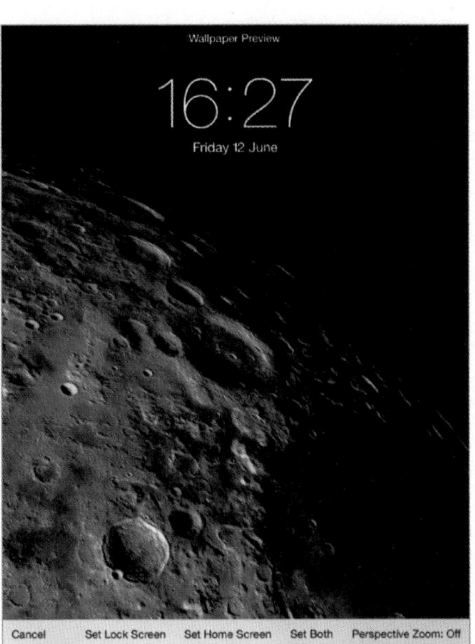

05 Top options

Use a pinch, reverse pinch and swipe to position the image and then pick from the options at the bottom of the screen: Set Lock Screen, Set Home Screen or Set Both.

06 Check it

Once you've tapped an option, you'll be taken back to the home screen where you can see your changes. Use the Sleep button if you wish to view the lock screen.

Find a misplaced iPad or iPhone

Keep all of your devices safe at any time and take action to render them impossible to use if they are stolen

Find My iPhone is an app that can be used on any Apply device and, despite the name, it has been tweaked to take full advantage of the bigger iPad screen. With this app you can quickly and accurately find any iPhone or iPad that signs in using the same Apple ID and which is currently connected to the internet. Location Services is used to pinpoint its exact location, at which point you can take different actions remotely.

Lost mode will lock the device completely and let you send a personalised message to the device lock screen, you can erase the device with a couple of taps or you can continually play a loud sound. All of this is very useful in deterring theft, but just in case you should at the very least already have a passcode set up on your device to stop others from seeing your data. You should also not try to retrieve the device yourself for obvious reasons.

If your device is powered down or in an area where data coverage is not available, you will not be able to track it, but when turned on Find My iPhone should prove to be useful again. It can make all of the difference between finding your precious device and losing it forever, so now is time to understand exactly how it works.

"Lost mode will lock the device completely and let you send a personalised message"

Find My iPhone Find devices from home

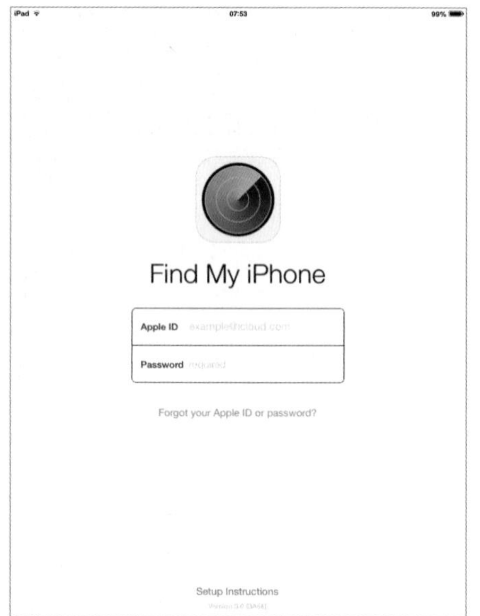

01 Signing in

Find and install Find My iPhone on the App Store and, when opened, you will be prompted to sign in with your Apple ID. Do this with each device your family owns that uses the same Apple ID.

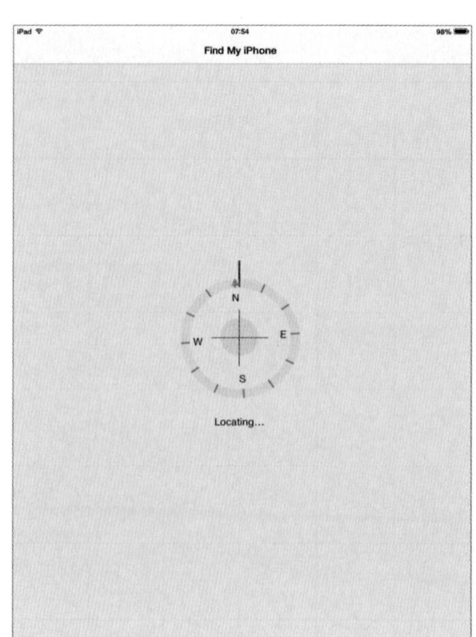

02 A quick search

The iPad will start searching for devices that are connected to the internet. Initially, this could take some time, but in future searches they should appear very quickly within the main interface.

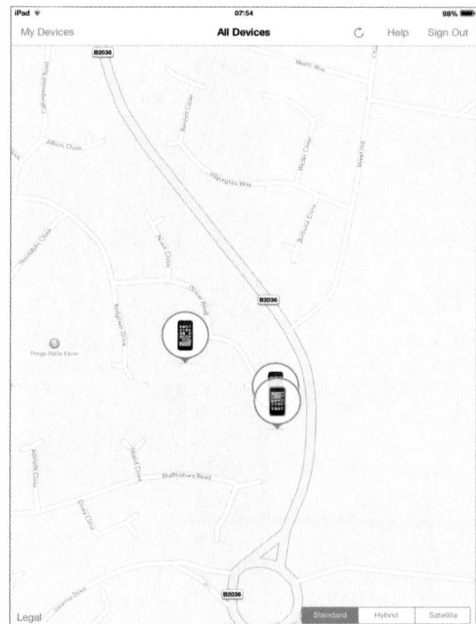

03 Here they are

As if by magic, your devices will appear on a real-time map within Find My iPhone. As the devices move, you will see this reflected on the map so you always know exactly where they are.

A logical interface

Keep all of your precious devices safe all the time

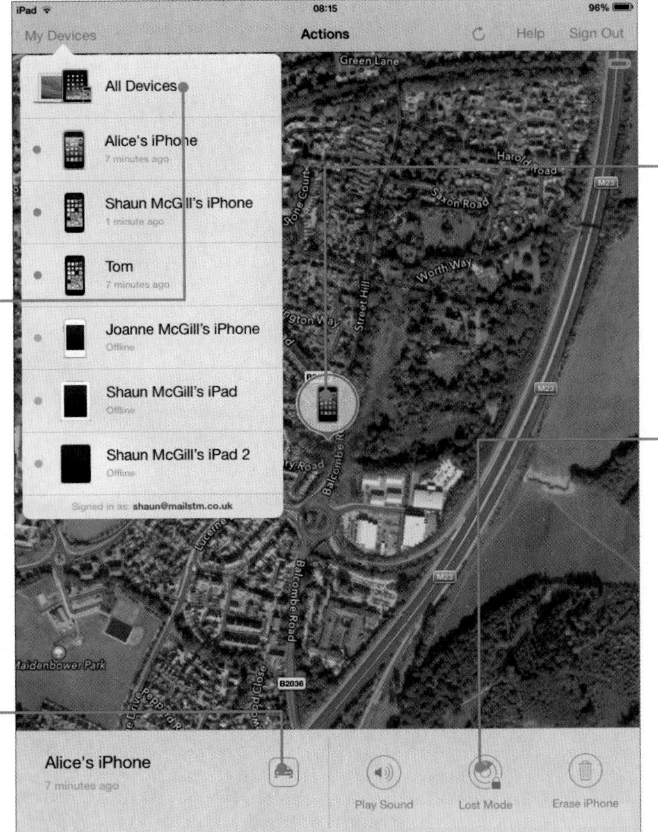

Every device covered
All of your devices should be set up with the Find My iPhone app just in case any of them gets lost or is ever stolen

A perfectly tracked phone
Each device will be shown on the map in its exact location any time it is connected. It is a highly accurate and useful solution

Erase a device
If the iPad is stolen, you can put it into lost mode or erase it immediately. This will stop whoever has it from using it

Time to travel
Tapping this icon will immediately open Apple Maps with a route pre-planned for you to travel to where the device currently is

Use it at home
The Play Sound option at the bottom of the screen is very useful if you lose your iPad at home. Tap the icon and a loud sound will start to play which should be enough to help you find the device immediately. This is sure to come in very handy!

04 Choose a device

Tap on any device and a new menu will appear at the bottom of the screen. The name of the device will be shown and you can tap the car icon to receive directions to travel to it.

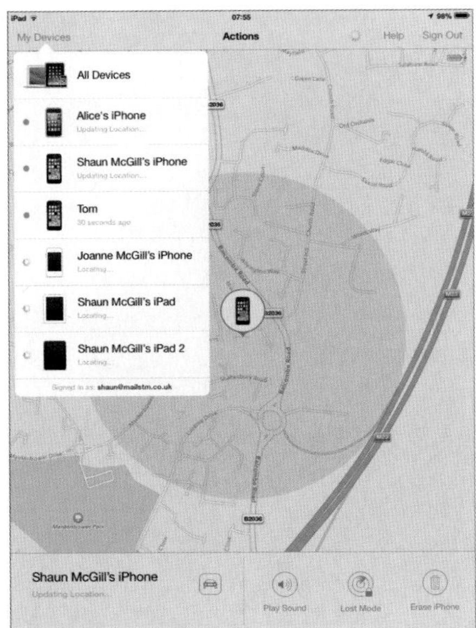

05 A handy list

When you tap My Devices at the top left-hand side of the screen, you will be able to see, and then select, all of your devices in one list. It also shows any devices that are not connected.

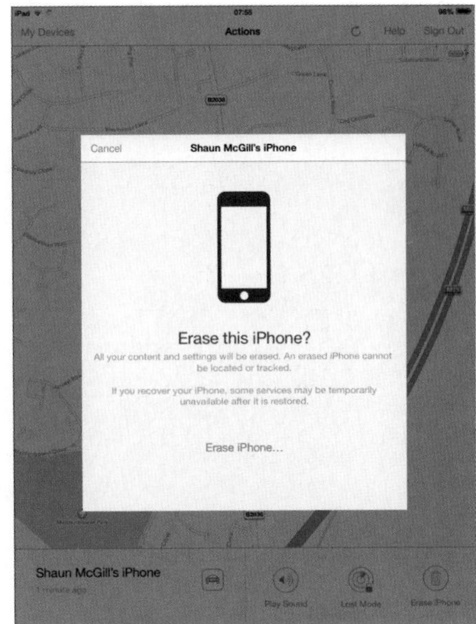

06 Take action

If your device has been stolen or you are concerned, you can put it in lost mode remotely or erase it immediately to stop others from seeing your personal information. It takes a couple of taps.

Get to grips with multitasking

Multitasking is extremely easy to use and there are many useful features available using just a swipe and a tap

Multitasking has been available on the iPad since the beginning, but recent changes mean that it is easier to use than ever before. Gone is the small strip of icons at the bottom of the screen when you double-tap the home button, and in its place is a full-screen display that lets you move between apps with ease.

Each app is obviously presented clearly thanks to the large screenshots that show the last position the app reached, and the app icons are displayed directly below each shot. You can swipe up on the main panel to close an app fully or tap it to open it immediately. This will help you leave tasks mid-flow to come back to later, when you will also be able to quickly assess the state of each task from a distance.

This may sound like a small change, but for a feature that you will likely use often, it really does make the daily process of navigating your iPad much quicker and more efficient when used often. Other enhancements have been added in the background which you will not see, but again they do add to the seamless nature of multitasking on an iPad running iOS 8 or higher.

It's time to show you how to use the feature so that you can benefit as well.

"You can swipe up on the main panel to close an app fully or tap it to open it immediately"

Multitasking Understand the multitasking features

01 Panels and icons

Double-tap the home button no matter what you are doing on your iPad and a series of horizontal panels will appear on the screen. Below each you will see an icon that's is designed to show what app you are looking at. The panels show where the app froze.

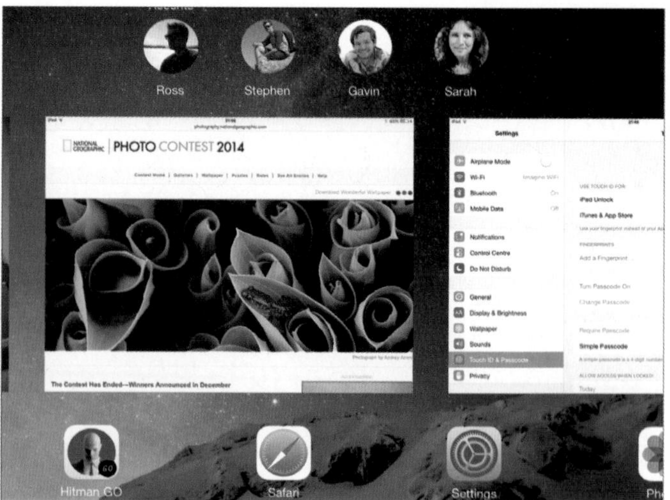

02 Switch between apps

To switch between apps, simply scroll your finger left and all of the recently used and open apps will be shown. You can now tap either the app icon or the main panel to jump straight to that app. It should start up in the exact position you left it in.

Multitask with ease

Learn to multitask in seconds

The Home screen
The Home screen is also available at the far left and will always be in that position. Do a long scroll to the right and you will be taken straight to it. A potentially useful shortcut which could save time

Contact view
Along the top of the screen you will also see your recent contacts. Tap one of the icons to open up options for each contact, so you can quickly message, call or FaceTime them

Swipe up
Swipe any panel to the top of the screen and the app will be closed immediately. This can be useful if your iPad is performing slowly or if you just want to close a few running apps

Use the icons
The icons may not seem to have a purpose, but they are particularly useful for switching between apps quickly. Swipe across the icons and your open apps will scroll much faster than simply swiping the app panels

In the background
When you use your iPad, a lot is happening in the background. The apps you use most often are intelligently updated so when you go to one of these they will show a more recent state. For example, a social network app could be updated in the background continually. The software uses your usage pattern to offer a balance between usability and power consumption.

03 Close an app

If you want to close an app, all you have to do it hold your finger on a panel and slide it to the top of the screen. The panel will disappear and the app to the right will slide over to take its place. The sheer size of the panels makes closing apps very simple.

04 Multitasking tips

If you want to swipe through your apps faster, swipe across the icons at the bottom of the screen rather than the panels at the centre. Another useful tip is that you can close multiple apps at once – simply place a finger on each app's panel and swipe them all up off the screen at once.

Introducing the Control Centre

Take advantage of the Control Centre to quickly change settings and access frequently used features

The new Control Centre introduced in iOS 7 was something that users had craved for a long time, but Apple's implementation is arguably even better than we could have hoped for. The elegance with which it works is astounding, with a raft of shortcuts and features are available to you with one swipe and a tap.

A lot is happening in a very small space on the iPad and it is surprising that it does not take up more screen real estate, but even this works because you do not have to move your finger much at all to access what you need. Within the pop-up panel you have access to music controls, the Clock app, the camera, AirDrop, AirPlay plus volume and brightness bars. Add to this icons for Airplane mode, Wi-Fi, Bluetooth, Do Not Disturb, Silent mode and screen lock and you can start to see just how effective it can be.

It takes no time to learn and once you start using it, you will wonder however you managed to navigate your device before it arrived. Let's now explore the new Control Centre and discover how you can make the most of its useful functions in just a few simple swipes.

"Once you start using the Control Centre, you will wonder how you managed before it arrived"

Control Centre understand the Control Centre

01 Where is it?

Your home screen looks normal until you start to move your finger upwards from below the screen. The Control Centre will start to appear no matter where you place your finger to swipe up and it will take up the bottom portion of the screen. Notice the semi-transparency of the panel.

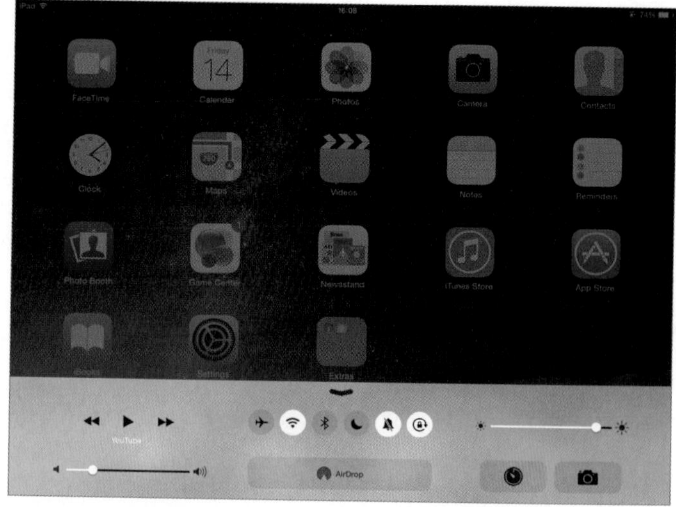

02 Use the settings

The six icons in the middle of the panel will be used the most and, as you tap each one, text indicators will appear above them. You can use these icons to manage Airplane mode, Wi-Fi, Bluetooth, Do Not Disturb, Silent mode and the screen rotation lock. Tap each to turn on and off.

Keep in control

Every useful control you need

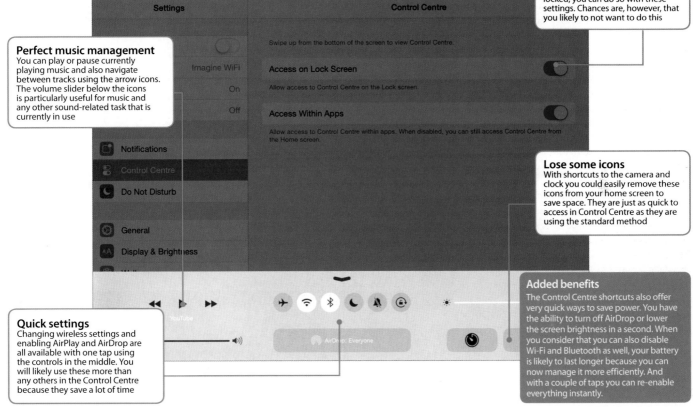

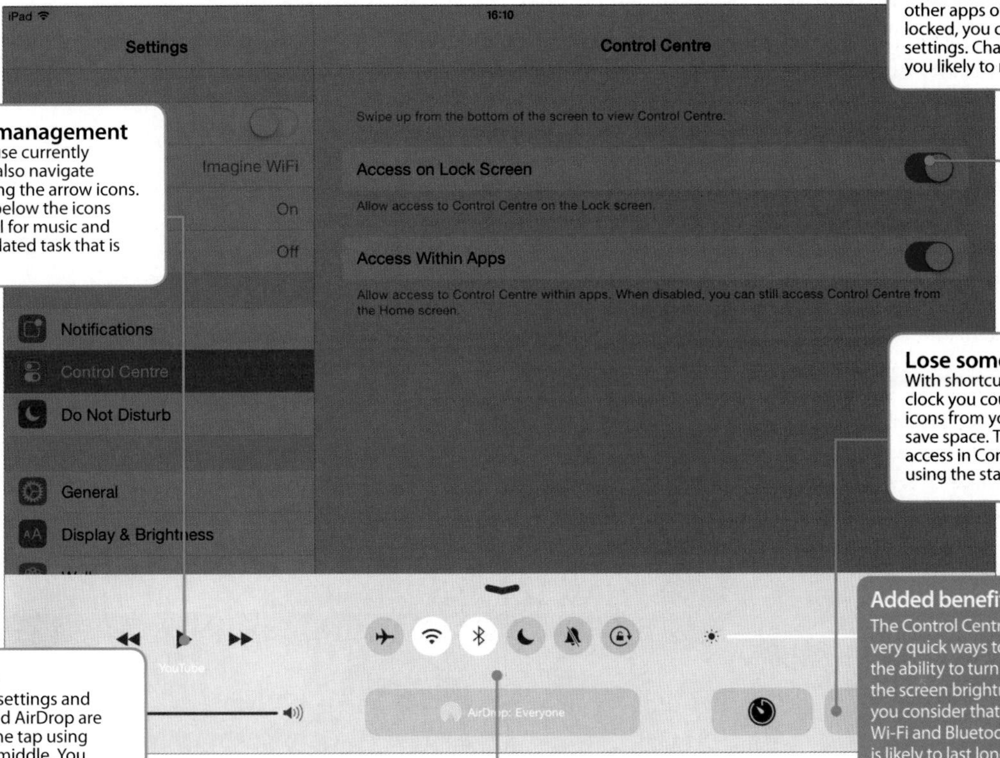

Setting it up
If you have need to limit the use of the Control Centre when using other apps or when the screen is locked, you can do so with these settings. Chances are, however, that you likely to not want to do this

Perfect music management
You can play or pause currently playing music and also navigate between tracks using the arrow icons. The volume slider below the icons is particularly useful for music and any other sound-related task that is currently in use

Lose some icons
With shortcuts to the camera and clock you could easily remove these icons from your home screen to save space. They are just as quick to access in Control Centre as they are using the standard method

Quick settings
Changing wireless settings and enabling AirPlay and AirDrop are all available with one tap using the controls in the middle. You will likely use these more than any others in the Control Centre because they save a lot of time

Added benefits
The Control Centre shortcuts also offer very quick ways to save power. You have the ability to turn off AirDrop or lower the screen brightness in a second. When you consider that you can also disable Wi-Fi and Bluetooth as well, your battery is likely to last longer because you can now manage it more efficiently. And with a couple of taps you can re-enable everything instantly.

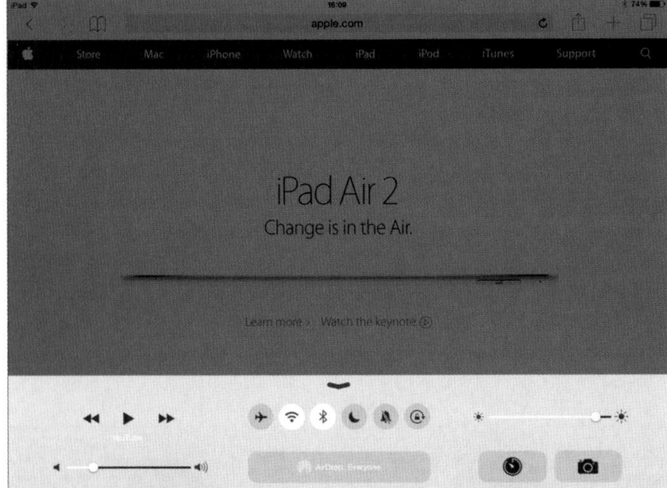

03 Extra controls

To the left you will see icons that can manage music play and volume. Simply use the slider for volume and the icons to pause, play and jump between tracks. Over to the right you will find icons to quickly access the camera and clock, plus a brightness control.

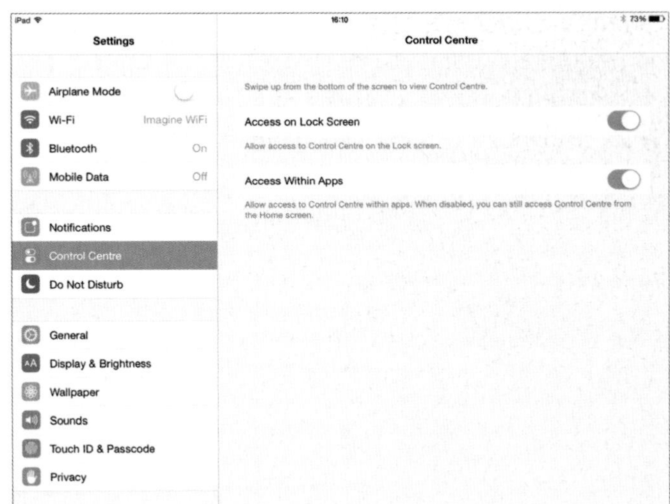

04 Set it up

Go to Settings>Control Centre and you will be given two options. The first lets you choose whether to allow access to the Control Centre from the lock screen and the second does the same when you are using a different app. We would advise to turn both on.

Access email on your iPad

While email works perfectly well on the iPhone it really comes into its own on the iPad's larger screen

In today's digital age, using email is one of the most essential ways of being able to stay in touch with friends and family, as well as being a pretty vital tool in the business world. While both the iPhone and iPod Touch are perfectly capable of displaying email, the iPad is just so much better due to its larger size, making it a much superior option. What's more, the virtual keyboard makes it far easier and quicker to type on (especially when you need to write longer mails), making it far more practical to use.

This step-by-step tutorial will not only show you how to set up a new or existing email account for use on the iPad and beyond, but will also take you through the fundamentals of reading and sending email on your device. Once set up you'll be able to use existing accounts at will, quickly reply to and forward mail that you receive, and, most importantly, ensure that you stay in touch with friends and loved ones.

In short, we will show you how to integrate your iPad into your lifestyle in a way that will make you feel closer to the people you care about, rather than further away. Let's get started and learn how to get going with email.

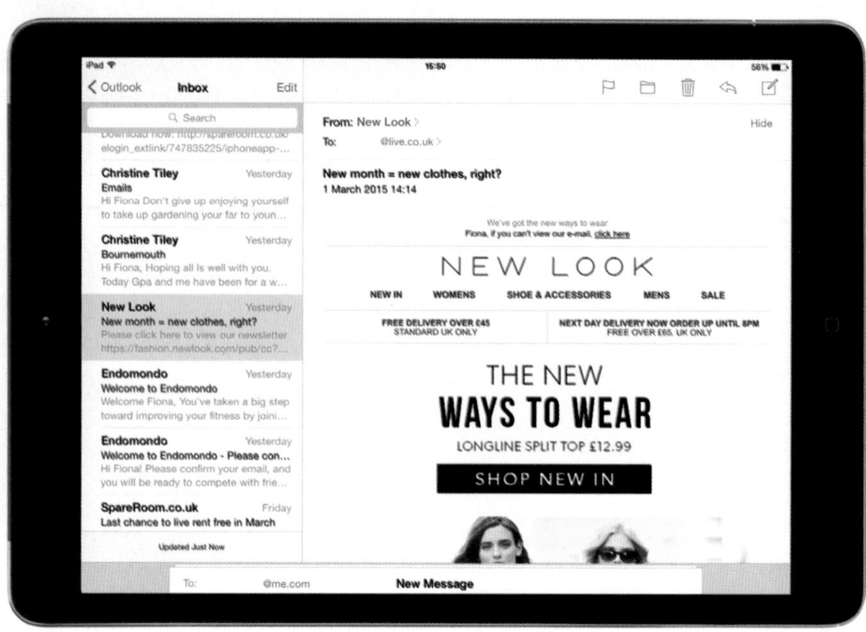

"While both the iPhone and iPod Touch can display email, the iPad's size makes it so much better"

Mail Set up an email account on your iPad

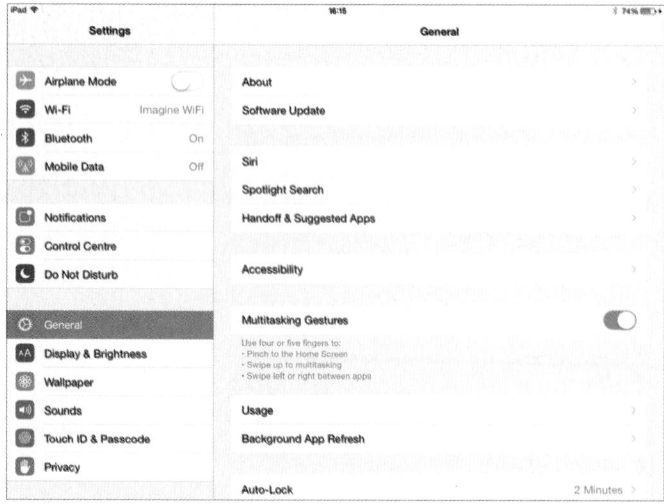

01 Set things up

In order to set up an email account you will need to first enter the Settings app of your iPad. Look at the icons on the home page of your iPad until you find one with a large, grey cog. Tap on it to continue to the Settings menu. It may be located on the Dock at the bottom of the screen.

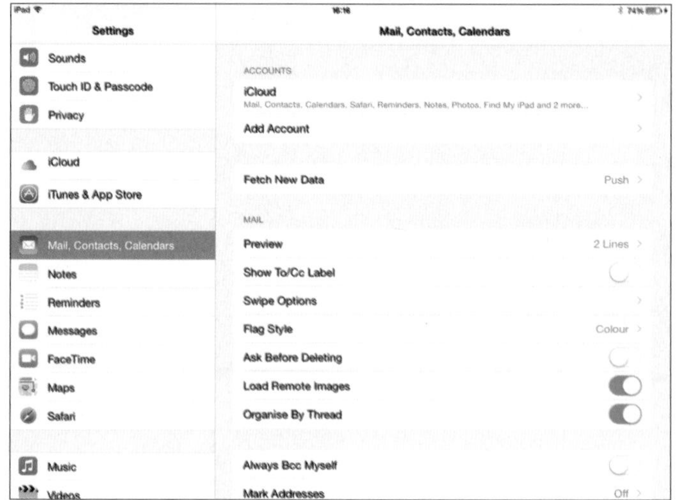

02 Find your mail

Upon entering Settings, you'll find a row of different icons down the left-hand side of the screen. Look for and select 'Mail, Contacts, Calendars' in order to continue. Now look on the right-hand side of the screen and tap Add Account.

Viewing mail

Learn about your email viewing options

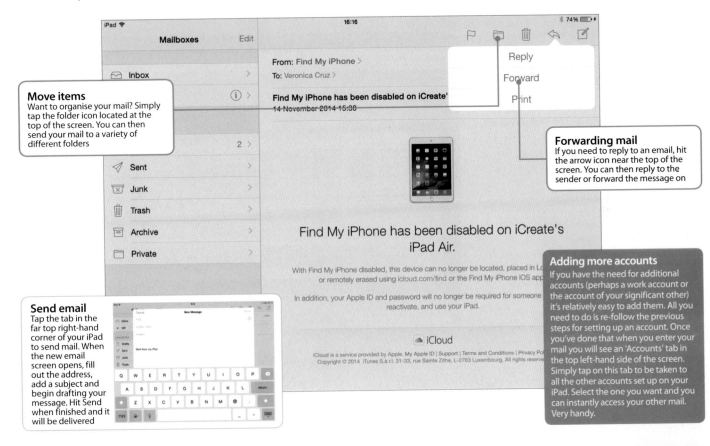

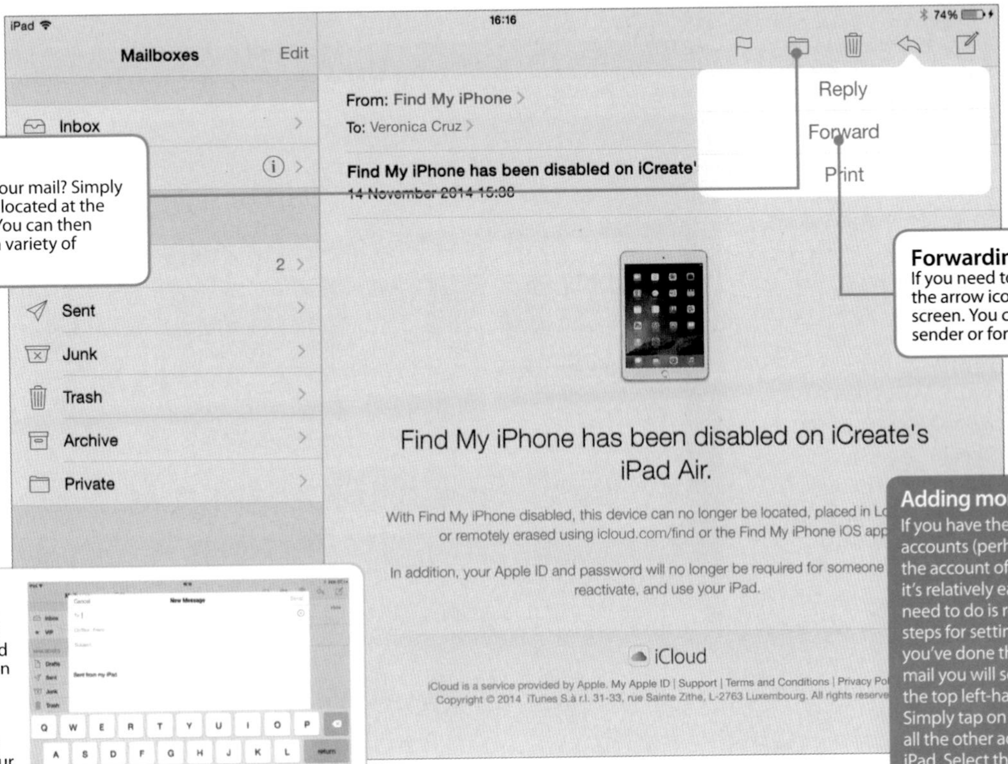

Move items
Want to organise your mail? Simply tap the folder icon located at the top of the screen. You can then send your mail to a variety of different folders

Forwarding mail
If you need to reply to an email, hit the arrow icon near the top of the screen. You can then reply to the sender or forward the message on

Adding more accounts
If you have the need for additional accounts (perhaps a work account or the account of your significant other) it's relatively easy to add them. All you need to do is re-follow the previous steps for setting up an account. Once you've done that when you enter your mail you will see an 'Accounts' tab in the top left-hand side of the screen. Simply tap on this tab to be taken to all the other accounts set up on your iPad. Select the one you want and you can instantly access your other mail. Very handy.

Send email
Tap the tab in the far top right-hand corner of your iPad to send mail. When the new email screen opens, fill out the address, add a subject and begin drafting your message. Hit Send when finished and it will be delivered

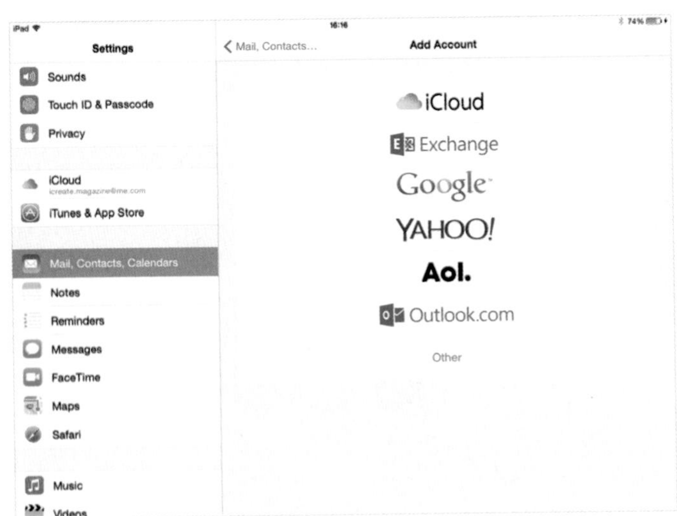

03 Make your choice

You'll now be presented with seven email provider options. They are iCloud, Microsoft Exchange, Google Mail, Yahoo! Mail, AOL, Microsoft Hotmail and Other (which lets you access accounts like Zoho Mail). Whether you want to create a new account or add an existing one, the process is as follows…

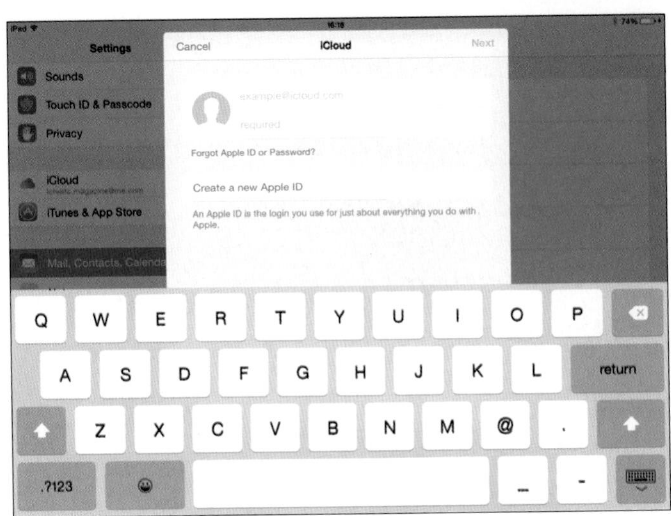

04 You've got mail!

After choosing your preferred provider you'll be presented with the following screen. All you need to do here is fill in the relevant information for each section. Once this is done, simply tap Next in the top right-hand corner. Congratulations, you have mail!

Install iTunes on your desktop

Although connecting your iPad to your computer is no longer necessary, installing iTunes has some benefits

Since the release of iOS 5, all of Apple's devices, including your iPad, can be used straight out of the box without the need to connect them to your computer via iTunes, as was previously the case. However, installing the latest copy of iTunes on your computer is still recommended as it allows you to perform a series of useful tasks.

Primarily, through iTunes you can convert your CD collection and copy the files to your iPad, but the latest version, 12, fully embraces Apple's iTunes in the iCloud service so that any music you purchase through iTunes – be it on your iPad or Mac – is automatically pushed to all of your devices wirelessly. What's more, through iTunes Match you can also access your entire iTunes library from any device, stream individual tracks or download them for offline listening for a small annual cost (£21.99/$24.99). You can also connect your iPad to your computer via USB and perform essential backup and syncing processes.

In this tutorial we guide you through the process of downloading and installing the latest version of iTunes for your desktop.

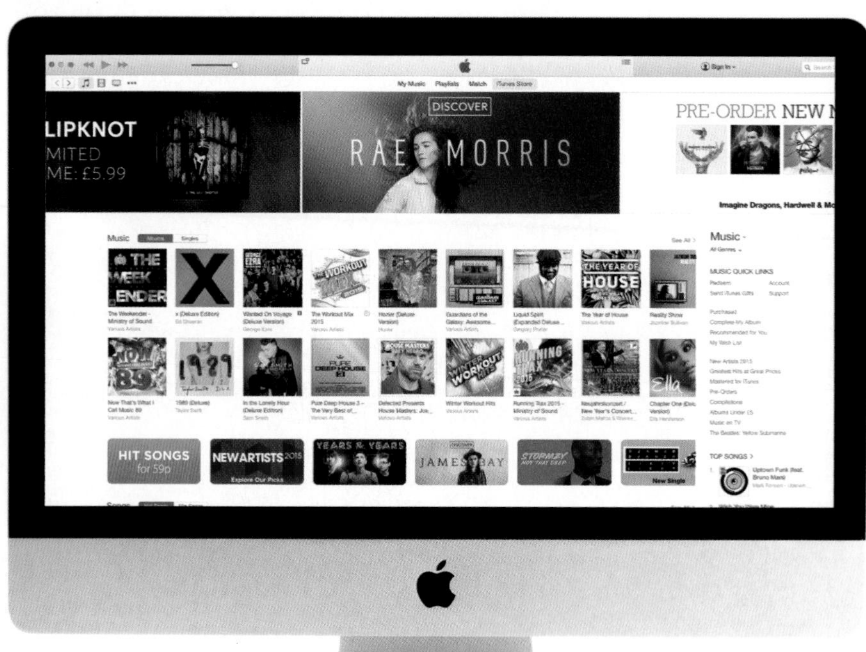

iTunes Installing iTunes on your Mac or PC

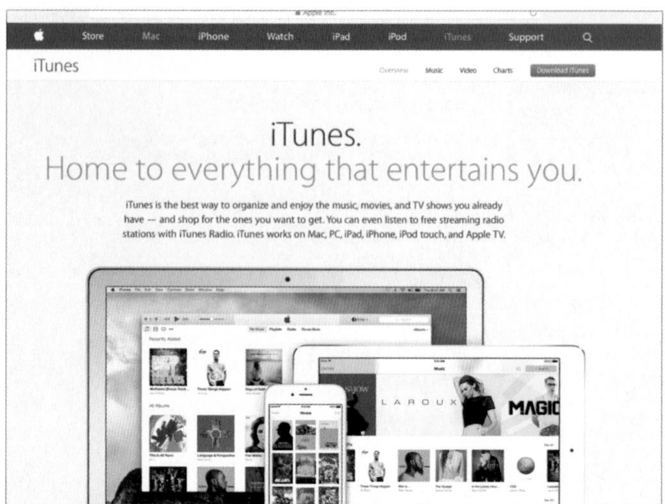

01 Get online

Your first step is to launch your favourite web browser and point it in the direction of **www.itunes.com**. The layout of the page changes regularly, but there will be a 'Download iTunes' button somewhere within it (currently, it's located in the top-right of the page).

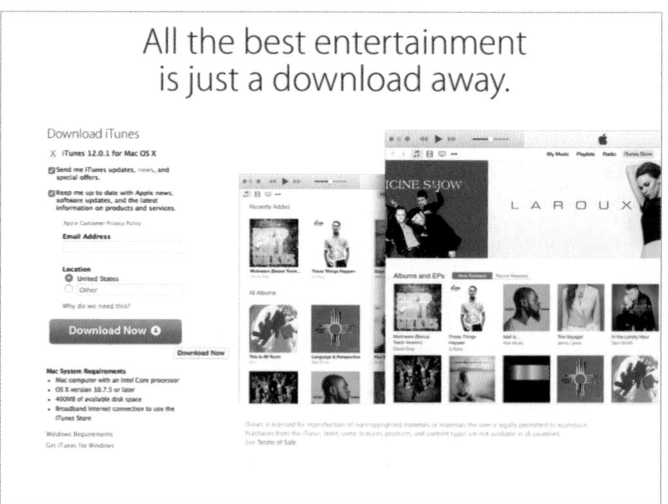

02 Download now

This will lead you to the official download page. Your browser will recognise the type of computer you're on so you won't be offered any choices that could lead to confusion. You'll see a single 'Download Now' button. Be sure to double-check you're happy with the options to receive emails from Apple.

The iTunes Download page

Navigate the basics of the Download page

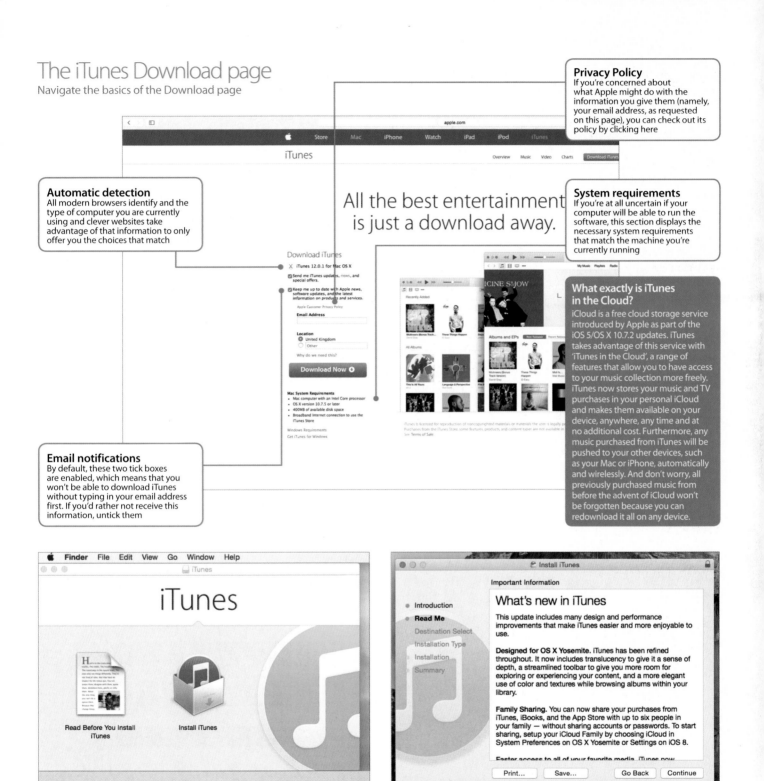

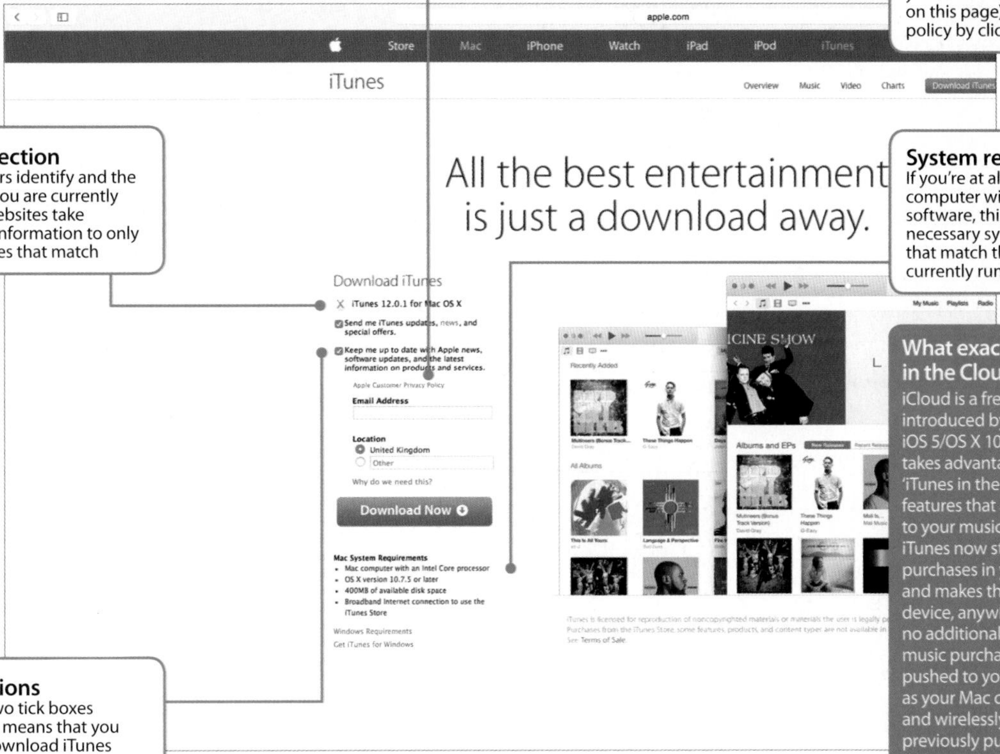

Privacy Policy
If you're concerned about what Apple might do with the information you give them (namely, your email address, as requested on this page), you can check out its policy by clicking here

Automatic detection
All modern browsers identify and the type of computer you are currently using and clever websites take advantage of that information to only offer you the choices that match

System requirements
If you're at all uncertain if your computer will be able to run the software, this section displays the necessary system requirements that match the machine you're currently running

Email notifications
By default, these two tick boxes are enabled, which means that you won't be able to download iTunes without typing in your email address first. If you'd rather not receive this information, untick them

What exactly is iTunes in the Cloud?

iCloud is a free cloud storage service introduced by Apple as part of the iOS 5/OS X 10.7.2 updates. iTunes takes advantage of this service with 'iTunes in the Cloud', a range of features that allow you to have access to your music collection more freely. iTunes now stores your music and TV purchases in your personal iCloud and makes them available on your device, anywhere, any time and at no additional cost. Furthermore, any music purchased from iTunes will be pushed to your other devices, such as your Mac or iPhone, automatically and wirelessly. And don't worry, all previously purchased music from before the advent of iCloud won't be forgotten because you can redownload it all on any device.

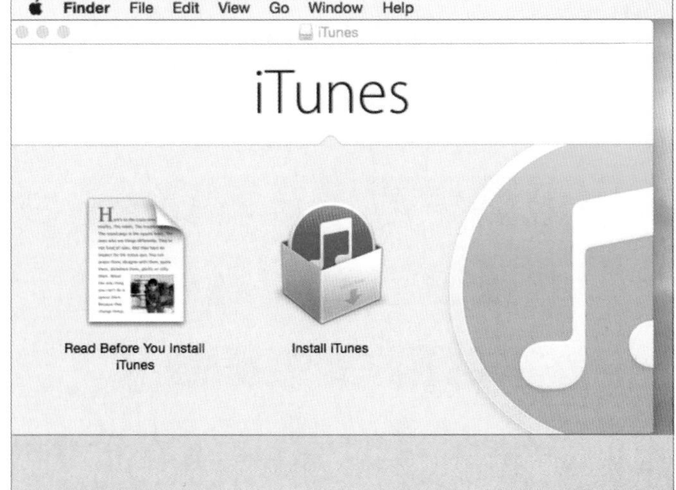

03 Installing

Once the download has completed, a new window will open up with a semi-transparent iTunes logo inside it. The 'Read Before You Install iTunes' document gives you the minimum requirements, without which the program will not function. Double-click 'Install iTunes' to proceed.

04 Licence Agreement

Once iTunes has been installed, its icon should appear in your Dock or Desktop. If it hasn't, you'll be able to locate it in your Applications or Program Files folder. The first time you double-click on it, you'll have to agree to the licence agreement. Agreeing grants you access to the software.

Get to know the iTunes interface

iTunes is capable of storing any media you'd care to enjoy, all while being the gateway to Apple's online store

The first version of iTunes was released well over a decade ago, back on 9 January 2001. Apple had purchased Casady and Greene's SoundJam MP two years previously, realising that it had missed the boat with regards to the CD ripping and burning that was going on at the time. Back then, the iPod didn't even exist. Three years later, however, the iTunes Music Store was born, along with Apple's ambitions as an online entertainment retailer.

It's only recently become the case that you can use your iPad without installing iTunes on your computer, and since the release of iOS 5 you can activate your device and get all the latest system updates without the need to manually connect it to your computer.

However, there is a lot more to iTunes than allowing iPad functionality, not least the ability to convert your CD collection to MP3 format and copy the tracks to your device, browse for all the latest entertainment and apps at the iTunes and App Stores and enjoy the many new features that iCloud provides. Here we show you the basic essentials to help you navigate iTunes and get acquainted with its media-storing capabilities.

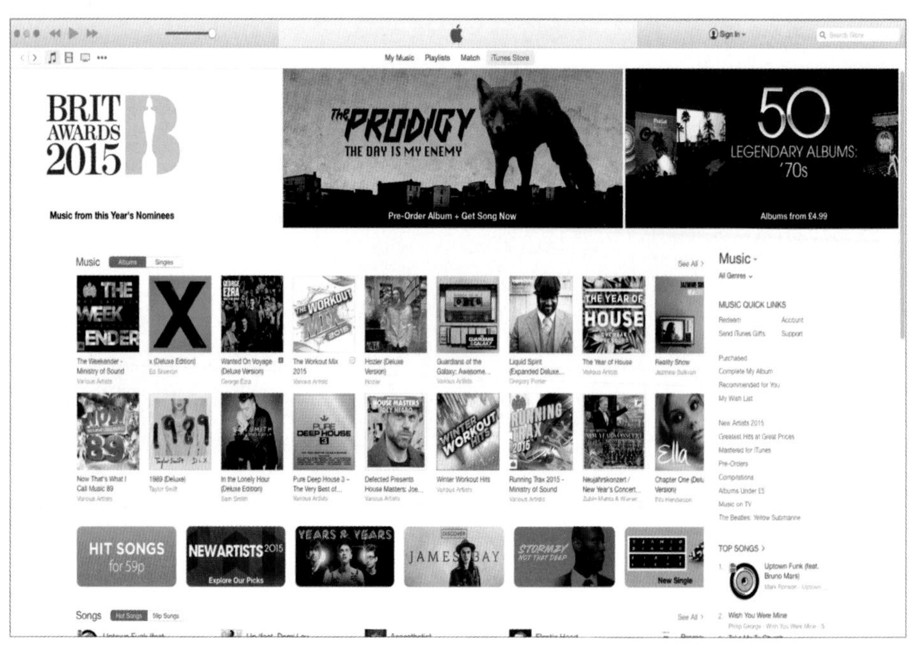

"It's only recently the case that you can use your iPad without installing iTunes on your computer"

iTunes Getting to know the software

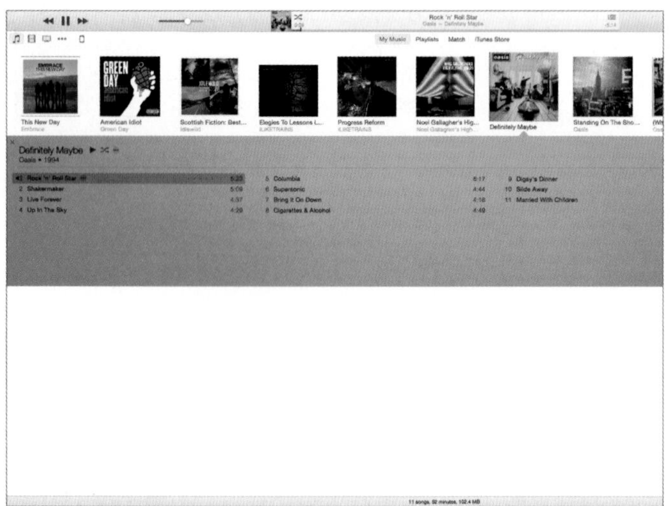

01 The Library

Your media is broken down by type – ie music, films, television shows, podcasts, books and apps for your iOS devices – all of which you can acquire from the iTunes Store. To sort between these, simply click on the current category button and select a new one from the drop-down list.

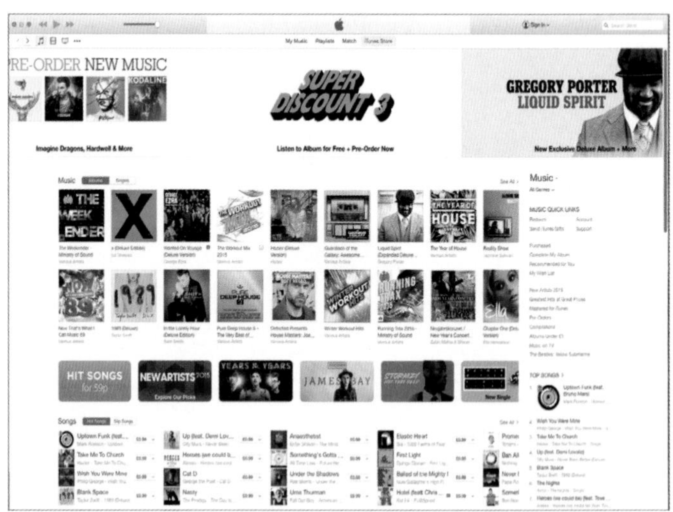

02 The Store

To access Apple's online media store, move your cursor up to the right-hand side of the top menu bar and click on 'iTunes Store'. The front page is geared towards entertainment, showing you the latest and most popular songs and albums, films and TV shows (books can only be read on your iOS device).

Browsing the App Store

Helping you find the apps you need in seconds

Search and find
If none of the recommendations are of any help, you can always use the good old-fashioned search field. Start typing and a list of options will appear for you to choose from

Latest releases
Sometimes a recommendation is all you need, and the Best New Apps section shows you a selection of staff favourites that you may feel suit your exact needs

Quick Links
Under your iTunes account details, the App Store Quick Links gives you a speedy way to access App Store collections and essential categories to help you find some great apps

Categories
Narrow down your search by browsing through a specific category. To access this menu, click on the App Store button and select your choice

How do I choose what to add to my iPad?

By default, iTunes is designed to take care of that for you. Even if you have more media than can fit in your iPad, it'll choose which ones to add, and which to leave behind. But if you'd like more control over the process, start by clicking on the iPad button near the top of iTunes. From there, you'll have options in the various tabs to select which songs, films or apps you'd like to include. There are multiple ways of doing this, which will be explained in other parts of this book.

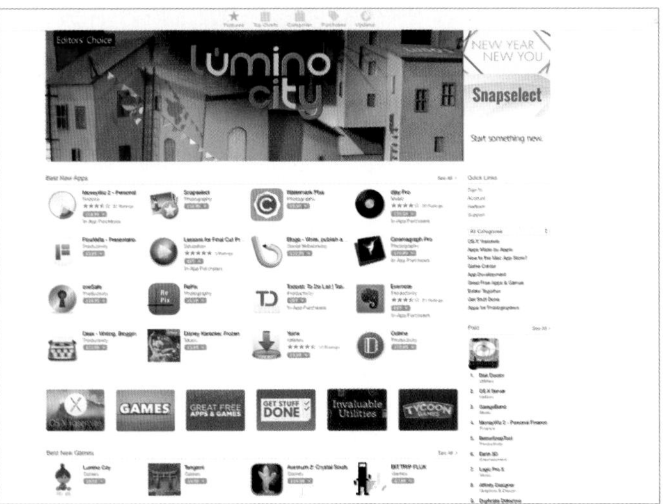

03 Finding the apps

To get to the App Store and start browsing for applications for your iPad, head back to the row of buttons just above the main content window in iTunes and click on 'App Store'. Once there, you'll see two buttons centred immediately below the menu bar. Click on 'iPad' to view the iPad apps.

04 Connecting your iPad

After activating your iPad, it'll appear on the right-hand side of the top menu bar in the main library view. Click on its name and you'll gain access to your device's sync settings. You can use that section to select which media to add and which apps to install, or just let iTunes add everything automatically.

Sync your music from iTunes

Here's how easy it is to sync your music collection from a computer to your iPad

Playing music on your iPad might not be the first use that comes to mind if you own an iPod too, but it's certainly possible. In fact, your iPad may be the best option for playing music during a party or when entertaining other people, allowing them to make a selection too. The larger display makes it easy to browse the music library, album artwork looks gorgeous when viewed full-screen, and the Library found in the desktop version makes a comeback, giving you quick access to podcasts, audiobooks, Genius mixes and more. It's the closest thing you'll get to using the full desktop version of iTunes while on the go. Getting music onto your iPad is a simple process through iTunes. It's possible to sync tracks, albums or your entire music library. iTunes remembers your settings, so whenever your iPad is plugged into the computer it automatically syncs any new music tracks to the device. By spending just a few minutes setting up your music sync options, you'll never have to manually transfer tracks and albums again.

iTunes Get your music on your iPad

01 Import tunes

First, ensure you have some music in your iTunes Library. You can rip tracks from your CD collection or purchase songs from the iTunes store.

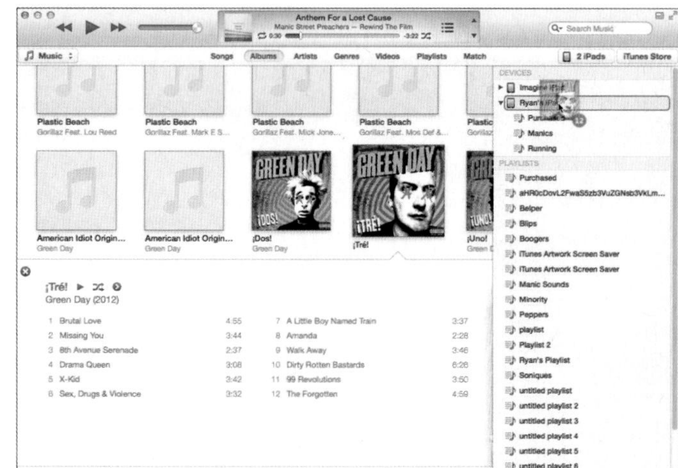

02 Get to your music

Connect your iPad to your computer and then you can either drag songs manually from your library to your device or click on Music in its settings.

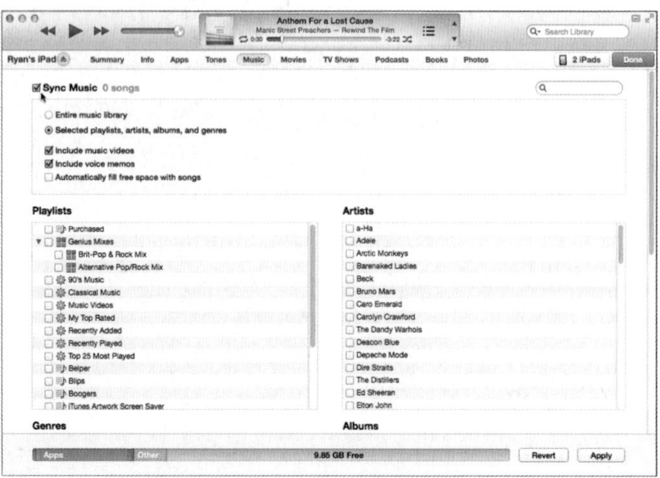

03 Choose what to sync

From here you can choose what to sync. Once you're happy with the selection, click the Apply/Sync button at the bottom-right of the screen.

04 Get playing

Once the syncing process has been completed, turn on your iPad and open the Music app located on your home screen.

Transfer movies using iTunes

We explain how easy it is to copy movies from your desktop computer to an iPad

Movies look amazing on the iPad screen. Whether you're lying in bed or sitting on a train with the iPad in your hands, the display shows off movies with vivid clarity.

The experience of watching films on your iPad gets even better if the movie has been purchased or rented through the iTunes Store, as the iPad will display detailed information about the film and enable users to skip directly to a particular chapter with just one tap of the finger. For those with an Apple TV it's also possible to wirelessly stream any movie to the device from your iPad, which will allow you to watch films on a big screen – preferably on a high-definition TV – and control the playback using the iPad's touch screen display, but we will explain more on that later.

In this tutorial we'll explain how easy it is to sync movies from your desktop computer to the iPad using iTunes. In next to no time you'll be up and running with a selection of great movies on your iPad.

iTunes Sync your movies to your iPad

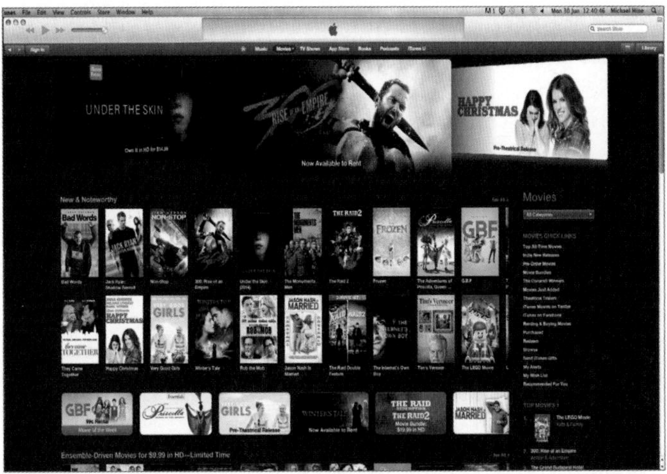

01 Get ready

Ensure you have movies to sync in iTunes. Films can be purchased from the iTunes Store or copied to your iTunes Library in MOV or MP4 format.

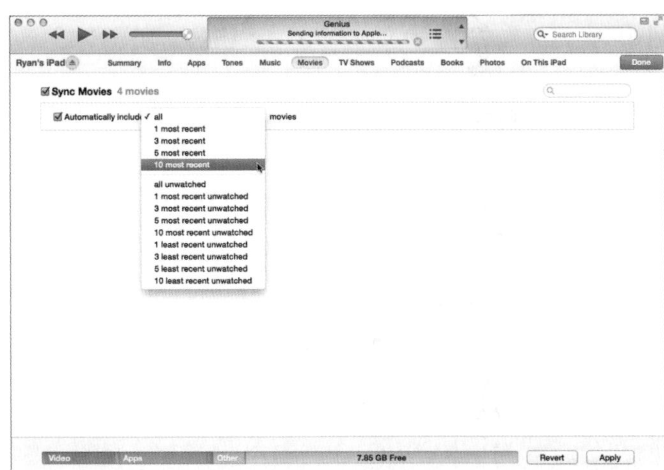

02 Select films

Connect your iPad and click on it in iTunes, then select the Films tab at the top of the screen. If unselected, check the top Sync Films button.

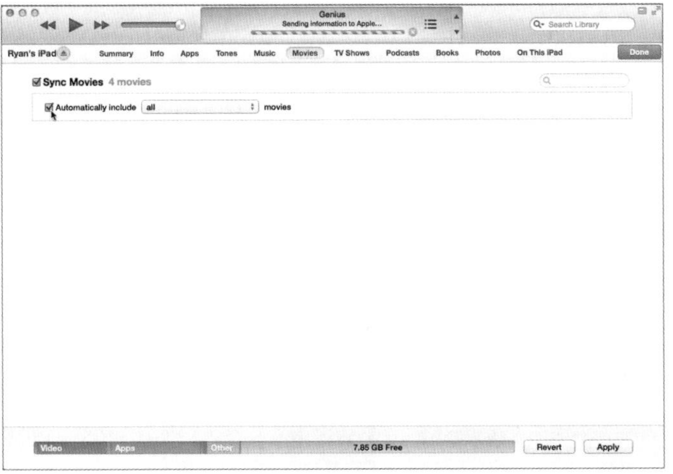

03 Sync!

Select the films that you wish to sync, but be aware of their file sizes. Once you're happy, click the Apply/Sync button at the bottom of the screen.

04 Get watching

Once the films have copied you can watch them from the Videos app. If purchased from the Store, they will include chapters for easy navigation.

Sync your books through iTunes

Find out how to sync books with your iPad, and where to download the latest titles

Before the iPad was even announced, media pundits were declaring it to be the saviour of print media. Even against the competition from other tablets and e-readers, the iPad is a fantastic device for reading books and magazines for a number of reasons. The iPad's display makes reading text a joy, particularly when combined with the Retina display on the iPad; the vivid colour screen makes images look even better than their printed counterparts; its support for multimedia means videos and web links can be embedded in books; and it's possible to change the font and text size, look up words with a dictionary and easily control the brightness for when reading in a low-lit environment. The list goes on.

e-Books can either be synced from a desktop computer or purchased directly from Apple's iBooks app – and if downloading books to your computer, you can also use the Automatic Downloads iCloud feature (go to Settings>Store and activate the options). Here we show you how to sync from iTunes.

iTunes Sync e-Books to your iPad

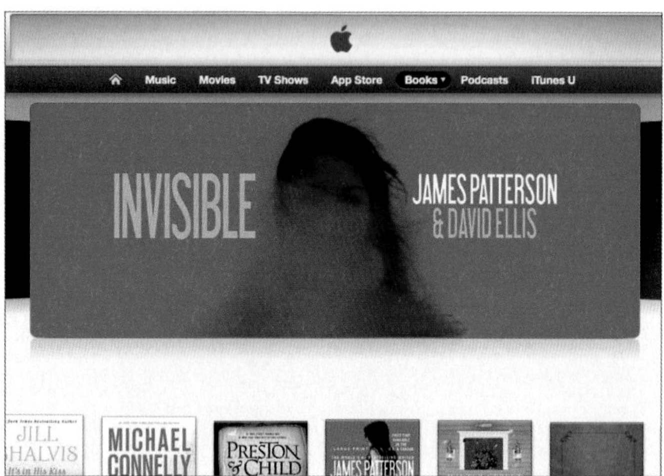

01 Go shopping
Go to the iTunes Store and click on the Books tab at the top of the screen. Books you purchase and download will be added to the Books section in your library.

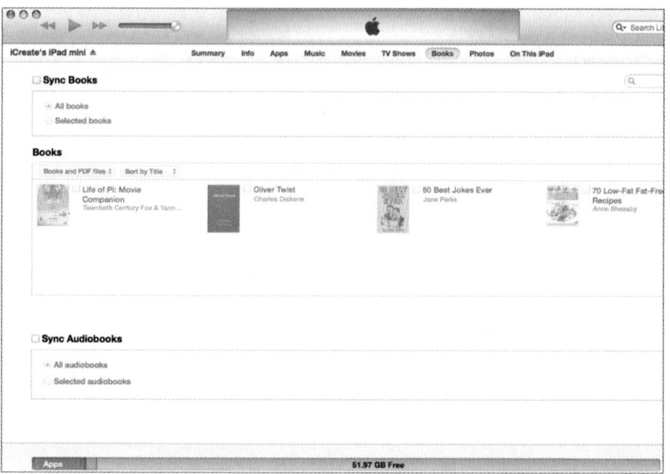

02 Books window
Turn on your iPad and plug it into the computer. After syncing, click on the iPad button from the top of iTunes, then select the Books option, also at the top.

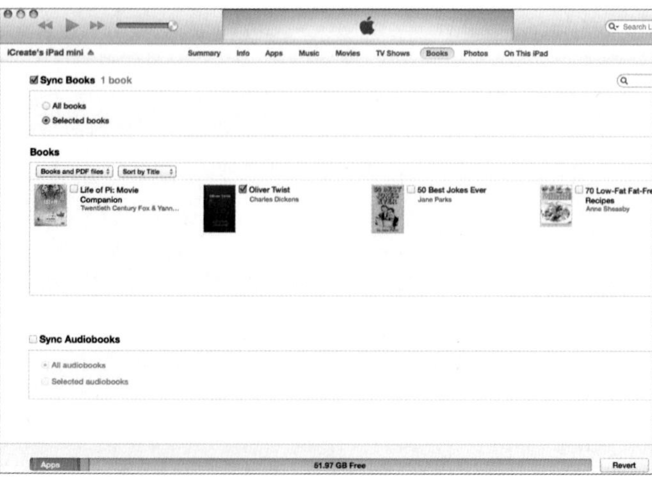

03 Choose your books
You can sync every book by checking the All Books button, or alternatively select your books of choice. Click the Sync/Apply button once you're ready.

04 Download in iBooks
If you install the free iBooks app on your iPad then you can also download books from within by tapping the Store button in the top-left corner.

Put photos on your iPad

Discover how easy it is to sync photographs from your Mac/PC to an iPad

The iPad is the perfect device for displaying photos. Thanks to its Multi-Touch support it's easy to swipe through images, zoom into areas and create slide-shows. It's by far the best way to show off your latest holiday snaps as the device can be passed from person to person, and because the Photos app is so intuitive it can be used by anyone – even children.

There are a handful of ways to get your favourite photos onto your iPad. They can be synced from a Mac/PC, emailed or imported from an SD card and, thanks to the wonder of iCloud's Photo Stream feature, even beamed wirelessly to your device automatically. In this tutorial we'll explain how easy it is to transfer batches of images from your computer using iTunes.

iTunes Get your photos on your iPad via iTunes

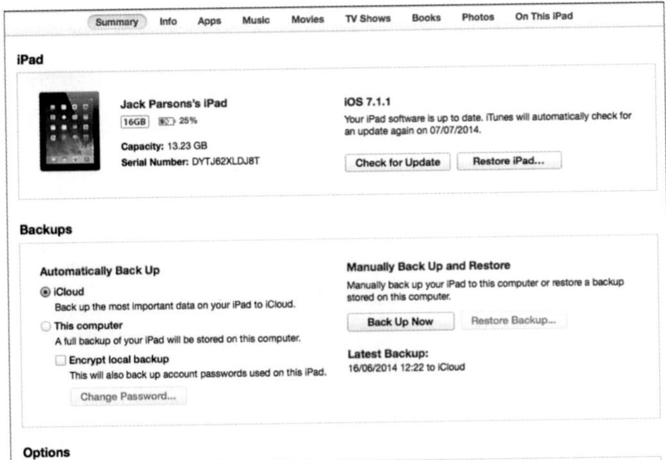

01 Plug in

Open iTunes on your Mac/PC, then plug the iPad into the computer and they'll sync. Once done, click on your iPad button in the top-right of iTunes.

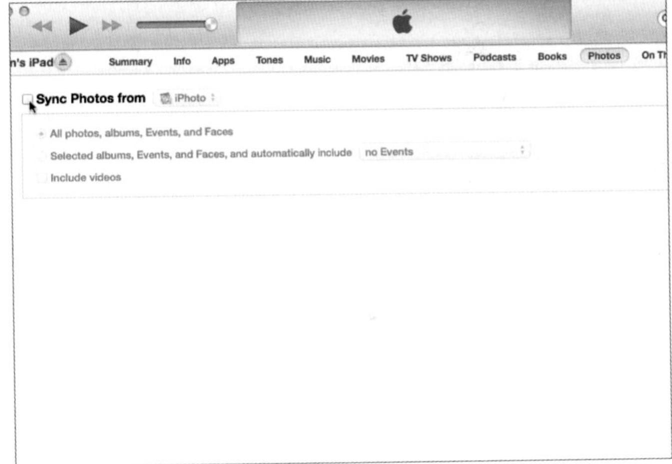

02 iPad summary

You'll see a summary of your iPad. At the top of the screen are various buttons for syncing media – click on the Photos button at the far end.

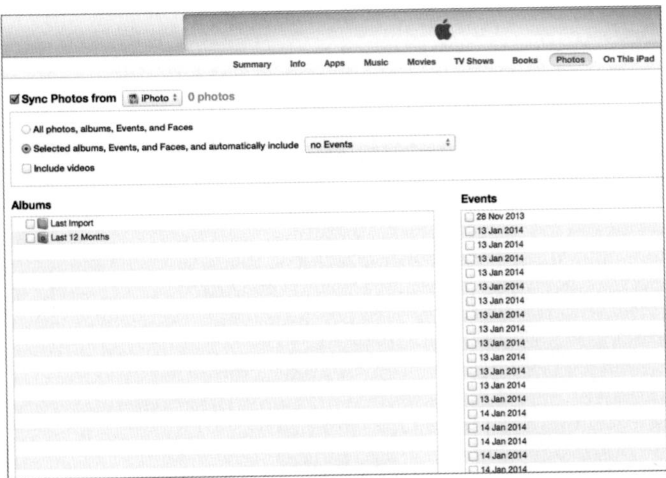

03 Choose your photos

Here you'll see an option to sync photos from your Mac or PC. Click on the check box and choose a folder from your computer. When correct, click OK.

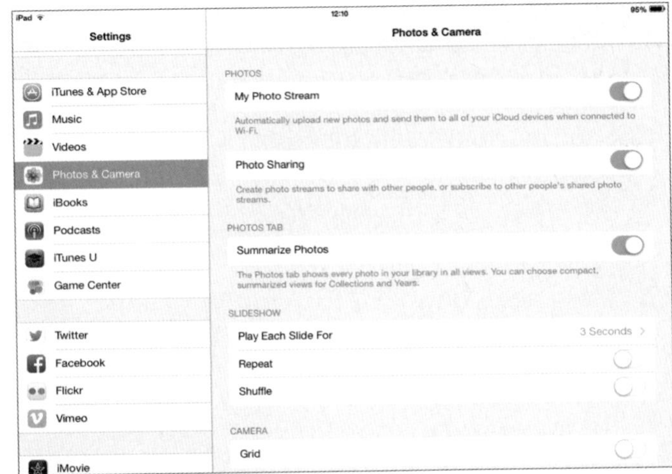

04 Activate Photo Stream

To get all photos automatically pushed to your iPad from your computer or iPhone, go to Settings>Photos and turn Photo Stream on.

Getting started

"It mixes a simple UI with some seriously advanced features"

66 Add an event

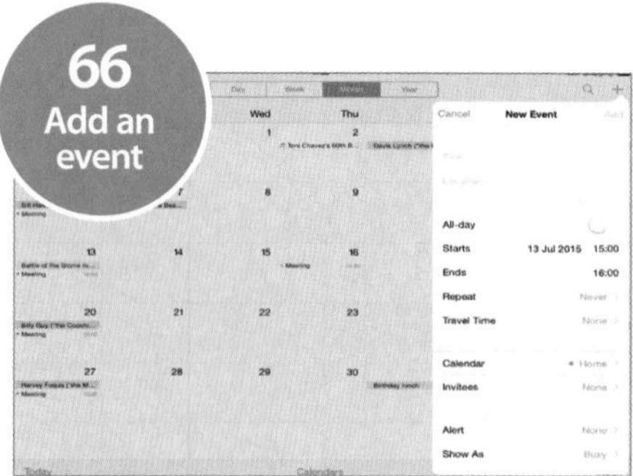

82 Navigate with Mapsi

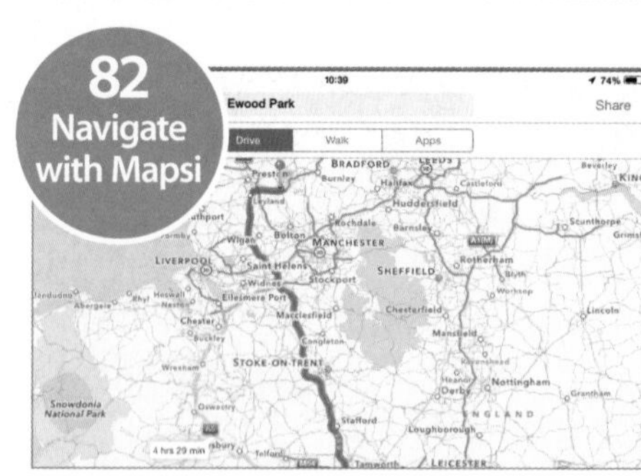

86 Utilise Spotlight

90 Download media

Albums

The Desired Effect
Brandon Flowers

Hot Songs

Bills
LunchMoney Lewis - B

Together
Ella Eyre - Together - S

All the basics are covered right here to get you in control of your iPad

See All >

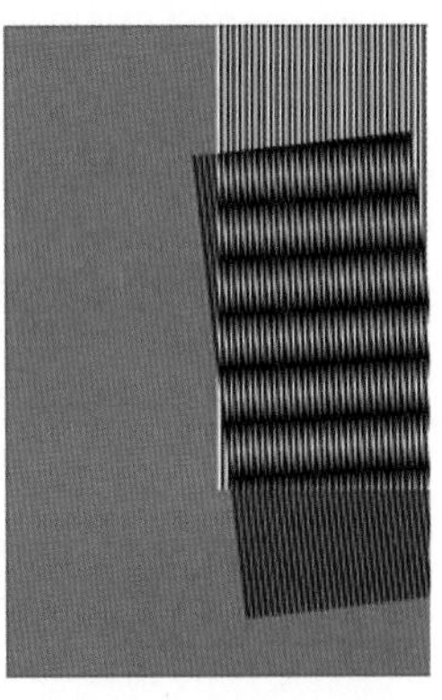

ts
rs

Pitch Perfect 2 (Original Motion Picture Sound...
Various Artists

Blurryface
twenty one pilots

Why Make Sens
(Deluxe Edition)
Hot Chip

See All >

gle £0.99

£0.99

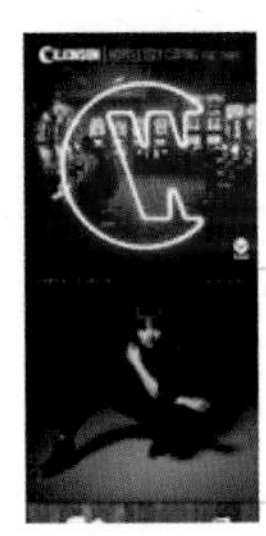

Hopelessly Coping (feat. Thabo)
Wilkinson - Hopelessly Coping (feat. Thabo) - Si...

Light Up the Dark
Gabrielle Aplin - Light Up the Dark (Deluxe Edition)

Move icons and use folders

Discover how to organise your apps and keep your iPad tidy

Whenever a new app is installed, its icon just gets added to the end of the existing list, or if there's a gap anywhere on your interface, it can appear there. This is fine when you only have a handful of apps, but after a couple of months with your iPad, the screen will probably start to fill up, making it all look quite disorganised and messy.

Fortunately, there is flexibility in the position of each of your apps, and with some thought you can devise a system for organising them that works for you. You could order them by groups depending on whether they perform similar functions. For a example, you could arrange games on one page, utilities on another and reference apps on a page as well. Much like a desktop, it is also possible to create folders in which to group similar apps to make your display very neat and tidy.

You can reorganise your iPad screens using iTunes, where it is easy to create extra screens, even if the current ones are full, but it's also possible to move icons around directly on the iPad. The final benefits are that unwanted apps can be deleted and must-have apps can be added to the Dock bar at the bottom of every screen.

"You can bundle apps together to make your display very neat and tidy"

Home screen Keep your iPad organised

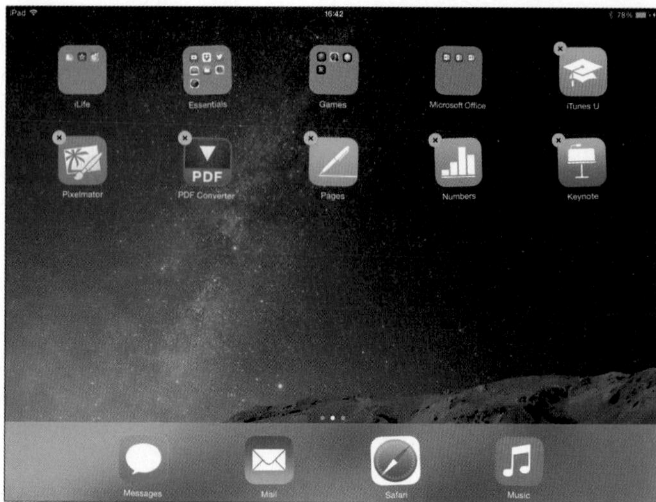

01 Activate the wiggle

Turn your iPad on so that you are looking at your home screen. If you have lots of apps then the icons for them will be spread over subsequent screens. To arrange them together tap and hold an app you want to move until all the apps start to wiggle.

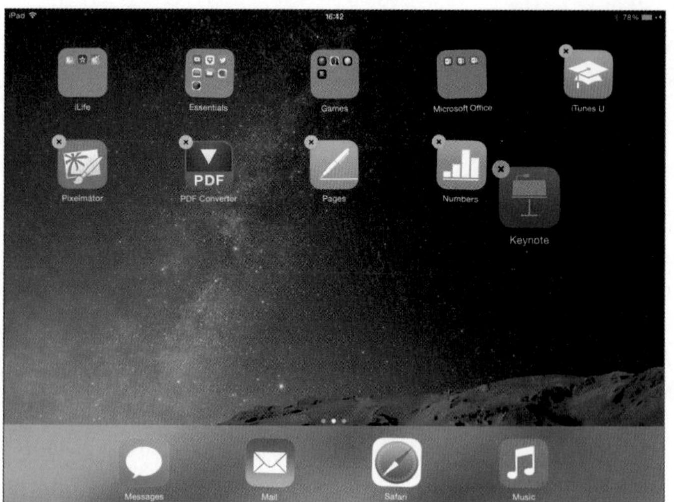

02 Move the app

Still holding down on the app, drag your finger to the edge of the screen you want to move to. The apps will then scroll sideways to pull the next screen into view. Now move your finger over the place where you want the app to go and then let go of it.

Inside the new folder display

Edit the folder name and move apps inside it

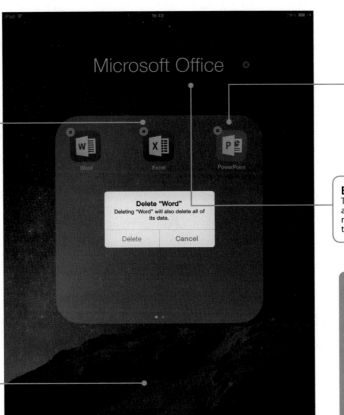

Delete an app in a folder
To remove an app that is inside a folder, simply tap on the 'X' icon in the top-left corner. You will still have a backup inside iTunes

Rearrange apps
If there are lots of apps inside a folder, rearrange them by tapping and holding and then dragging to a new position. The other apps will shuffle along and move

Edit the folder name
Tap a folder to open it. Tap and hold an app inside to go into wiggle editing mode. You can now remove or change the folder name

Take an app out
While in wiggle mode you can drag an app out of the folder again simply by tapping and holding and then moving outside the folder area

Favourite and unwanted apps

When in wiggle mode, a little cross appears on the top-left corner of all the apps. Tap on this to delete the app directly from your iPad. You can't delete the ones the iPad comes with. The Dock bar at the bottom of the screen comes with six slots for your favourite apps. Again, in wiggle mode you can move them around, drag them on or off the bar or simply add your new, favourite app to the ones there by dragging and releasing the app over it.

03 Create folders for common apps

Press the Home button to return your iPad to normal. To create folders, drop an app over the top of one you want it to appear in a folder with. A folder is then instantly created and a name is added above it that reflects the type of apps included if they are fairly similar.

04 Rename the folder

If the folder name isn't to your liking, simply tap on the 'X' icon to delete it and tap in the text field to enter your own. When complete, press the Home button twice to exit. To add more apps to the same folder in future, you simply need to drag and drop them into it.

Discover the features of Safari

Following its recent makeover for the iOS 8 update, we reveal the most useful features of the Apple browser

Safari has long been considered one of the best mobile browsers. It mixes a simple user interface with great functionality and plenty of additional features to keep everybody happy. Apple isn't a company to stand still, and the iOS 8 rollout predictably saw Safari given a tidy new facelift.

The main features revolve around the continued move to cloud computing and the aim of seamlessly syncing between various devices. To do so, Apple has introduced iCloud Tabs, which means you'll never need to email a link to yourself. Flicking through a webpage on your iPhone at work, but you want to view it on your iPad at home? iCloud Tabs ensures that a webpage is instantly loaded in any browser linked with your iCloud account.

iCloud Tabs is just the tip of the iceberg though. There's also the Offline Reading List function, which lets you view webpages regardless of whether you are connected to the internet. Meanwhile Facebook and Twitter integration into the Safari experience also makes life easier for those always sharing online content with friends and family.

Here we take you through these features in a bit more detail, as well as a few more to boot.

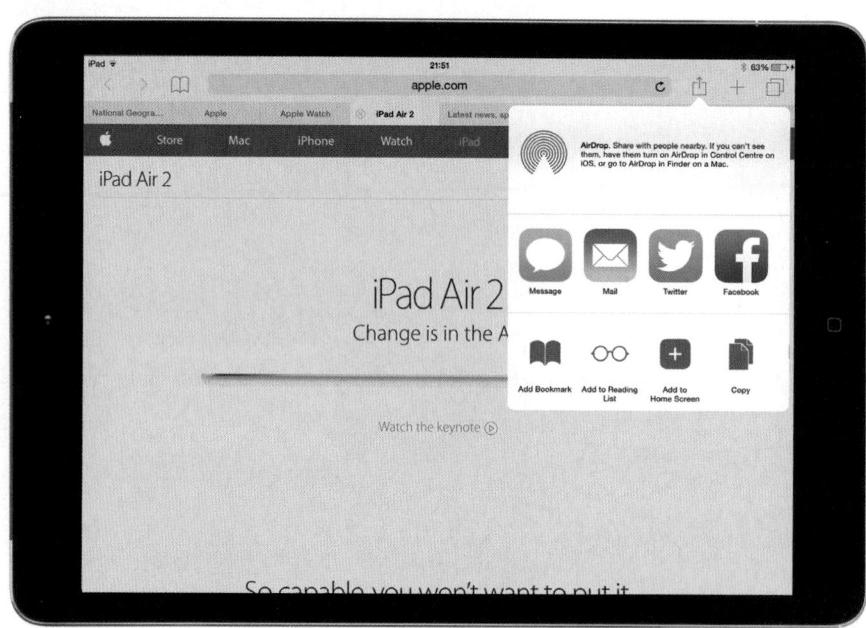

"The main features revolve around the move to cloud computing and the aim of syncing between devices"

Safari Explore Safari's best features

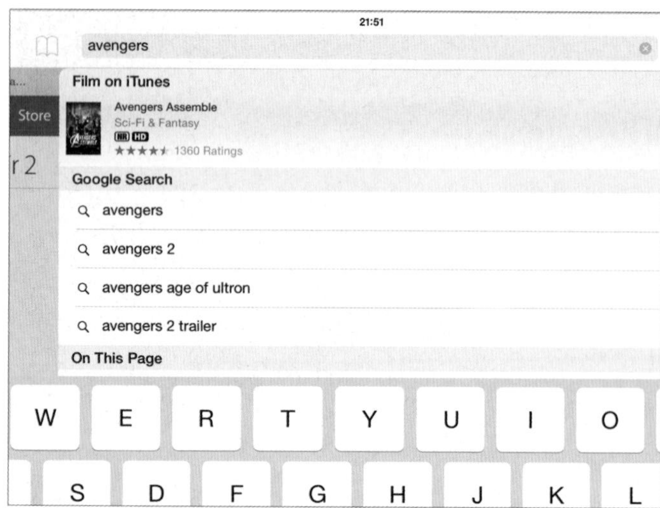

01 Smarter search

When you start typing a search term into Safari's new Search bar, the app will now suggest results from all kinds of locations, including Wikipedia entries, apps from the App Store, and even location results. Tap one of these entries and you'll be taken to the relevant page, or directed to another app.

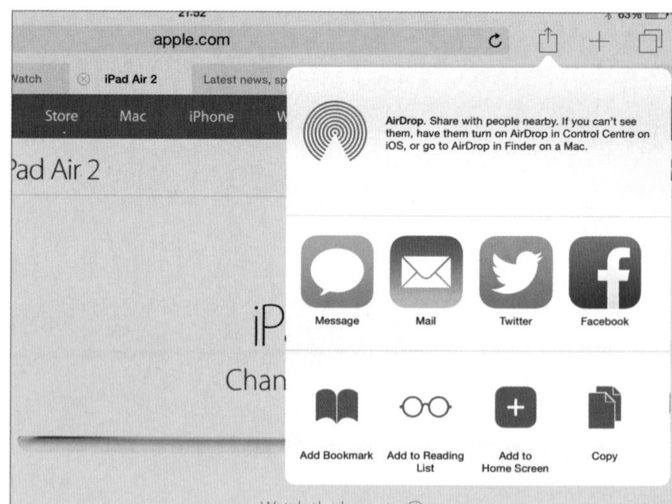

02 Offline Reading List

When you save an article for reading later, it's saved to your device so you can view it even if you're offline. Find an article, hit the Share icon (the arrow and box next to the right side of the address bar) and tap the 'Add to Reading List' option to get started.

Inside Safari

A closer look at the best features

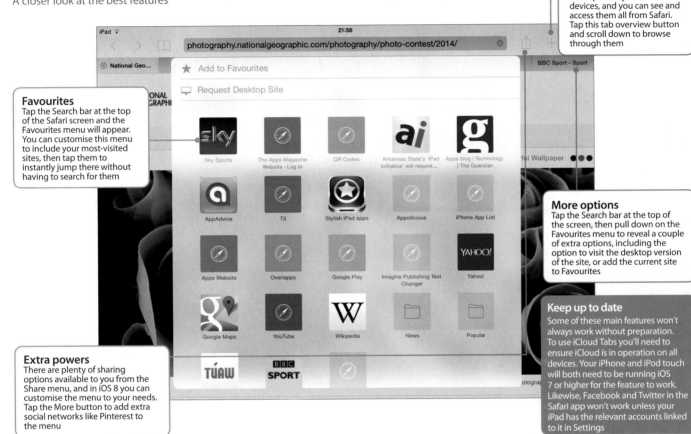

iCloud Tabs
iCloud will keep track of the tabs open on your other devices, and you can see and access them all from Safari. Tap this tab overview button and scroll down to browse through them

Favourites
Tap the Search bar at the top of the Safari screen and the Favourites menu will appear. You can customise this menu to include your most-visited sites, then tap them to instantly jump there without having to search for them

More options
Tap the Search bar at the top of the screen, then pull down on the Favourites menu to reveal a couple of extra options, including the option to visit the desktop version of the site, or add the current site to Favourites

Keep up to date
Some of these main features won't always work without preparation. To use iCloud Tabs you'll need to ensure iCloud is in operation on all devices. Your iPhone and iPod touch will both need to be running iOS 7 or higher for the feature to work. Likewise, Facebook and Twitter in the Safari app won't work unless your iPad has the relevant accounts linked to it in Settings

Extra powers
There are plenty of sharing options available to you from the Share menu, and in iOS 8 you can customise the menu to your needs. Tap the More button to add extra social networks like Pinterest to the menu

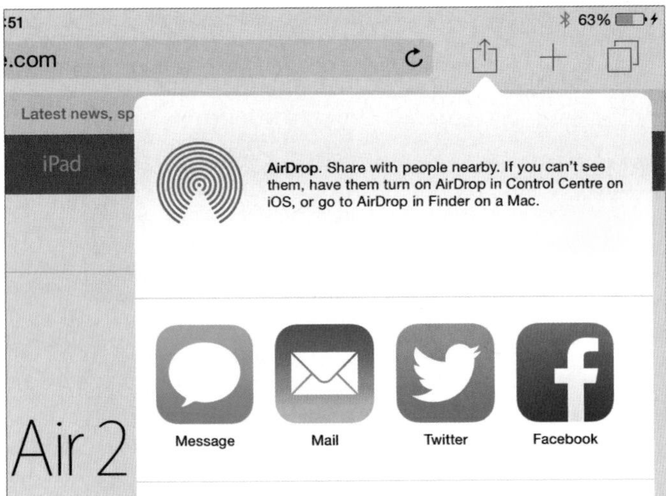

03 Social integration

As well as being able to update Twitter and Facebook straight from Safari by tapping on the share icon, you can also instantly view the links that your friends have shared on their favourite networks. Simply tap the book icon and then selecting the '@' tab in the window that appears.

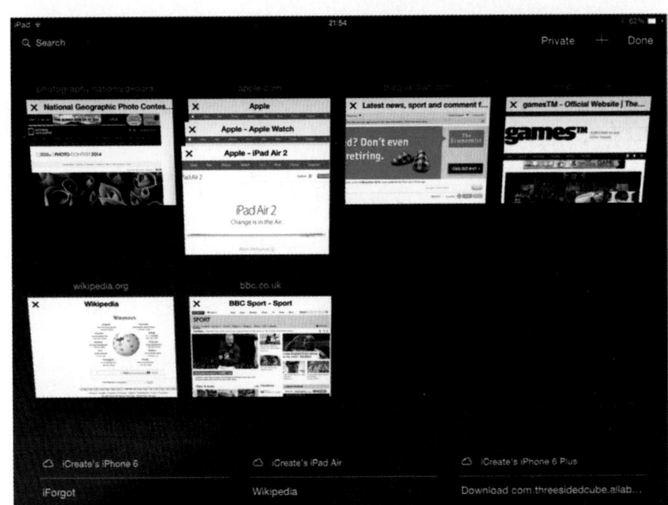

04 New Tab view

iOS 8 brings an all-new tab view to Safari on iPad – tap the button in the top-right of the screen or pinch your fingers together on the page to view this screen. You can tap a tab to open it instantly or swipe a tab off the left-hand side of the screen to close it down.

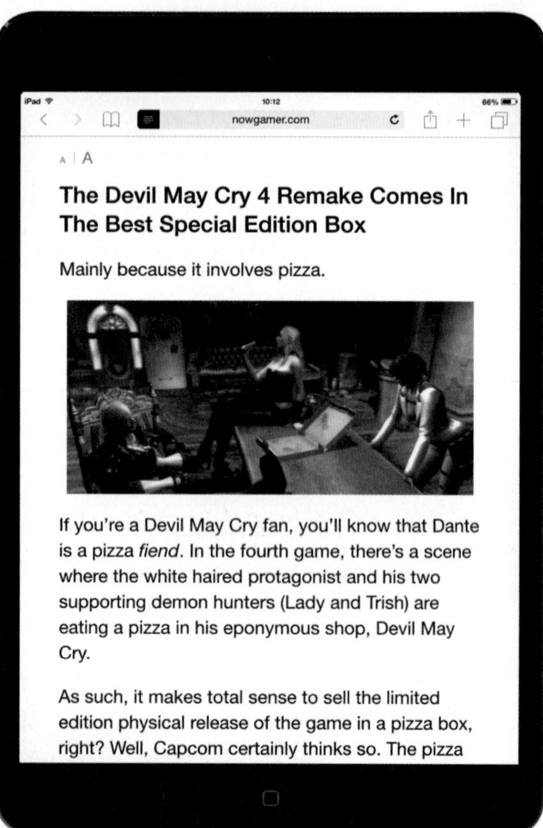

nowgamer.com
The Devil May Cry 4 Remake Comes In The Best Special Edition Box
Mainly because it involves pizza.
If you're a Devil May Cry fan, you'll know that Dante is a pizza fiend. In the fourth game, there's a scene where the white haired protagonist and his two supporting demon hunters (Lady and Trish) are eating a pizza in his eponymous shop, Devil May Cry.
As such, it makes total sense to sell the limited edition physical release of the game in a pizza box, right? Well, Capcom certainly thinks so. The pizza

De-clutter the web with Safari Reader

Thanks to a new Safari feature, you can read fresh web content devoid of intrusive ads and page furniture

Browsing webpages through Safari on your iPad is a pleasurable experience, thanks to its intuitive interface and useful features designed to make surfing the internet as effortless as possible.

The Safari app has got even better over time with previous updates introducing key elements such as Reading List and Reader that are still going strong in the most recent software updates. The Reader feature enables you to read and enjoy web articles completely free from clutter, such as intrusive ad banners and links. If you have accessed a page that can benefit from the Safari Reader function then a Reader icon will be visible to the left of the address bar. Tap on it and the page will undergo an instant transformation into a cleaner, easier-to-read format.

What's more, you are able to increase the font size to make it even easier to read and not get distracted by page furniture. It is a very quick and easy-to-use feature. To add to its simplicity, when you have finished reading the article and want to return the page to its original state, you just tap the Reader icon again and carry on as normal. Read on to find out more about this cool feature.

> "The Reader feature enables you to read and enjoy web articles completely free from clutter, such as intrusive ad banners and links"

Safari How to use Reader

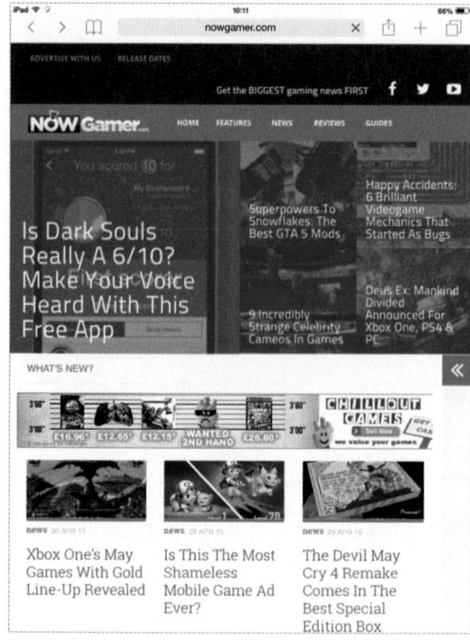

01 Launch Safari

Launch your Safari app and begin browsing the internet. Keep an eye on the address bar for the Reader icon, which signifies that the page you are on is compatible.

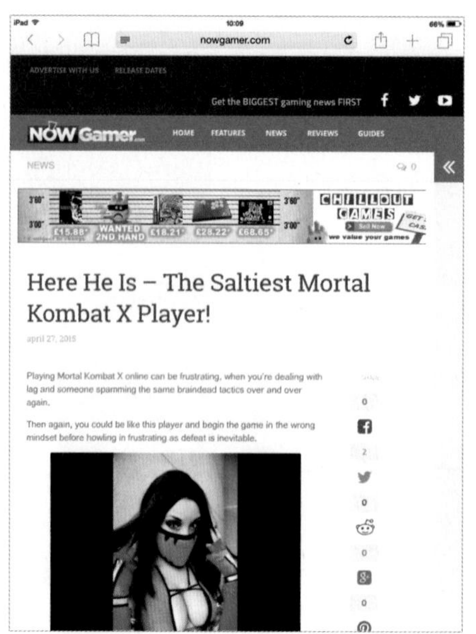

02 Find a page or story

Not every page on the internet is compatible with Reader. You will know when one is, though, because it will display a small list icon to the left of the URL.

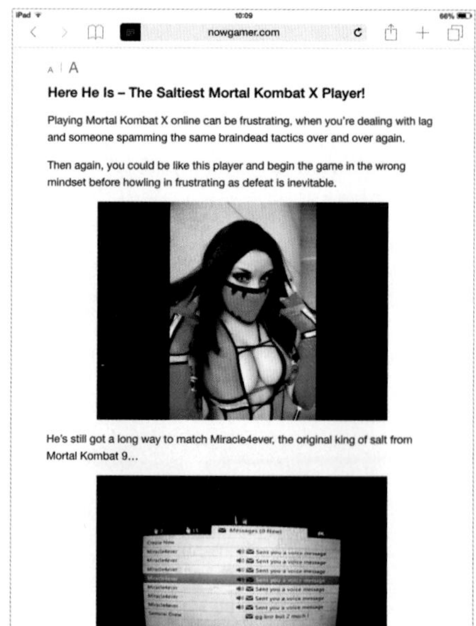

03 Tap Reader

When you find a page that displays the Reader icon, all you need to do is tap on it in order to instantly transform the page into a clear, easy-to-read format. It's as simple as that.

Make pages easier to read

Make web articles cleaner with the tap of a button

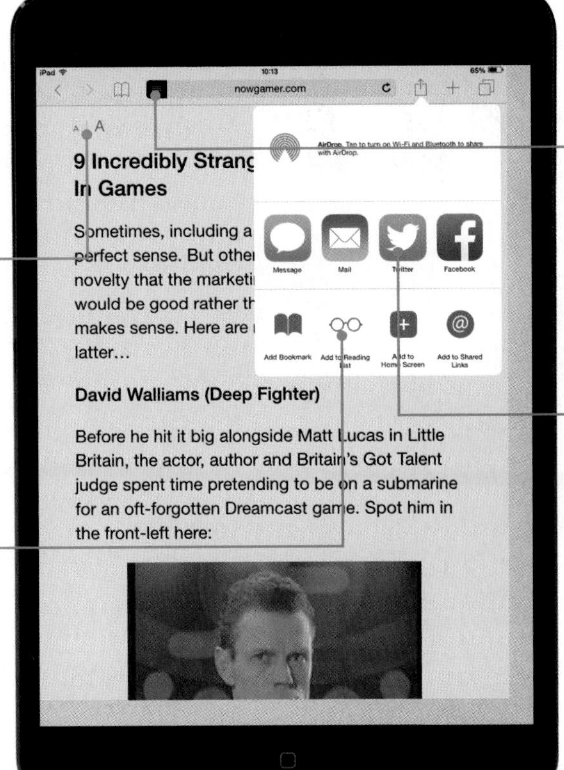

Change font size
Tap either of the 'A' icons at the top of the Reader page to increase or decrease the size of the text and make it easier to read

Reading List
To store the article safely, without having to create a new bookmark, tap on the sharing icon and choose Add to Reading List

Enable/disable Reader
Tap on the list icon that appears to the left of the URL in order to enable or disable Reader. Not all web pages boast this feature

Share icons
If a page or article that you come across is particularly interesting, you can share it with others via email, Facebook or Twitter. To do so, simply tap the Share icon and select an option from this menu

iCloud compatability
Safari is fully compatible with your iCloud, so all of your bookmarks and Reading List articles will be automatically synced, meaning you can continue exactly where you left off on a different device.

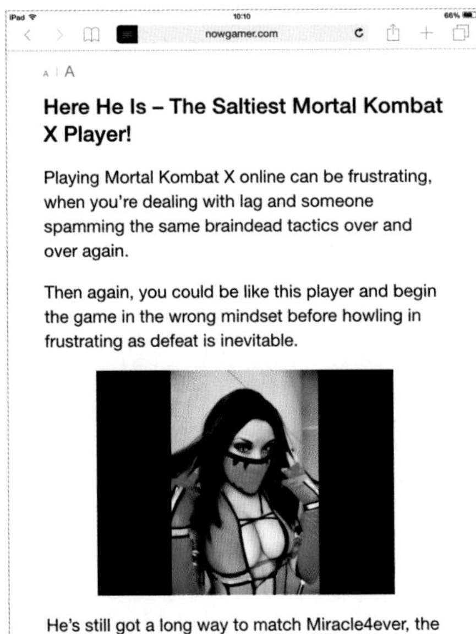

04 Change the text size

After dropping the option to change the text size in iOS 7, Apple has reinstated it for iOS 8. Repeatedly tap on either of the two 'A' icons at the top of the page to increase or decrease the text size.

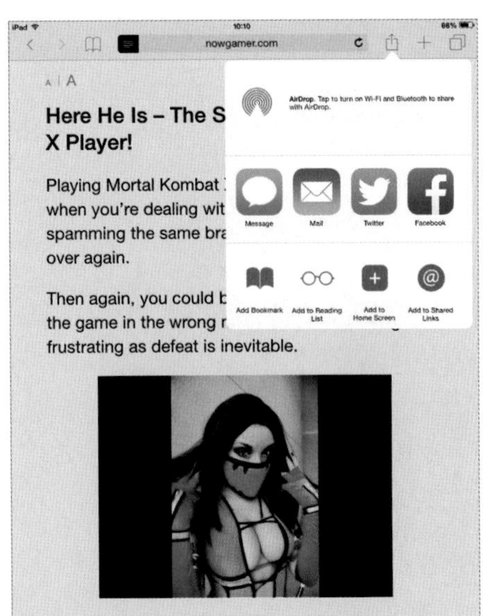

05 Add to Reading List

If you do not have time to read an article, you are able to add it to your Reading List. Just tap the sharing icon at the top of the screen and choose Add to Reading List.

06 Return to normal

When you have read the article, simply tap the list icon to the next of the URL again and your page will return to normal, so you can then continue browsing as usual.

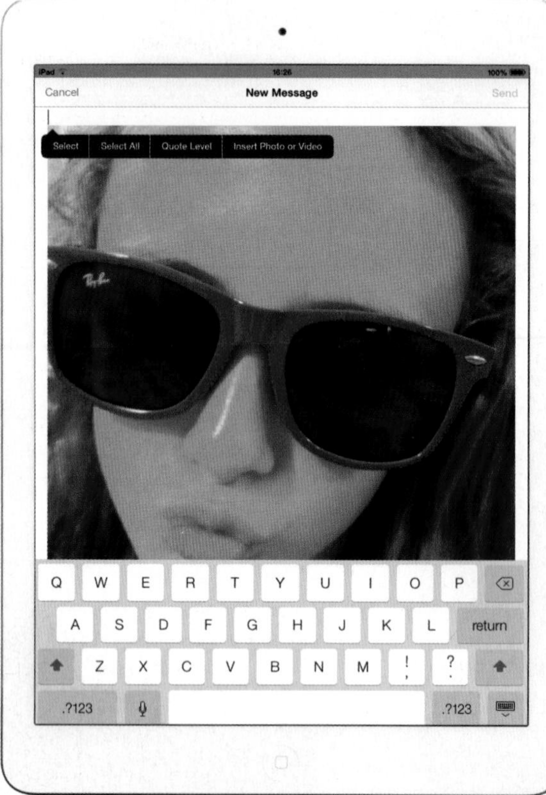

Explore the Mail app

iOS 8 brought new features to Apple's Mail app, so managing your emails is now even easier

When it comes to the way people use their iPads, one of the most convenient functions to perform on a tablet is managing emails. The large touch screen makes it a beautifully simple way to view your email, and with messages capable of displaying photos inside the message itself, it's much more engaging.

In iOS 8, Apple didn't change the formula of Mail too much. The popular app displays your messages in much the same way, but there have been a few subtle but useful changes that will make it much easier to stay in touch in this way.

Swiping left on a message now allows you to quickly delete or flag it, while swiping right lets you mark an email as Unread. These gestures are simple, but they're so intuitive that they make managing your inbox a breeze. It's also quick to add images to messages by simply tapping in your message and then tapping the Insert Photo or Video option from the pop-up menu. Finally you can define VIPs. This is a great feature for contacting friends and family; their messages will appear starred, and will be sorted into a separate inbox with customisable alerts so you know as soon as they've got in touch.

"The app still displays your messages in much the same way, but there have been a few subtle but useful changes"

Mail Use the latest features of Mail

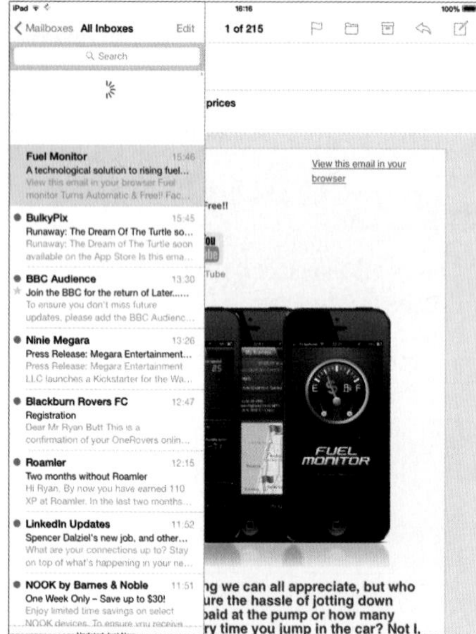

01 Pull to refresh

If you swipe down on your inbox list to the left, you can pull the list of current emails down. This gesture prompts Mail to refresh and check the server for newly received messages.

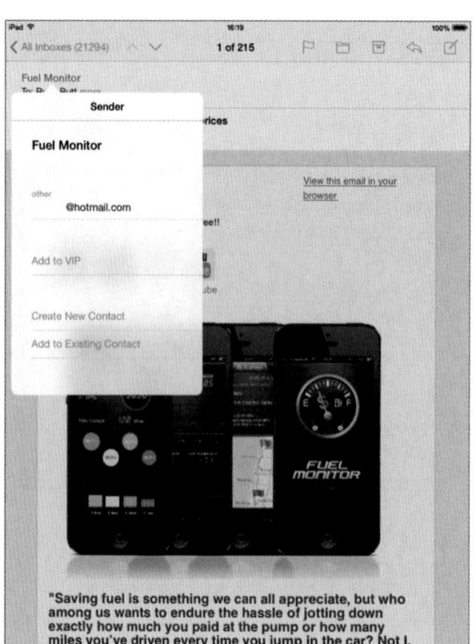

02 VIPs

To make a contact a VIP, tap their name and choose 'Add to VIP' from the bottom of the list. This means you'll be alerted when an email from them arrives, and it will be sorted in the VIP inbox.

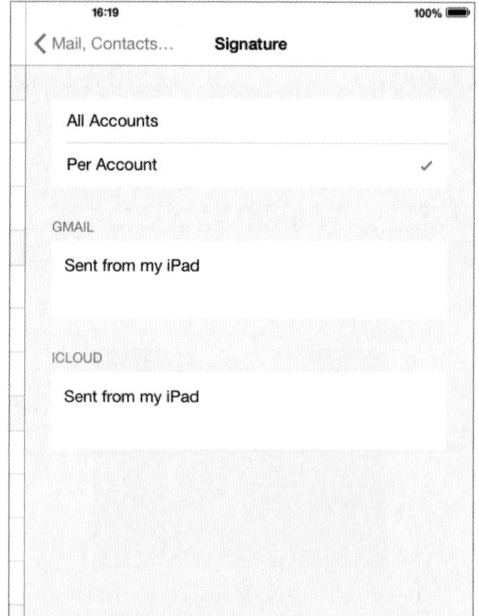

03 Multiple signatures

You can also add multiple signatures to your accounts in the Settings app by going to 'Mail, Contacts & Calendars', choosing Signature and then Per Account, before typing out a signature.

Mail's essential features

How will the latest features affect you?

Pull to refresh
It might seem like a small thing, but Pull to Refresh really will revolutionise the way you read emails on your iPad, with a simple, time-saving gesture

Starry eyes
VIPs are sorted from other email senders with a star next to the emails they send. Unread messages have blue stars, while read messages have these grey ones

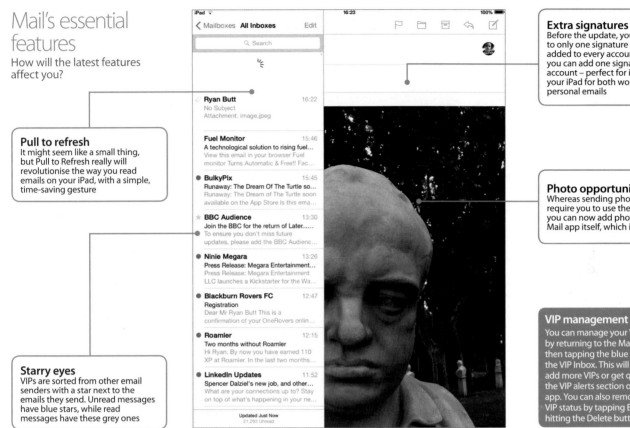

Extra signatures
Before the update, you were limited to only one signature that was added to every account. In iOS 8 you can add one signature for each account – perfect for if you use your iPad for both work and personal emails

Photo opportunity
Whereas sending photos used to require you to use the Photos app, you can now add photos within the Mail app itself, which is very useful

VIP management
You can manage your VIPs within mail by returning to the Mailboxes section, then tapping the blue arrow next to the VIP Inbox. This will allow you to add more VIPs or get quick access to the VIP alerts section of the Settings app. You can also remove a contact's VIP status by tapping Edit, then hitting the Delete button.

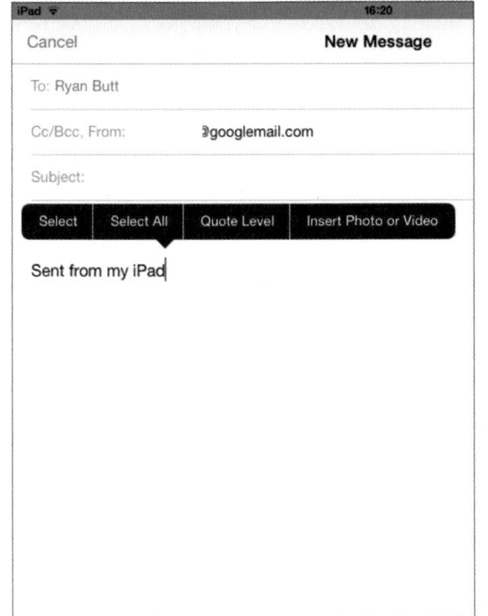

04 Inline images
It's very easy to add an image to an email; simply double-tap and then choose 'Insert Photo or Video'. Then select your image from that pop-up menu and hit Add.

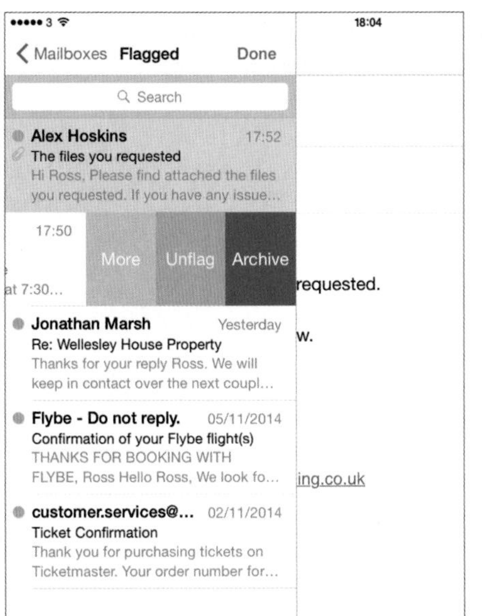

05 Inbox gestures
Swiping left on a message will allow you to quickly flag or delete it, while tapping the More button brings up a host of other options. Swiping right lets you mark a message as read or unread

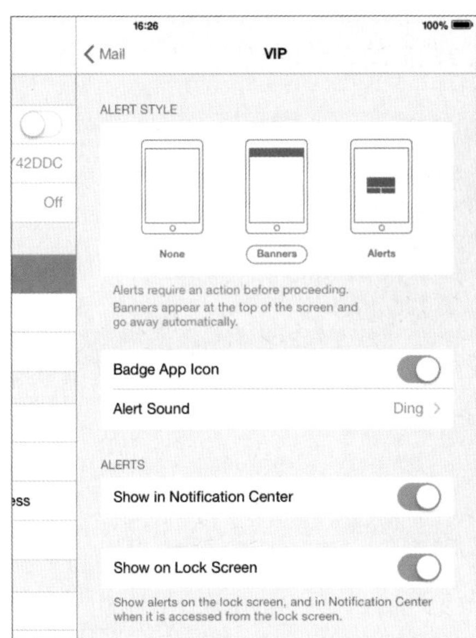

06 Customised notifications
You can customise Notifications for VIP messages in the Notifications section of the Settings app. This way you will always know when your VIPs send you an email.

Add photos and videos to Mail

Adding media attachments to emails is no longer a battle; now it's the work of a couple of clicks

It may be hard to believe, but it was once quite a hassle to email images and videos to friends and family from your iPad. In those dark days, you had to adopt an awkward workaround: first open up the Photos app, then select the video or picture you want to send and finally email it from within that app. When you think about it, it was an odd way to go about things; surely you should be sending email attachments from Mail?

Well, since the iOS 7 update, things are more like they should be. You can treat media attachments in the same way as you would in an email application on your computer – by adding them within the body of an email message. With a couple of taps inside your email message, you can open a media browser, add the video or image to the email, and send it. This means that the recipient will be greeted by the attachment as soon as the message is opened.

What's more while there was once a limit on the number of videos or images you could send at one time, with the latest version of Mail you can add as many as you want. So let's get started in making your emails that little bit more interesting!

"Treat media attachments in the same way as you would in an email app on your computer"

Mail Adding photos or video to email

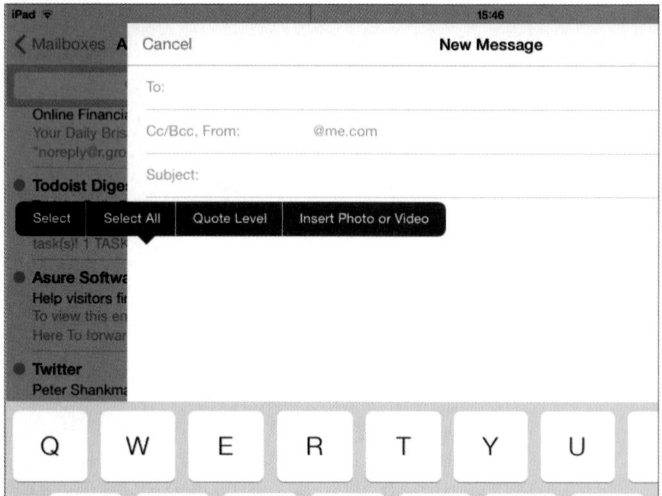

01 Edit the message

To add a photo or video inside the body of an email, open up the Mail app and tap the Compose button to start drafting a new message. Tap inside the empty body of the message to bring up a popover menu. From this menu, choose 'Insert Photo or Video'.

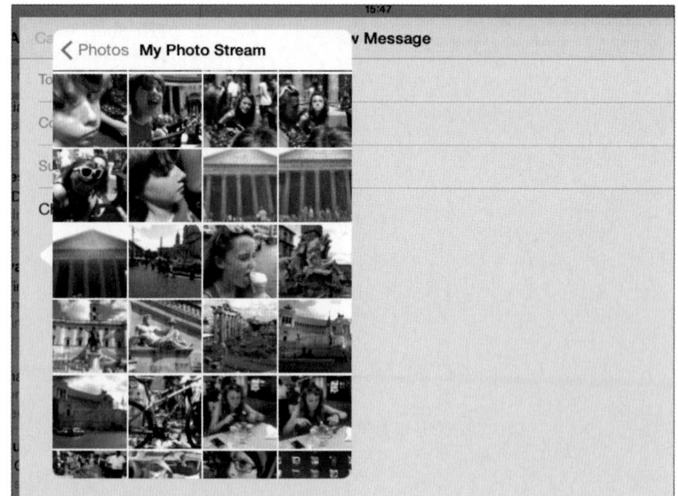

02 Select the media

You can then choose the video or photo you want to add, either from your Camera Roll or from your Photo Stream. Tap the thumbnail preview of the one you want to add and it will appear in a Preview window. To add it to the email, tap Use.

Adding media to emails

Grabbing images to send by email

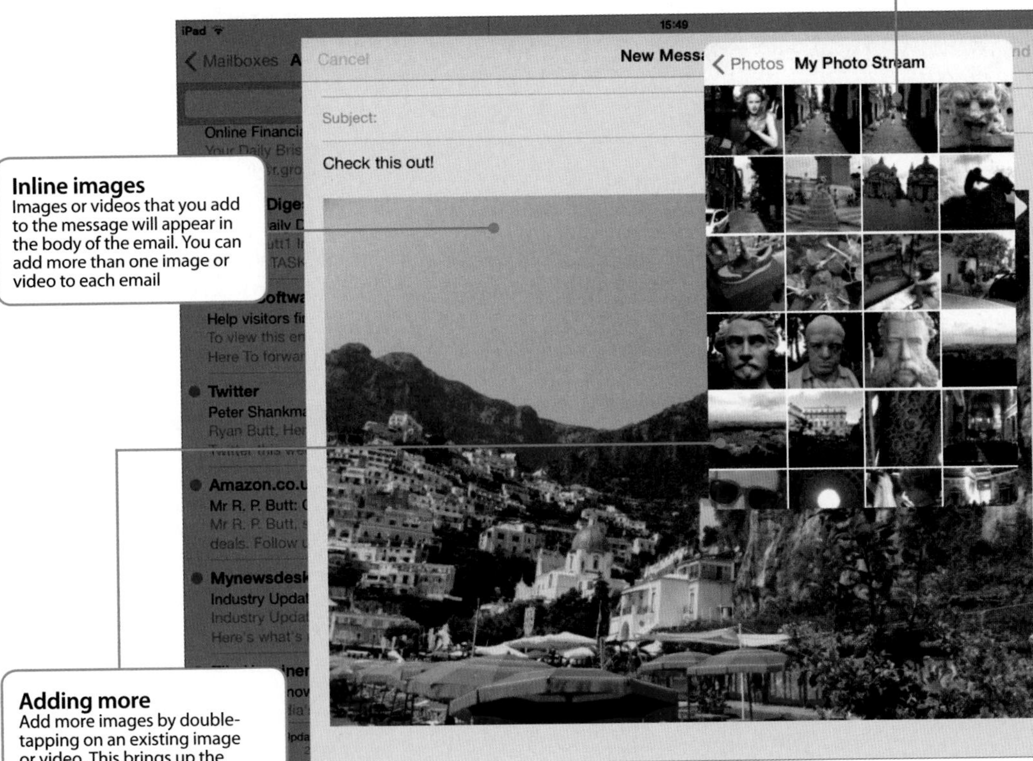

Preview images

You can preview images in this window before committing to adding them to the email message. If you like what you see, tap the Use button. If you tap Cancel you can return to choose another image

Inline images

Images or videos that you add to the message will appear in the body of the email. You can add more than one image or video to each email

Adding an image

Tap in an empty area of the email body to bring up the popover menu. This menu lets you add images or videos directly into the body of your email

Using the Photos app

Though this new method is great, you can still use the old method of sending media via the Photos app. To do this, open Photos, tap the 'Edit' button, tap the thumbnails of the media you want to send, select the 'Share' button at the bottom and tap the 'Mail' option. That's still handy to know, because the older method has a significant advantage in one area: it's easier to select and add several images quickly. By contrast when you create your message in Mail, you can't add more than one image or media file at a time.

Adding more

Add more images by double-tapping on an existing image or video. This brings up the popover menu, which will let you insert a photo or video nest to the media you just tapped

03 Add more images

The image or video should now appear inside your email message. To add more images or videos to the email, just repeat the processes in Steps 1 and 2, tapping inside the email message and then selecting the 'Insert Photo or Video' menu option.

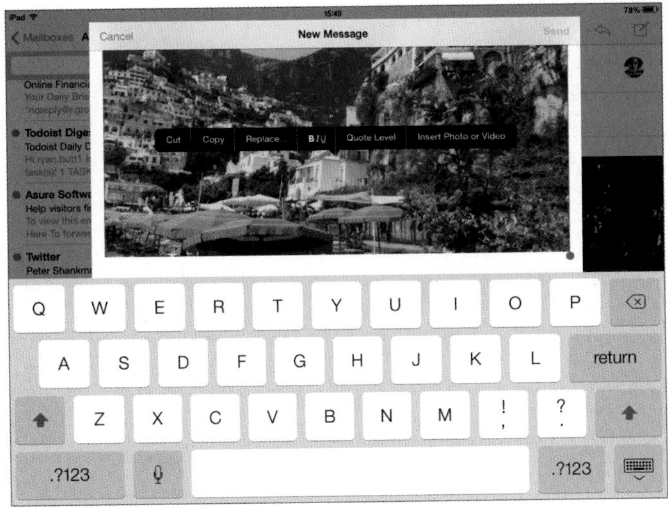

04 Cut images

If you change your mind, you can delete media from your email message. Tap and hold on the image so it's highlighted and then select Cut from the popover menu. When you've finalised your image selection, tap Send and it should be with your recipient in no time.

Add an event in Calendar

If you often struggle to remember your schedule, make sure you never miss an important event with your iPad

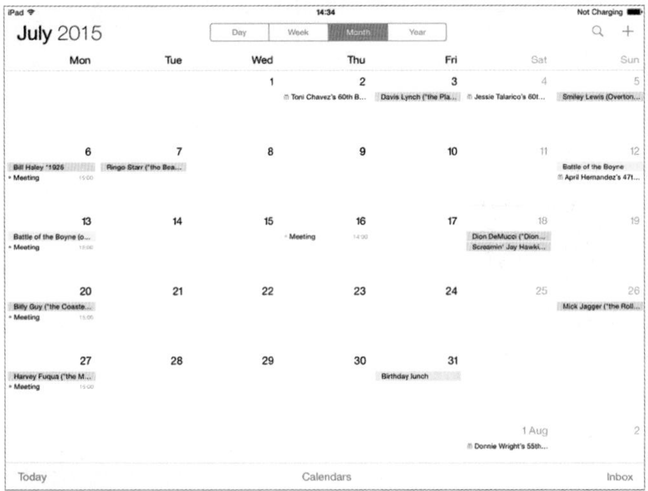

Tuesday 10 **The Calendar app on the iPhone is pretty useful and very easy to use, but it is dwarfed by the sheer scale of the iPad equivalent.** Like the Contacts app, Apple has gone with the classic analogue look and made the app look like an old-school, physical calendar. Of course, this digital version has a multitude of advantages over a real one. Firstly, you get the beauty of typeface rather than scrawled handwriting. Secondly, it's easy to undo mistakes. Thirdly, you can view it in a number of different ways.

Like all the iPad apps, the Calendar app is easy to use. So easy to use that you'll want to document every move you make using it, from eating breakfast to scheduling business meetings. Adding an event is simplicity itself, and the large screen size means that pop-up windows replace the screen shunting right or left as it does on the iPhone. All you need remains in front of you at all times. Once your events are created, you can edit and then view them in a number of ways as you change orientation via the top tabs of the app.

"You get the beauty of typeface rather than scrawled handwriting"

Adding an event

You're never more than a few taps away from adding or editing an event in your calendar, and the interface is extremely simple

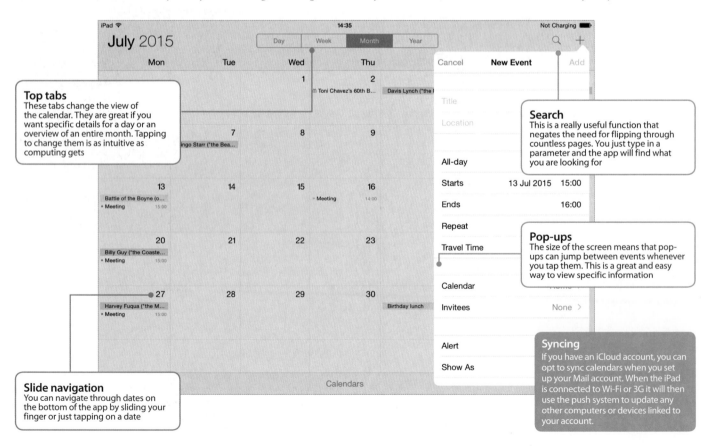

Top tabs
These tabs change the view of the calendar. They are great if you want specific details for a day or an overview of an entire month. Tapping to change them is as intuitive as computing gets

Search
This is a really useful function that negates the need for flipping through countless pages. You just type in a parameter and the app will find what you are looking for

Pop-ups
The size of the screen means that pop-ups can jump between events whenever you tap them. This is a great and easy way to view specific information

Slide navigation
You can navigate through dates on the bottom of the app by sliding your finger or just tapping on a date

Syncing
If you have an iCloud account, you can opt to sync calendars when you set up your Mail account. When the iPad is connected to Wi-Fi or 3G it will then use the push system to update any other computers or devices linked to your account.

Calendar Add an event

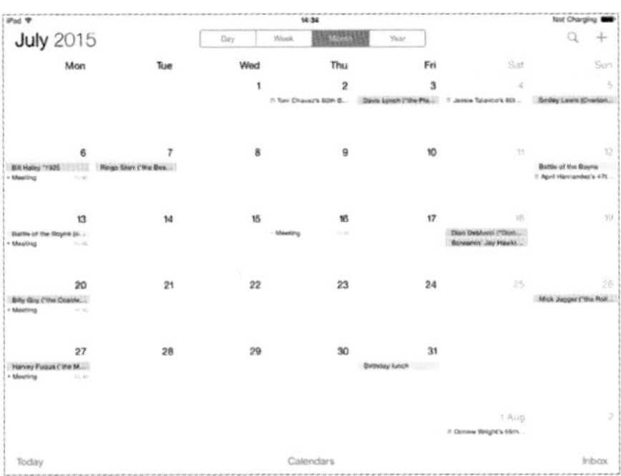

01 Open the app

Open the Calendar app and turn the iPad horizontal to see the dual-page layout. Navigate to the day you want and then tap the '+' button in the top right corner.

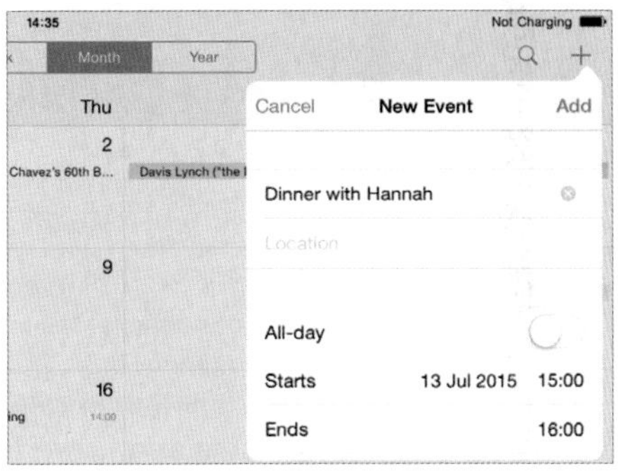

02 Name your event

A small pop-up window appears in the centre of the screen, as does the keyboard. Tap the field you wish to edit – such as 'Title' – and then name your event as you please.

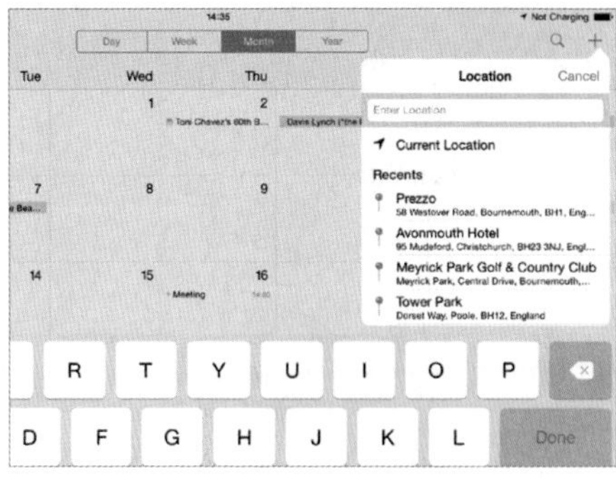

03 Add details

You can add as much or as little detail as you want, including the location of the event. You will have access to a full keyboard so you can go to town on the detail.

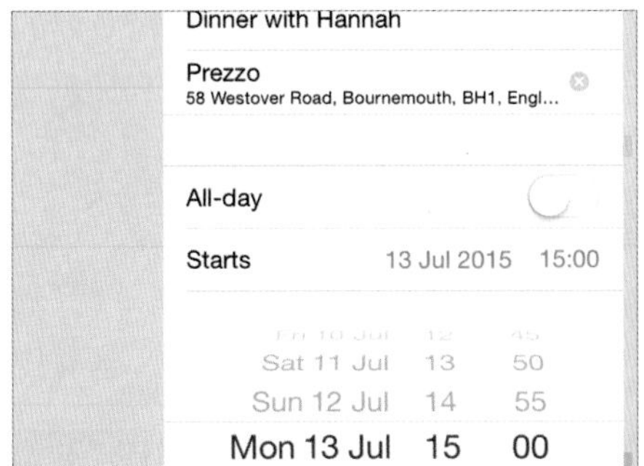

04 Give it a date

You now need to add the start and end date of your event, just to make sure you don't miss it! Tap on the relevant field to see the pop-up change into a new window display.

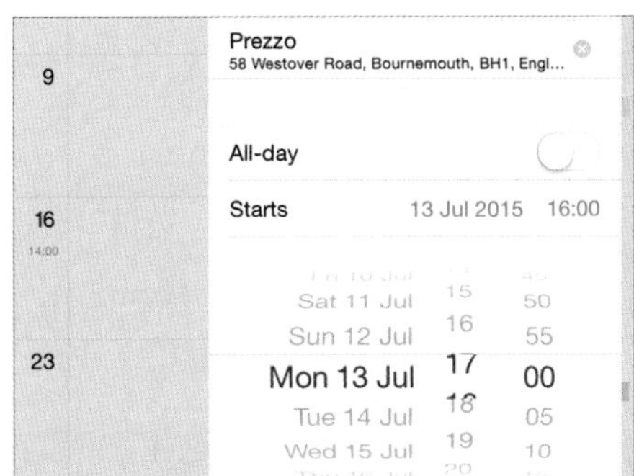

05 Select times

Use the wheels to select the date and both start and end times for the event. Otherwise you can toggle the 'All-day' button if the event is likely to take up the entire day.

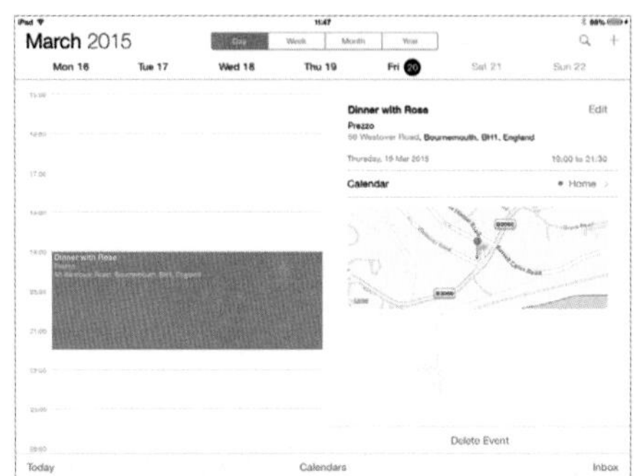

06 Tap Done

When you have everything in place, you need to tap the 'Done' button located in the top-right corner of the window. Alternatively you can cancel it to return without saving.

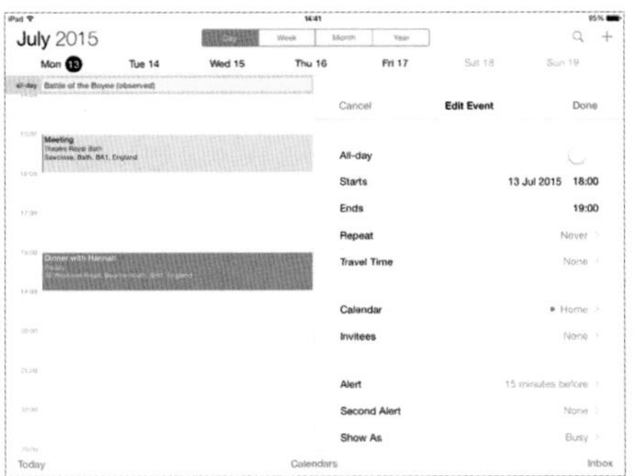

07 Set reminders

Tap the 'Alert' field to set reminders for the event. These will help ensure you don't miss an appointment. Alerts pop up on your iPad at the times you set them.

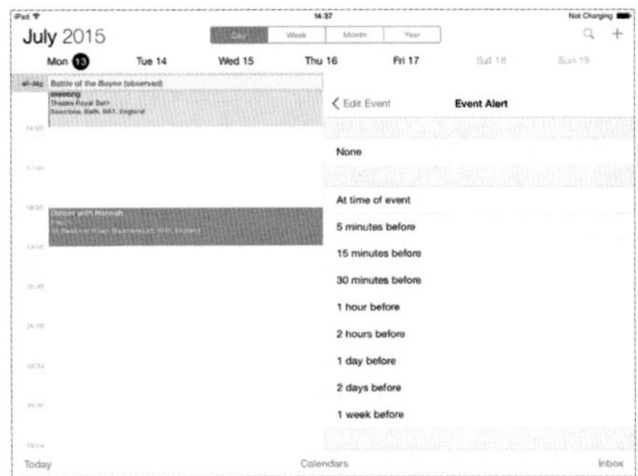

08 Tap it, save it

There are a number of options for alerts, ranging from at the event time to two days before. Tap on the option you wish to use and a tick will appear. Save your progress by clicking 'Done'.

09 Save and view

Save your event and it will appear on the page. Tap on it to see the full details and to make changes. If you change your mind, tap the red 'Delete Event' button at the bottom.

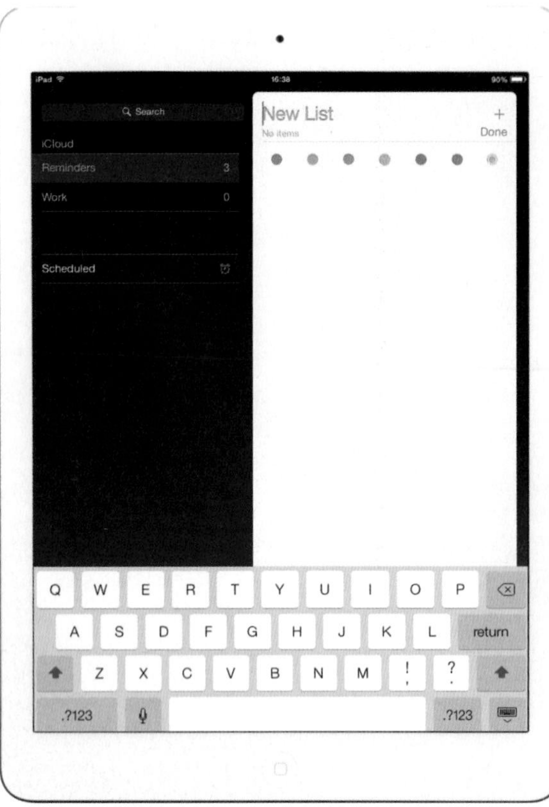

Never miss an event by using Reminders

Thanks to Apple's task management app, you have no excuse for forgetting birthdays

We all like to think that our minds operate like super-computers. As such, we utter the words, "Don't worry, I'll remember…" on an all-too-regular basis, only to forget whatever it was we said we'd never forget. To help, Apple has created its own task management app, and it's a cracker.

Reminders is an app that helps you organise your life by sorting your tasks into To Do lists, complete with due dates, notes and reminders to ensure that you never forget when something important is coming up. Simply jot down tasks, record when you need to do them by, then tick each one off as you complete it. A great touch is that Reminders is location-based, so if you need to pick up something from the supermarket, you can be reminded with an alert as soon as you get close to the shop in question.

The app is also fully integrated with your Calendar, Outlook and iCloud apps, meaning that any changes you make to your Reminders list will update automatically across each of these facilities. In this tutorial, we guide you through the process of setting your own reminders and managing your To Do lists to enhance your day-to-day efficiency.

"The Reminders app also works with Calendar, Outlook and iCloud"

Reminders Setting yourself reminders

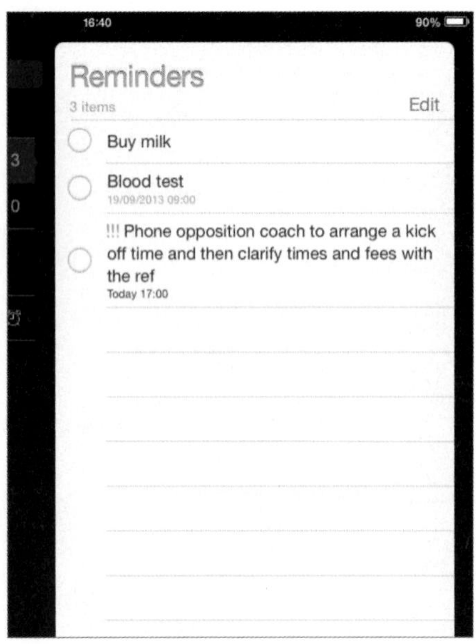

01 Add a reminder

Within the Reminders app, you can immediately start compiling a To Do list by tapping either the paper, or the '+' button in the top-right corner. Use the default keyboard to type your reminder.

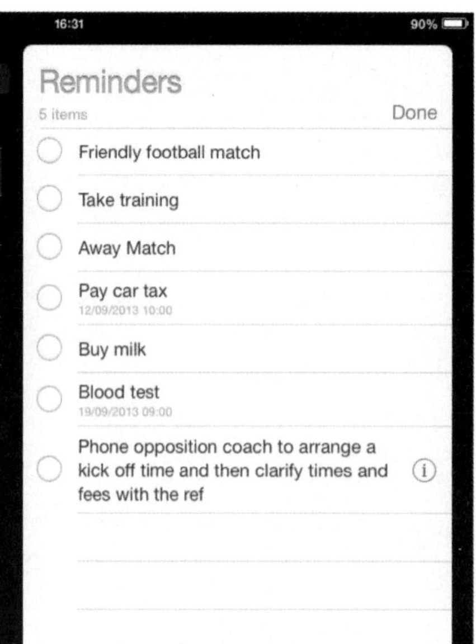

02 Make lists

Add reminders to your To Do list by tapping the page or on Edit. The lines on the paper will even expand to neatly contain all of your text – just in case you have a complicated task to complete!

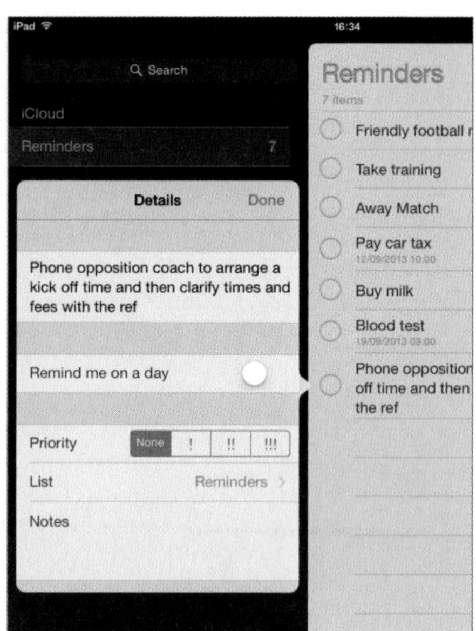

03 Add details

Select a task and tap on the 'i' icon to view details. Tap 'Remind me on a day' to On, then use the trusty wheels and hit the date to choose when your device should alert you.

Adding reminders

Never miss anything you had planned again!

Search
If you end up with vast lists of reminders – new and old – search for a specific reminder by entering some key words into the search window

Your lists
You'll be able to access all of your reminder lists from the main menu. You can also create new lists to add to this section

Your reminders
Tap the page or the '+' icon to add new reminders, and they will be presented as an easy-to-manage To Do list

Tickboxes
Once you have completed a task, place a tick in the box and it will be removed from your reminders list and added to your Completed list for future reference

Your system
By default, your tasks are arranged into Reminders or Completed sections. If you want to change the names of these categories or create new folders in which to store your reminders, tap the Edit button in the top-left corner, and start creating new places for your filing system.

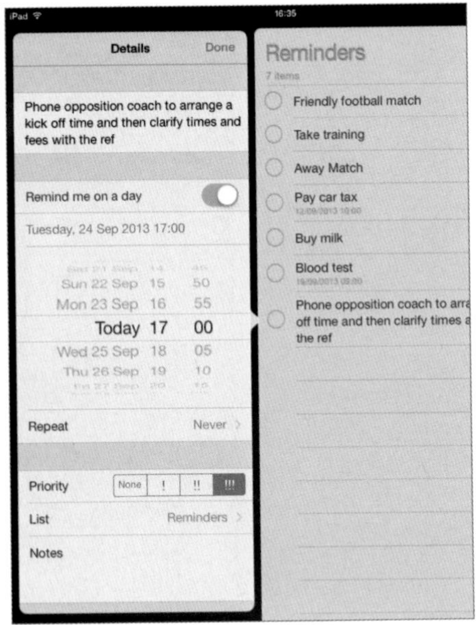

04 More options
You can set various other options, such as the level of priority, and add notes that relate to each task if you feel you may need more information. Tap Done when you're happy.

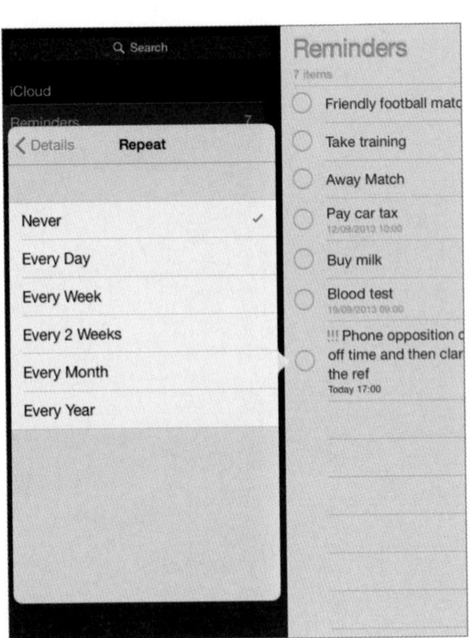

05 Repeat events
If the item you need reminding of is a frequent occurrence, you can also tap on Repeat and set yourself a timescale for repeating the reminder, such as every week.

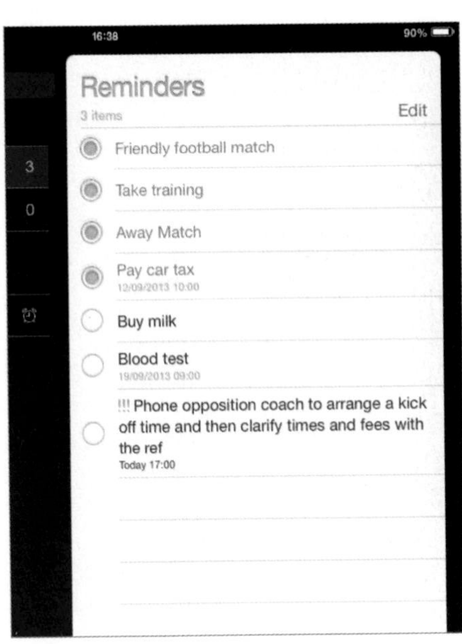

06 Tick them off
Whenever a task is completed, tap the box next to it to add a mark. Reminders that have been marked will be added to your Completed list, making you feel good about progress!

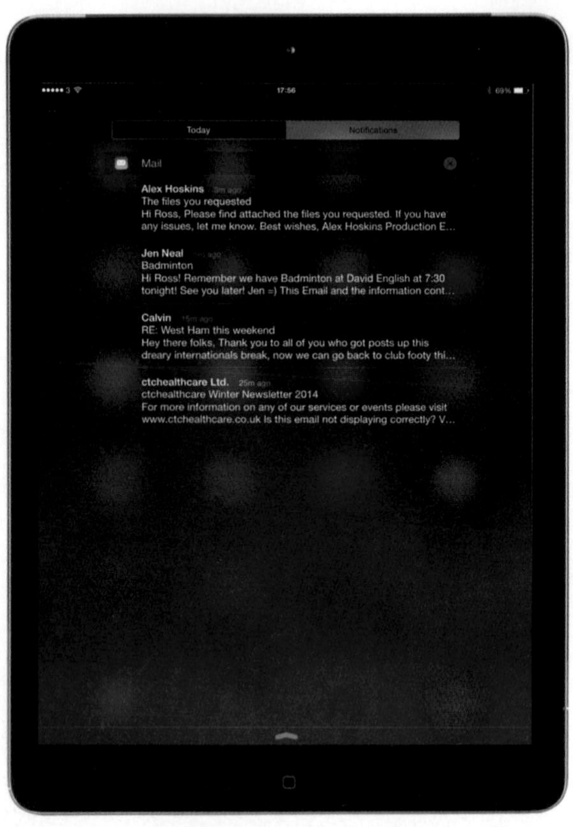

Customise your Notifications screen

Make sure you never miss a thing by setting up your very own personalised Notifications screen

Your iPad has always been good at notifying you about updates, messages, events and so on. The system introduced in iOS 5 features an enhanced suite to allow you to tailor all aspects of how your device gets messages to you. However, iOS 8 has truly embraced the concept of personalised notifications to make sure your iPad becomes a fully-integrated lifestyle tool that you can depend on.

For example, you can opt to receive alerts on messages, notifications, news stories and even the latest scores – all of which can be delivered to the top of your screen without disturbing the task you are in the middle of completing.

All you have to do in order to set up your own personalised notifications is go to Settings, choose the apps, and then select the order in which you would like them to appear in your Notification Centre and how you want them to alert you. To stay in the loop, simply swipe down from the top of the screen and you will be presented with a list of notifications for all of the apps you have chosen to feature. Here, we will show you just how to get the most out of this fantastic feature and stay up-to-date at all times.

"Tailor all aspects of how your device gets messages to you"

Notification Centre How to set up and use your Notification Centre

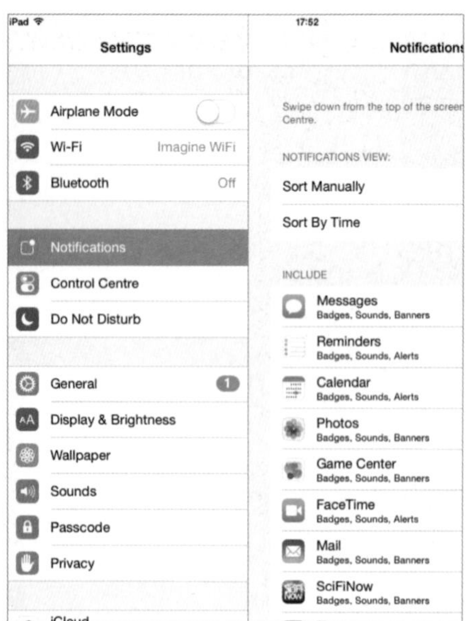

01 Go to Settings

From your iPad's home screen, tap 'Settings', which is housed in your dock by default, then tap on 'Notifications', which should be the fourth option down on the list.

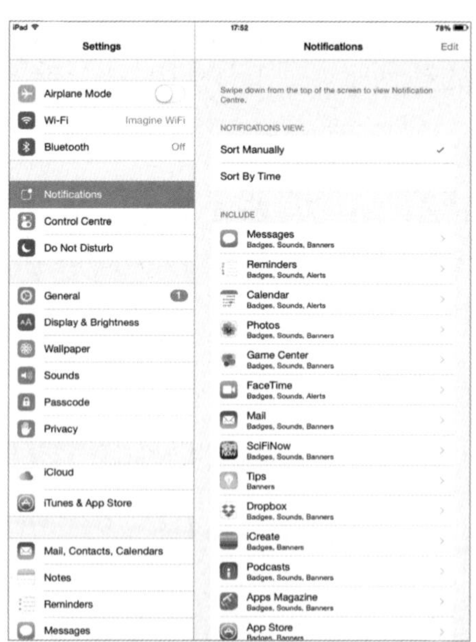

02 Add items

In Settings, you can choose which apps are featured in the Notifications centre. Tap 'Edit', then hold the right-hand edge of each app strip and drag it into the desired position.

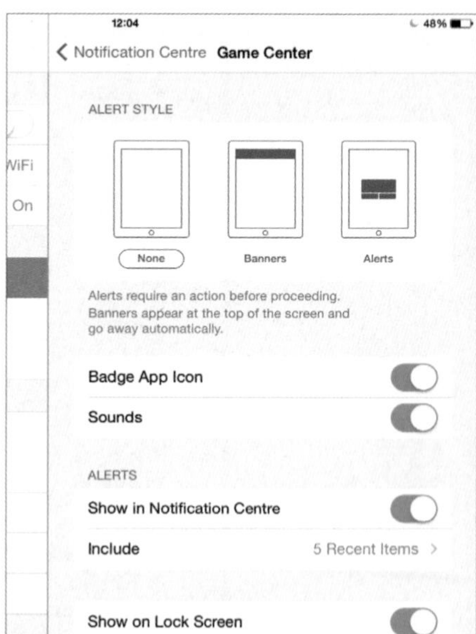

03 Tailor notification options

Tap the arrow next to an app and you will see options that are specific to that app. Choose how many items relating to that app are displayed when a notification arrives.

Setting up your Notification Centre

Tailoring the news feed that's all about you

View in lock screen
This option determines if alerts appear on your device's lock screen. It is good to have this activated so that you never miss a thing

Badge icons
This slider will determine whether the icon for the app that is notifying you is displayed in the alert. It looks better if they are on

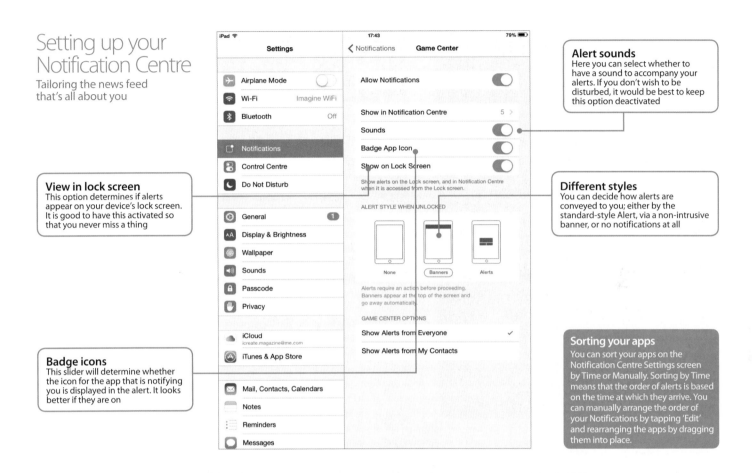

Alert sounds
Here you can select whether to have a sound to accompany your alerts. If you don't wish to be disturbed, it would be best to keep this option deactivated

Different styles
You can decide how alerts are conveyed to you; either by the standard-style Alert, via a non-intrusive banner, or no notifications at all

Sorting your apps
You can sort your apps on the Notification Centre Settings screen by Time or Manually. Sorting by Time means that the order of alerts is based on the time at which they arrive. You can manually arrange the order of your Notifications by tapping 'Edit' and rearranging the apps by dragging them into place.

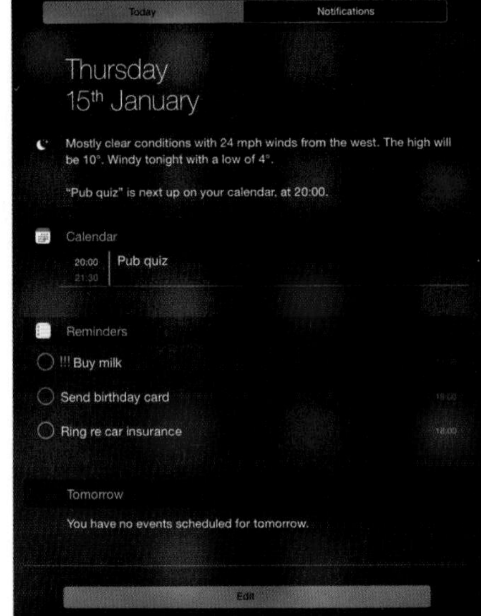

04 Access Notification Centre
Simply swipe down from the top of the screen to call up the Notifications Centre. In iOS 8 you can tap 'Edit' to choose any widgets you'd like to show on this screen, like Calendar and Reminders.

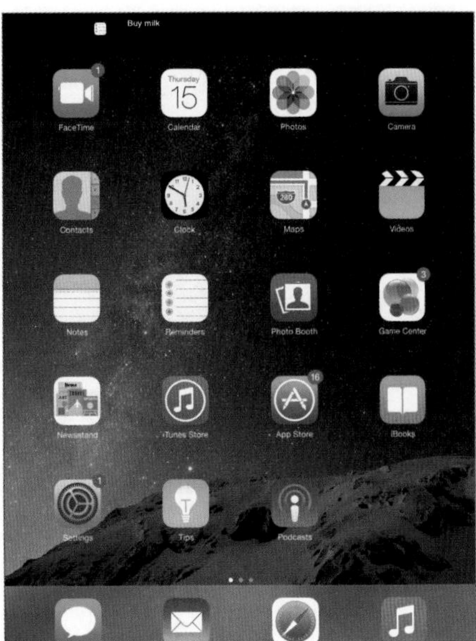

05 Your alerts
Notifications arrive in the form of a message at the top of the screen and don't intrude with the app you are currently using, giving you the option to ignore it if you so wish.

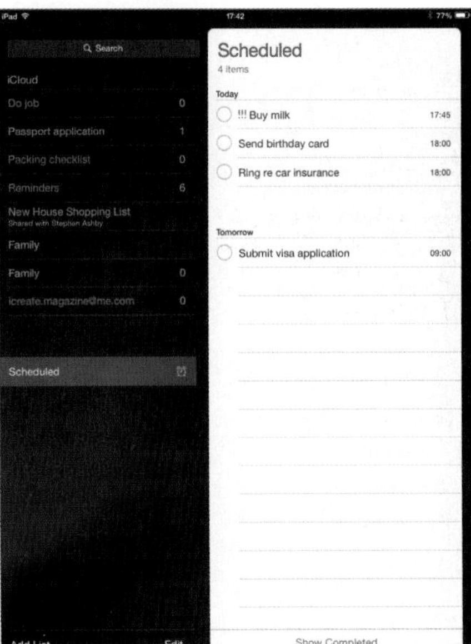

06 Go to app
If you need to respond to a notification immediately, drag down your Notifications Centre and tap on the notification. You will then be taken directly to the specific app to carry out your desired action

Instantly respond to notifications

If you receive a message or email, there is no need to leave the app you are in to deal with it...

Your iPad can be used as a great communicative tool, but what happens if you receive important emails while you're in the middle of doing something else on your device? Not a problem, because by tailoring Notification Center, you can respond to notifications without ever leaving the app that you're in or abandoning the task you're completing.

To get started, launch your Settings app from the Home screen and tap on the Notifications section in the left-hand column. You will see all of the apps in your Notification Center (which is normally accessible by swiping down from the top of the screen), so tap on one, such as Messages, and then ensure that the Allow Notifications slider is moved to the On position. You can then select how you wish the notifications to appear on screen, such as Banners.

Once this is activated, whenever you receive a new message from that specific app, a banner alert will appear at the top of the screen to notify you. Depending on how urgent the message is, you can either launch the respective app to read and respond to the message, or swipe down on the message to read it and reply.

"You can respond to notifications without ever leaving the app that you're in"

Notification Center Deal with notifications instantly

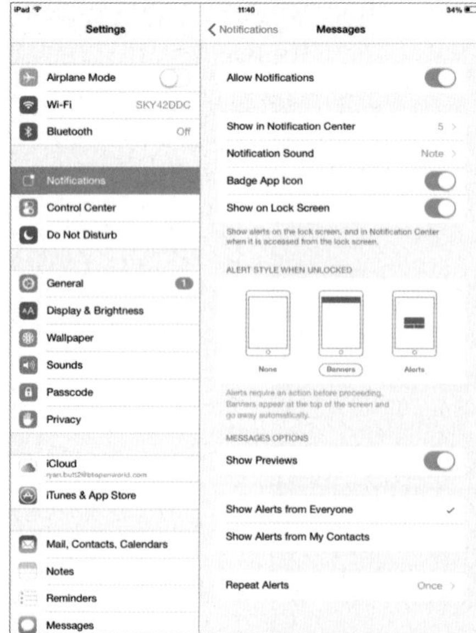

01 Refine your settings

Launch the Settings app and go to the Notifications section. Ensure services such as Messages and Mail are included and set the alert style to Banners so that they appear at the top of the screen.

02 Assess notifications

When you receive messages, non-intrusive banner notifications will flash up at the top of the screen. You can ignore them, but if you see that it needs an urgent response you can tap on it and pull down.

03 Quick reply

Pulling down on the notification provides a means of responding to the message, no matter which app you are currently in. A text field will appear into which you can write your response.

Respond quickly to notifications

Reply to messages without leaving the app you're working in

Message notification
With your Notification Center settings configured correctly, banner alerts will appear at the top of the screen when you receive new messages

Dictate your response
To make replying to messages easier you can do it hands-free. Tap on the microphone icon and speak your response to have it converted into text

Predictive responses
The system is clever enough to provide quick responses based on the content of the message. Tap one of these to make responding quicker

Reply instantly
Pull down on the message notification to bring up the option to reply. Here you can add a subject and body text without leaving the app you are in

Notification options
If you find that notifications crop up more regularly than you can manage, or if you receive important messages from particular apps, you can always set up audio or vibrate alerts. If you find this too intrusive, you can also activate the Badges option, whereby the app icon will display a number relating to the number of messages waiting for you to read and respond to.

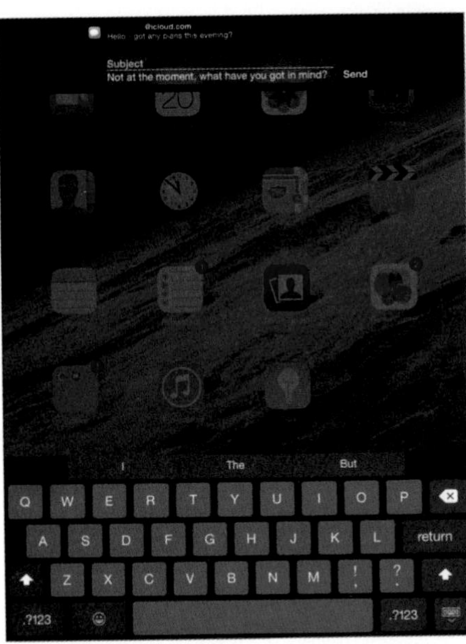

04 Do not disturb!
Enter a response and tap on the Send button to fire back the response. You can continue what you were previously doing with very little distraction, safe in the knowledge that your response has been sent.

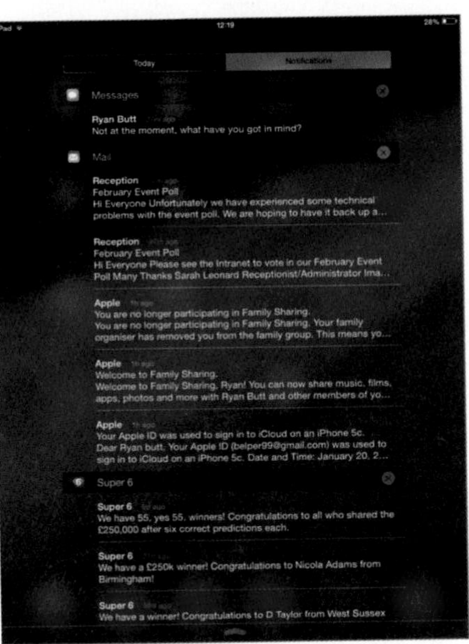

05 View notifications
If you miss the banner notifications, you can still respond to messages and emails from your Notification Center. To access this, simply swipe down from the top of the screen.

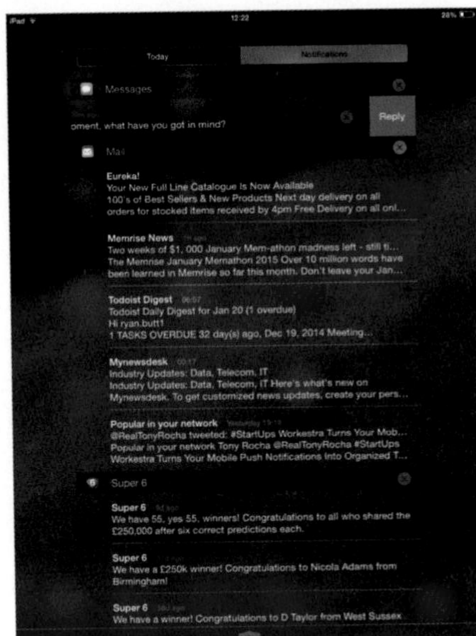

06 Manage notifications
Tap on Notifications to see messages and emails and swipe to the left on any entry to see options to Reply (for messages), Mark as Read or Archive (for emails). Close the Notification Center by swiping up.

Make calls using FaceTime

Here's how you sign up to FaceTime and call someone for a video conversation

The addition of dual cameras to the iPad 2 was one of the worst kept secrets and yet (or perhaps because of this) it was also one of the most anticipated features of the device's launch. Not so much for the ability to go out and take pictures with your iPad, as the large device is not exactly built for this purpose, but instead for apps that can handle video calling, video capture and transmission.

Yes, FaceTime is available on the iPad and it has its very own app. If you're used to the FaceTime iPhone app then you'll be right at home here. The cameras are the same resolution, so if you think your main screen image looks soft, it's because it's being displayed at the huge iPad size, not a tiny iPod touch screen size.

The first thing you need to have in place before any calls are made is to register FaceTime using your Apple ID. This is the ID that is used by Apple and the App Store for purchases. Once the Apple ID is set up for the FaceTime account, an email address needs to be assigned to it. This is the one that you will use to call other people and that they will use to call you. Once you're set up with that, you can speak face-to-face with all your friends.

"Before any calls are made, you must register FaceTime using your Apple ID"

FaceTime Register FaceTime and make calls

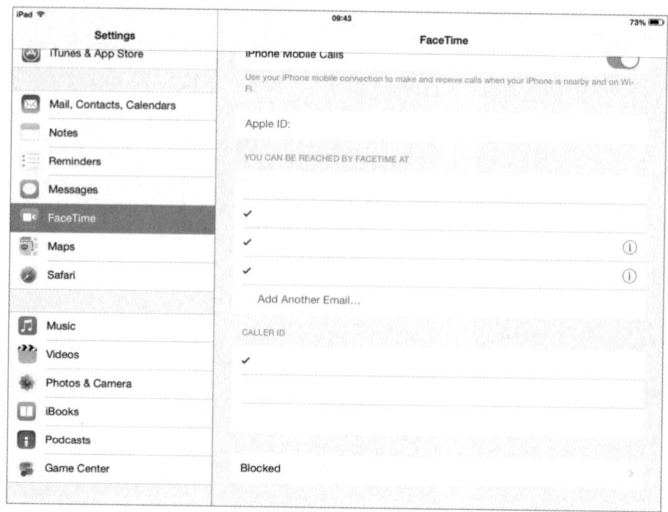

01 Register your details

To register your details, tap on the Settings app and scroll down the list of built-in apps until you get to FaceTime. Tap on this and toggle FaceTime On. You will be required to enter your Apple ID. Enter the email address and the password and then tap Sign In to get started.

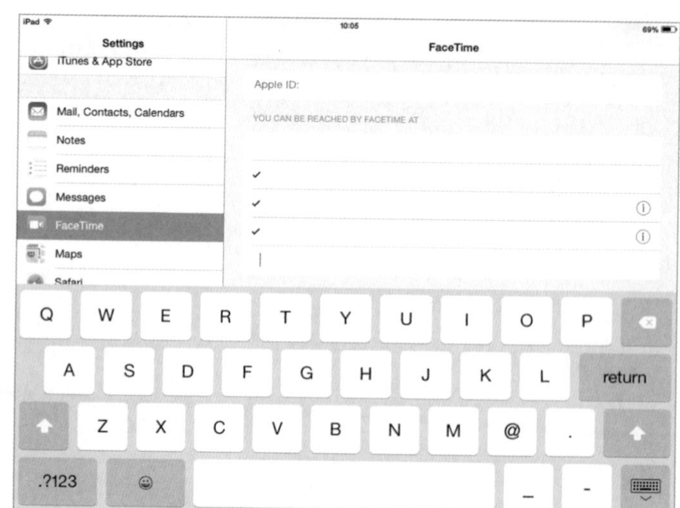

02 Select an address

FaceTime can use different email addresses. Enter the one that you would like to use for your calls. If it's the same as your Apple ID account, it will be verified immediately. However, if it is a different email address, a verification link will be sent to that address.

Making a call

It's easy to make FaceTime calls. Just find contacts who use it and call away

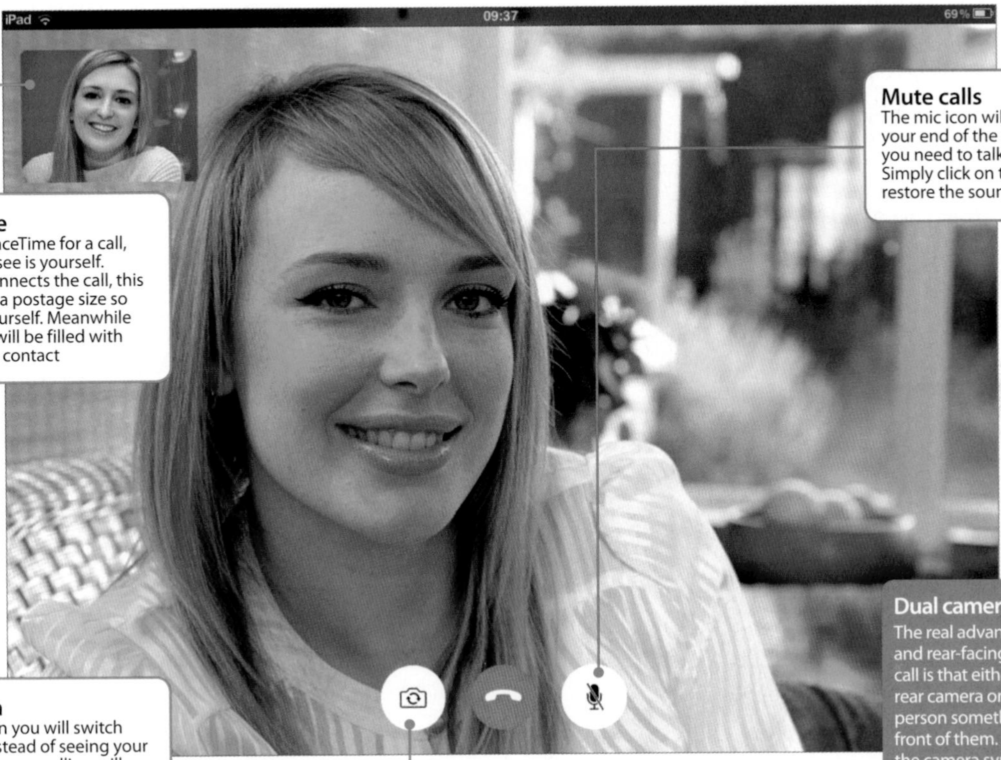

Cameras in use
When activating FaceTime for a call, the first thing you see is yourself. When FaceTime connects the call, this window shrinks to a postage size so you can still see yourself. Meanwhile the main window will be filled with the video from the contact

Mute calls
The mic icon will mute the sound from your end of the call. This is useful if you need to talk to people off camera. Simply click on the same icon again to restore the sound as normal

Switch camera
By tapping this icon you will switch cameras so that instead of seeing your face, the person you are calling will see what you are pointing your iPad at. Good for showing off items

Dual cameras
The real advantage of having front and rear-facing cameras in a FaceTime call is that either person can turn the rear camera on to show the other person something that is going on in front of them. All you need to do is tap the camera symbol with the rotating arms to switch your camera from front facing to rear facing.

03 Get into FaceTime

Once verified, your details will be displayed and FaceTime will be on. Exit Settings and tap on the FaceTime app. This will show the display from the front-facing camera and a list of recent contacts sorted by Video and Audio calls. To bring up a full list of contacts, tap the '+' icon in the top-left corner.

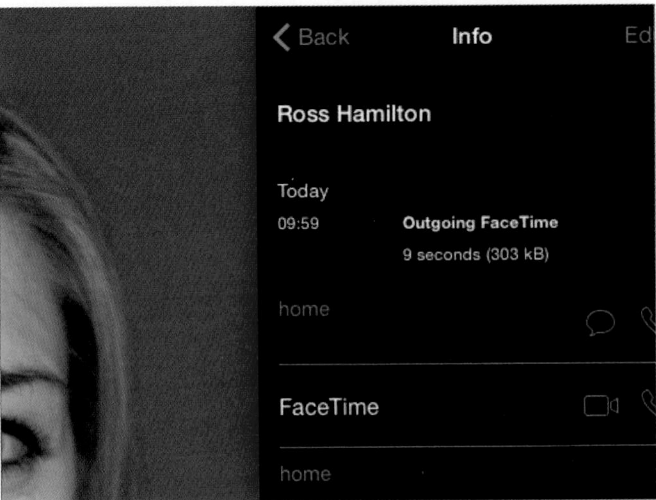

04 Make a call

Tap on the person whom you would like to call. If they have a FaceTime account then they will have a FaceTime option beneath their phone number. Tap on either the video camera to make a FaceTime video call, or the phone to make a FaceTime Audio call.

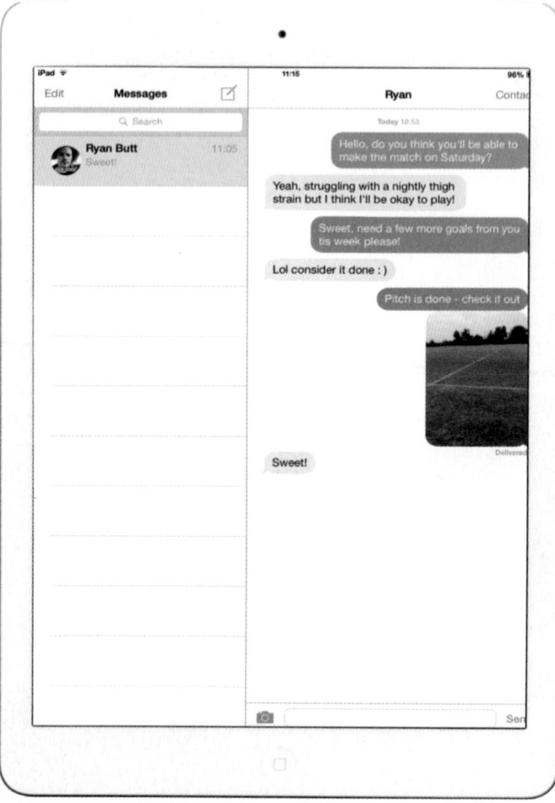

Stay in contact using iMessage

Get to grips with Apple's messaging service and send unlimited text messages to your friends

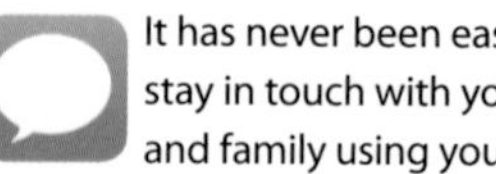

It has never been easier to stay in touch with your friends and family using your Apple device. Thanks to iMessage, you can send unlimited text messages to everyone you know for free, so long as you have a Wi-Fi, 3G or 4G connection.

The app works exactly like the iPhone Messages app, letting you share photos, videos, locations and contacts around your social circles. This is a great feature for keeping everyone in the loop via group messaging. To start, tap the New Message button and enter the Apple IDs of the people you wish to contact. Then simply enter your message into a text field, hitting the camera button to attach media, and tapping Send.

The interface of iMessage is fabulously intuitive. Most importantly, the service is absolutely free! So as long as both you and your friends have iOS 5 or above installed on your Apple devices, you can text without worrying about incurring a hefty bill. All messages can be tracked with delivery receipts, and thanks to the iCloud, you can start a conversation on one device and finish it later on another. Here we guide you through the process of using iMessage for the first time.

"It's never been easier to stay in touch with your friends and family"

iMessage How to text for free

01 Create a message

To kick things off you will need to tap the New Message icon (a piece of paper and a pen), and you'll be prompted to enter the Apple ID of the person you wish to send a message to.

02 Type and send

Tap on the text field and type your message into the window. When you have finished writing what you wish to say, hit Send and your message will be delivered instantly.

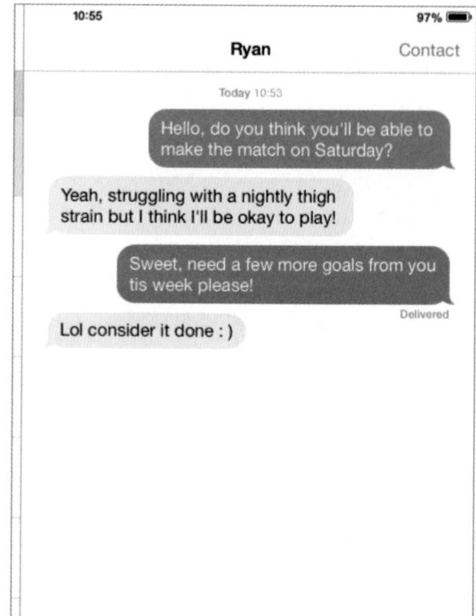

03 Quick conversations

The conversations will be neatly displayed in the main window, and the text will be colour-coded so you know who said what – blue will be your message and grey that of the recipient.

Free and easy messaging

Quickly conversing has never been so easy

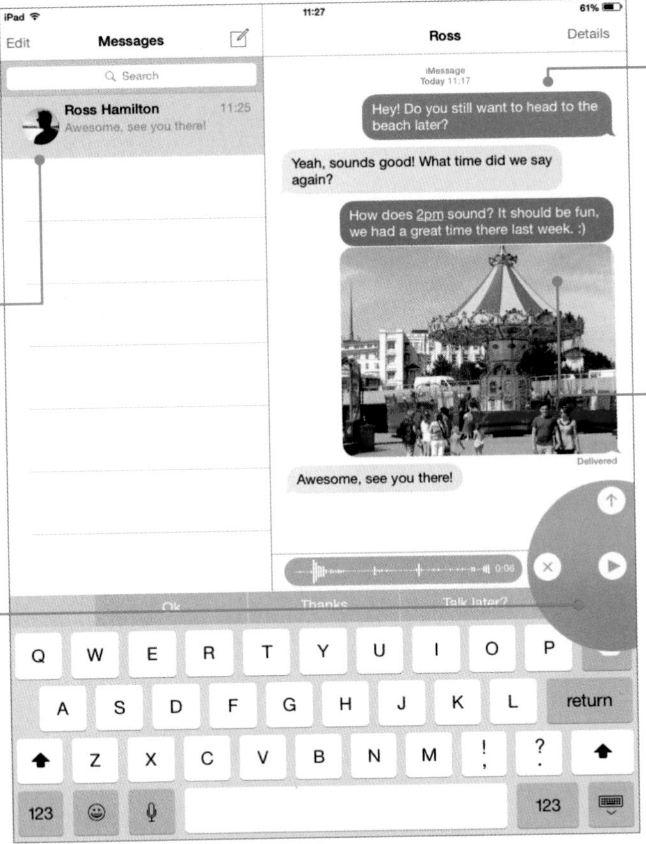

Delete messages
Delete messages by holding on the message and choosing More. Now select the message and tap on the trash icon

Your recipients
All of your friends will be listed in the column to the left of the window. You can even bring in more people for group conversations

Instant messaging
Sending messages is easy. Just tap on the text field, type what you want and hit the Send button. Each text bubble is colour-coded to make it easy to see who said what

Voice messages
New in iOS 8 is the ability to send quick voice messages in the iMessage app. Simply hold down the microphone button to start recording and release when you're done. You can then replay your recording, swipe left to delete it, and swipe up to send it

Adding photos
Images and videos can be added and attached to your messages. Just type your message as normal, and then tap the camera icon to select and send your chosen media. You can add multiple pictures or videos too.

04 Add images

Once you have typed your message, tap the camera icon, pick a photograph you wish to send from your Camera Roll, and then tap Use to include it in your next message.

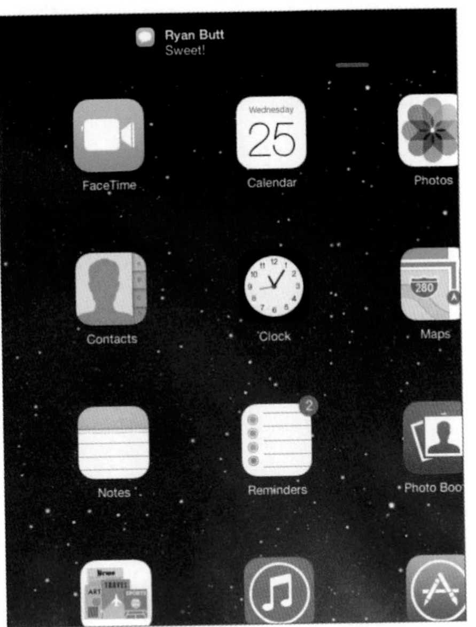

05 Notifications

iMessage is automatically integrated with your Notifications, so if you receive any new messages you will be instantly notified. Drag down to reply straight away or tap to be taken to the app.

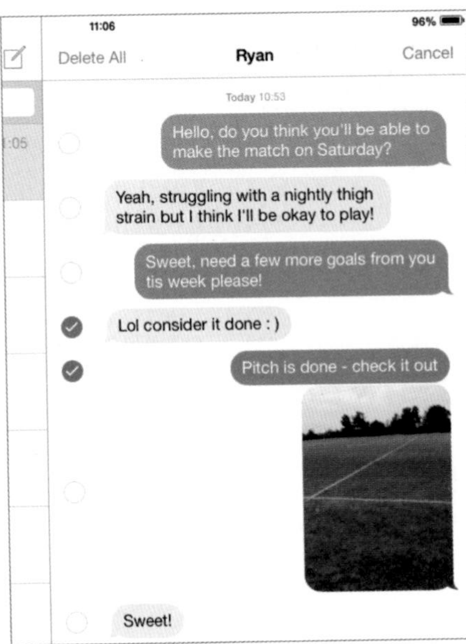

06 Deleting messages

If there are parts of conversations you want to delete, press and hold on the message then tap More. You can now select messages to delete. Once selected, tap the trash icon.

Make notes on your iPad

Jot down ideas on your iPad more easily than a full word-processing suite using the built-in Notes app

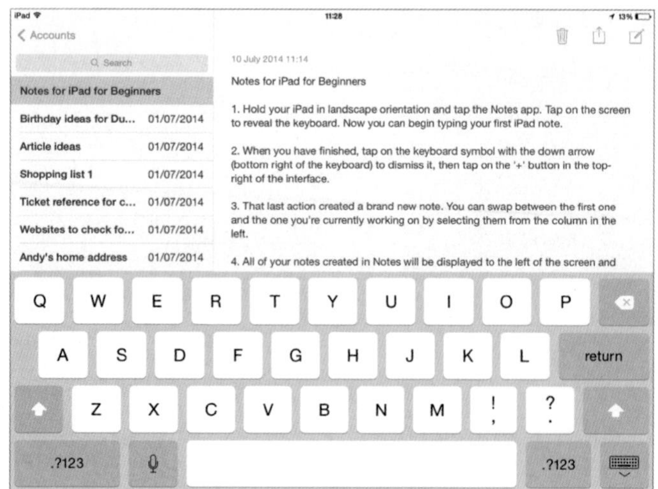
Accounts
Search
10 July 2014 11:14
Notes for iPad for Beginners
Birthday ideas for Du... 01/07/2014
Article ideas 01/07/2014
Shopping list 1 01/07/2014
Ticket reference for c... 01/07/2014
Websites to check fo... 01/07/2014
Andy's home address 01/07/2014
1. Hold your iPad in landscape orientation and tap the Notes app. Tap on the screen to reveal the keyboard. Now you can begin typing your first iPad note.
2. When you have finished, tap on the keyboard symbol with the down arrow (bottom right of the keyboard) to dismiss it, then tap on the '+' button in the top-right of the interface.
3. That last action created a brand new note. You can swap between the first one and the one you're currently working on by selecting them from the column in the left.
4. All of your notes created in Notes will be displayed to the left of the screen and
return
.?123

Despite the fact that some people view the iPad as a device designed merely to consume media, just spending a few minutes with it will make you realise that this isn't true. With the help of a few choice programs, the iPad is capable of being used to create drawings, edit photos or write essays. But you don't need to purchase anything for the latter, as the Notes app comes bundled with the iPad and is a really great place to start exploring how you can handle typing on glass.

Notes is remarkably similar to the program bearing the same name on the iPhone and iPod touch, it has simply been expanded a little to take advantage of the additional space the iPad screen provides. This step-by-step tutorial will show you how it works, what you can do with it, and how it could help you in your day-to-day activities.

> "Notes comes bundled with the iPad and is a great place to start exploring how you can handle typing on glass"

Using Notes

The Notes app is great for jotting down ideas on the go, and even copying text from the web to read later

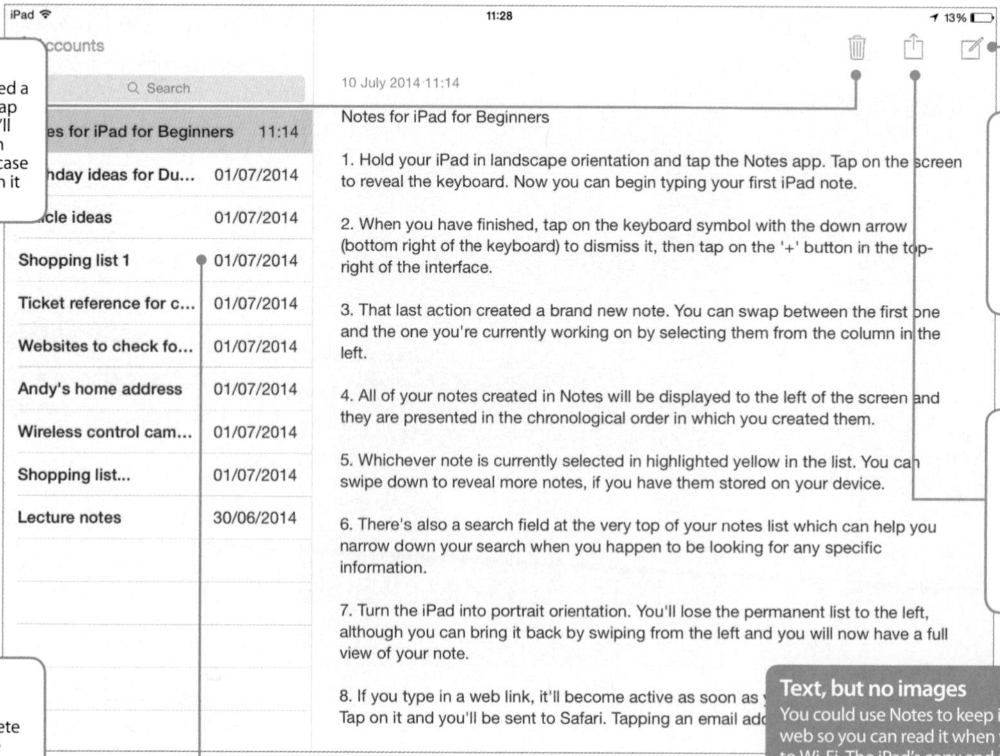

Delete

If you no longer need a note, select it and tap on this button. You'll be asked to confirm your choice just in case you have tapped on it by mistake

Add

You can add as many notes as you need in this app. Whether you're in the landscape or portrait orientation, this button is always in the top-right corner of the screen

Emailing

Notes lets you email the content of your pages without you having to copy and paste the information over yourself. Tap on this icon to create an email message

Swipe

You don't have to select a note to delete it, just swipe its title to reveal a Delete button – just like the messages in Mail

Text, but no images

You could use Notes to keep information from the web so you can read it when you don't have access to Wi-Fi. The iPad's copy and paste system works perfectly for this, but be aware that it only lets you copy text – you can't add images to Notes.

Notes Use Notes to write down ideas

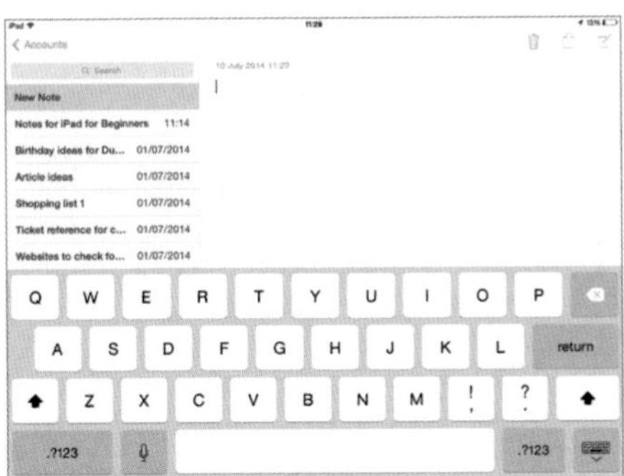

01 The look of Notes

Hold your iPad in the landscape orientation and tap the Notes app. Tap on the screen to reveal the keyboard. Now you can begin typing in your very first iPad note.

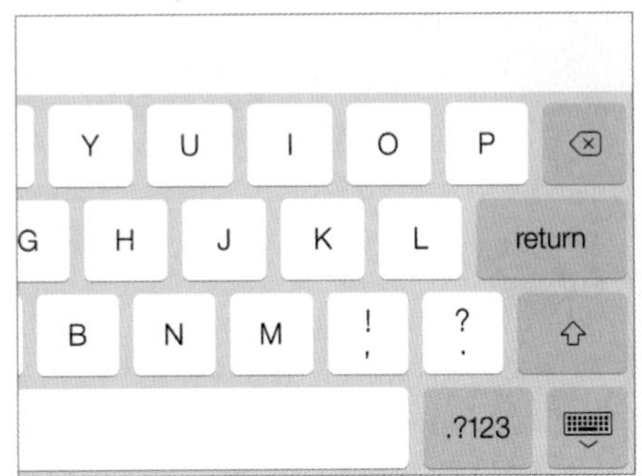

02 The note icon

When you have finished, tap on the keyboard symbol with the down arrow (bottom-right of the keyboard) to dismiss it, then tap on the '+' button in the top-right of the interface.

03 From one to another

That last action created a brand new note. You can swap between the first one and the one you're currently working on by selecting them from the column on the left.

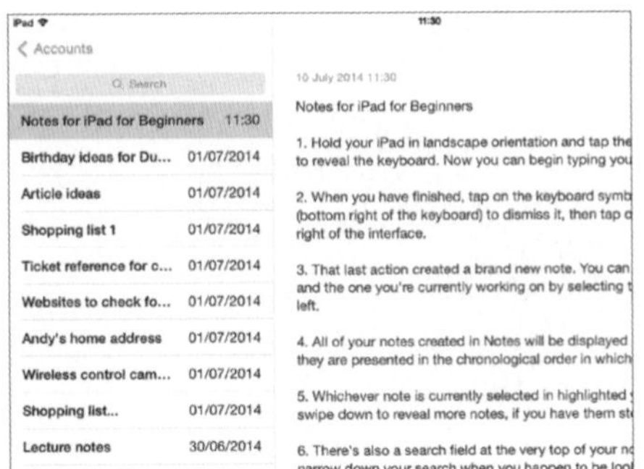

04 Your notes

All of your created notes will be displayed in the list to the left of the screen and they are all presented in the chronological order in which you created them, making them easy to find.

05 The selected note

Whichever note is currently selected is highlighted in yellow in the list. You can swipe down the list to reveal more notes, if they are on your device. One line of the note can be seen for easy recognition.

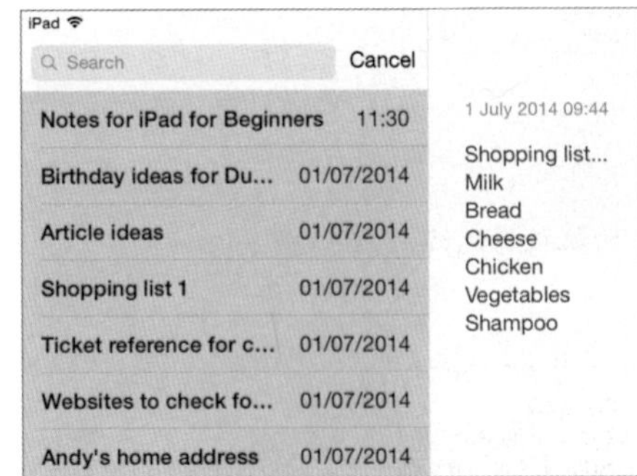

06 Searching

There's also a search field at the very top of the notes list, which can help you narrow down your search when you happen to be looking for any specific information.

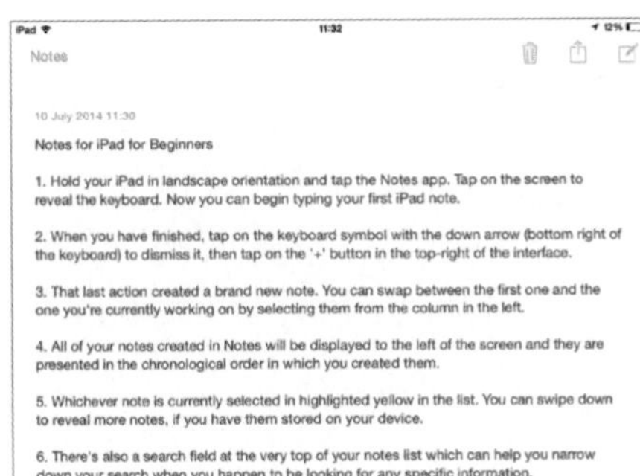

07 Portrait

Turn the iPad to the portrait orientation. You'll lose the permanent list to the left (although you can bring it back by swiping from the left), and you will now have a full view of your note.

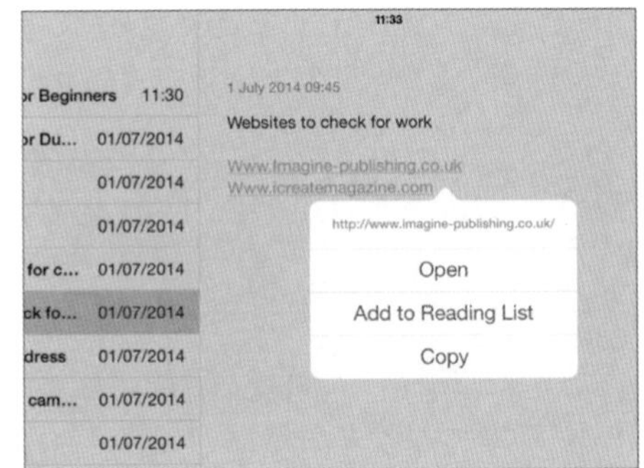

08 Tappable links

If you type in a web link, it'll become active as soon as you hide the keyboard. Tap on it and you'll be sent to Safari. Tapping an email address sends you to Mail.

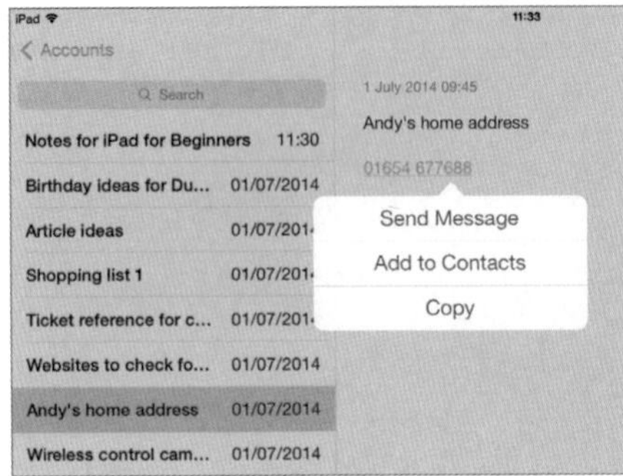

09 Save numbers

Your iPad recognises phone numbers too. As you can't phone people, you're offered the options to Create New Contact or Add To Existing Contact instead. For places, you can select Open in Maps.

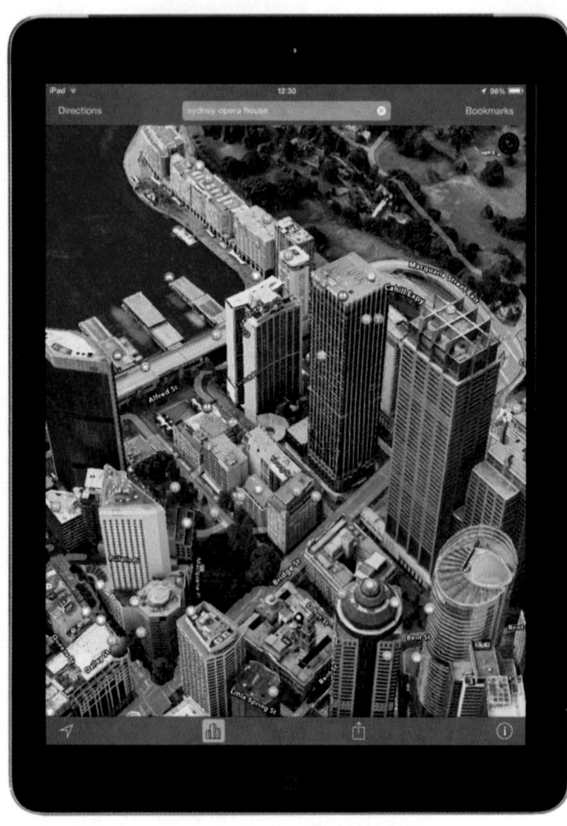

Get to know the Maps app

Everything you need to know about the fresh new face of the Maps app for iPad

Ever since the iPhone and the iPad first launched, Google had provided the mapping experience on iOS. Then, with the release of iOS 6, Apple struck out on its own and created an app from the ground up. They started completely from scratch when they began designing the app, and along with data from Yelp and TomTom, it has created a beautiful application with some amazing features that will certainly boost your experience.

Maps now includes turn-by-turn navigation, effectively transforming your device into a handheld satellite navigation system. With a 3D view and Siri integration on the new iPad, you can simply tell it where you want to go and follow the instructions as they are read out to you.

The new app also includes a 3D view of major cities around the world; when you're viewing a city in the top-down view, dragging two fingers upwards will allow you to effectively fly through the city and pan around in 3D.

We've taken a look at all the brilliant new features below, so read on to find out more about this fantastic app. Before you know it you'll be wondering how you got around before it was a part of your life!

"Apple has struck out on its own and created Maps from the ground up"

Maps Get the latest maps data

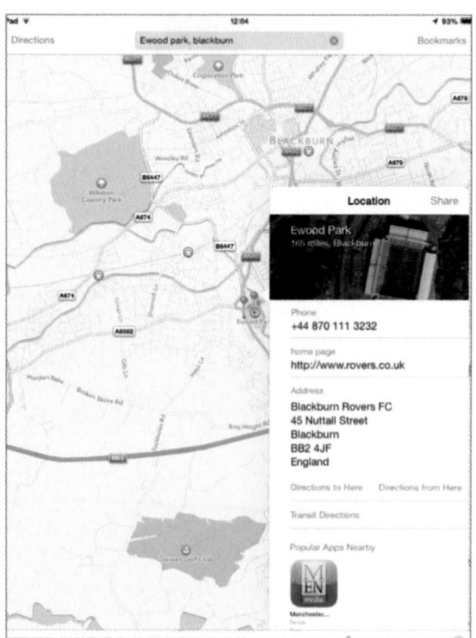

01 Information

With the help of Yelp, there are now over 100 million added points of interest around the world – tap one and this useful window will appear, showing information and options.

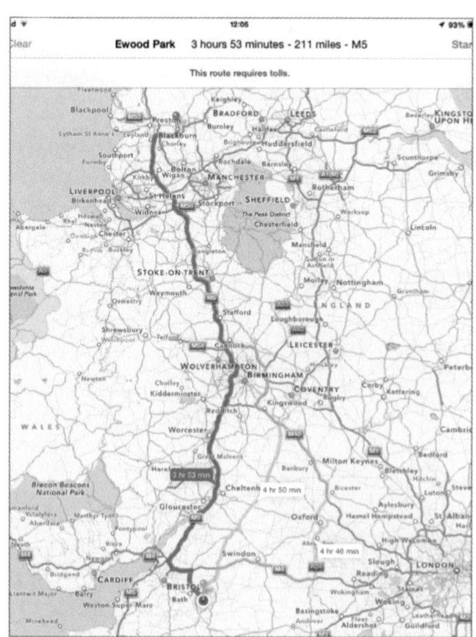

02 Directions

In the top-left of the screen you will see the Directions button. Tap this and you can get directions instantly – you'll even get a sat nav-style 3D view to help you navigate the landscape.

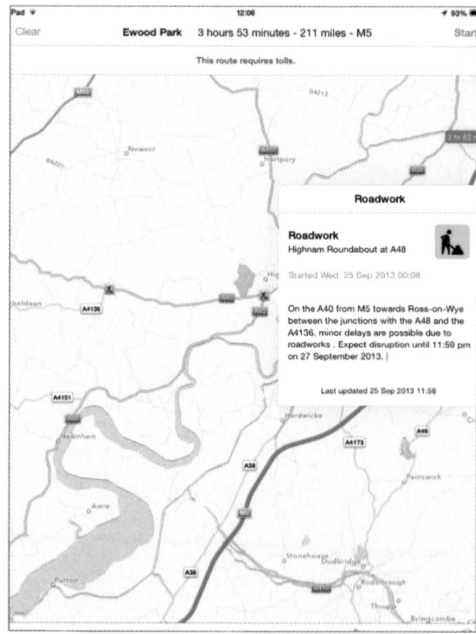

03 Traffic

The TomTom data also includes updates on any traffic problems. Tap an icon and you can view the time and details for each hold-up, enabling you to plan your journey around it.

The new Maps interface

It's Maps, but not as we know it

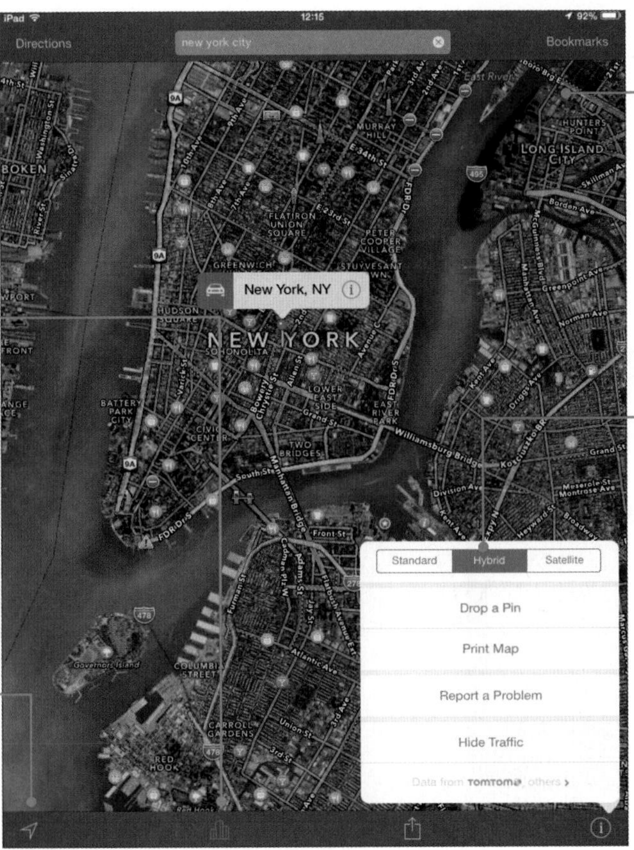

3D mode
To move into 3D mode you can either drag two fingers upwards to change the angle, or tap the 3D button in the bottom-left to change it automatically

Location data
The app still allows you to find your current location using the button in the bottom-left, with your location shown as a blue dot

Re-aligned
If you rotate the map with two fingers, you can realign the map to face north by tapping the compass icon in the top-right of the map

View options
Tap the icon in the bottom-right and you will see more options. You can view the map in different ways or show or hide traffic information

Always developing
The Maps app is still in early development with Apple. While there are some features that are missing, and locations that can't be found through a search, the whole maps database will only improve in coming years. It's constantly evolving, and there's plenty more to come.

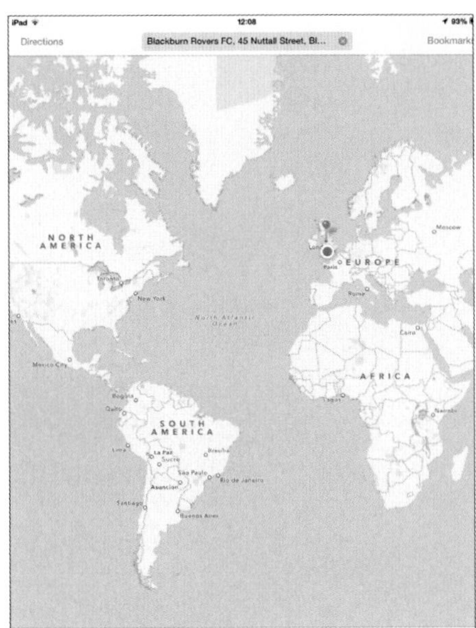

04 The world

In the iOS 8 Maps app you can no longer zoom out to the extent of seeing the entire globe, but you can zoom out to see most of the world, then you can simply swipe to scroll around it.

05 Bookmarks

Just like in Google Maps, your recent searches will be saved to the app's Bookmarks menu for quick access. You can also find your contacts and bookmarked locations included here.

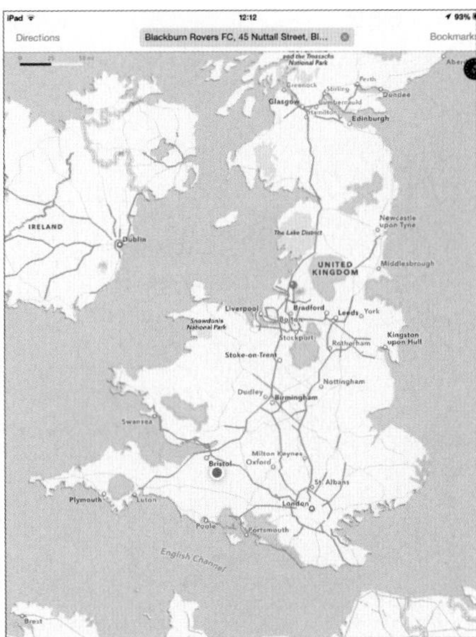

06 Rotation

Just as in Google Maps, the new Maps app lets you use two fingers to twist the map around. This is perfect if you're following directions or need to get your bearings.

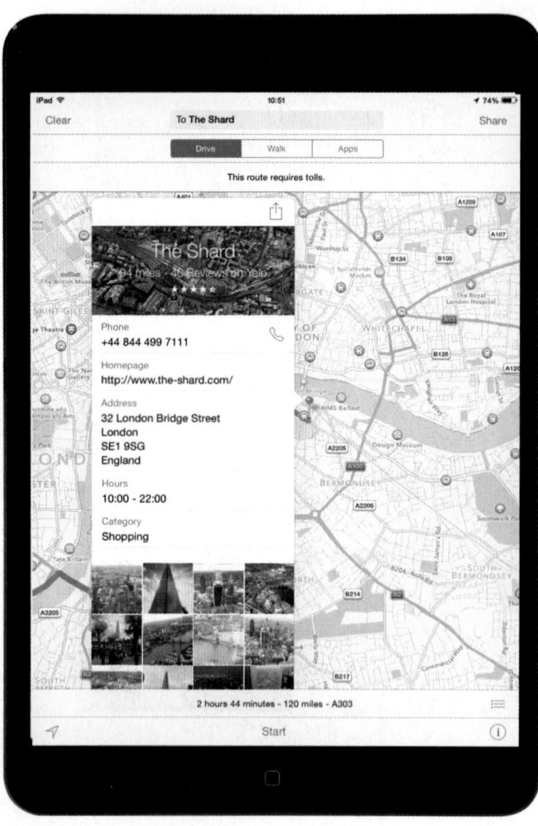

Find your way with the Maps app

Apple's very own Maps app has been completely redesigned in order to compete with other maps applications around

Recently completely redesigned from the ground up, Maps app revolutionises the way you view the world. Constantly being refined, the map elements are now vector-based, so graphics and text are incredibly detailed, even when you zoom in, and the panning is super-smooth. You can also get visual and spoken turn-by-turn navigation, real-time traffic updates and even soar over cityscapes to see the sights from the air in amazing, high-resolution quality in the new 3D Flyover mode. However, at present only a small selection of cities have been adequately rendered for this purpose and only iOS devices containing an A5 processor will be able to handle the feature (which rules out the original iPhone 4).

There are still plenty of exciting new features to enjoy though, even if you don't have the latest Apple device to run it on – such as turn-by-turn navigation. Now your iPad can operate just like an expensive satnav system by superimposing large signs and arrows over the map and speaking each direction to you, so you can concentrate on the road ahead, safe in the knowledge that your iPad will get you to your destination on time.

"Graphics and text are incredibly detailed, even when you zoom in, and the panning is super-smooth"

Maps Get to grips with Maps

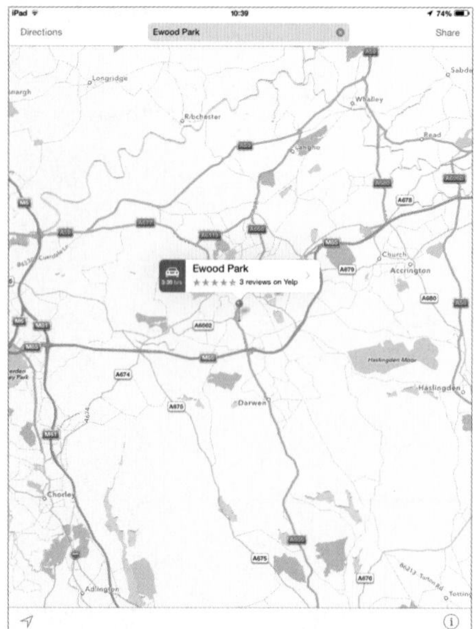

01 Drop a pin

You should use the search field in Maps in order to enter an address or postcode. When the location is displayed, press and hold the screen in order to drop a pin.

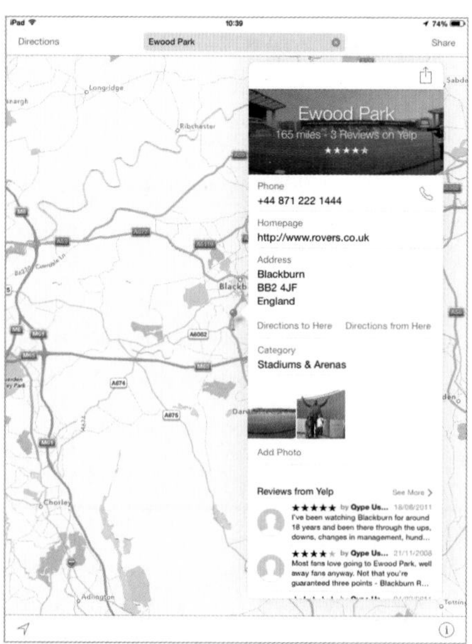

02 Get Info

Tap the pin in order to bring up the name of the location and then tap the blue arrow to get information about the place, plus options to share or add it to Contacts.

03 Find a route

Tap on the car icon on a pin location and a route will be plotted there from your current location. Use the tabs at the top of the screen to choose your mode of transport.

Discover the new features

The updated app is packed full of options to help you get where you need to go

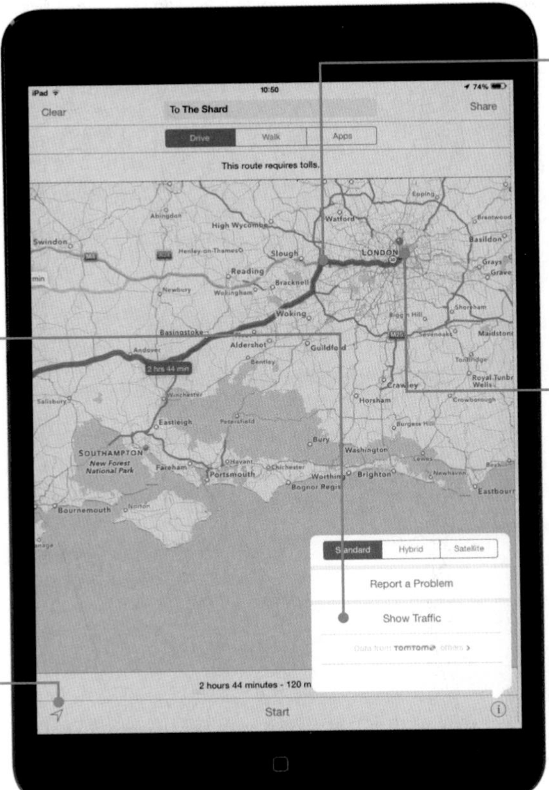

Hands-free directions
Large signs and arrows superimposed over the image show you which way to go and how long it's going to take you to get there, even if your screen is locked

Show Traffic
You can get real-time traffic information to calculate your ETA. Maps gives you details on what's causing a backup, so you can tell if there's a major accident or just a minor delay

Find locations
It is easy to find locations, either by dropping pins or entering details in the search field. You can then tap on 'pinned' locations to get info and share them via Facebook, Twitter and whole host of other mediums

Turn-by-turn navigation
Spoken directions informing you of every upcoming turn on route to your destination, a 3D view and real-time traffic information will ensure you reach your destination with time to spare

Flyover
With the new Flyover mode, you can see major metro areas from the air with photo-realistic, interactive 3D views. Explore cities in high resolution as you zoom, pan, tilt and rotate around the city and all of its famous landmarks.

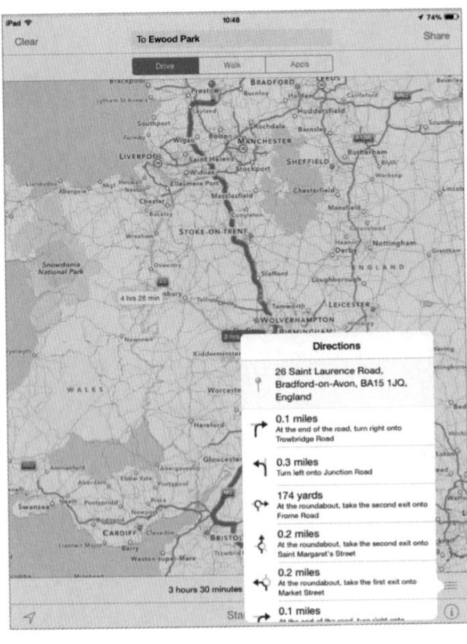

04 Start directions

Tap on the small list icon that is situated in the lower-right corner of the route screen the screen to get your directions relayed to you in list form. Tap on a step to enter turn-by-turn mode.

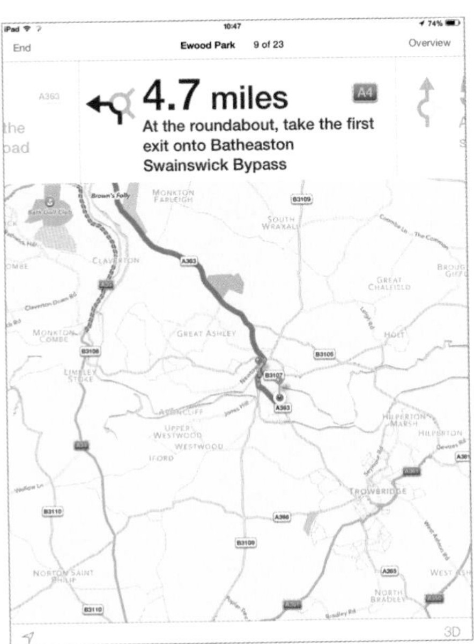

05 Start your journey

If you want to go straight to turn-by-turn mode, return to the route map screen and tap on the Start button. The directions will then be overlayed on the screen.

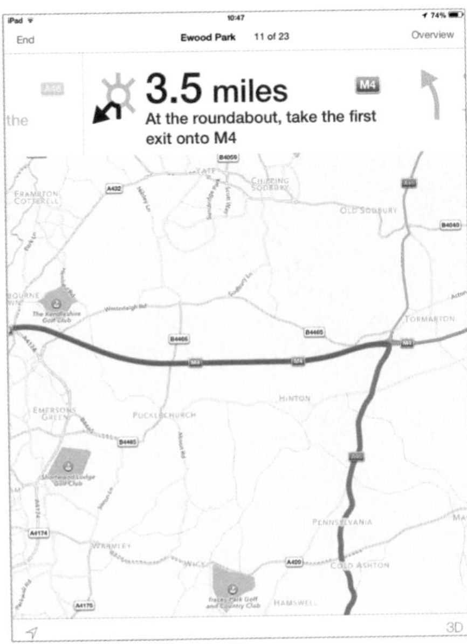

06 Get directed

When you are approaching a turn, the Maps app speaks directions, so you are able to keep your eyes on the road and be confident that Maps will lead the way.

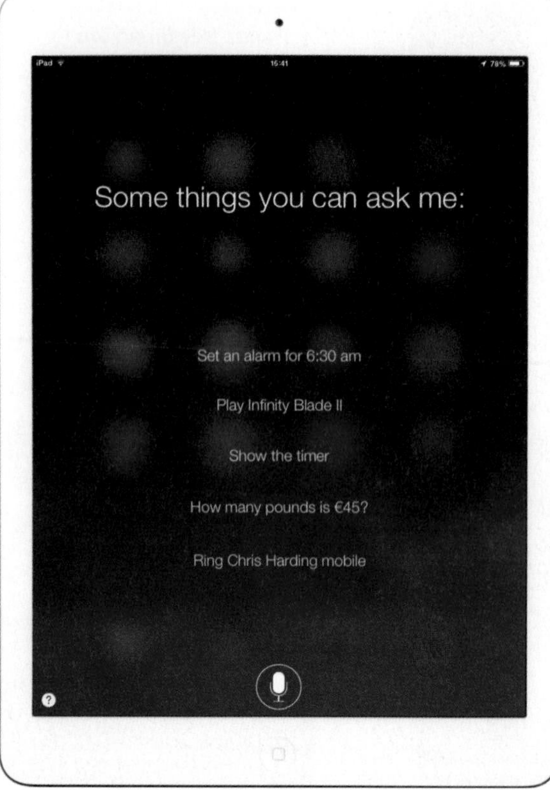

Talk to your tablet with Siri

Enjoy more control over your iPad with a host of great new voice commands with Siri

When it was first introduced, Siri seemed almost futuristic. Not only could you talk to your device, but it would talk back and do things for you! Siri has stuck around, but it hasn't always been the most useful feature. Fortunately, iOS 8 brought with it a number of new Siri commands that help you to really make the most of your iPad as your own virtual personal assistant.

Siri now has far more access to your iPad's key settings and apps. Control Centre might be a quick way to access your brightness settings, but if you're struggling to see a recipe mid-way through cooking and don't want to get your iPad dirty, Siri will sort it for you. It can now also search Twitter for tweets from specific users and even find images online, all without forcing you into Safari or any other app. It's an exciting change of gear that'll see us take another step closer to the futuristic vision we've been dreaming of for years.

Here's our pick of some of the best Siri features for you to try out. You'll need to be connected to the internet and have a compatible device, but otherwise, it's just a case of tapping and holding that Home button in order to launch Siri and get going.

"Siri now has far more access to your iPad's key settings and apps"

Siri Go hands free with your iPad

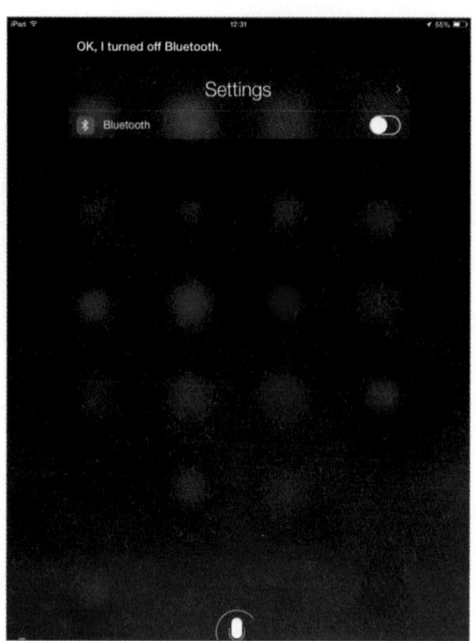

01 Change your settings

Asking Siri to 'Turn Bluetooth off' is now the quickest way to toggle that connectivity setting. It works for Wi-Fi, too, as well as a few other Settings app controls.

02 Check the gossip

Integration with Twitter and Facebook allows you to post directly to the sites; just say 'tweet' or 'post to Facebook'. Search for a specific user's tweets by asking: 'What is [user name] saying?'

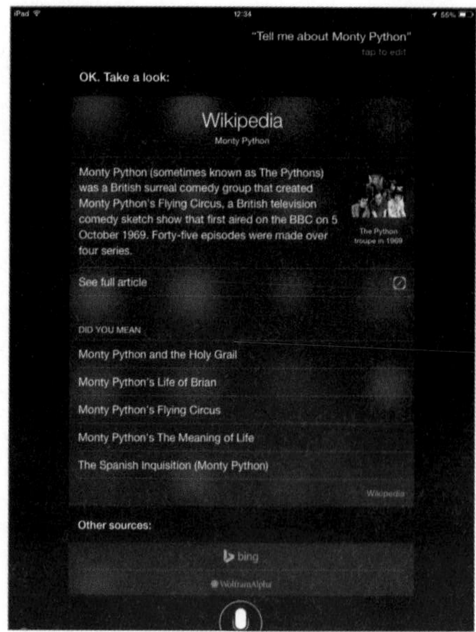

03 Search on Wikipedia

Whether it's settling a debate, impressing your mates or simply swotting up, Siri can help. Ask about any person or subject to be shown a Wikipedia entry.

More Siri commands

Make the most of Siri's intelligent audio request options

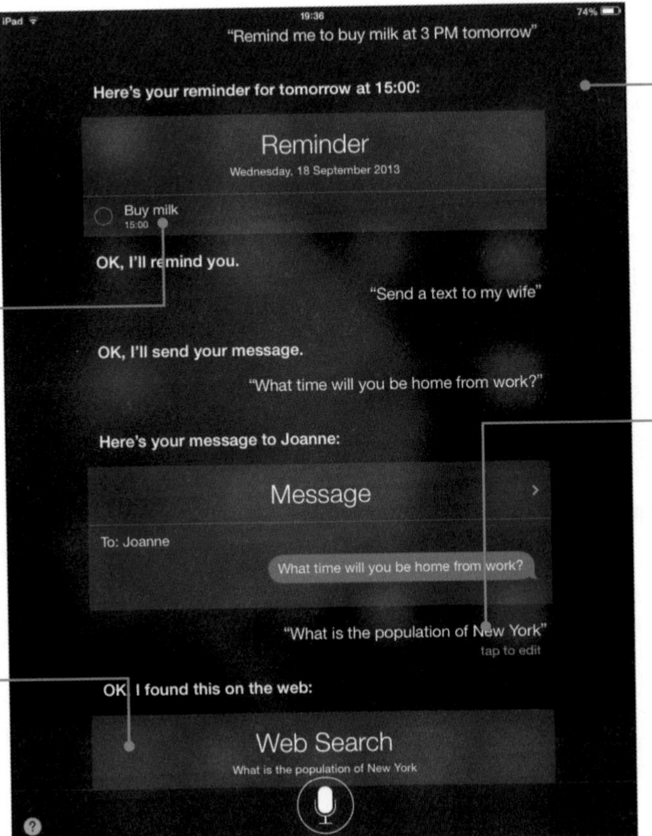

"Remind me to buy milk at 3 PM tomorrow"
Here's your reminder for tomorrow at 15:00:
Reminder
Wednesday, 18 September 2013
Buy milk
15:00
OK, I'll remind you.
"Send a text to my wife"
OK, I'll send your message.
"What time will you be home from work?"
Here's your message to Joanne:
Message
To: Joanne
What time will you be home from work?
"What is the population of New York"
tap to edit
OK, I found this on the web:
Web Search
What is the population of New York

Hey, Siri
Now if your iPad is plugged into power, you can activate Siri hands-free simply by saying 'Hey, Siri'. Shazam integration means it's a quick and easy way to find out what's playing

Classic commands
Like the Siri of old, classic commands and requests such as local information still work, and things seem to be a little snappier since iOS 7, so you will not be going hungry

Tap and edit
If Siri doesn't quite catch your request, you can always tap to edit and use the iPad's software keyboard to tweak the interpretation and get the right answers

A new wave
Siri is no exception to iOS 8's redesign and now features a far cleaner interface with a sound wave that reacts to your voice when you speak your commands

Teaching Siri
To make Siri even more practical use phrases like, 'John Smith is my Dad' to teach relationships between people in your Contacts app and yourself. That way, you can say commands such as, 'FaceTime my Dad' to speed things up.

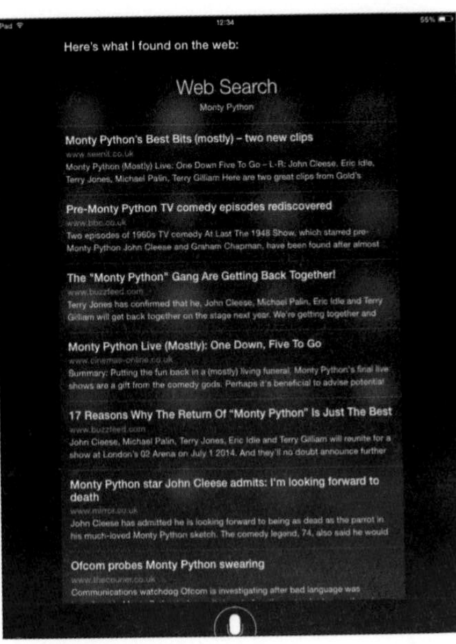

Here's what I found on the web:
Web Search
Monty Python
Monty Python's Best Bits (mostly) – two new clips
Pre-Monty Python TV comedy episodes rediscovered
The "Monty Python" Gang Are Getting Back Together!
Monty Python Live (Mostly): One Down, Five To Go
17 Reasons Why The Return Of "Monty Python" Is Just The Best
Monty Python star John Cleese admits: I'm looking forward to death
Ofcom probes Monty Python swearing

04 Stay away, Safari!

Instead of taking you straight to Safari for web results, Siri displays searches via Bing within its own interface, meaning you can carry on asking questions or tap any result.

"Launch photos"

05 Launch an app

Siri's powers have even extended to launching apps and, while it might not be quicker than tapping an icon, if you're already asking questions another one can't hurt.

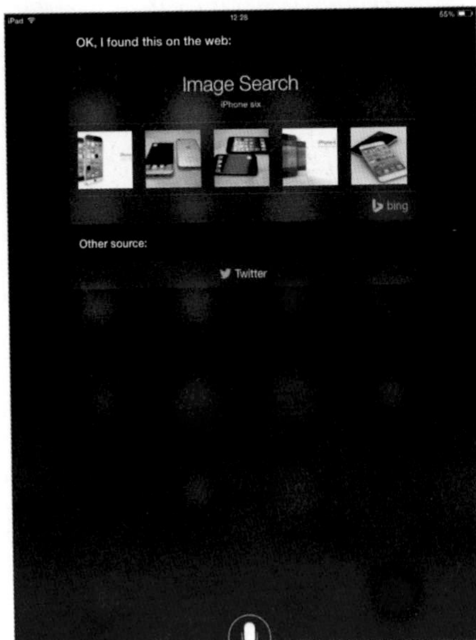

OK, I found this on the web:
Image Search
bing
Other source:
Twitter

06 Find a photo

Asking Siri, 'Show me images of [a place/person/animal/etc]' will take you straight to Bing's image results, again, without throwing you into the Safari app, which is handy.

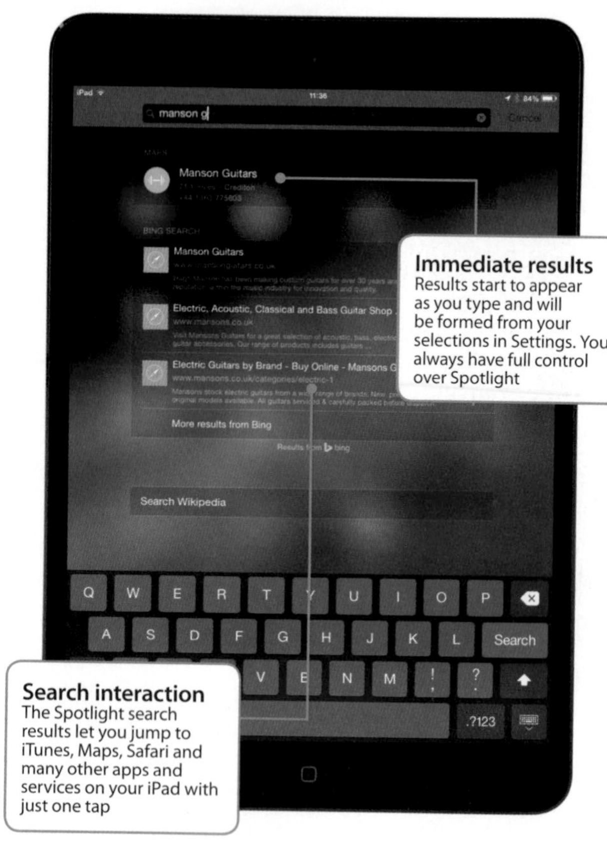

Immediate results
Results start to appear as you type and will be formed from your selections in Settings. You always have full control over Spotlight
Search interaction
The Spotlight search results let you jump to iTunes, Maps, Safari and many other apps and services on your iPad with just one tap

Search and find apps with Spotlight

Spotlight is the perfect addition to the iPad home screens and it can help you find anything you need in a matter of seconds

To put it simply, Spotlight is your handy search tool that is available on your iPad. It has been out there for a while, but the most obvious recent change in Spotlight is the ability to swipe downwards in any home screen to bring up the search facility. Simple swipe down and start typing to immediately see relevant results appear. You get to control what is displayed, and in what order on the list, and you can then jump to see more detail or access the app that the result is in if it is stored locally on your iPad. For instance, if you want to search for a particular artist without scrolling for a while through your list of music, you can tap in their name and it will appear on the screen.

The sheer speed of Spotlight makes it a highly useful addition to any iPad and, potentially, you will find yourself opening apps through Spotlight if you have many installed. It is a feature you will use multiple times a day once you start using it and an iPad without it just isn't the same.

The time has come to get to grips with the power of Spotlight; just follow our guide to get started.

"The sheer speed of Spotlight makes it a highly useful addition to the iOS home screen"

Spotlight Find what you need with Spotlight

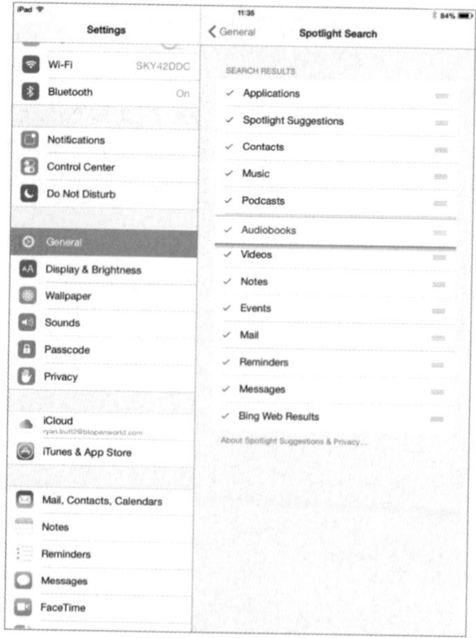

01 Spotlight settings

Go to Settings>General>Spotlight Search and tick the options you want to see in your search results. You can also hold and move each option to change the order for what you want to see appear first.

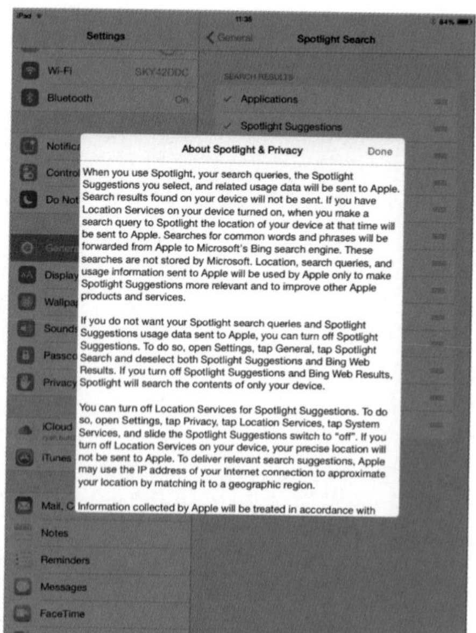

02 Understand the process

Tap 'About Spotlight & Privacy' to read the legal text. There is some useful information held within this screen which may be worth reading so that you understand all of your search options.

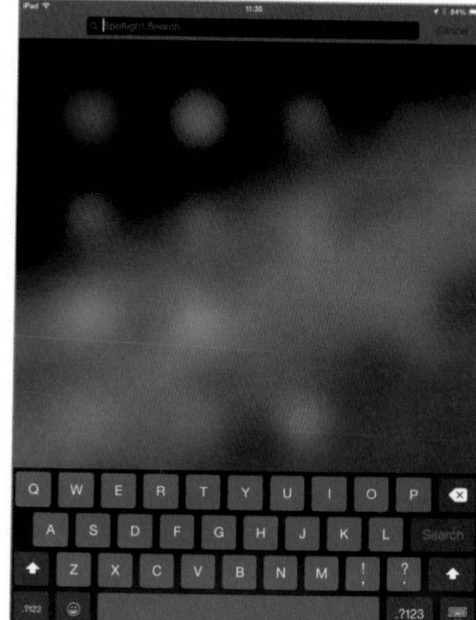

03 Your first search

When on any home screen, swipe downwards within the main part of the screen and a search bar will appear at the top of the screen. The keyboard will pop up ready for you to type a search phrase.

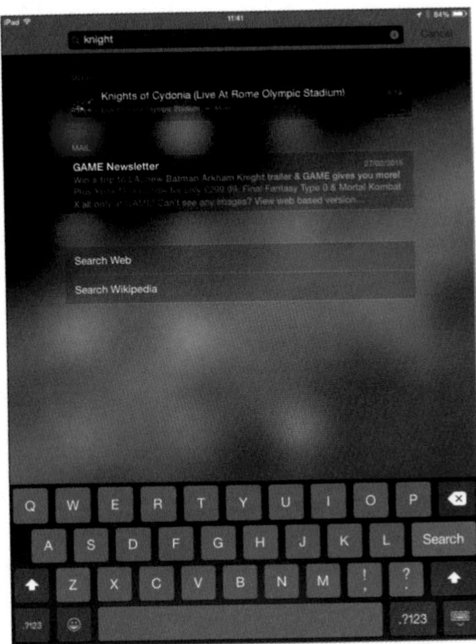

04 As you type…

Results appear as you type, in the order chosen in the first step. If subjects are missing, it's because there are no results. For example, songs which don't match your phrase may not be installed.

05 Interactive results

All of the results take you to another place rather than just provide information. For example, tapping a song will open the Music app and start playing the song with the full album art on display.

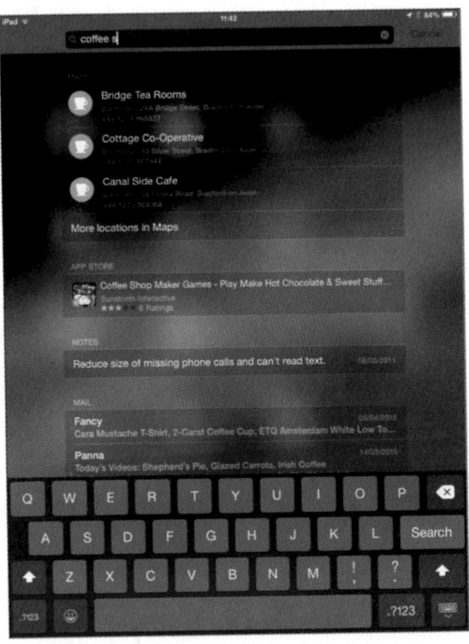

06 Find a location

If you search for an establishment or a location, the results detail the distance from you and have contact numbers if available. Tap a result and Maps will open to let you navigate to the establishment.

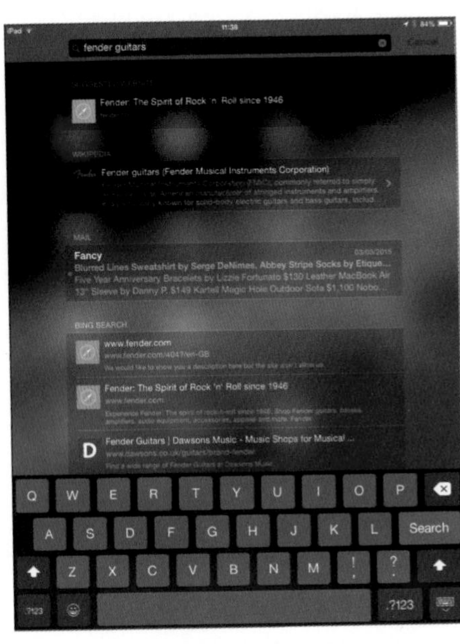

07 Web searches

Standard web searches will appear using Bing as the search provider, with no option to customise. Wikipedia is also used to offer immediate and detailed information about the term searched for.

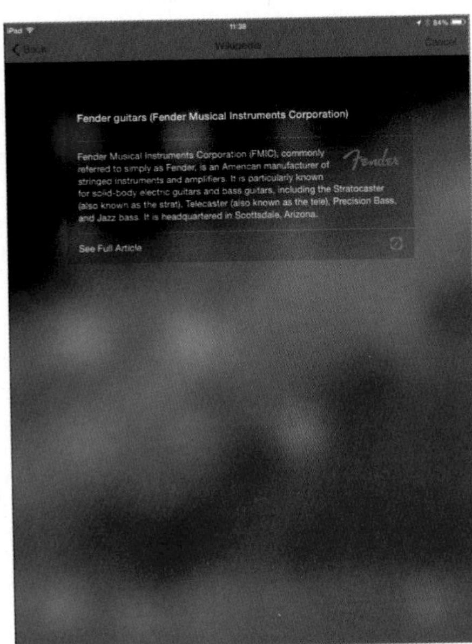

08 See summarised detail

For some results you will see a summary offering the main detail in a concise form. This may be enough for you to get what you need, but a link will be included to the full article as well.

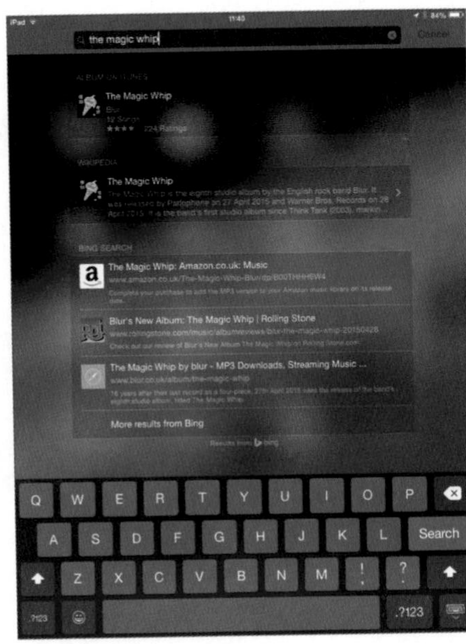

09 Find iTunes media

Films, TV shows and music will be shown in the results as well, which means you can tap once to go to iTunes and make a purchase. Spotlight works in tandem with the main Apple apps and services.

Explore the App Store

The iPad's App Store underwent an exciting revamp as part of iOS 8

As part of the huge iOS 8 update, all Apple mobile stores received a substantial make-over. The new App Store has been tweaked and enhanced in order to produce a more efficient user experience, and it has certainly succeeded. The App Store on your iPad is now easier than ever to navigate and purchase items from.

Of the new features, perhaps the most significant is being able to download new apps inside the App Store, rather than being taken to one of your home pages. There's also a new intuitive Genius bar to give you clever recommendations based on what you have downloaded previously.

Other new features include being able to view each app's update history, as well as individual developer pages. Facebook integration is also present, while the ability to view app screenshots in full screen mode is a big positive.

Contrary to some rumours, this is definitely not an upgrade to worry about, but one to embrace. All your favourite options remain, but most have received a little sprinkle of Apple's magic dust to give you a better user experience. Let's have a closer look at four of the most important changes.

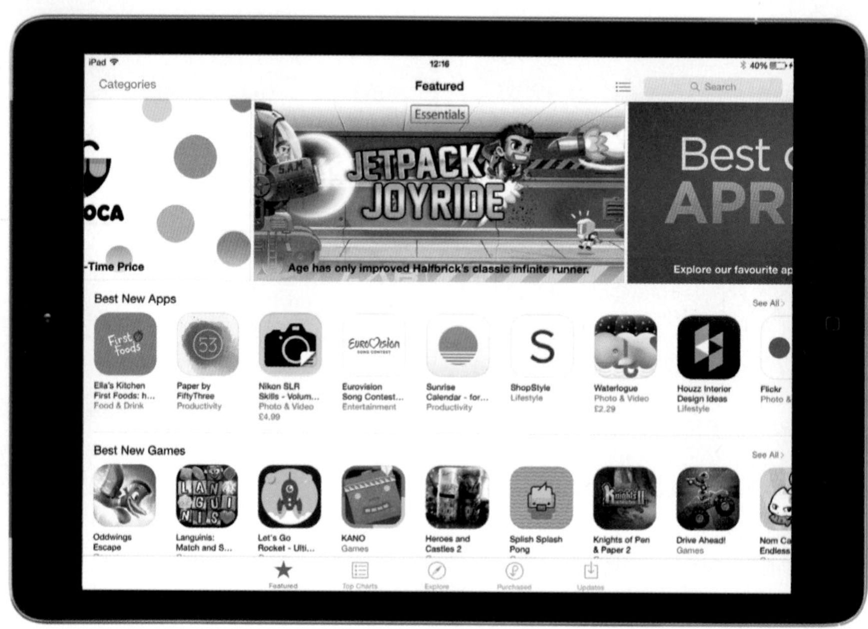

"It has been tweaked and enhanced in order to produce a more efficient user experience"

App Store So what's new?

01 Stay put

The biggest change to the App Store is based on purchasing new apps. Instead of being whisked away to your home screen from the app when you hit the buy button, you can now watch the installation process inside the App Store itself. It's a welcome addition!

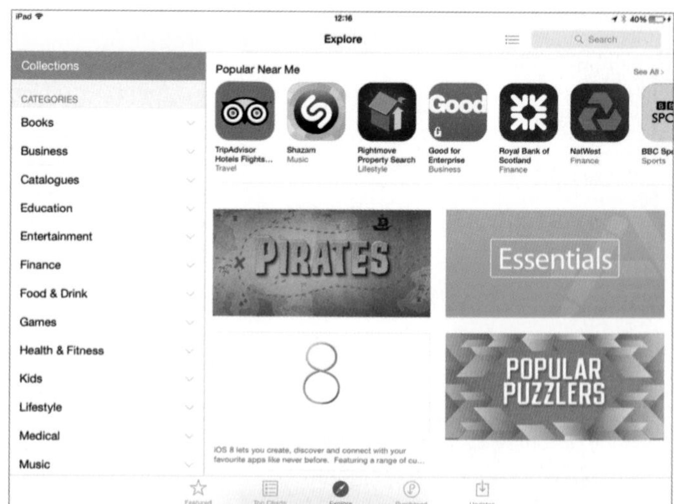

02 Popular near you

A new feature of the App Store is Near Me. Tap on this at the bottom of the interface and you can opt to display apps that are popular near your current location. Particularly useful in a zombie apocalypse when you are after hints on useful apps to help you survive!

Top Charts

Downloading your first apps

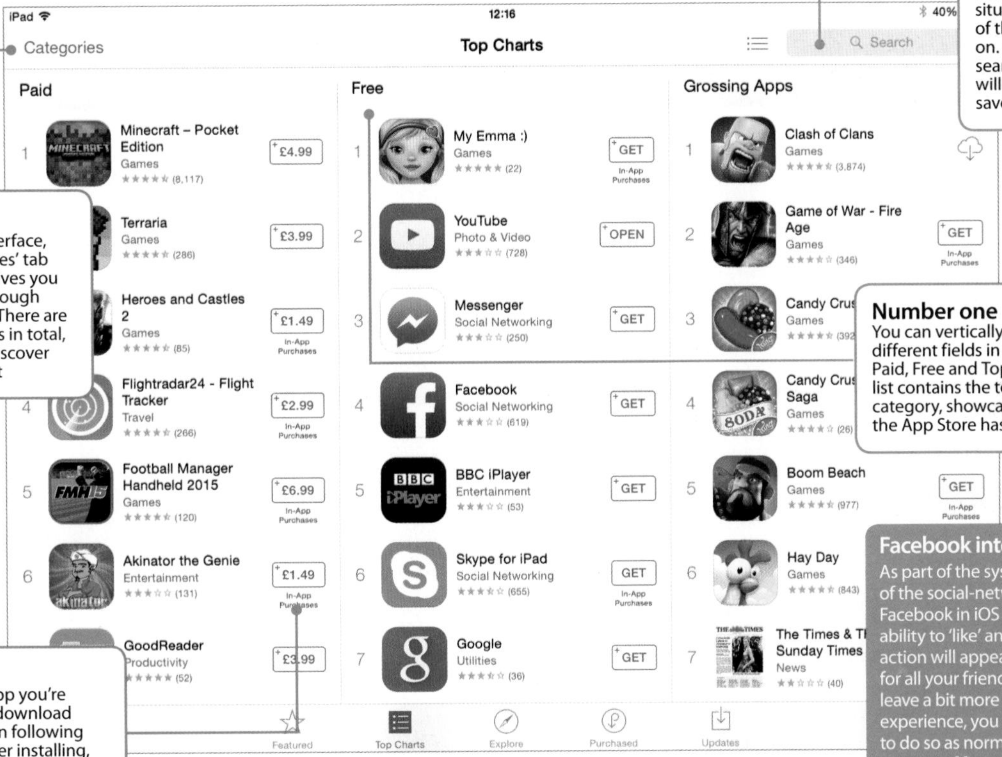

iPad 12:16 40%

Categories | Top Charts | Search

Paid		Free		Grossing Apps	
1 Minecraft – Pocket Edition, Games (8,117)	£4.99	1 My Emma :), Games (22)	GET In-App Purchases	1 Clash of Clans, Games (3,874)	
2 Terraria, Games (286)	£3.99	2 YouTube, Photo & Video (728)	OPEN	2 Game of War - Fire Age, Games (346)	GET In-App Purchases
3 Heroes and Castles 2, Games (85)	£1.49 In-App Purchases	3 Messenger, Social Networking (250)	GET	3 Candy Crus… Games	
4 Flightradar24 - Flight Tracker, Travel (266)	£2.99 In-App Purchases	4 Facebook, Social Networking (619)	GET	4 Candy Crus… Saga, Games (26)	
5 Football Manager Handheld 2015, Games (120)	£6.99 In-App Purchases	5 BBC iPlayer, Entertainment (53)	GET	5 Boom Beach, Games (977)	GET In-App Purchases
6 Akinator the Genie, Entertainment (131)	£1.49 In-App Purchases	6 Skype for iPad, Social Networking (655)	GET In-App Purchases	6 Hay Day, Games (843)	
GoodReader, Productivity (52)	£3.99	7 Google, Utilities (36)	GET	7 The Times & T… Sunday Times, News (40)	

Featured | Top Charts | Explore | Purchased | Updates

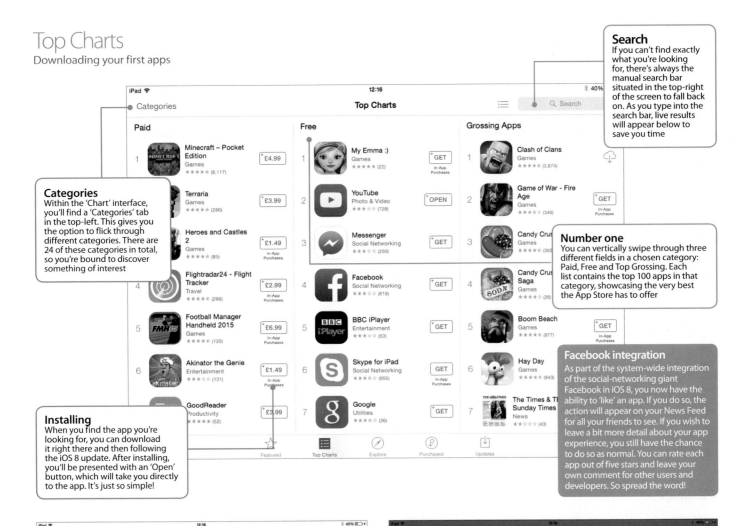

Search
If you can't find exactly what you're looking for, there's always the manual search bar situated in the top-right of the screen to fall back on. As you type into the search bar, live results will appear below to save you time

Categories
Within the 'Chart' interface, you'll find a 'Categories' tab in the top-left. This gives you the option to flick through different categories. There are 24 of these categories in total, so you're bound to discover something of interest

Number one
You can vertically swipe through three different fields in a chosen category: Paid, Free and Top Grossing. Each list contains the top 100 apps in that category, showcasing the very best the App Store has to offer

Installing
When you find the app you're looking for, you can download it right there and then following the iOS 8 update. After installing, you'll be presented with an 'Open' button, which will take you directly to the app. It's just so simple!

Facebook integration
As part of the system-wide integration of the social-networking giant Facebook in iOS 8, you now have the ability to 'like' an app. If you do so, the action will appear on your News Feed for all your friends to see. If you wish to leave a bit more detail about your app experience, you still have the chance to do so as normal. You can rate each app out of five stars and leave your own comment for other users and developers. So spread the word!

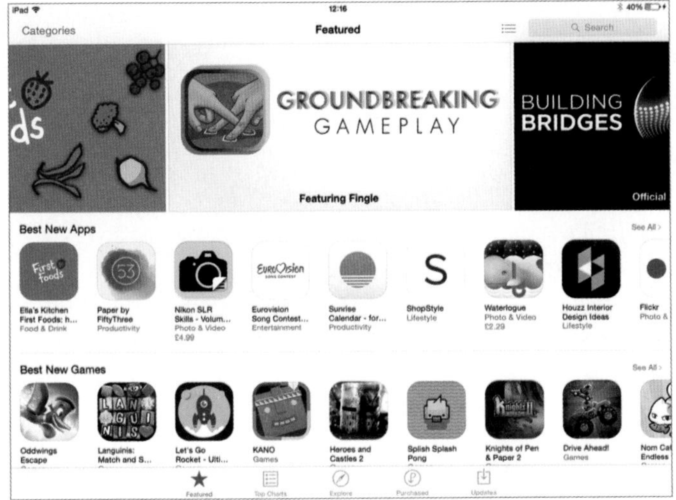

03 Revamped UI

The new-style App Store has been built from the ground up. It's a comprehensive re-design that ultimately makes it easier than ever before to navigate. Menus can be intelligently swiped through, and it all looks perfect on the large real estate your iPad provides.

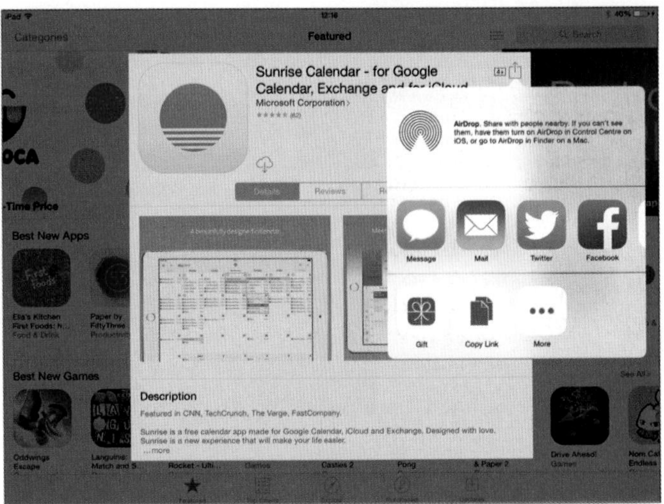

04 Sharing options

If you come across an app you're fond of, or one that you think everyone needs to know about, however well known, iOS 8 has added a selection of sharing options for you to utilise. Simply hit the share icon to view your options for various channels by which to spread the word.

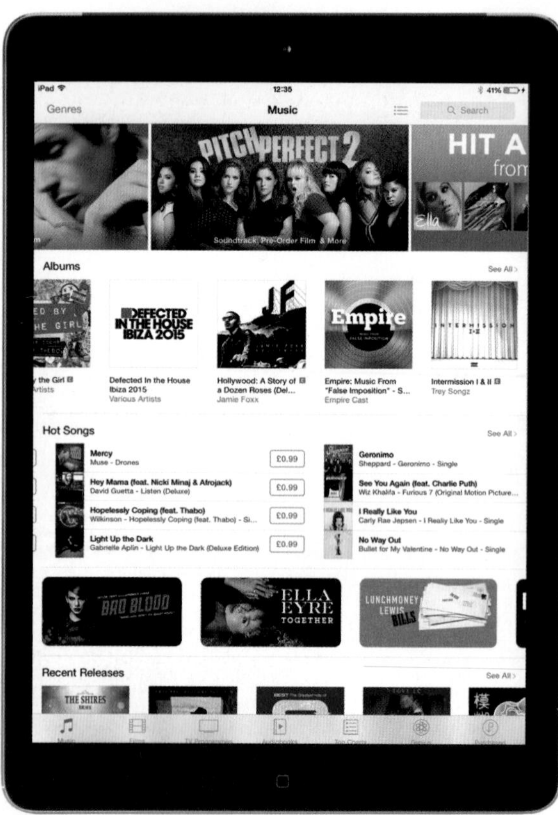

Use iTunes to download media

We show you how to use Apple's virtual superstore to purchase music, films and other assorted media

The birth of iTunes signalled a significant change in the way we shop for music and media. Everything can now be bought whenever and wherever we are – and it's all thanks to iTunes.

The iTunes app for your iPad is a friendly and welcoming portal to a thriving online marketplace, where you can shop at your leisure and not be suckered into slinging cheap tat that is on display next to the tills into your basket. You can go in, get what you want and, within minutes, be listening to it through your iPad's Music app or watching it through the Videos app. All from the comfort of your own home, or even while out on the go.

Using iTunes really couldn't be easier. Everything is well laid out and easily accessible, while all of your past and present purchases are within arm's reach at all times. The hardest part, if there even is a hard part, is ensuring that all of your billing information remains up-to-date so you can continue making purchases at will. When you know your details are all present and correct, all of the sonics and flicks you could ever want will be available at your fingertips. Here we guide you through this essential app.

"iTunes is a friendly and welcoming portal to a thriving online marketplace"

iTunes How to browse and buy media

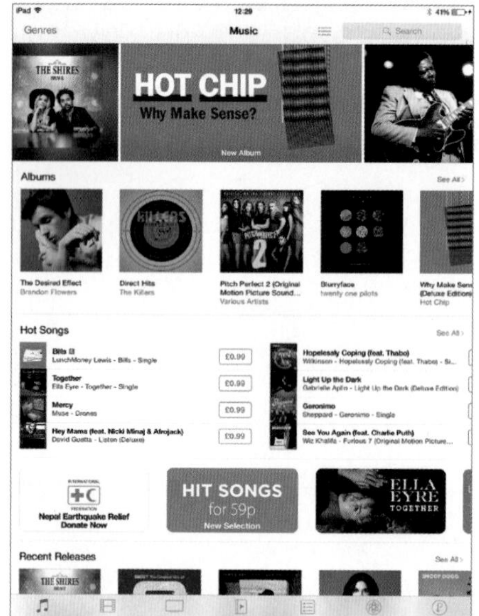

01 Launch iTunes

When you launch the iTunes app you will be taken straight to the main storefront, which is the Music Store by default. All of the categories in the store are laid out across the bottom of the screen.

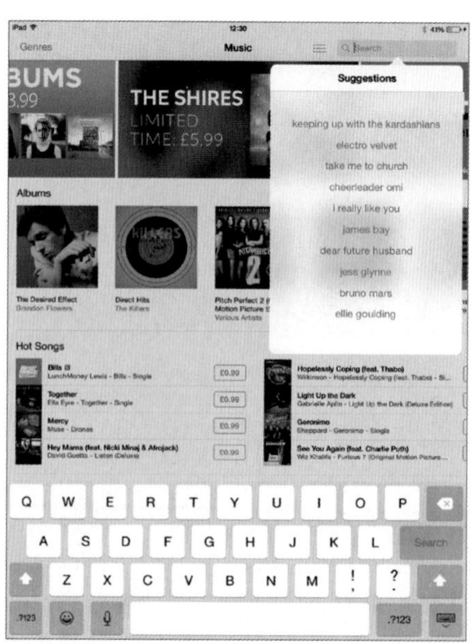

02 Browse the store

The newest, most exciting media will always be displayed on the main page. If you don't find what you want there then you can search for artists and albums by using the 'Search' window.

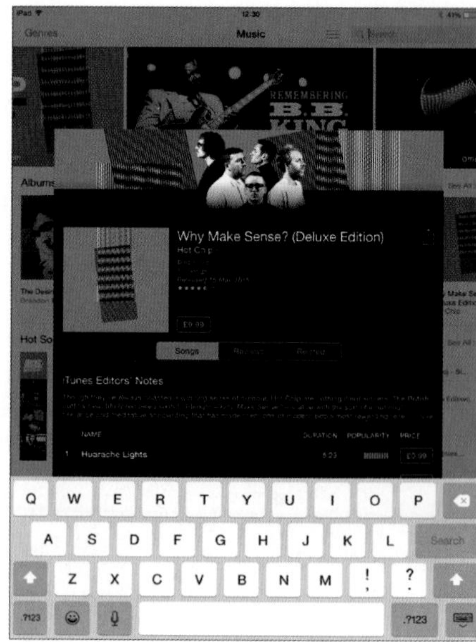

03 Purchase music

When you find what you want, tap on it to bring up a window. Then tap the price at the top to buy the entire album, or tap on the price next to the separate tracks to download them individually.

Exploring the iTunes app

Navigating the user-friendly interface

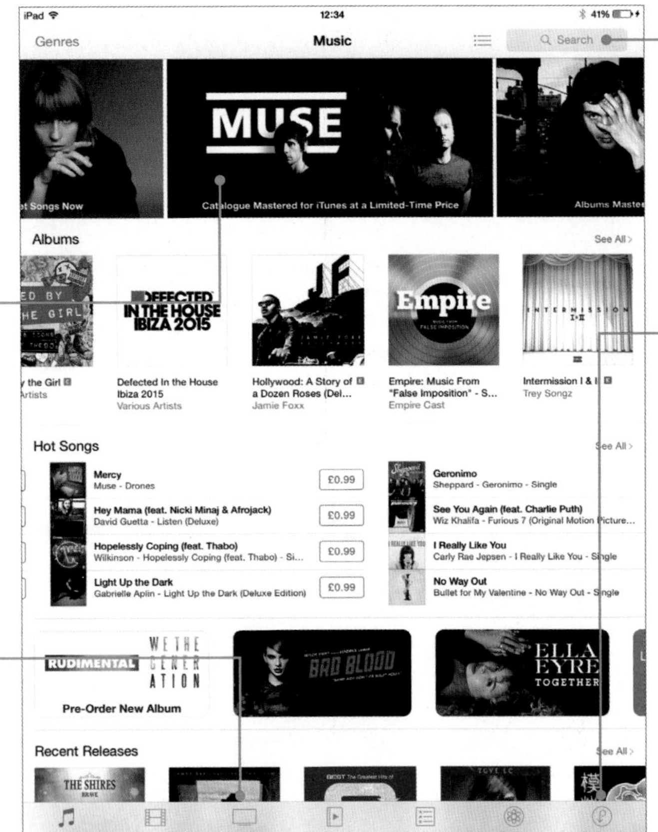

Search for content
You can use the Genre tabs at the top of the screen to narrow down your search, or you can enter specific keywords into the Search engine to instantly find what you are looking for

Featured content
All of the most recent, hottest releases will be displayed in the top area of the screen that appears when you first tap on each store section

Previous
When you purchase a song, film or other media from iTunes, a Downloads tab will appear in the bottom-right. You can see their download progress by tapping on the icon here

Store categories
All of the different store categories, such as Music, Films, TV Shows, etc, are displayed as icons along the bottom of the screen. Tap on one to access it

Get past purchases
With iCloud integration, it isn't just your current purchases that are pushed to your other iOS devices. A section in the iTunes app, called 'Purchased' will allow you to view all media downloaded through your Apple ID instantly download it again onto your current device.

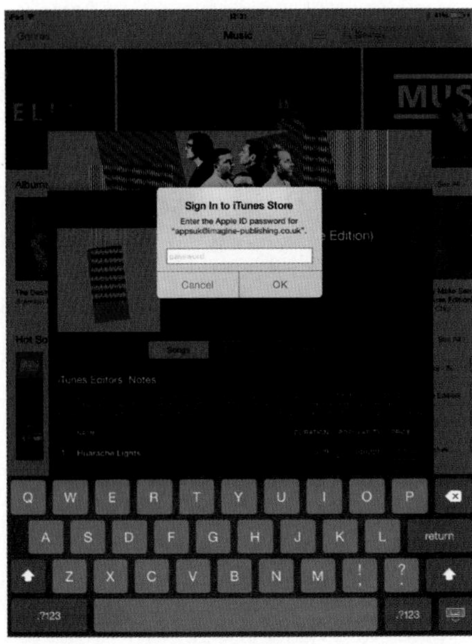

04 Authorise download

After opting to download an item, you will be required to sign in using your Apple ID to authorise the purchase. You may also be required to enter billing information.

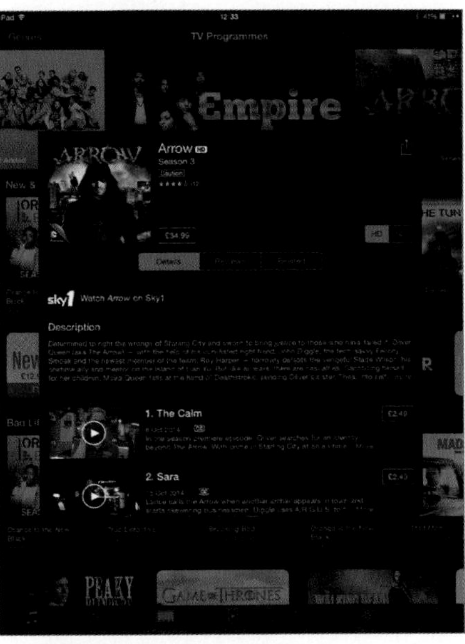

05 Buy more media

You can also purchase films, TV shows and audiobooks through iTunes. The main difference being that with movies you can choose to rent as well as buy your favourite titles.

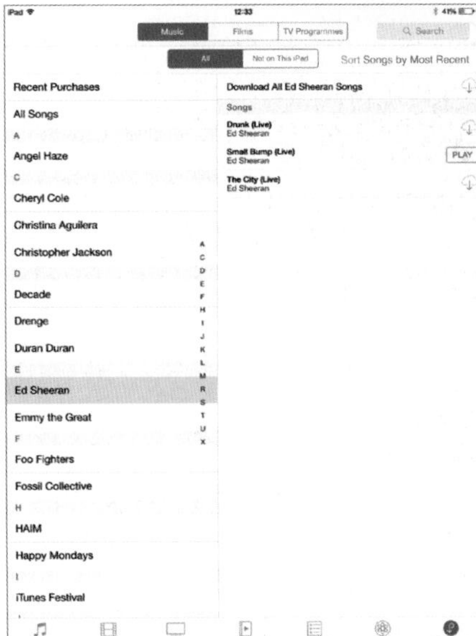

06 iTunes in the Cloud

The iTunes app is compatible with your personal iCloud account, so anything you purchase from the store can be automatically pushed to all of your other iOS devices free of charge.

The next step

Have fun, become more productive and get more from your iPad

"With iCloud pushing downloads onto all of your iDevices, your iPad becomes a hub for videos, music, games and more"

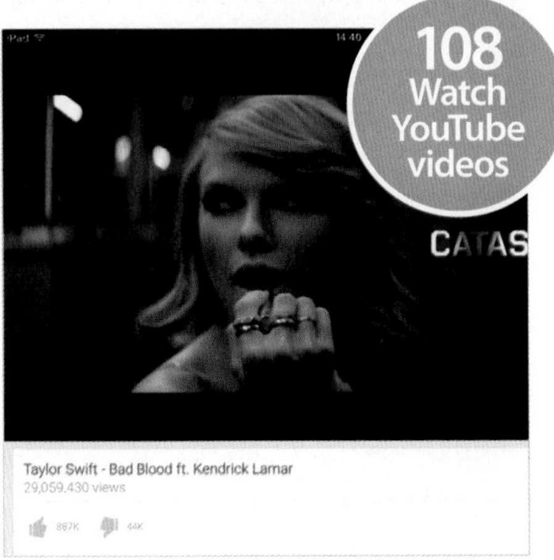
108
Watch YouTube videos
Taylor Swift - Bad Blood ft. Kendrick Lamar

Take photos and videos on your iPad

When you need to capture a moment, your iPad is capable of everything you might need it for

The iPad camera is not an obvious feature mainly because of the size of the tablet itself, but if you happen to have it with you and want to grab a quick snap, you might as well know how it all works. Despite specifications that are meagre in comparison to standalone cameras and some smartphones, your iPad is still capable of capturing decent quality photos and videos if you take the time to make it work properly.

There are certain options for perfecting stills and videos that you might be execting, but some other features are more out-of-the-box. For example, there is the choice to capture perfectly proportioned photos using the Square option. The resultant images could be used for scanned documents or anything else, and this simple addition of a unusual shape adds some charm to the experience. HDR will also help you deal with unusual lighting and, just like everything else in the interface, it is just one tap away at all times.

Indeed, it is surprising how functional and fully-featured iPad cameras are, and since iOS 8 everything has been upgraded just a little to make the final results even better than before.

"It is surprising how functional and fully-featured iPad cameras are"

Camera iPad photos and videos

01 A new style

Tap the Camera icon and you will see a different look in the main interface. Swipe along the right-hand bar to select the available options.

02 Focusing

Tap the screen on the particular spot where you would like it to focus and the lens will do the hard work for you. This spot will be highlighted by a yellow square on the screen.

03 Capture videos

Slide the right-hand bar down to go into the video mode. When it's recording, the capture button will be transformed into a red square within a circle and a timer is displayed.

A simple photo-taking interface

Use the right-hand bar

Time-lapse photos
The new time-lapse feature creates a brilliant effect by taking photos every few seconds. Keep your camera still, point it at a moving scene and watch it go

See your snaps
Tap this small icon to quickly jump to your camera roll to see all of your photos. This is great for quickly checking your last shot

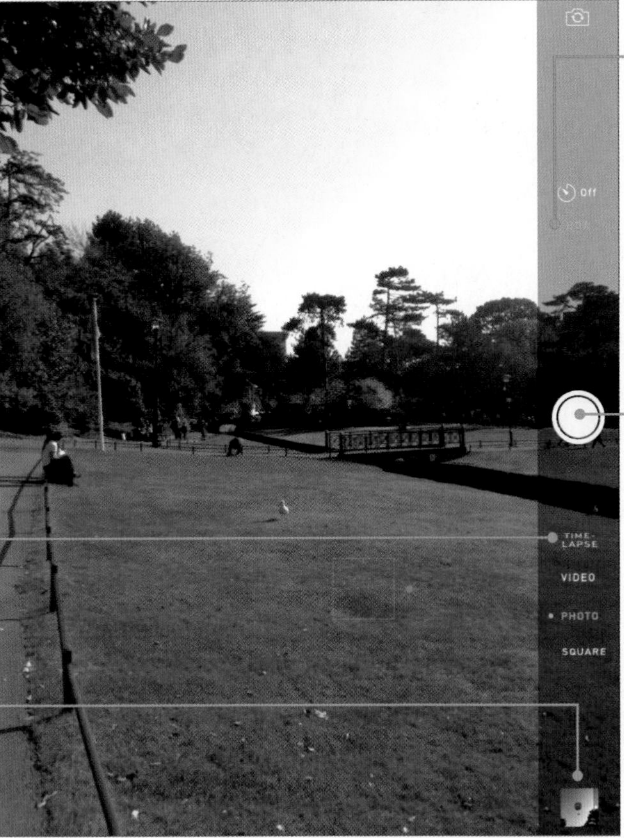

HDR
Turning the HDR option on is particularly helpful when you are taking landscape shots with varied light sources. It can greatly improve any photo

The capture button
The capture button is logically placed for ease of use and will turn red when you are recording video. Hold it to take burst shots

Timer delay
Pressing the timer icon allows you to set a countdown of either three or five seconds between when you press the capture button and when the photo is taken. It's a cool feature that lets you organise shots from behind the camera before jumping in yourself.

04 Turn it around

Tapping the top right-hand icon will swap to the front-facing camera on the screen face of the iPad, which is useful if you want to snap a picture of yourself to see how you look.

05 Take a timed shot

If you want to give yourself a few seconds to line up the perfect shot, tap the Timer icon in the top-right corner. Choose to enact either a three or ten-second delay after pressing the capture button.

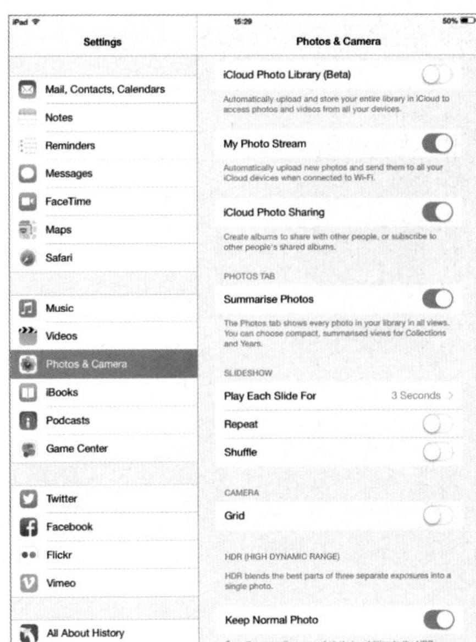

06 Tweak the settings

Go to Settings>Photos & Camera and you will be able to fiddle with the camera settings. You could add a grid to the camera view and save a standard shot when snapping HDR photos.

Edit images in Photos

Make the most of your iPad's camera and take advantage of the built-in photo-editing feature

Since the release of iOS 5 back in 2011, you have been able to edit your images directly from the Photos app. Admittedly, the editing software isn't going to turn your photos into works of art with just a couple of taps, but it does help to enhance both photos taken with the camera and photos already on the device. Fortunately, iOS 8 has improved on this significantly.

The editing features available include the ability to rotate images from portrait to landscape. There's also an enhance option, which can adjust the colour depth, brightness and contrast, transforming a relatively dull photo into something that is altogether more pleasant to look at. The last few options should prove to be useful as well; the first of these allows you to add stylish filters to your images, the second removes the notorious red-eye that you get in photos overloaded with flash, and the third enables you to crop images.

For this tutorial, you need to have upgraded your iPad to at least iOS 5, but preferably to iOS 8 as not all of the features highlighted are available with earlier operating systems. Head to the Settings app and tap General>Software Update to keep up-to-date.

"It isn't going to turn your photos into works of art, but it does enhance them"

Photos Edit your photographs on your iPad

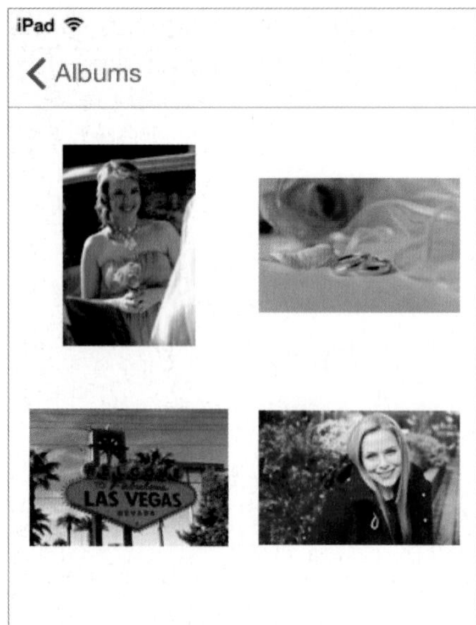

01 Select your photo

Launch the Photos app from the home screen and you will automatically see all your pictures and videos. Pick one you want to make amendments to, and then tap Edit.

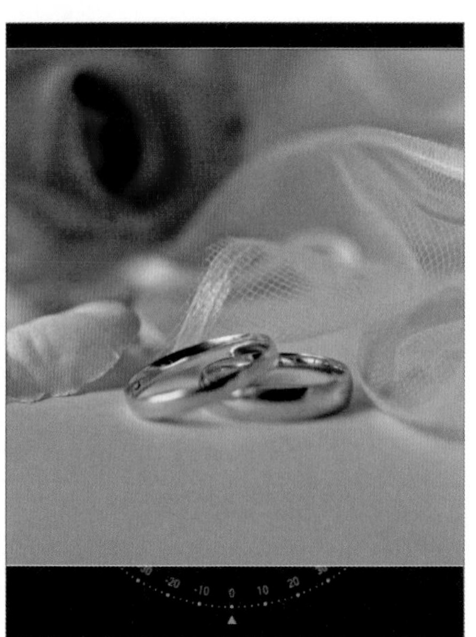

02 Rotate the photo

From the Edit screen, use the Crop tool (second from the left or the top), and then the Rotate icon on the left-hand side. Drag the wheel left or right to rotate the image. Tap Save when you're done.

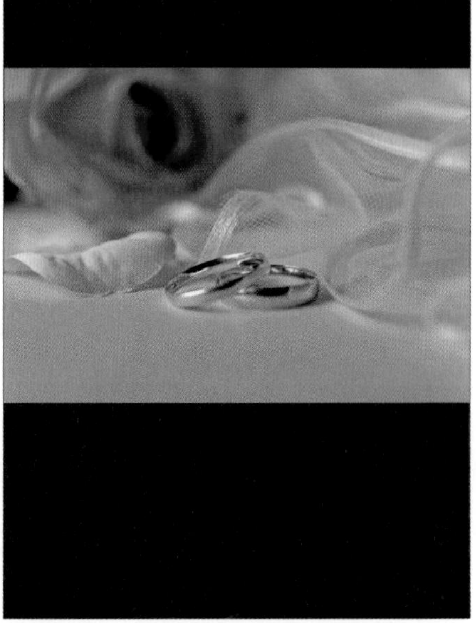

03 Enhance the image

If you choose the wand icon, the software will adjust the colours of the image. Tap the same option again to cancel the changes or tap Save to finish instead.

Editing interface

Editing your photos is as intuitive as the iPad itself

Multi-touch controls
Before you choose how you want to edit a photo, you can use the multi-touch pinch controls to zoom in to focus on the areas you want to improve

Crop photos
The Crop tool is another underestimated feature of Photos. You can chop out parts of the photo (such as a blurred section or distraction) that you don't want anymore or focus on a particular part of the shot

Undo any changes
Thanks to the intuitiveness of the iPad, you can easily revert back to the original image by pressing cancel, and then quickly resave it

Enhance
On the surface this seems like a basic option compared to most dedicated editing packages, but in practice it's a great feature that can transform your photo within moments

Sharing photos
Once you have made changes to your photo, you can use the share option to assign the photo to a message, use it as your wallpaper, email, tweet or even print it. iOS 8 even lets you share images using other apps, such as Pinterest and Evernote, directly from Photos as long as you have the option enabled in Settings.

04 Remove red-eye

Select an image where people have red eyes, then tap on the Red-Eye option (the icon with the eye). Next, simply tap on each person's eyes to remove the red. Click Save to finish.

05 Crop the photo

Select an image to edit and tap the crop option. Drag your finger to resize the photo and swipe the dial below to adjust the orientation. Tap the icon to the right to constrain your selection.

06 Use filters

You can now also add filters to your image with ease. These range from black and white filters to a trendy retro selection. Tap the filters icon and make your selection.

Organise your photos

Organise and keep all of your most important photos in order on an iPad with ease

Treasured photos will always have a special place in our hearts, but it is very easy to take and collect so many that you often miss the truly special moments. On an iPad with the Photos app you have the ability to organise your collection logically to ensure that the ones you view most often are always available.

Some of the organisation can be done in iTunes on a Mac or PC connected to your iPad, but for quick tweaks and for making changes on the move you have everything you need on the iPad to keep all of your photos in logical order. What's more, iOS 8 introduced some new organisation features, for example individual photos can now be favourited and you can hide photos and videos from Moments.

The iPad is the perfect tool for viewing photos thanks to the superb screen and portable form. With its larger screen and capability to show more detail than other devices that it is possible that you will prefer to view your photos on it more than any other device. Here we will offer some tips on the best ways to keep order and the steps you need to take, but there is nothing here that is difficult to understand or hard to remember.

"The iPad is the perfect tool for viewing photos"

Photos Manage your photo collection

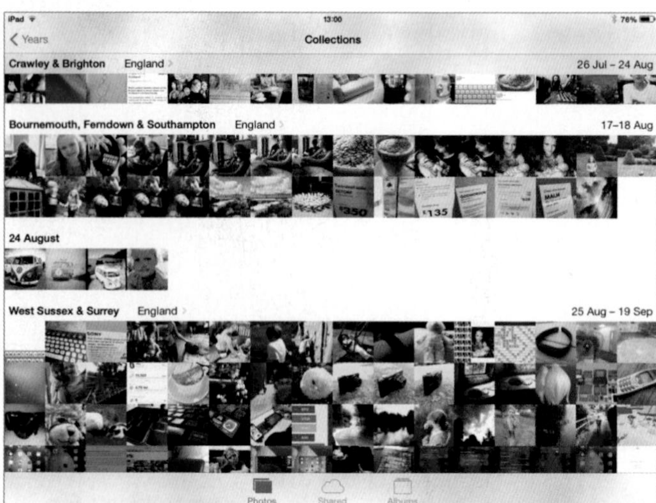

01 Photo collections

In iOS 8 all of your iPad photos are available to view by date using the Photos icon at the bottom. They will be broken up by the date, time and location in which they were taken, which is a completely automatic process. Tap the Albums icon to continue.

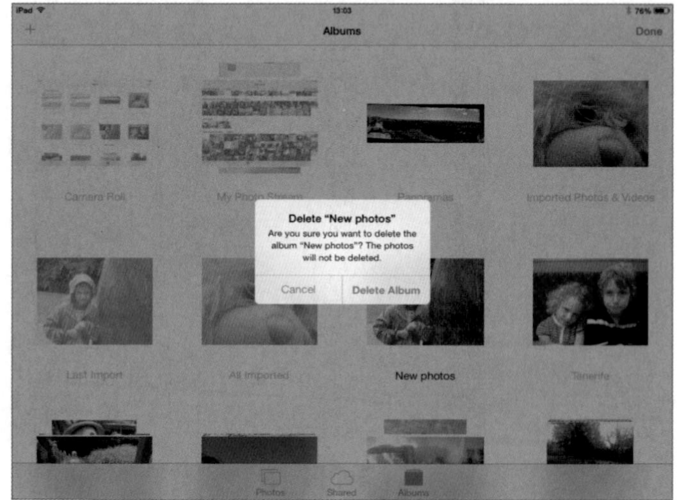

02 Static albums

Most of your albums will be static and tapping the Edit button will not enable changes, but some may show a small 'x' next to them. Tap this to delete an album. But don't worry when you do this as the photos within it will not be deleted and will remain available on the iPad.

Multiple organisation options

Take control of your photo collection

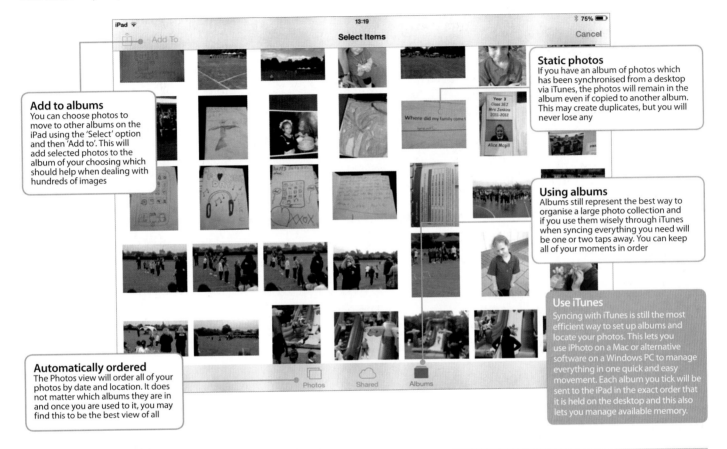

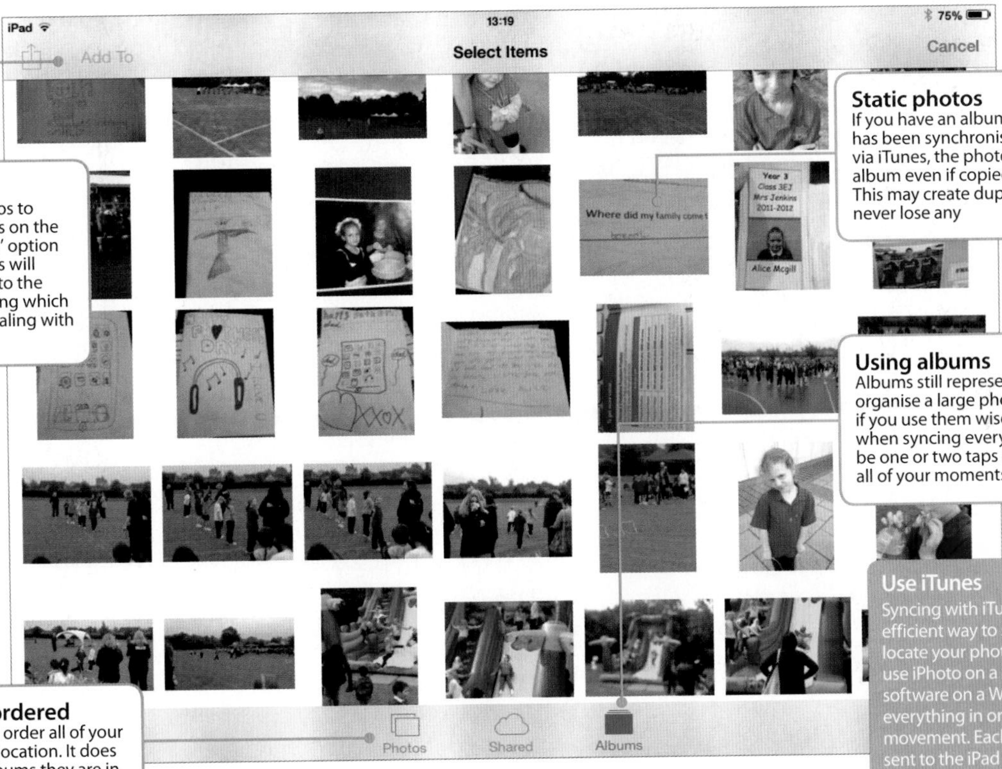

Add to albums
You can choose photos to move to other albums on the iPad using the 'Select' option and then 'Add to'. This will add selected photos to the album of your choosing which should help when dealing with hundreds of images

Static photos
If you have an album of photos which has been synchronised from a desktop via iTunes, the photos will remain in the album even if copied to another album. This may create duplicates, but you will never lose any

Using albums
Albums still represent the best way to organise a large photo collection and if you use them wisely through iTunes when syncing everything you need will be one or two taps away. You can keep all of your moments in order

Automatically ordered
The Photos view will order all of your photos by date and location. It does not matter which albums they are in and once you are used to it, you may find this to be the best view of all

Use iTunes
Syncing with iTunes is still the most efficient way to set up albums and locate your photos. This lets you use iPhoto on a Mac or alternative software on a Windows PC to manage everything in one quick and easy movement. Each album you tick will be sent to the iPad in the exact order that it is held on the desktop and this also lets you manage available memory.

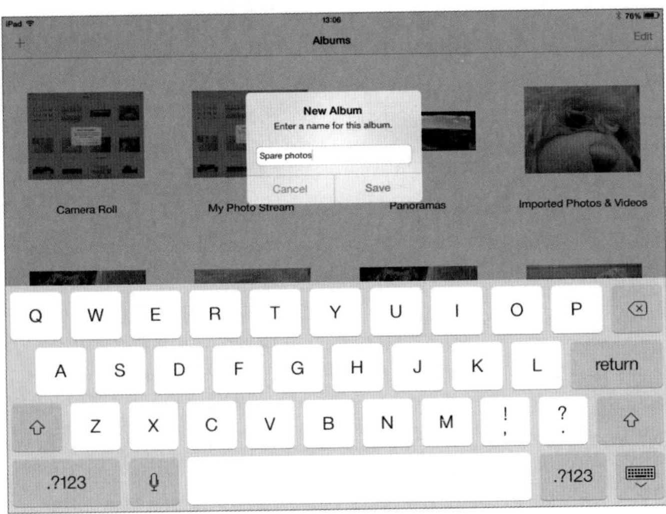

03 Create new albums
When in the Album view, tap the '+' icon top-left to create a new album. You will be asked to give it a name before giving the option to specify which photos you want to be included in the album. The photos you add will still stay in their original albums as well.

04 Copy between albums
Tap the Select option and choose a few photos. Now tap the Add To option in the top-left to move the selected photos to a different album. As in the previous step, the original photos will remain in the album you have copied them from as well as appearing in the new location.

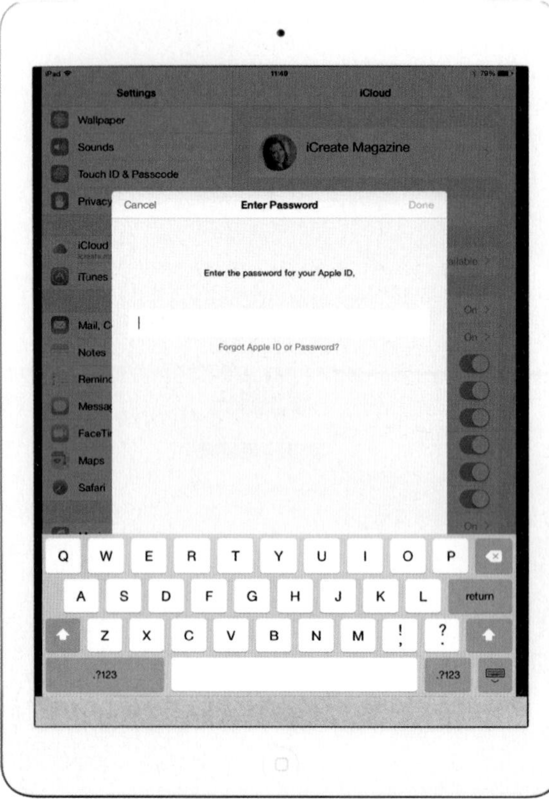

Use Photo Stream to sync your photos

Take advantage of Apple's iCloud service to get your photos automatically pushed to all of your devices

One of the handiest features of iOS is Photo Stream. Using your own personal iCloud, with Photo Stream activated, you can get photos transported automatically – and totally wirelessly – to all of your Apple devices on the same Wi-Fi network. So if you take a picture on your iPhone, within seconds it will appear on your iPad. If you take some snaps on your iPad then they will be beamed to your iPhone and your Mac without you having to lift a finger.

The whole process eradicates the need to email individual images or copy them onto portable storage devices to transport to other devices. It's a convenient process that runs in the background.

In order to set up Photo Stream, you must first set up your iCloud account. This is a free service that replaced Apple's MobileMe service, and it provides a host of great features such as the option to sync documents and files, music, bookmarks, contact details and calendar events across all of your devices, as well as backing up your important data. Setting up iCloud is easy: you go to Settings, tap on the iCloud section and then log in with your standard Apple ID (the same email address and password that you use for your other Apple services, such as the App Store and iTunes). In this tutorial we guide you through the process.

Photos How to activate your Photo Stream

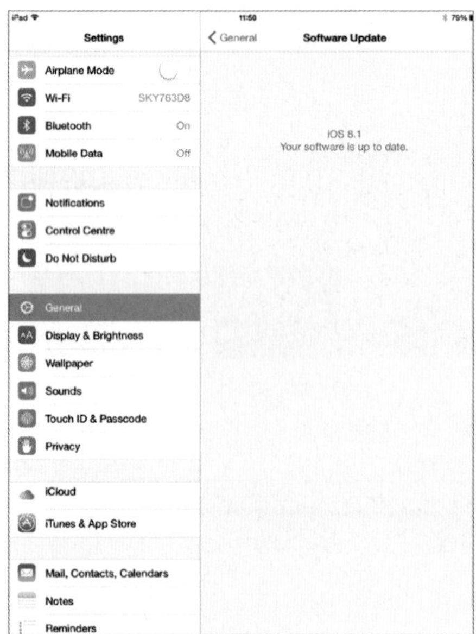

01 Update

Photo Stream comes as part of iOS 5 and above, so connect your device to your computer through iTunes and ensure that you have the latest free software update installed on your device.

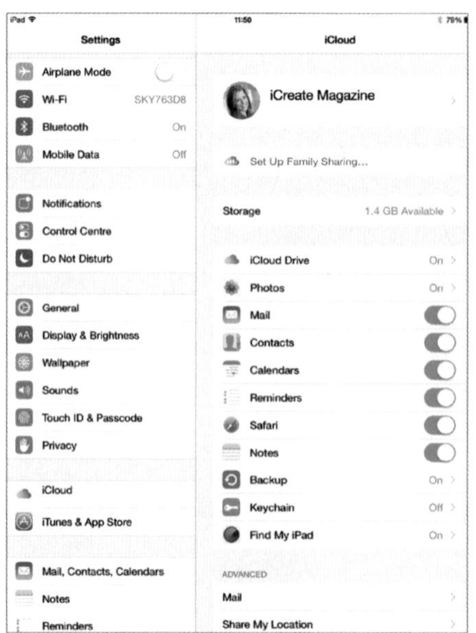

02 Activate your iCloud

Go to Settings>iCloud and activate your free iCloud account by logging in with your Apple ID (the same email address and password that you use to log in to the other Apple services).

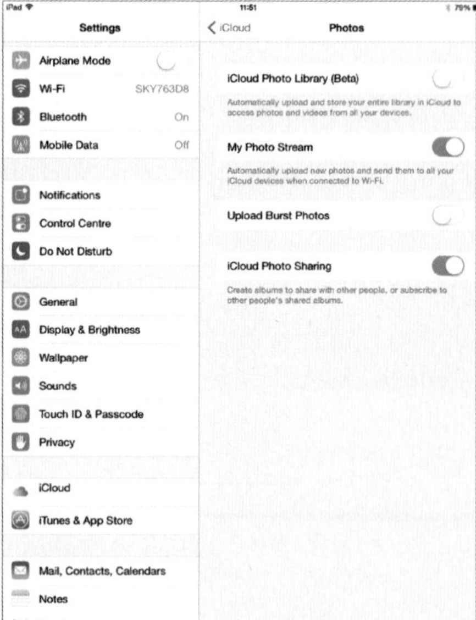

03 Turn on Photo Stream

You have full freedom over which services you use by toggling on or off from Settings>iCloud. Photos i included in the list of compatible apps. Tap this then move the Photo Stream slider to On to activate it.

Your synced photos

Thanks to Photo Stream you need never manually transfer your photos again

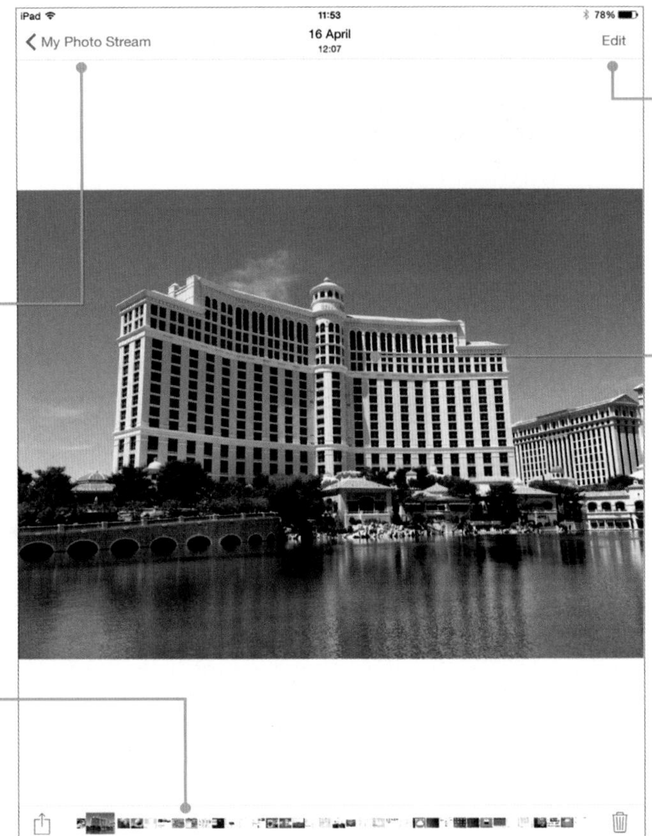

Get editing
When you've tapped on an image in your Photo Stream, you can then tap here to edit it. You can rotate, crop and enhance it to make sure it looks its best before sharing it

Photo Stream
Once activated, Photo Stream will automatically update your Photos app with all of the images captured across all your devices

Tap, pinch, expand
All images that are automatically imported into your Photo Stream album can be tapped on, expanded and pinched to shrink like normal through your Photos app

Your photos
Your Photo Stream album will be updated as and when new images are captured on other devices linked to your iCloud. Take pictures, sit back and watch the magic happen

All cameras supported
Photo Stream isn't restricted to iDevices. If you plug a non-Apple digital camera into your Mac (which is running at least Mac OS X 10.7.2 with iCloud enabled), all of the images on that camera will also be automatically whipped off and pushed straight to your Photo Stream too. Now that really is impressive.

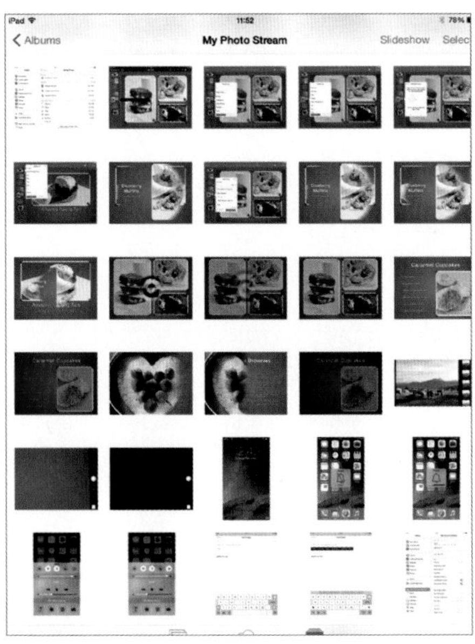

04 Take pictures
Repeat the previous steps on your other iDevice and then start taking photos. Within minutes, open up the Photos app on your iPad and then tap on the new My Photo Stream album.

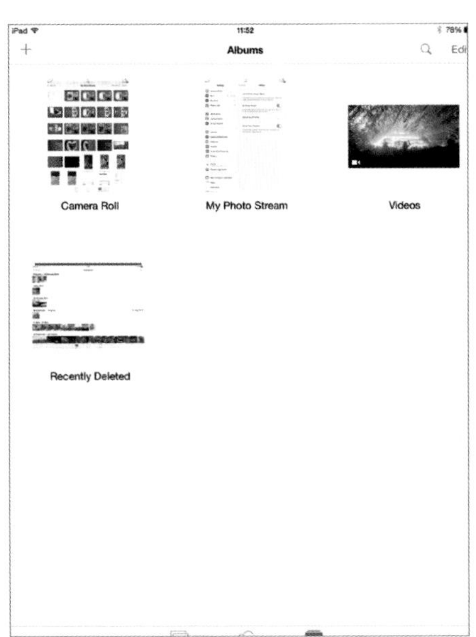

05 Instant transferral
All of the photos that you've taken on your iPhone will start appearing in your Photo Stream album, doing away with the need to manually transfer images by email or copying them across.

06 View and edit
You now have complete access to all of the photos taken on all of your devices. You can now edit and sharing them with others, which will save you hours of time and effort in the long run.

Learn to set up Family Sharing

Link family members to one account so that all downloaded media can be shared between devices

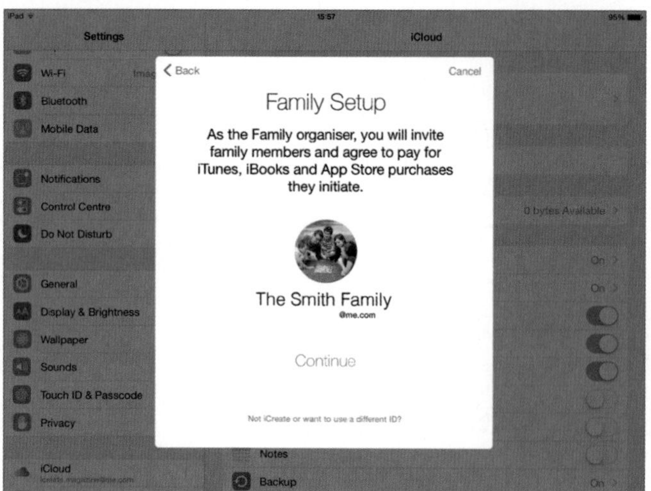

Family Sharing is a new way to bring you closer to your family, keep a eye on their purchases and even share their media downloads. Available for up to six people, this facility allows family members to share purchases from iTunes, iBooks and the App Store without sharing accounts. Set up by one family member, known as the organiser, all of the family purchases can be paid for with the same credit card. A permission alert will notify the organiser, who can then approve or deny the request to purchase that media, if suitable. This means that young children won't be able to make purchases without the organiser's permission, helping to curb spending and restrict access.

There are numerous other benefits of using this service; you can share photos quickly and easily within the household, mark up events on a central family calendar and even help track down missing devices. Once set up, family members get instant access to each other's downloads without the need to share Apple IDs and passwords.

> "Family members get instant access to each other's downloads"

Activate Family Sharing

Learn how to enact controls over your family members' purchasing power

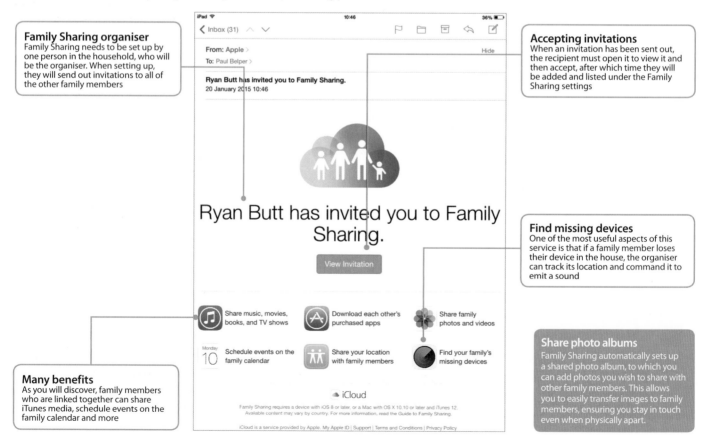

Family Sharing organiser
Family Sharing needs to be set up by one person in the household, who will be the organiser. When setting up, they will send out invitations to all of the other family members

Accepting invitations
When an invitation has been sent out, the recipient must open it to view it and then accept, after which time they will be added and listed under the Family Sharing settings

Find missing devices
One of the most useful aspects of this service is that if a family member loses their device in the house, the organiser can track its location and command it to emit a sound

Many benefits
As you will discover, family members who are linked together can share iTunes media, schedule events on the family calendar and more

Share photo albums
Family Sharing automatically sets up a shared photo album, to which you can add photos you wish to share with other family members. This allows you to easily transfer images to family members, ensuring you stay in touch even when physically apart.

Settings Get Family Sharing working on your iPad

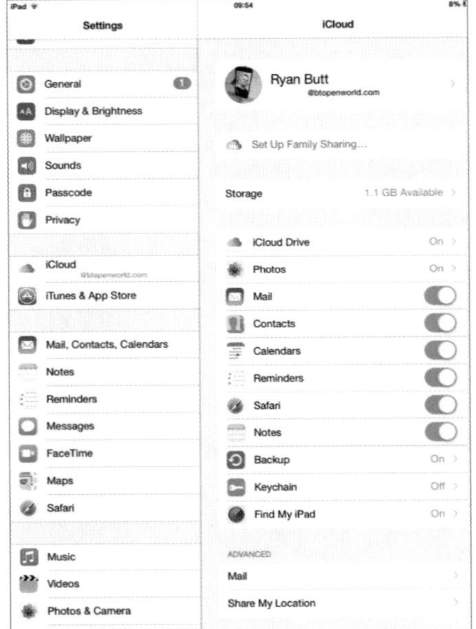

01 Get started

Launch the Settings app and scroll down the categories in the column on the left until you come to the iCloud section. Tap on this and you will see the option to Set Up Family Sharing at the top.

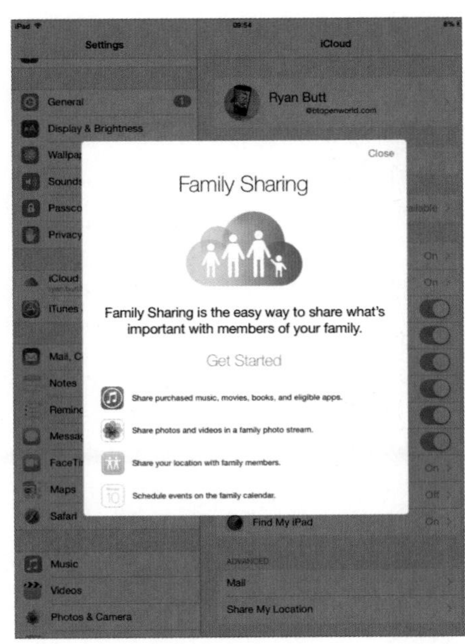

02 Login to Family Sharing

Tap on the Set Up Family Sharing option followed by Get Started. Now sign in using the Apple ID that you wish to use in order to share iTunes, iBooks and App Store purchases throughout your family.

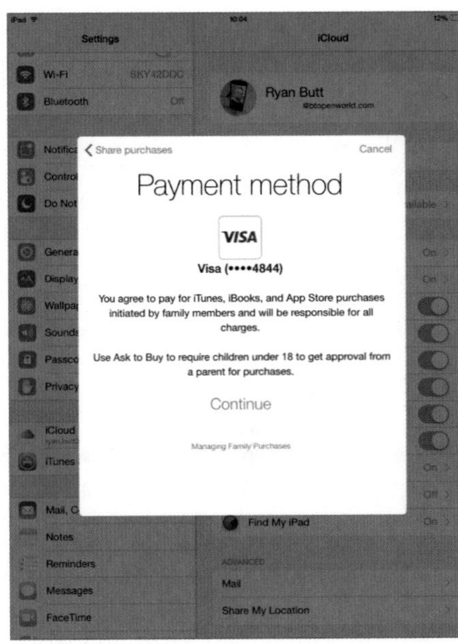

03 Check payment details

You will have to check the payment method to authorise all iTunes, iBooks and App Store purchases in your household, or enter payment details if they aren't already linked to your Apple ID.

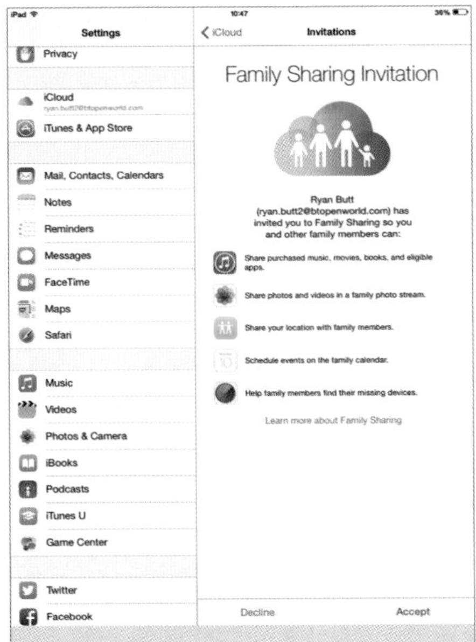

04 Share your location

The next step involves sharing your location with family members using Messages and the Find My Friends app. Delay this process until later if you wish by tapping on Not Now if you prefer.

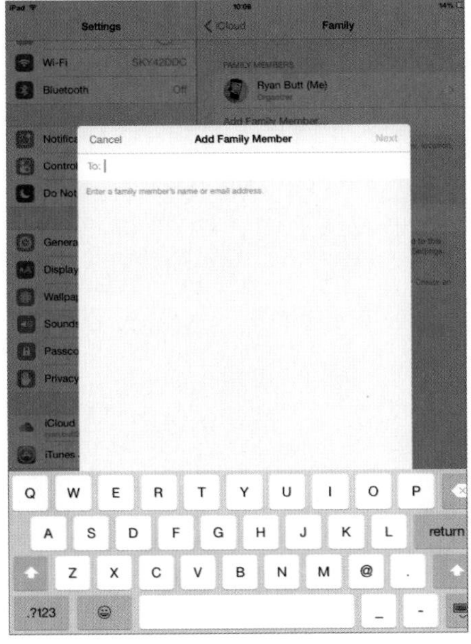

05 Connect with family

You will be taken back to the Settings screen to start adding family members by entering their name or email address. An invitation will be sent and, when accepted, the member will join.

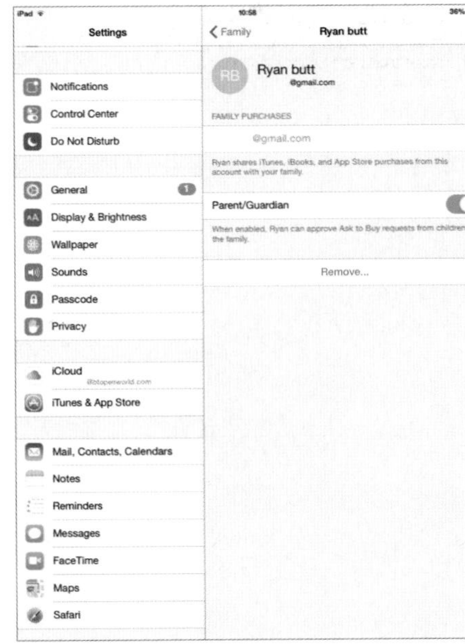

06 Establish boundaries

From the organiser's Family Settings screen, you can tap on the names of attached family members to grant/revoke certain app-buying privileges or remove people from the Family Sharing circle.

Set up a Game Center account

Enter into a world of fun games, fierce competition and social gaming with Game Center

Apple's Game Center is a multi-purpose gaming service that gives users a platform to befriend other gamers, engage in multiplayer modes, compete for online leaderboard supremacy and earn unlockable achievements. The app comes preloaded on Apple devices, and it significantly enhances your iPad as a gaming platform.

Once you have followed the initial set-up instructions, there are a wealth of options available to you. From the top menu you can clearly see your friend, game and achievement counters displayed, while the bottom tab bar lets you access Game Center's menus. 'Games' is by far the most in-depth, displaying all of your Game Center-enabled games, as well as your global ranking on the online leaderboards, something many people can become obsessed with.

Within each game's menu, you can also see how many achievements you have unlocked, get details on locked achievements and recommend the app to a friend. It's a solid service that brings together the best games available on one dedicated platform. So look no further to get started on this gaming platform.

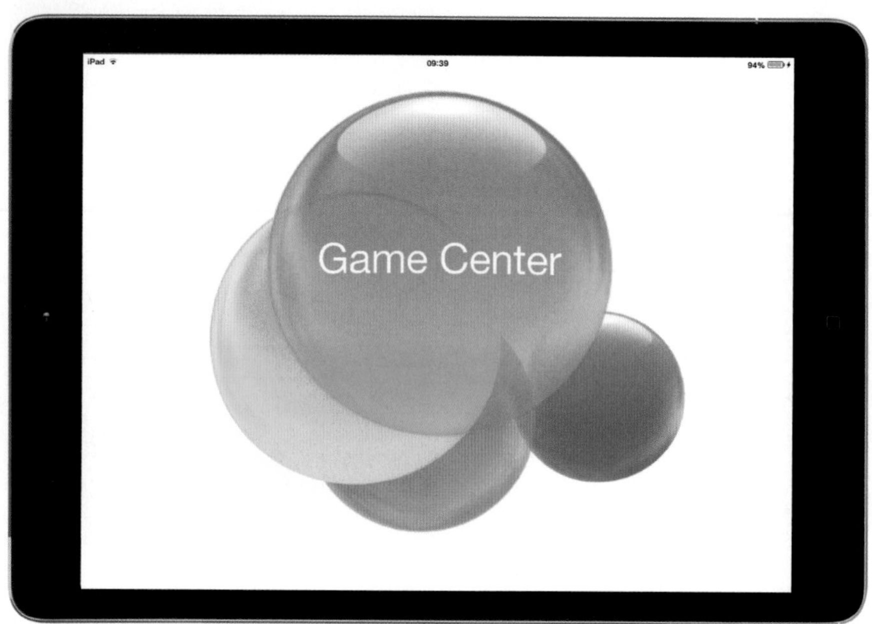

"The app comes preloaded on Apple devices, and it significantly enhances your iPad as a gaming platform"

Game Center Set up your new account

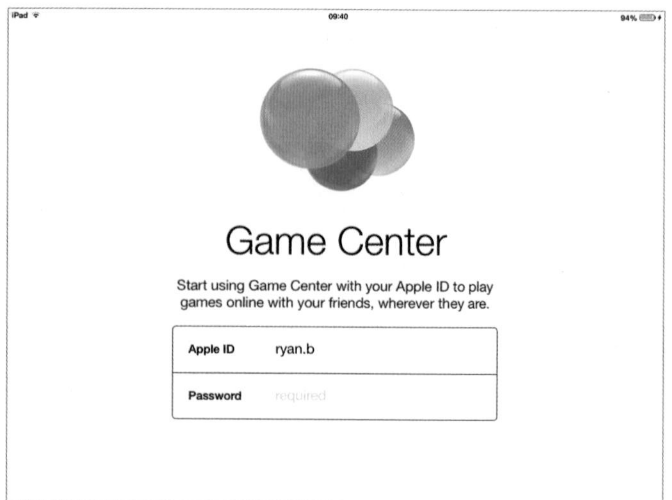

01 Sign in

As you will enter an Apple ID when setting up your iPad for the first time, this will be automatically applied to the Game Center app. If not, you will be prompted to sign in with your Apple ID the first time you launch the app. Enter your email address and password.

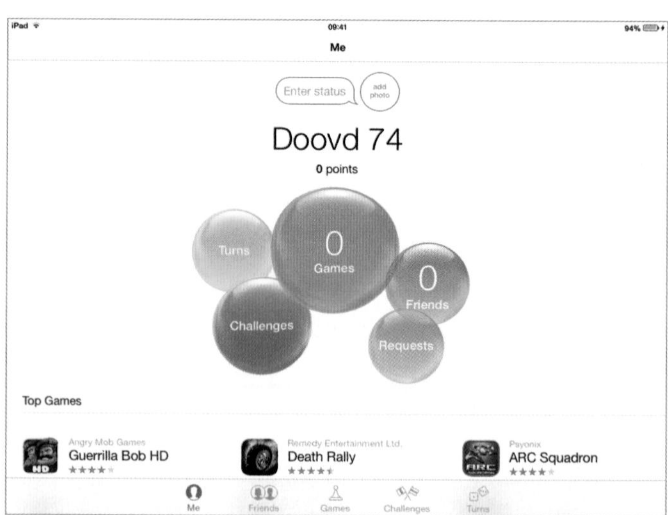

02 Your Game Center

Once signed in you will be taken to the main tab of your Game Center app. This screen will provide easy access to your games, friends, challenges, turns (a feature introduced in iOS 7) and friend requests. Either tap on the bubbles or use the tabs at the bottom of the interface.

Welcome to Game Center

Enter a world of fun and friends

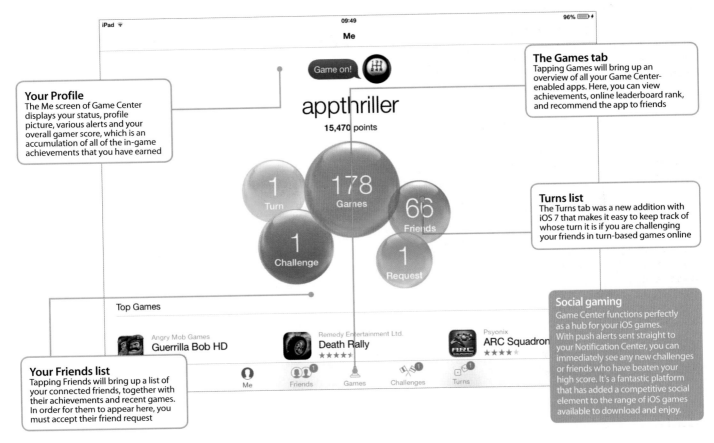

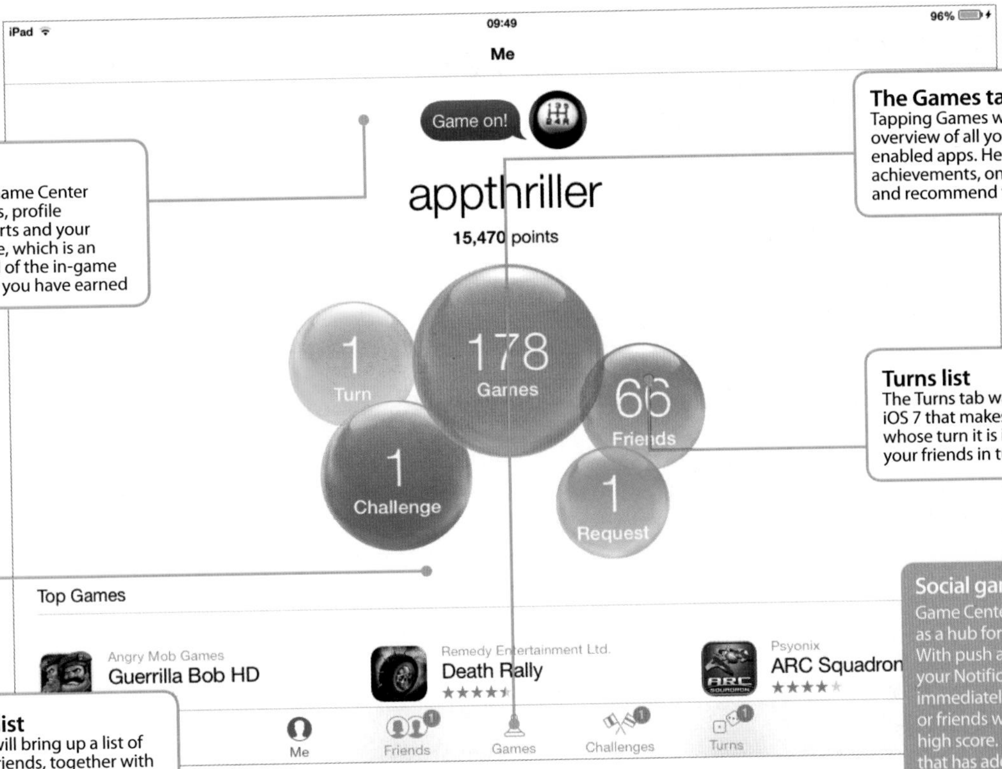

Your Profile

The Me screen of Game Center displays your status, profile picture, various alerts and your overall gamer score, which is an accumulation of all of the in-game achievements that you have earned

The Games tab

Tapping Games will bring up an overview of all your Game Center-enabled apps. Here, you can view achievements, online leaderboard rank, and recommend the app to friends

Turns list

The Turns tab was a new addition with iOS 7 that makes it easy to keep track of whose turn it is if you are challenging your friends in turn-based games online

Your Friends list

Tapping Friends will bring up a list of your connected friends, together with their achievements and recent games. In order for them to appear here, you must accept their friend request

Social gaming

Game Center functions perfectly as a hub for your iOS games. With push alerts sent straight to your Notification Center, you can immediately see any new challenges or friends who have beaten your high score. It's a fantastic platform that has added a competitive social element to the range of iOS games available to download and enjoy.

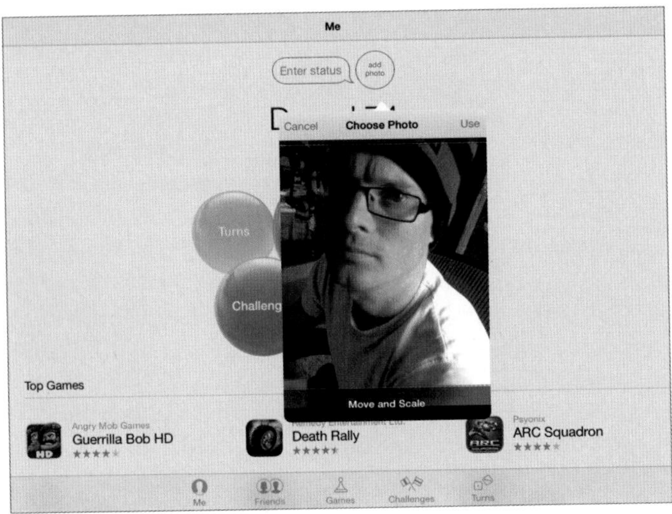

03 Enter status and photo

Tap on the Enter Status speech bubble to post something to your page that all of your friends can see. You can also tap on the Add Photo circle to put a face to the name. You can then opt to either choose a photo from your library or take a new photo in-app.

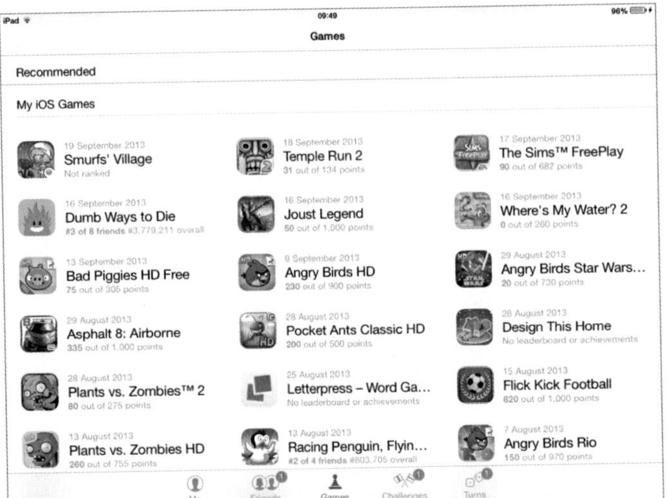

04 Start playing today

In the Games tab you can get your account started properly as you will be given recommendations as to which games to download and start your collection with. You can also search for new games by tapping the Search field and entering keywords.

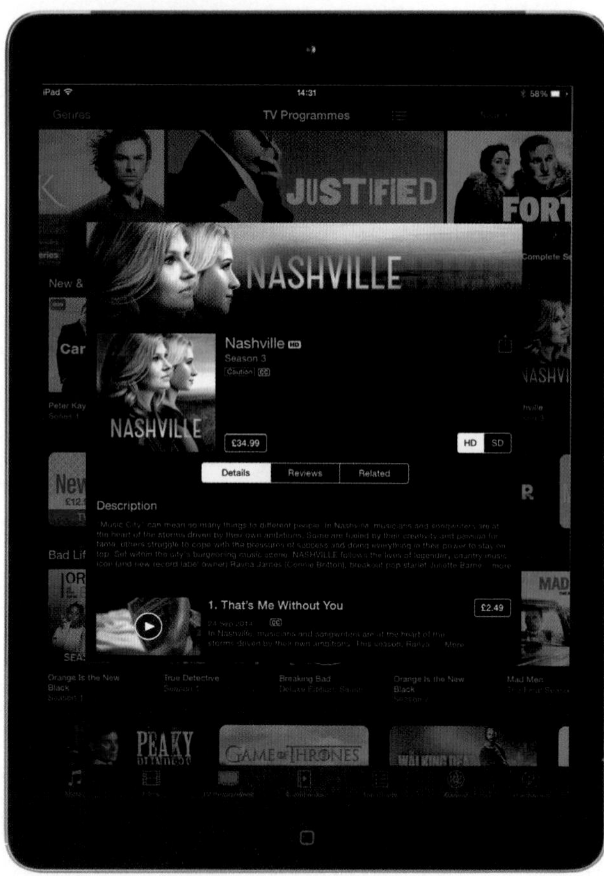

Get the most out of Videos

The iPad is perfectly designed for the mobile movie experience thanks to its large screen

The Videos feature alone has the potential to keep you occupied on long plane journeys, in hotels or waiting rooms, and adds a use to the iPad that could justify half of the cost straight away. It has been designed for ease of use, as most Apple software has, and takes care of many of the niggles found in competing devices. For example, it will automatically play a film from the point you left it, and expanding the screen requires a simple double tap. These small touches may seem small to you now, but once you get going with this facility you will realise their impact on user experience right away.

Everything in Videos is designed to help you get the most from the experience, but some tips are still a useful help to getting you off to a flying start. In this step-by-step guide we will show you how to obtain new movies, how to transfer them to your iPad and how to make the most of the viewing experience.

We are sure you could easily do all of this yourself, but in this instance a little knowledge certainly goes a long way, as missing out on the movie capabilities of the iPad would be a real shame. These few steps will get you started and the intuitiveness of your iPad will keep you going problem-free.

"The Video feature alone adds a use to the iPad that could justify half of the cost straight away"

Videos Make the most of movies

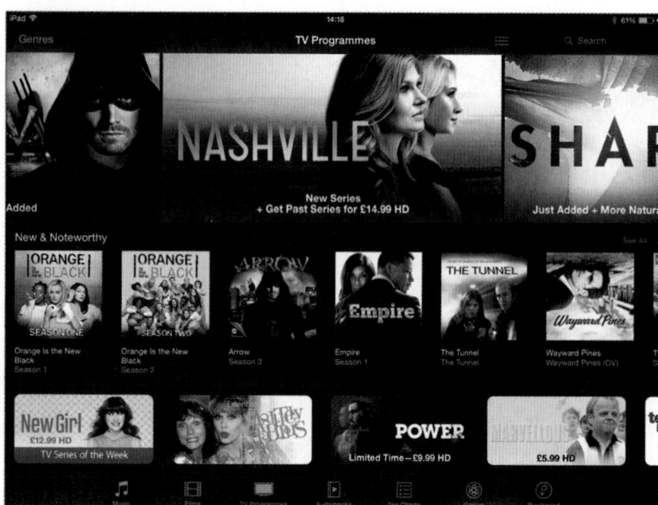

01 Grab a film

The easiest way to obtain the highest-quality content is via iTunes. Navigate to the Films or TV Programmes section of the store and choose the film you would like to rent or buy. You can also try some free trailers to get an idea of what you want to watch before you spend any money.

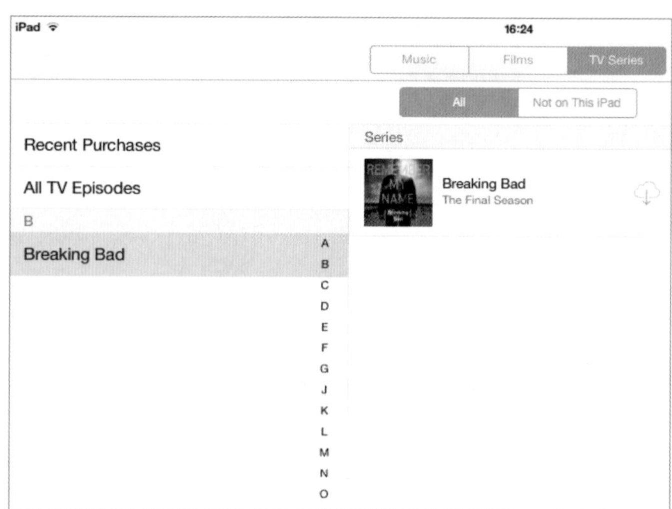

02 Put it on the iPad

Your purchases will be downloaded and stored on your iPad. If you have iCloud activated then they will also automatically be pushed to your other devices wirelessly, such as your Mac or iPhone, allowing you to view them on those devices too.

Watch movies on your iPad

Get the most out of the Videos app

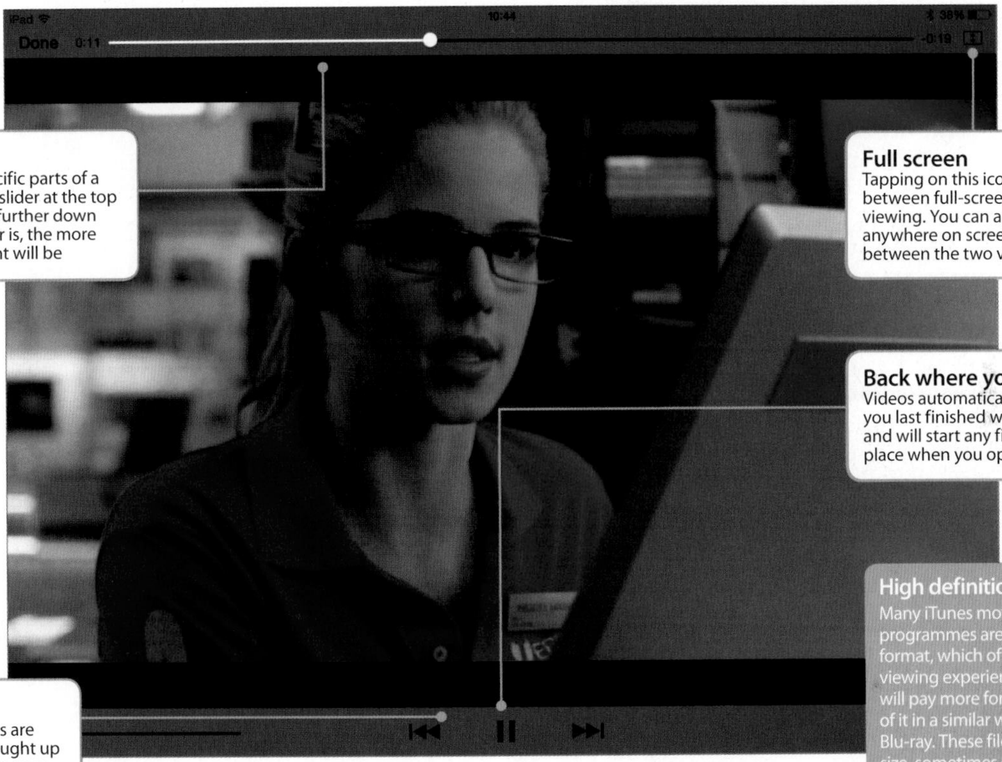

Full control
You can move to specific parts of a video by moving the slider at the top with your finger; the further down the screen your finger is, the more precise the movement will be

Full screen
Tapping on this icon will alternate between full-screen and widescreen viewing. You can also double tap anywhere on screen to achieve toggle between the two views

Back where you left off
Videos automatically remembers where you last finished watching something and will start any film at that exact place when you open it up again

High definition
Many iTunes movies and TV programmes are now available in HD format, which offers a much crisper viewing experience. Sometimes you will pay more for the video, but think of it in a similar way to paying more for Blu-ray. These files will also be larger in size, sometimes significantly, so make sure that you have adequate space on your iPad before you buy.

Main controls
The main control keys are standard and are brought up by tapping the screen once. You can play, pause, forward or rewind when you need to

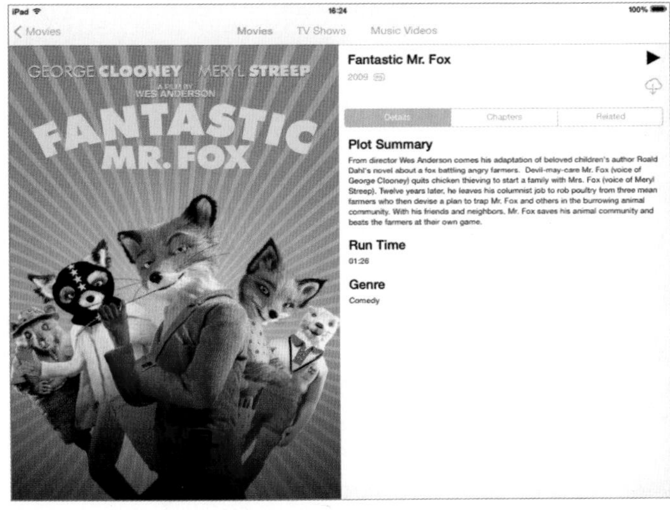

03 The fun starts here
All you need to do now is simply tap the Videos icon in your home screen and choose the film you want to watch from the list of videos you have installed onto your iPad. The film (or TV programme, for that matter) will then start to play immediately from the beginning.

04 Small changes
Double-tapping the screen will make the movie fill the whole screen, and doing so again will take it back to standard format (which is useful for widescreen films). The rest of the on-screen tweaks are obvious in their implementation, such as play, pause, etc.

Access video content via YouTube

Discover how to get the most out of YouTube on your iPad

Apple no longer includes YouTube as a standard, built-in app, but thankfully Google has worked hard to create its own custom app for the tablet device. The result is a more streamlined experience, with a brand new interface and a number of new features that give the user more control.

The sidebar on the left of the screen stays hidden in portrait, so you can access it when you need it. It helps you navigate through the various video categories and view your Profile information if you wish to log in. The new app also includes a voice search option, allowing you to speak aloud to search for a video in seconds.

The app may no longer be integrated into iOS, but since YouTube videos will play within Safari, this is only a small concern. For those that want the full YouTube experience on their tablet, however, the app is unmissable. The app itself is simple to use and easy to pick up, and with just a few taps millions of videos will be at your fingertips.

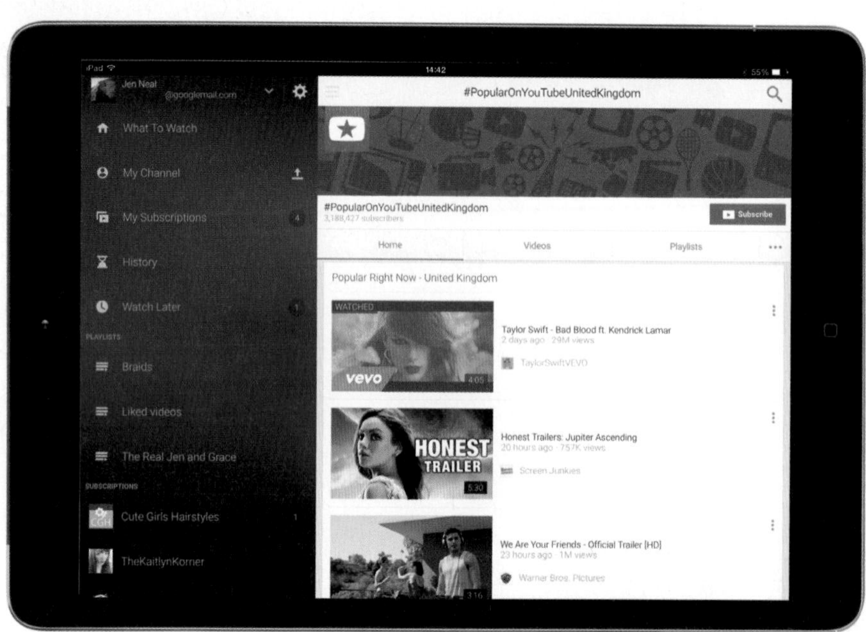

YouTube Make the most of YouTube

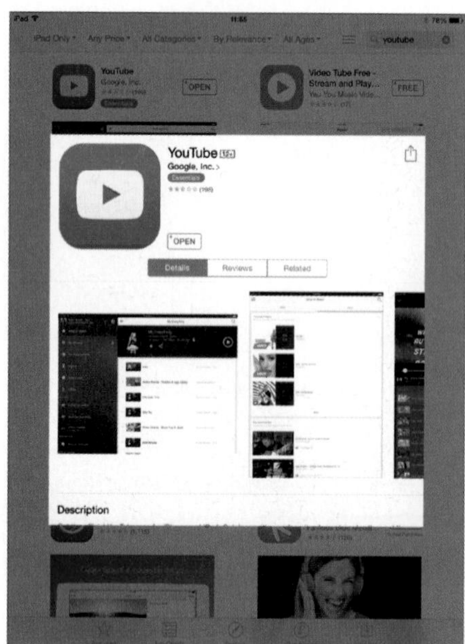

01 Get started

To start using YouTube on your iPad, head into the App Store and search for YouTube in the search bar. Download the free app and open it to start browsing videos.

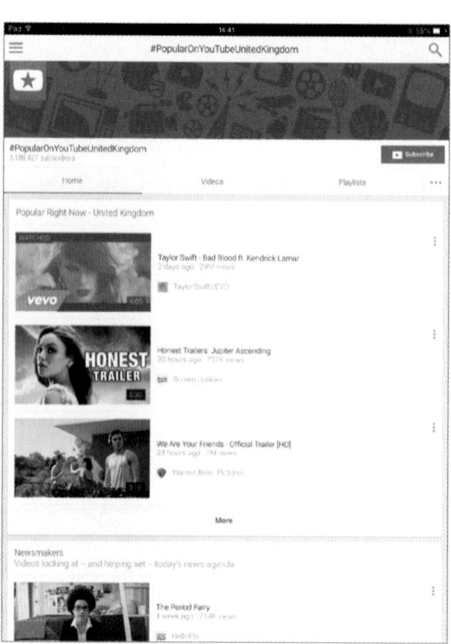

02 Popular videos

When you first open the app you'll see a range of the most popular videos on YouTube at the moment. Pull the list down to refresh it or tap a video to watch it.

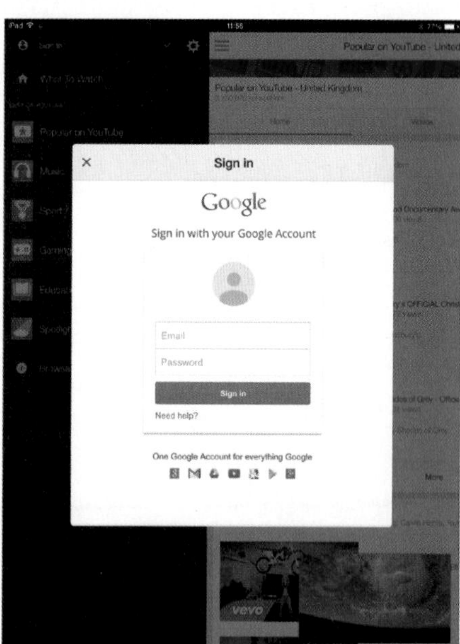

03 Sign in

To access your account, swipe across the top of the screen from left to right and you'll see a number of options. Simply tap Sign In and input your Google information to log in.

YouTube on iPad

The YouTube app is incredibly easy to use, with everything you could need in one place

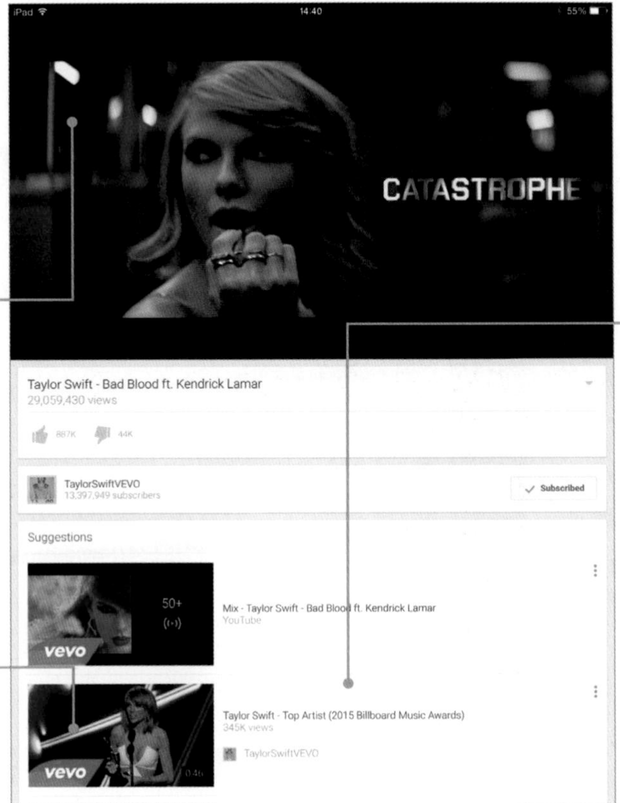

Swiping
No matter where you are in the app, it's possible to view the options sidebar by swiping across the screen from left to right

Related videos
YouTube will suggest a list of related videos based on your watching habits. Tap 'More' to extend the list and find even more great watches

Comments
Comments are visible when you watch a video, but you can access them by tapping this button. From here you can add your own comments, too

Streaming
Streaming video wirelessly is very bandwidth-hungry, and overuse on 3G alone could cause you to break the limit on your data account. Your network provider is then within its rights to send you a warning. When possible, try to use Wi-Fi because this will not only perform better, but it could potentially save you a lot of money.

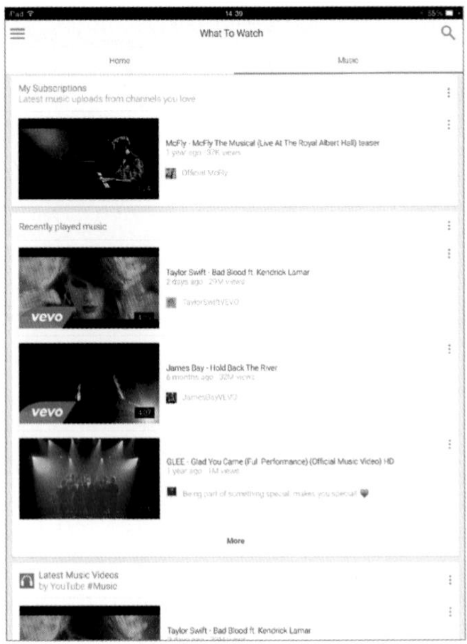

04 Explore the content

You will now see videos from users you're subscribed to in the main stream. Alternatively, swipe left to right again and pick a different category of video.

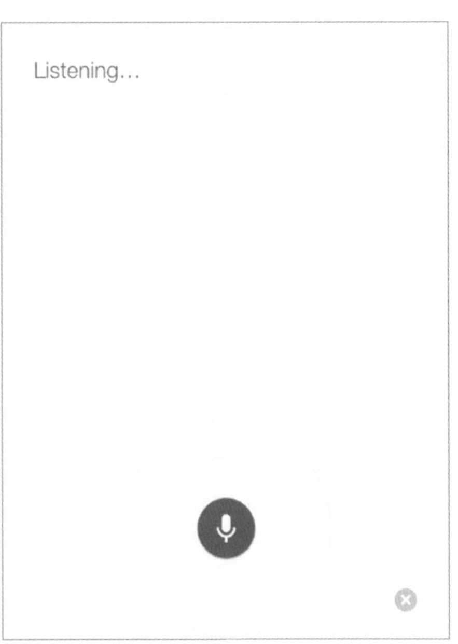

05 Voice Search

Tap Search and then tap the mic icon on the keyboard. Now simply dictate the name of the video you want to watch. The app will analyse your words and find relevant results.

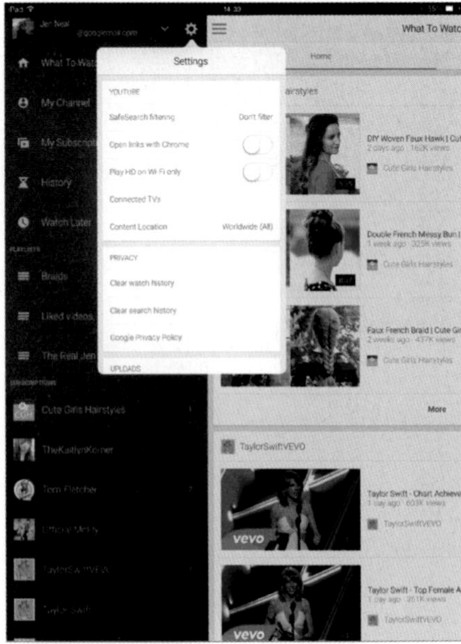

06 Settings

You can access a range of account settings from the sidebar as well. Tap the Settings section, or the arrow next to your user name, to see choices like the app used to open links.

Get to know the Music app

We guide you around your iPad Music app and show you how to make a playlist

The iPad Music app is your mobile music player and superstore all rolled into one. With a clean, simple, easy-to-manipulate interface, you can play any track stored in your library by tapping on it and using the playback controls. Create your own Playlists on the fly and even visit the iTunes Store from within the app to buy something new. It will make you want to just sit there and spend hour after hour discovering new music.

What's more, if you have enabled your iCloud (the free cloud storage and syncing service that comes free with iOS 5 and above), any new music you purchase will be pushed to all of your iOS devices without you having to lift a finger. By the same process you can also access and download music that you have downloaded in the past at no extra cost.

In this tutorial we guide you through the intricacies of this versatile app and show you how to create Playlists, access your purchased music files and much more.

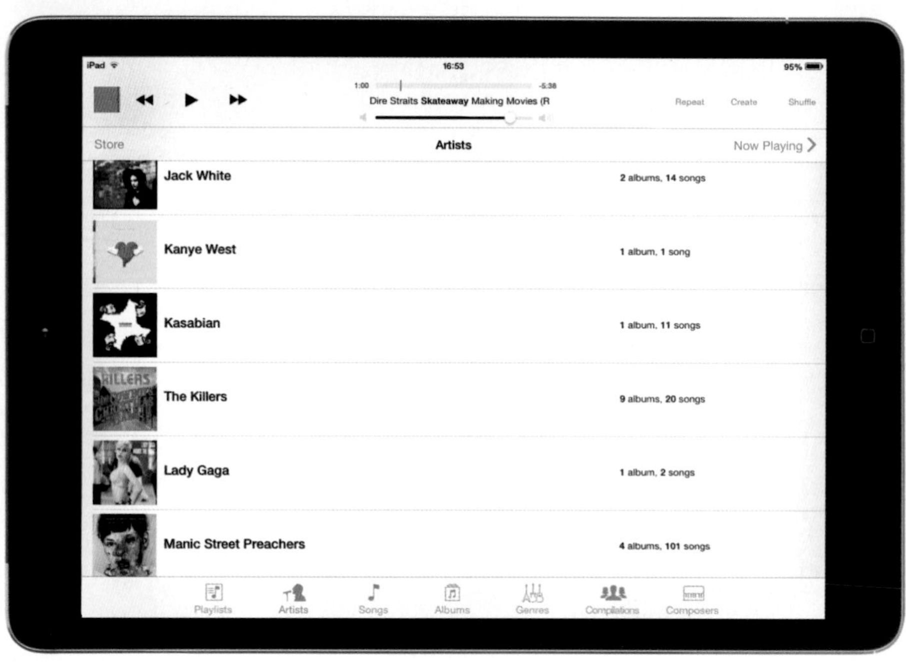

Music Create a playlist

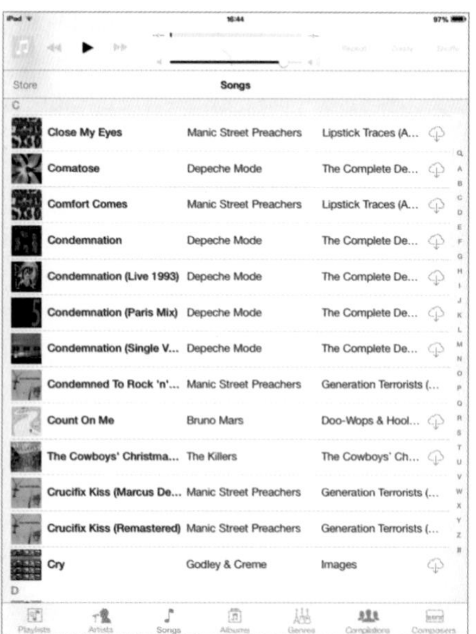

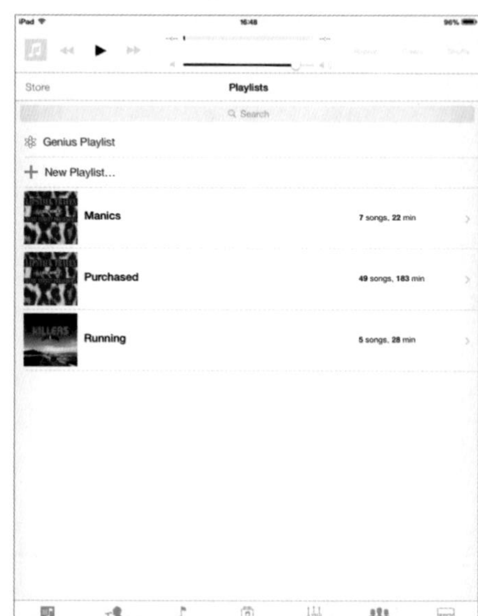

01 Launch the app

Your Music app can be found in your iPad's dock by default. To get started, tap on the icon to launch the app and then you'll be able to start listening to music on your device.

02 Browse songs

Use the tiles at the bottom of the screen to browse your music by Playlist, Songs, Artists or Albums. Tap on a song to start playing it. The playback controls are at the top of the screen.

03 Make a Playlist

Tap on the Playlist tile and then tap New Playlist in the top corner. Give your new Playlist a name, then add songs from your library, drag them into a preferred order and then tap Done.

Music while you're mobile

Setting up playlists on the iPad is a breeze

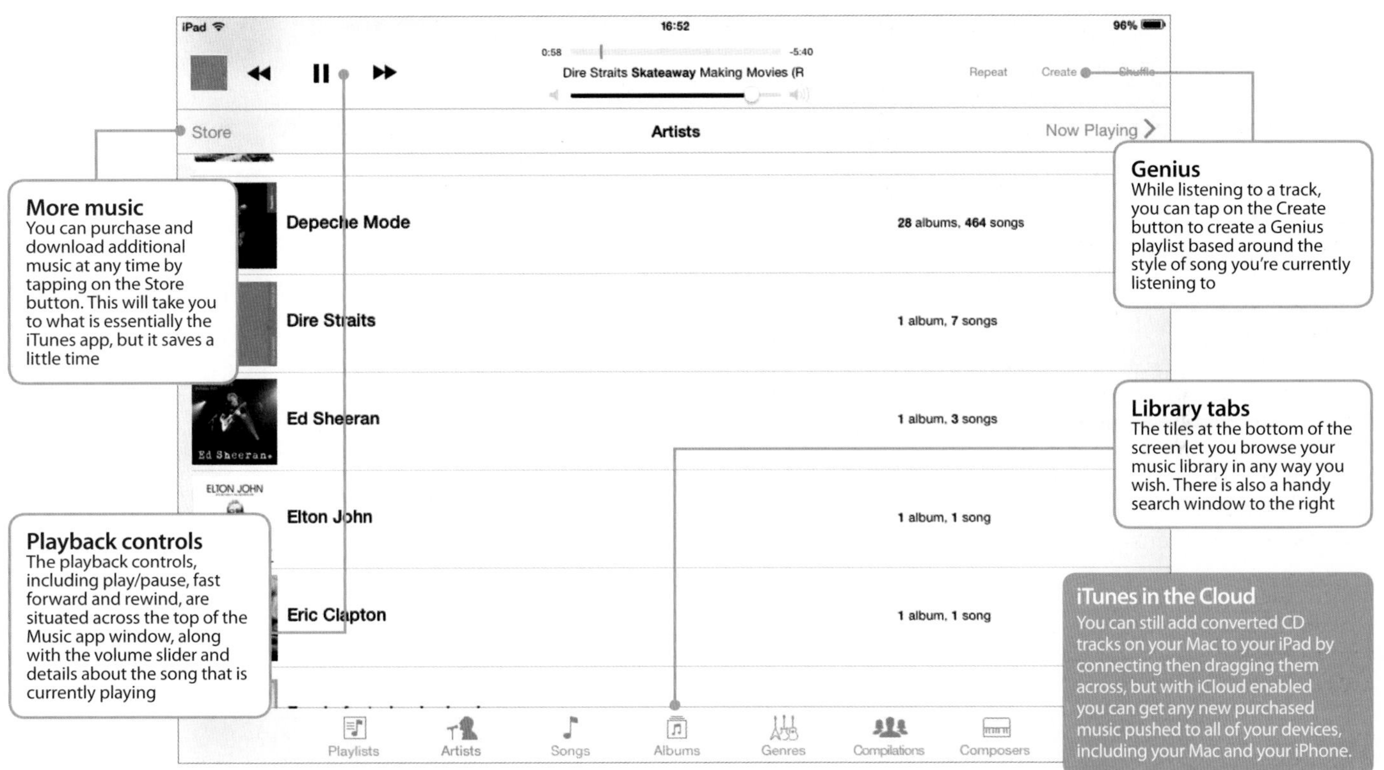

More music
You can purchase and download additional music at any time by tapping on the Store button. This will take you to what is essentially the iTunes app, but it saves a little time

Playback controls
The playback controls, including play/pause, fast forward and rewind, are situated across the top of the Music app window, along with the volume slider and details about the song that is currently playing

Genius
While listening to a track, you can tap on the Create button to create a Genius playlist based around the style of song you're currently listening to

Library tabs
The tiles at the bottom of the screen let you browse your music library in any way you wish. There is also a handy search window to the right

iTunes in the Cloud
You can still add converted CD tracks on your Mac to your iPad by connecting then dragging them across, but with iCloud enabled you can get any new purchased music pushed to all of your devices, including your Mac and your iPhone.

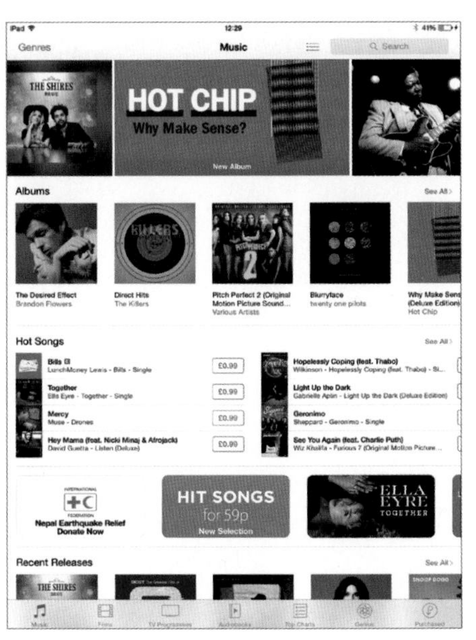

04 Visit the iTunes Store

You can make new purchases from within the Music app by tapping the Store button. You can then browse the full iTunes Store and download new tracks, albums and podcasts.

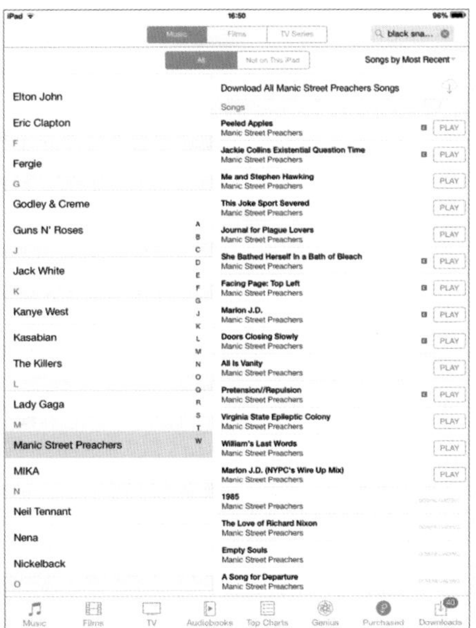

05 Connect to iCloud

Through iCloud you can get all of your previous iTunes purchases beamed directly to your iPad. Create an account and connect, then go to the Purchased category in the iTunes Store.

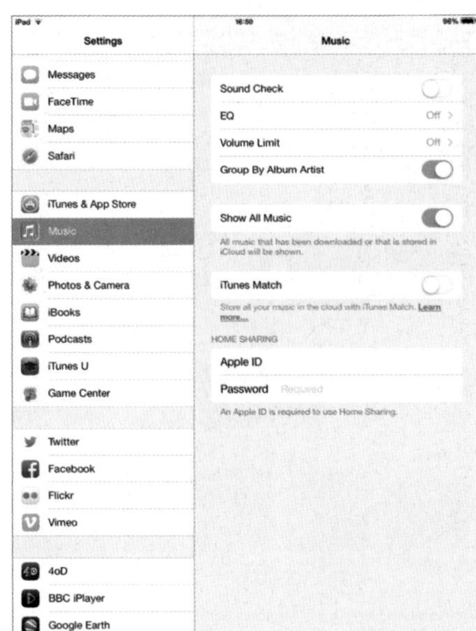

06 Get familiar with the settings

Go to Settings and then tap Music to access the app's preferences. Here you can set the EQ to the style of music you are playing, set a cap on how high the volume goes and more.

Listen to podcasts on your iPad

Search for, subscribe to, and listen to fantastically immersive podcasts on your iPhone

The iTunes store has recently become so big that it has had to migrate particular wings to their own standalone apps, such as iBooks, iTunesU and Podcasts. These apps now come as standard with iOS 8, so there is no reason not to jump right in to investigate what they can offer you. If you have used the iTunes app before, the Podcasts app will be immediately familiar.

Use the icons at the bottom of he screen to check out the Featured and Top Charts sections of the iTunes store and you will be able to start searching for popular podcasts. If you know what you want to subscribe to or wish to find podcasts that specialise in a particular area, tap on the Search option and enter keywords. When you find a suitable podcast, select it to view its info page and then tap on the Subscribe button to ensure that your are notified when a new episode is ready to download. You can also tap on the cloud icons to download individual episodes to your device.

To listen to your downloaded podcasts, tap on the My Podcasts icon and select a podcast, followed by the episode. You will then be presented with a familiar set of playback controls to Play/Pause and skip forward and back. You can also press, hold and drag the scrub bar at the bottom of the controls to fast-track to a particular point in any episode. Even if you have never listed to a podcast before, this app makes it an enjoyable experience.

Podcasts Download a podcast

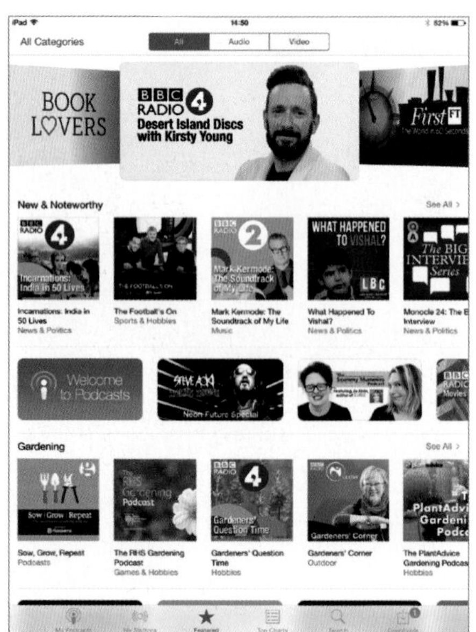

01 Start shopping

Tap on the Featured icon and you will be taken to the Podcasts wing of the iTunes store, where all of the latest podcasts will be displayed. Use the tabs to filter by Audio, Video or All.

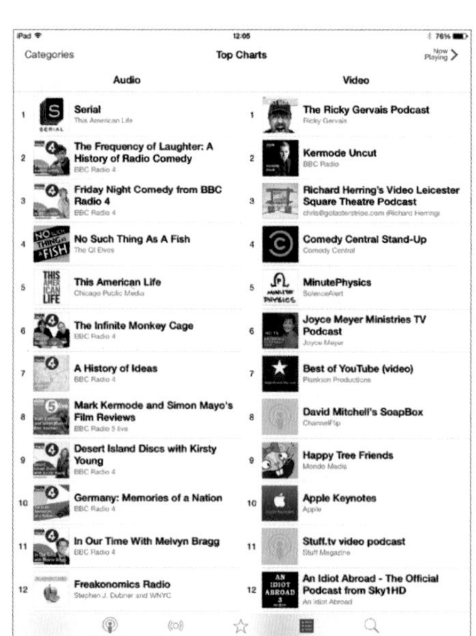

02 Explore the Top Charts

Tapping the Top Charts icon will list all of the podcasts that are currently popular. This is a good way to find content that is recent and that other users are listening to.

03 Subscribe to a podcast

When you find a podcast that you would like to subscribe to, tap on the Subscribe button and you will be notified whenever a new episode is ready to download and be listened to.

Getting to know the Podcasts interface

Explore the store and listen to content on your iPad

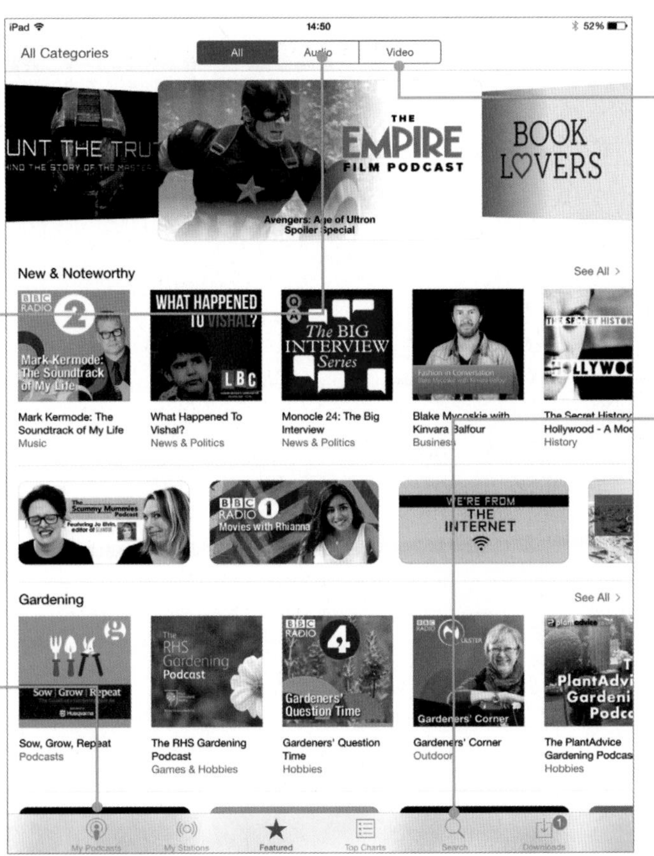

Store tabs
Podcasts come in two flavours, Audio and Video, which are self-explanatory. Use the tabs at the top of the Featured store window to view the latest and greatest podcasts in each category. When you find one, hit Subscribe

Your Podcasts
All of the podcasts that you have downloaded will be accessible through this section. Tap on a brand to view all of the podcasts inside and then tap an individual episode to start listening to it

Video
Podcasts don't just come in an audio format, you can also view video Podcasts. Just tap on the Video tab, and you can search and download in exactly the same way

Search
If you have a good idea of the sort of content that you would like to download and listen to then tap on the Search icon and start entering keywords to find content that matches quickly and easily

Creating podcast stations
You can line up a series of podcasts to listen to in one go by tapping on the My Stations icon, selecting the New Station option and then giving it a name. You can then pick individual episodes to make up your station or tap the Include All Podcasts option to feature every single podcast on your device.

04 Download episodes

You can also download individual episodes by tapping on the cloud icon next to a particular episode. All downloaded content will be accessible from the My Podcasts section.

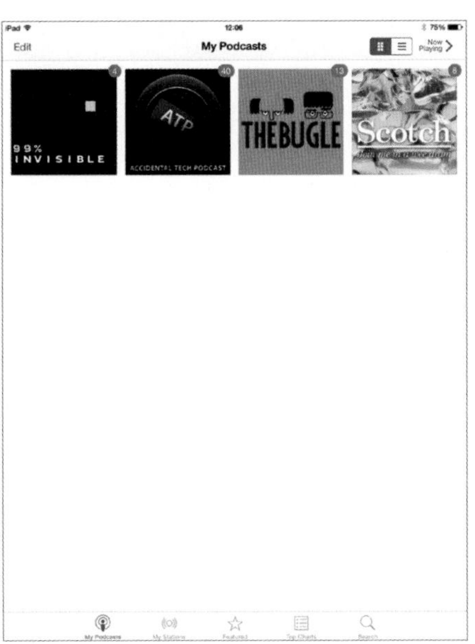

05 Play a podcast

When you are ready to start listening to a podcast, tap on the My Podcasts icon and select a podcast to listen to. Tap on an individual episode to start listening to it.

06 Playback controls

When you start listening to a podcast you will be presented with a familiar set of playback controls. You can also change the speed and use the scrub bar to jump to a particular point.

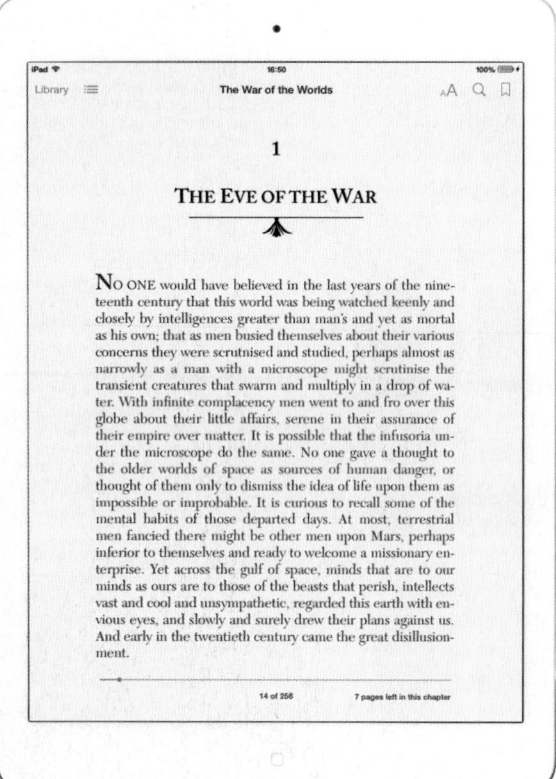

The War of the Worlds

1

THE EVE OF THE WAR

No one would have believed in the last years of the nineteenth century that this world was being watched keenly and closely by intelligences greater than man's and yet as mortal as his own; that as men busied themselves about their various concerns they were scrutinised and studied, perhaps almost as narrowly as a man with a microscope might scrutinise the transient creatures that swarm and multiply in a drop of water. With infinite complacency men went to and fro over this globe about their little affairs, serene in their assurance of their empire over matter. It is possible that the infusoria under the microscope do the same. No one gave a thought to the older worlds of space as sources of human danger, or thought of them only to dismiss the idea of life upon them as impossible or improbable. It is curious to recall some of the mental habits of those departed days. At most, terrestrial men fancied there might be other men upon Mars, perhaps inferior to themselves and ready to welcome a missionary enterprise. Yet across the gulf of space, minds that are to our minds as ours are to those of the beasts that perish, intellects vast and cool and unsympathetic, regarded this earth with envious eyes, and slowly and surely drew their plans against us. And early in the twentieth century came the great disillusionment.

14 of 256 7 pages left in this chapter

Purchase an iBook

Search for, subscribe to, and listen to fantastically immersive podcasts on your iPhone

One of the reasons for the iPad's popularity is for its ability to challenge the feats of Amazon's Kindle – and then some.

It's very easy to get lost in a world of crazy apps, accelerometers and multi-touch gestures, but the iPad was initially conceived as a fantastic e-book reader. The iPad obviously has a number of advantages over the Kindle in that it can do a great deal more than a dedicated device, but on a purely e-book-reading scale the iPad is still one of the most advanced out there. What's more is that Apple already has a tried and tested way to deliver e-books directly to its devices: namely the iTunes Store.

Apple hasn't just bundled the new books into that system, though, because it's created a separate space for these so that users can be sure of what they are downloading. iBooks is a fantastic resource on your iPad, holding all your e-books and giving you access to the custom-built iBooks Store to make purchases, which are downloaded directly. The system is simple, although unless you are running iOS 8 you may find you need to download the iBooks app from the App Store to kick things off.

This tutorial will take you through your first download from iBooks so you can get a feel for the system. It's then up to you to resist buying a library's worth of content!

"The iPad was initially conceived as a fantastic e-book reader"

iBooks Purchase a book

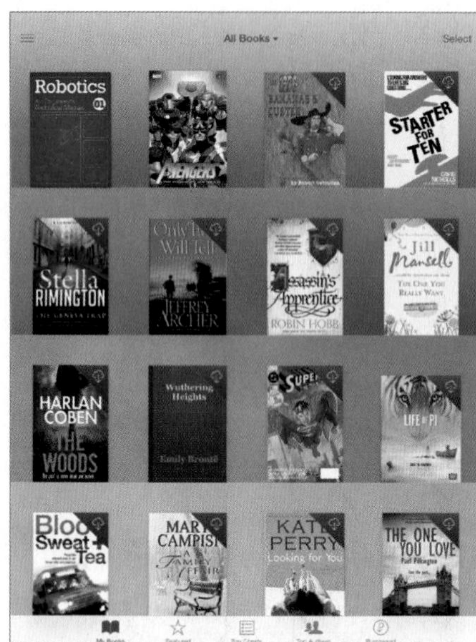

01 Load and launch

Find the iBooks icon on your Home screen, tap it, and once it's loaded you will be presented with blank shelves. To purchase your first book, hit the Store button at the top left.

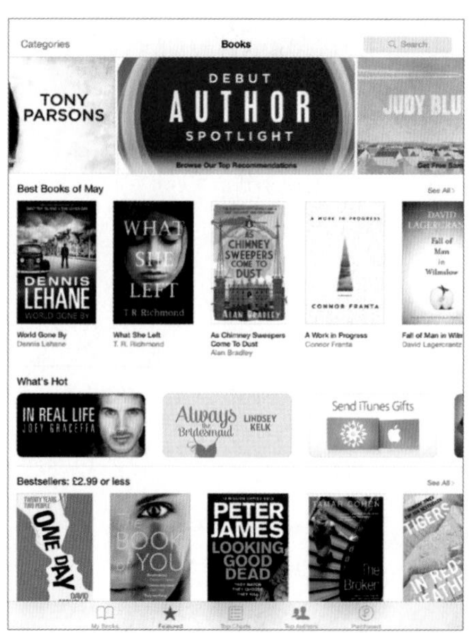

02 Familiar feel

Tapping the Top Charts icon will list all of the podcasts that are currently popular. This is a good way to find content that is recent and that other users are listening to.

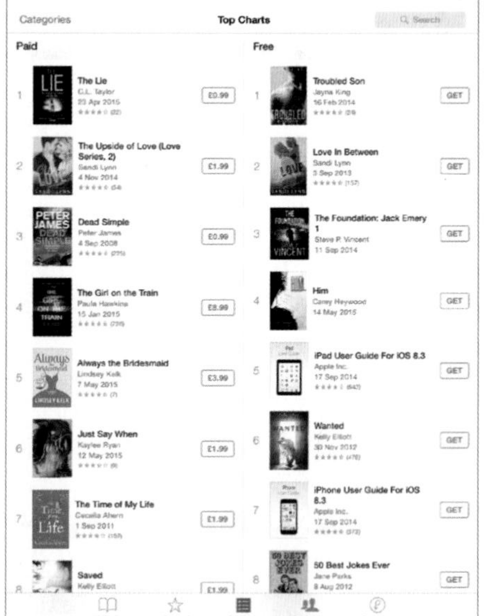

03 Top charts

The Featured section displays all of the latest releases of significance and you can also tap on Top Charts at the bottom of the screen to see which titles are currently popular.

The iBooks Store homepage

Find your way around your new home for digital books

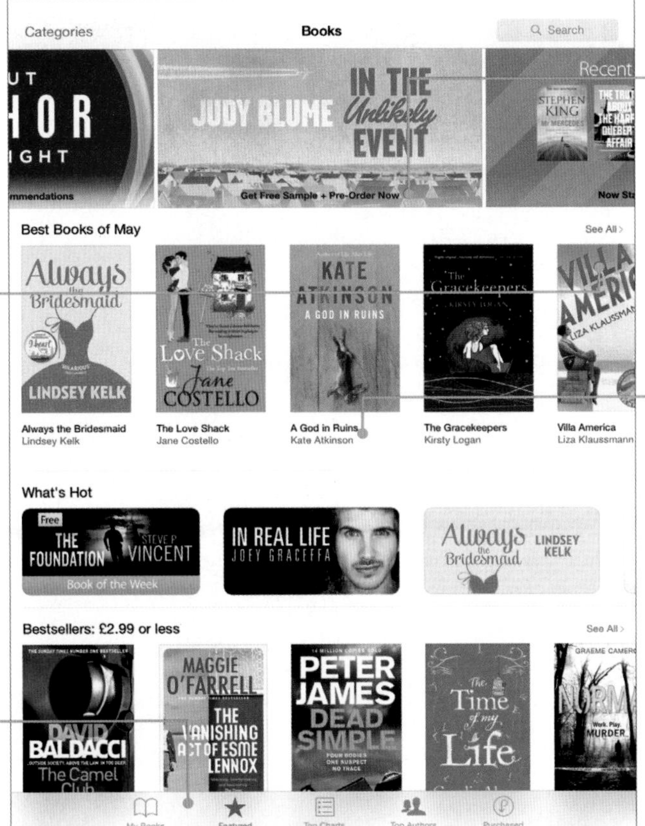

Promo perfection
Again, like the App Store, books are picked by Apple to be featured on the front of the Store. This positioning increases their sales no end, as you can imagine

See All
Use the See All button in order to get a bigger list from any given section. It's the same system that's used on the App Store

Easy navigation
Navigating through the Store with your fingers is easy. Tap buttons to see more and tap individual books in order to get more information

Tabs at the bottom
At the bottom of the interface there are four tabs, which will help you navigate through the Store and also see what you have already bought

iCloud
You can sync your book collection and bookmarks to iCloud, so that they will be available across all of your iOS 8 devices. Go to Settings>iBooks to activate and take advantage of these services.

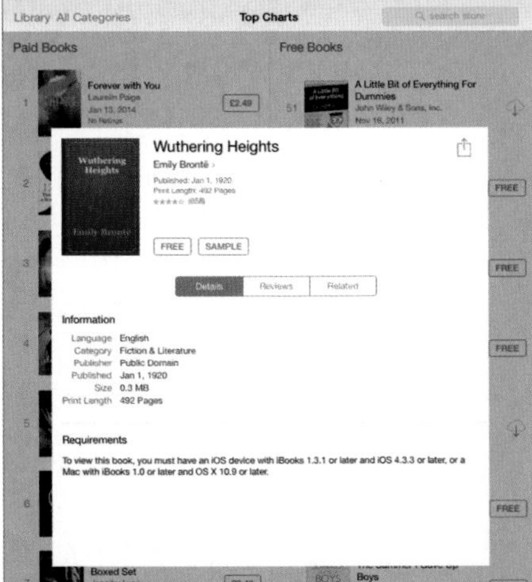

04 Free classics

Like the App Store, there are a huge number of free books. These tend to be the classics, so you can go ahead and get great content for nothing. Tap on the Free button and then tap Get Book.

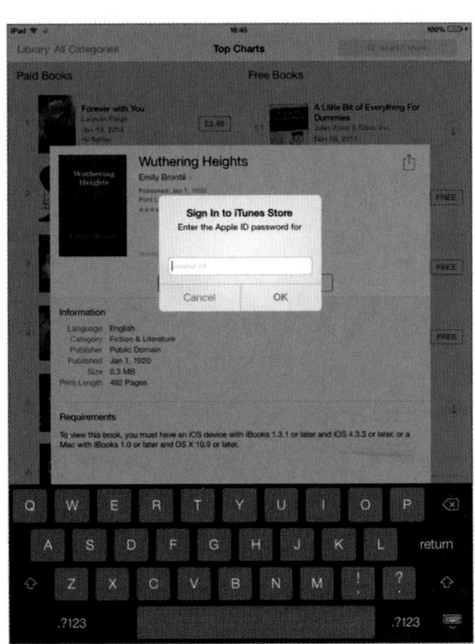

05 Password

You'll now be prompted to enter your iTunes account password to authorise the download. Do this and then tap the OK button to start downloading the book.

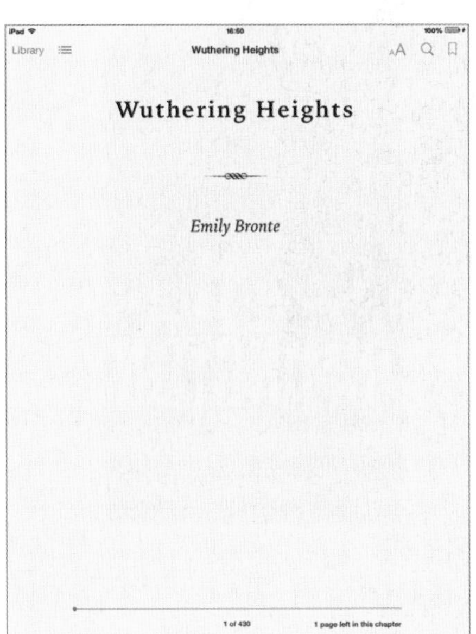

06 New books

Your new books will now appear on the bookshelf and you'll see a progress bar as they download. Once downloaded, the book will become available to read at your leisure.

Get to know iBooks

Having an e-Book reader on the iPad is very cool, so here's how to customise it to your liking

Despite the conjecture, if you've actually used the iPad you'll know full well that it's much more than just a large iPod touch. The size really does make it feel like you're holding a full-blown computer in your hands, and no other app exemplifies the difference more than iBooks.

When you're reading a book on the iPad it feels natural, it's easy to do, and you'll be certain to do a lot more reading now that it's so simple to carry your whole library around with you. The beauty of the iPad interface means that making changes to the way iBooks looks is very, very simple. Users can opt to make text bigger, change the font and alter the brightness of the page – without having to leave your place in the book you are reading. Try doing the same three operations on an iPhone and you will notice the difference; just see how many times you have to leave and return to the page you are reading.

iBooks is exceptional, so follow our quick tutorial on how to get more from the already excellent reading experience. While some people have found the transition from physical to digital books a slight challenge to overcome, the iPad will make this so effortless you'll be converted for life.

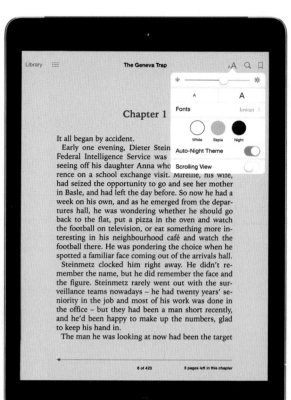

"Users can make text bigger, change the font and alter the brightness of the book"

iBooks Font, size and brightness

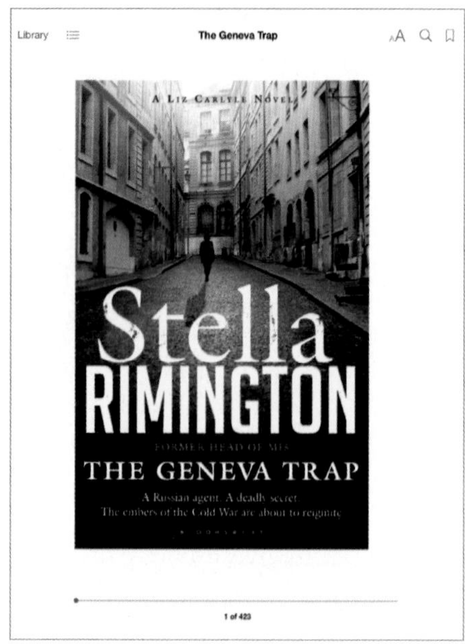

01 Open it up

From the Home screen, locate and open the iBooks app, then tap on the cover of a book on your shelf that you would like to read. The page is presented as if it were a real book but with options at the top and bottom.

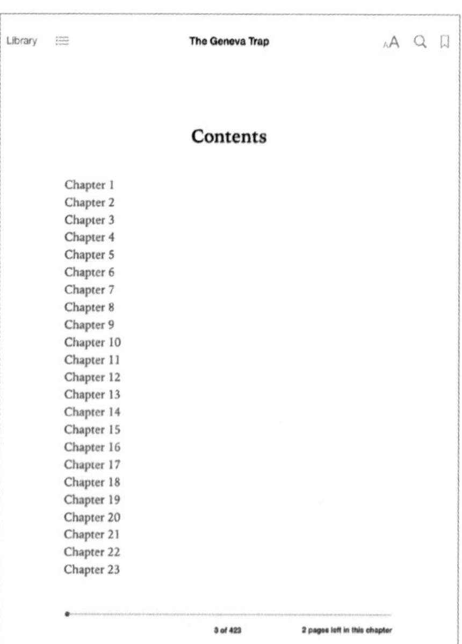

02 Contents

You can navigate to the contents page of any book by tapping the list icon in the top-left corner of the book page you are on. Move to a chapter by tapping on it. From here, you can also head to your own bookmarks and notes.

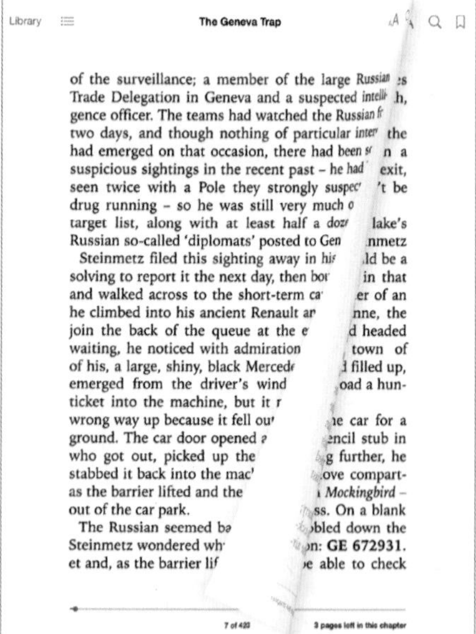

03 Curler

You can flip through pages by dragging from the right-hand side to the left, where you'll see the cool page-curl animation. It is as if you are flicking through a physical book. Alternatively you can tap on the right-hand side of the screen to flip the page.

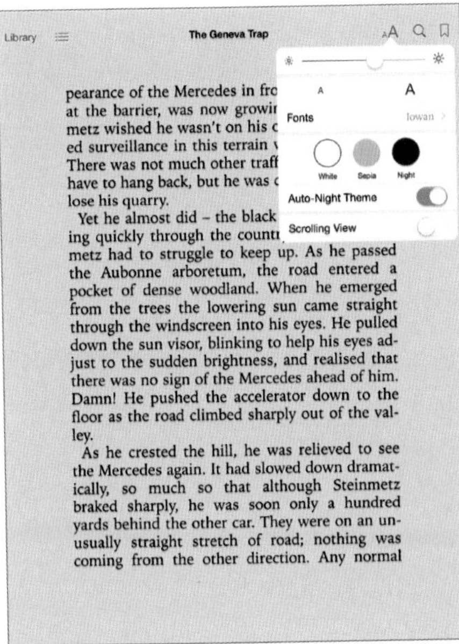

04 Font it

If you wish to alter the appearance of your font, tap on the 'AA' font button in the top right-hand corner of the page to access the menu where you can alter the book's font and text size. Tap the big 'A' to increase font size and the small one to decrease it.

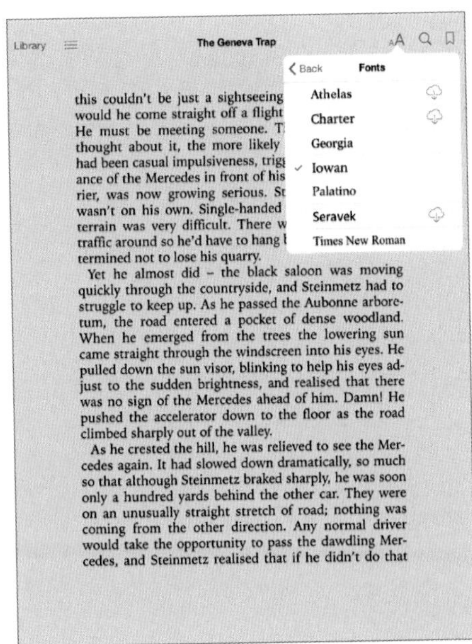

05 Font type

To change the font type, tap the Fonts button again in the top right-hand corner and pick from the available options that are listed in the pop-out window. The selection should provide an alternative that suits you.

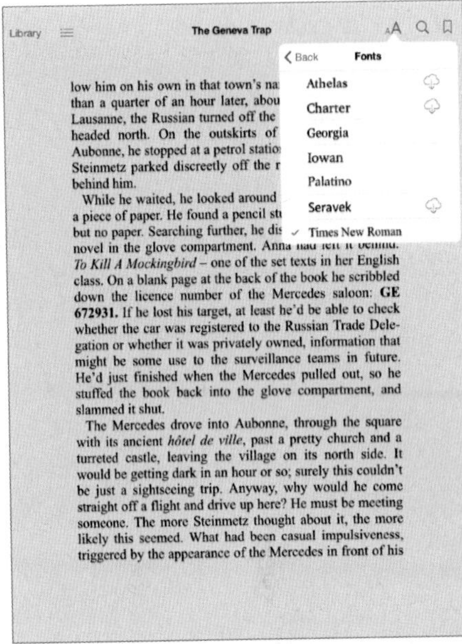

06 Tick it, watch it

Tap the font you wish to change it to and a tick will appear next to it. As with all the other changes you can make to the appearance of a book within iBooks, they will happen instantly and will stay that way until adjusted again.

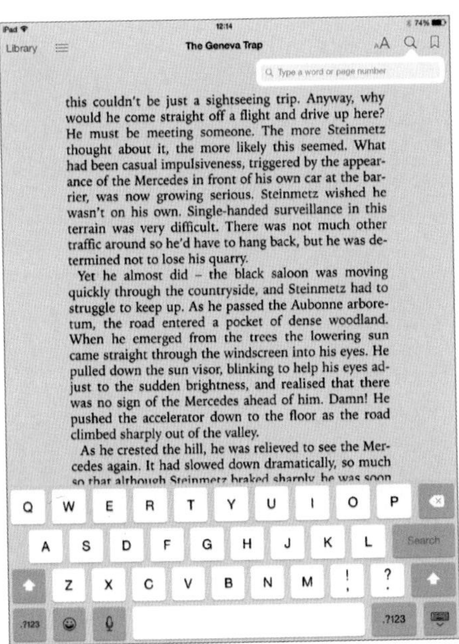

07 Spotlight index

Tap on the magnifying glass icon to bring up a search field. Every book in the iBook Store is fully indexed so you can instantly find individual words in a book, this is invaluable for jumping to specific sections of textbooks or dictionaries.

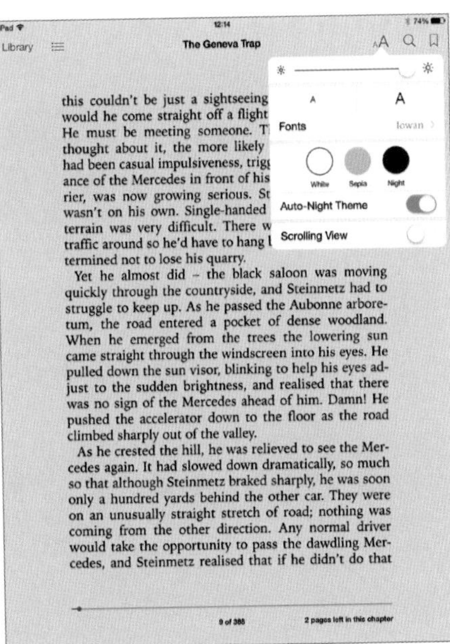

08 Brightness

Tap on the sunshine icon to bring up the brightness settings of the book. This only affects the brightness levels within the iBooks app itself and doesn't translate to the rest of the iPad, so you won't have to change it back.

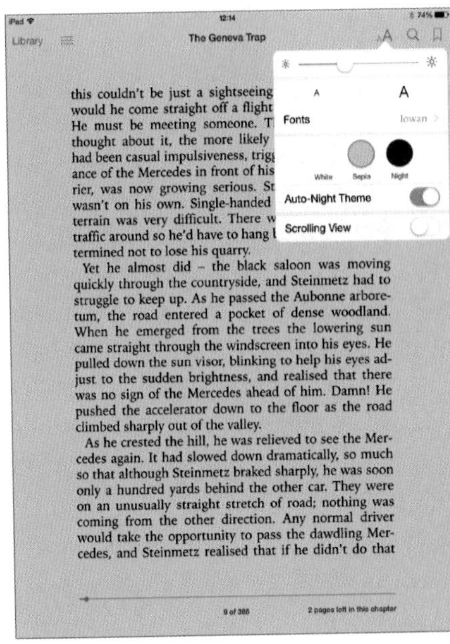

09 Suitable setting

Changing the brightness means that you can alter the reading light to whatever is most comfortable for your eyes. Depending on the ambient light of your surroundings, you may find yourself adjusting the brightness regularly to avoid eye strain.

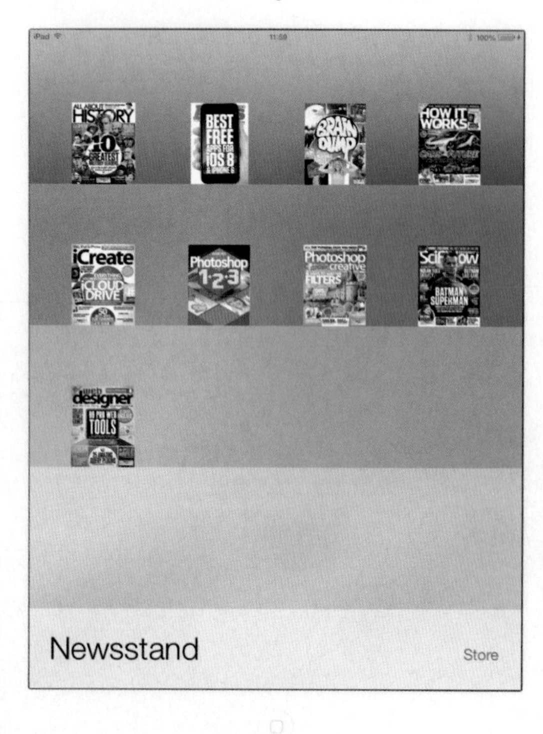

Set up a subscription on Newsstand

The built-in app allows you to subscribe to your favourite magazines and get the new issue on release day

One of the great built-in features of iOS 7 and above is the Newsstand app, which lets you keep on top of all your favourite reading material with ease. This app enables you to create your own personal magazine library, and has its own dedicated store for you to purchase and download from.

The excitement for Newsstand stems from the fact that it means new developers have started afresh on their tablet publications, learning from previous mistakes to provide a better reading experience this time around for iPad users.

The other big positive with Newsstand is that you can set up subscriptions to your favourite magazines, so you never miss an issue, and have each one download to your Newsstand library and be accessible to you anywhere.

More and more magazines are becoming available via Newsstand and the App Store, so the choice is growing constantly, with each publication trying to stand out from the crowd with the best interactive features and extra content. The process of setting up a subscription is simple and a good way to get your bearings if you are new to iOS.

"This built-in app enables you to create your own personal magazine library"

Newsstand Purchase a subscription

01 Open Newsstand

Tap the Newsstand icon to open up the app and see your library shelves. This is where all your downloaded items will be displayed. It's probably empty, but this will soon change!

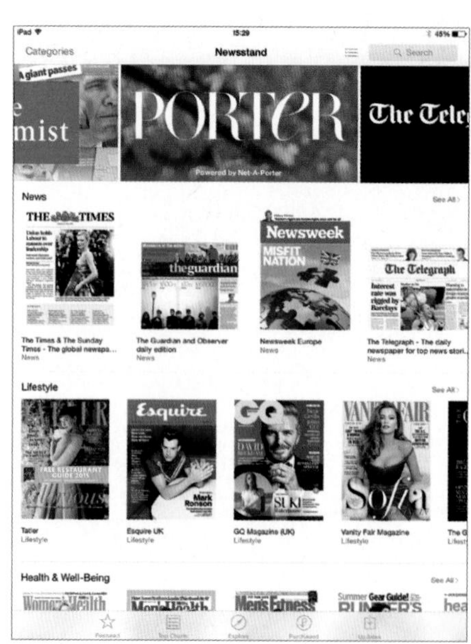

02 Visit the Store

To start your magazine search, tap the 'Store' button at the top-right of the Newsstand display. This will take you to the dedicated Newsstand wing of the App Store.

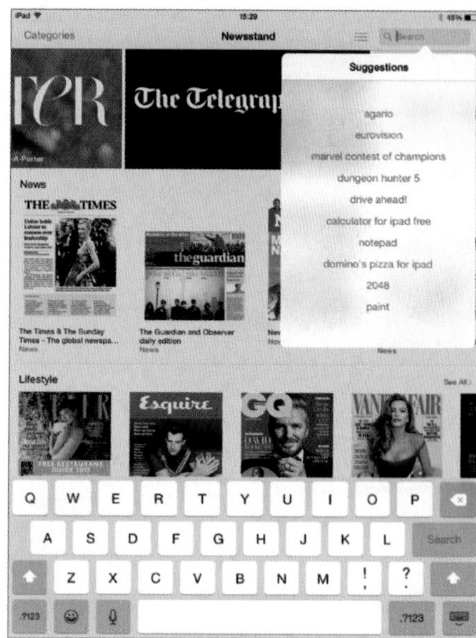

03 Search the Store

Here you can browse through all the magazines on sale – either using the various breakdowns provided by the Store, or tapping on 'Featured' at the bottom of the screen and searching the store.

Navigate the Newsstand shelves

Find your way around this magazine archive

Featured titles
At the top of this page is the animated Featured window, where a selection of the most popular titles are displayed. This is the by far the best place to start your browsing

Menu tabs
Along the bottom of the screen you have various tabs to help you navigate, including charts of the bestselling apps as well as Near Me, which shows popular magazines in your area

Search
If you want to search the store, you can hit any of the buttons at the bottom of the screen to see the Search bar appear

Get more info
When you find a magazine that you want, tap the icon to read extra info on the title, including user reviews and the cost of each issue

Auto Subscriptions
Always keep track of your subscriptions as some automatically renew without you physically tapping to do so. Make a note if a title you download tells you this, which it will do, so you don't get a nasty surprise when you get your bank statement six months after you thought a subscription had ended.

04 Install and download

Once you've found the title you were after, tap Install and enter your iTunes password to download it for free to Newsstand, where you can access back issues and set up subscriptions.

05 What's on offer

You can now tap the magazine to enter its personal library. You can buy individual issues, or tap the Subscribe icon to see what options and deals are on offer before purchasing.

06 Start reading

Once you've chosen your subscription and entered your password, the latest issue will become available in the magazine's library. Tap it to download, and start reading.

Join Twitter and get tweeting

Get into the phenomenon that is social media and connect with friends in an exciting way

It's not an exaggeration to say that Twitter is a social phenomenon. Whether you are already a part of the tweeting community or you are new to it, you will be aware of the terms 'hashtag' and 'trending topics'. And if you aren't, by the end of this tutorial, you will be! In iOS 8, Twitter comes as a part of the package. When you first set up you are given the option to connect your Twitter account or to join the social media service if you haven't already.

Some think of Twitter as 140 characters of mindless chatter, but there is a lot more to it than that. It helps keeps you connected with friends and family, while also allowing you to keep up with what's going on in the world around you. It is also a fantastic networking tool, allowing you to keep in touch with people with similar interests, as well as up-to-the-minute news, opinions and events relating to your field of interest.

In this tutorial we show you how to create an account, follow your favourite Twitter feeds and start sending your own tweets and direct messages to your followers. Discover the world of Twitter and start joining in and connecting to others in a way you ever thought of before.

"Some think of Twitter as 140 characters of mindless chatter, but there is a lot more to it"

Twitter Learn the essentials of the Twitter world

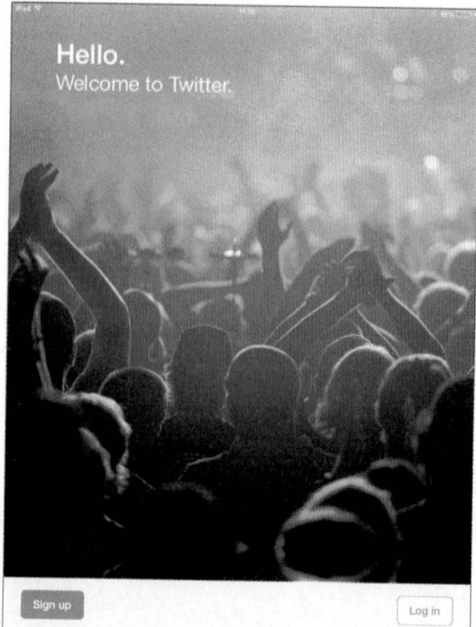

01 Get connected

Head over to the App Store, search for Twitter and tap Get>Install. Once it has installed, tap Open and it will take you to the app. You will be greeted with the option to Sign Up or Log In.

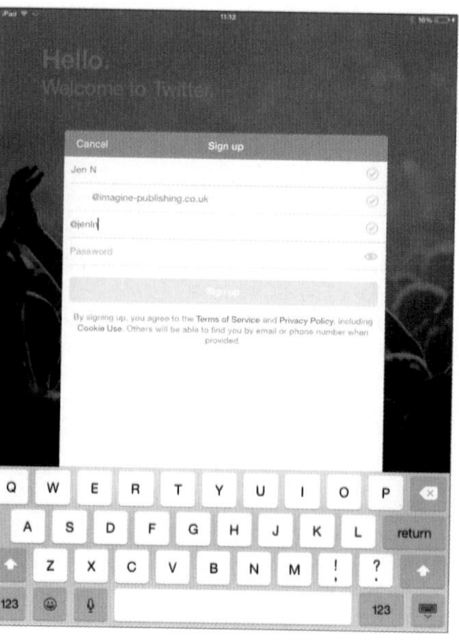

02 Create an account

If you are new to Twitter, tap on Sign Up and go to the Sign Up screen. Fill out your details and choose your Twitter handle (what you will be known as). If you already have an account, simply log in.

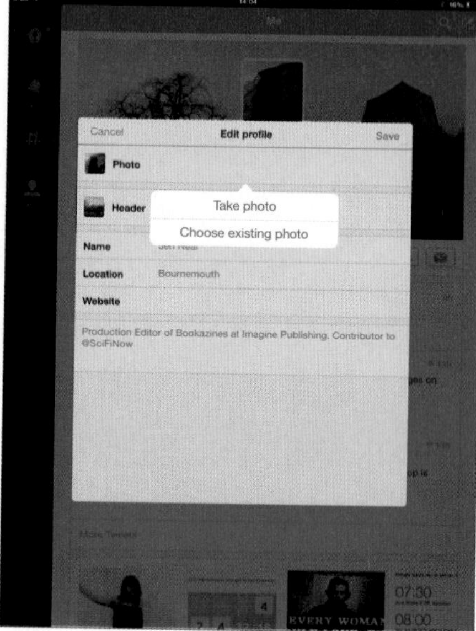

03 Design your profile

Fill out details such as your Bio, which will appear on your profile. To add a picture, tap the picture area and select one from your photos. This will appear next to your tweets on other people's feeds.

Understanding Twitter

Navigate the various options and actions available on your Twitter interface

Follow a user
To follow somebody, tap on the Follow button under their profile header. Once you have followed them it will read Following instead. To Unfollow, all you need to do is tap the button again

Followers
You can see if a user follows you back by the words Follows You next to their Twitter name

Favourite & retweet
You can favourite a tweet so you can find it again easily. If a user tweets something you wish to share, then you can hit the Retweet button to share with your own followers

Hashtags
Placing a hashtag before a word or phrase in Twitter turns it into a link that allows you to find and participate in a conversation on that topic. Make sure keywords or phrases with multiple words don't include a space between them. All you have to do is click on the keyword to see other Tweets on the same topic, and others who do the same will be able to see yours.

Statistics
This is where you see how many tweets, followers or followees a user has. Tap here to view the list of names

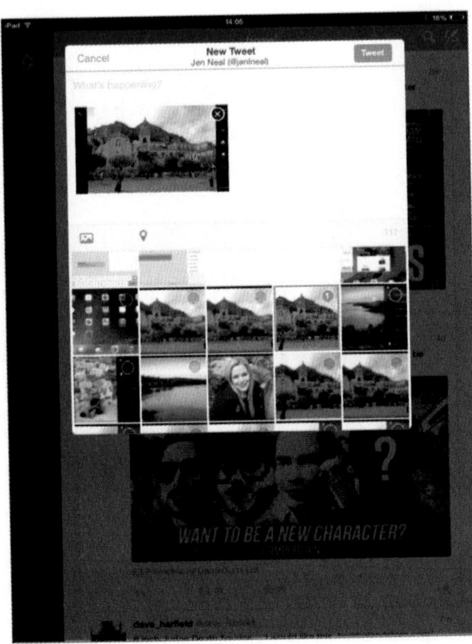

04 Tweet away!

To send a new tweet, tap on the quill square in the top-right. Type in your tweet and tap the Tweet button. This will now appear on your feed. You can add links to websites and pictures.

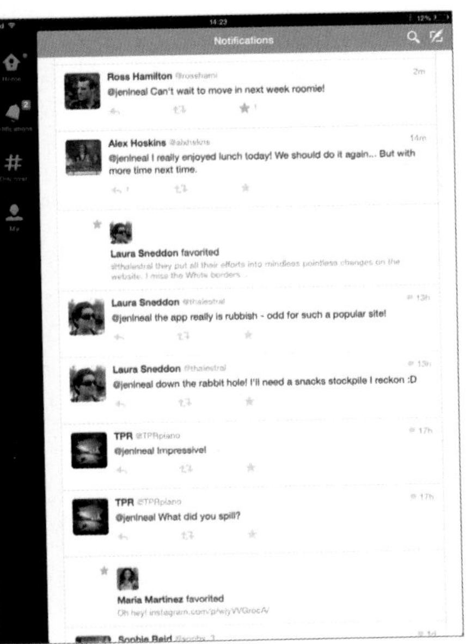

05 Get notifications

Tap on the Notification tab on the left-hand side of the screen to view replies, favourites and retweets. In order to reply, tap the arrow, or simply type '@ (username)' to talk to another user.

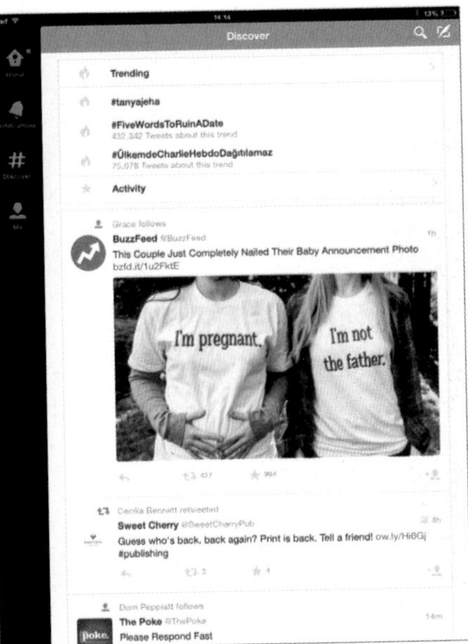

06 Join the conversation

The Discover tab is where you will see trending topics and popular tweets from the people you follow. There will be suggestions of people to follow and the most popular topics, or 'Trending topics'.

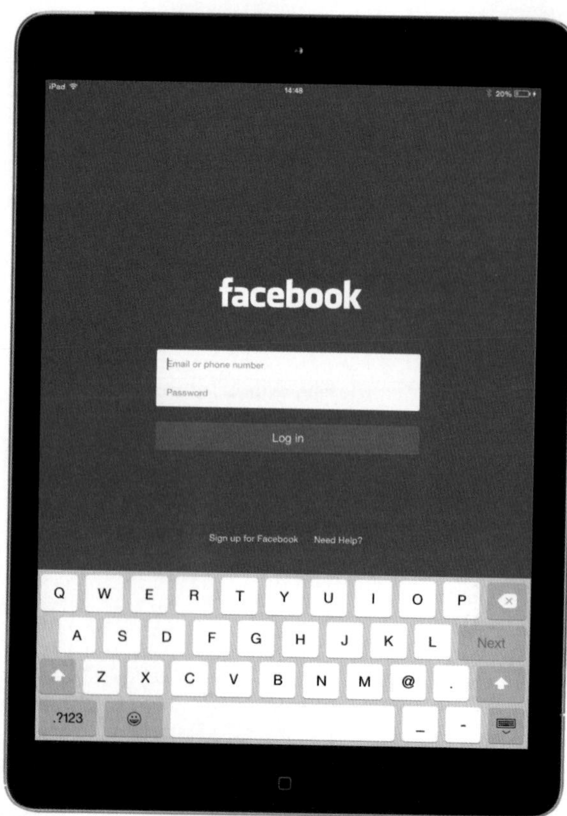

Facebook your friends & family

Get sociable with your friends and family on the biggest social network going!

Facebook is everywhere, from online trends laying their roots in the pages of the popular networking site, to news breaking to the masses using the system. And with such a large proportion of the adult population connecting with friends and family in this way, it is likely that you will be missing out on the conversation if you aren't a part of it too.

Posting to Facebook is simple. You can easily share any aspect of your life with all your friends on the news feed or directly on a specific person's timeline. From pictures of a recent project or holiday to personal thoughts and opinions, it is one of the best ways to keep your friends and family updated on your life.

Facebook even has the ability for you to link your interests with pages from a wide range of subjects, from TV shows to the more obscure hobbies. Here we will show you how to find what you are looking for to formulate a news feed that is perfect for you, and which you will enjoy engaging with on a daily basis.

So connect with your friends, like their pictures, comment on their statuses and generally keep up-to-date with what is going on in your social circles.

"It is likely that you will be missing out on the conversation if you aren't a part of it too"

Facebook Connect with your friends

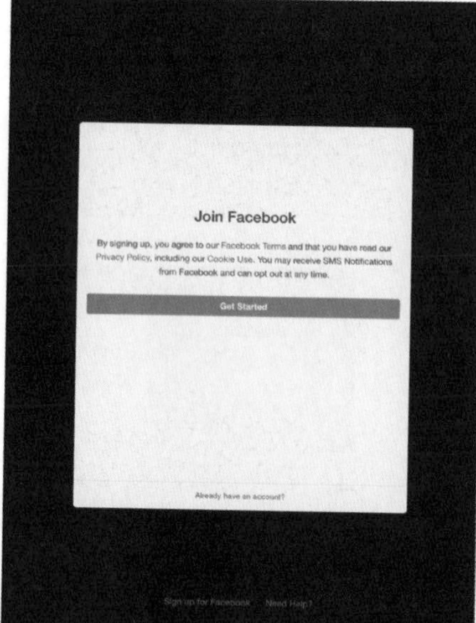

01 Join Facebook

Download the app from the App Store. Open the app and sign in if you have an account. If you don't, tap Sign up for Facebook at the bottom of the screen and follow the instructions.

02 Orientate yourself

Once you have signed up and added your first profile image, you will see your News Feed, which will fill up with your friends' statuses. To view your profile, tap your name in the top-right corner.

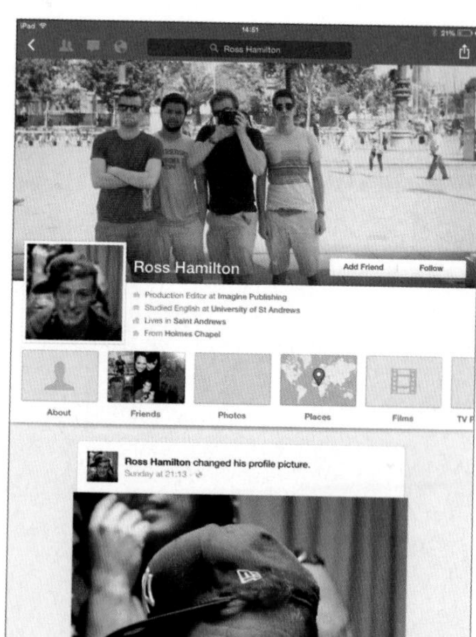

03 Connect with friends

To add new friends, type your friend's name in the search box. People with mutual friends will appear at the top, as will people with similar locations or job. Tap on Add Friend.

Stay in touch with Facebook

Familiarise yourself with the features of the Facebook news feed

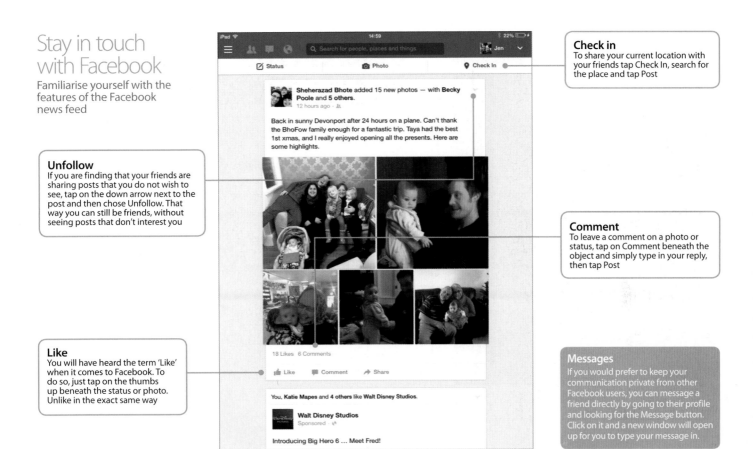

Check in
To share your current location with your friends tap Check In, search for the place and tap Post

Unfollow
If you are finding that your friends are sharing posts that you do not wish to see, tap on the down arrow next to the post and then chose Unfollow. That way you can still be friends, without seeing posts that don't interest you

Comment
To leave a comment on a photo or status, tap on Comment beneath the object and simply type in your reply, then tap Post

Like
You will have heard the term 'Like' when it comes to Facebook. To do so, just tap on the thumbs up beneath the status or photo. Unlike in the exact same way

Messages
If you would prefer to keep your communication private from other Facebook users, you can message a friend directly by going to their profile and looking for the Message button. Click on it and a new window will open up for you to type your message in.

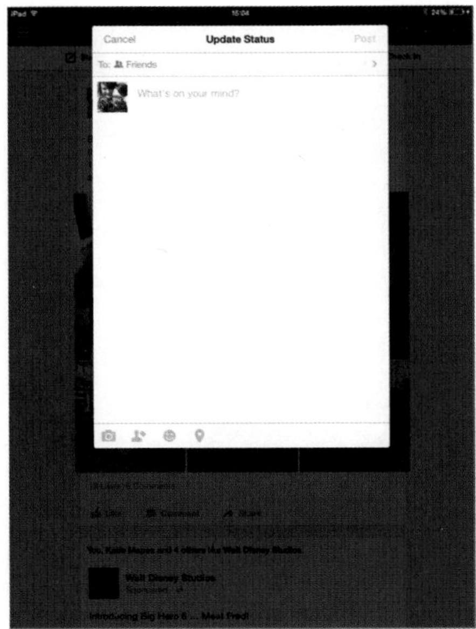

04 Status update

To share something with your friends you need to update your status. Simply tap on Status and type out your update. You can add photos, tag friends, and add locations to your posts at the bottom.

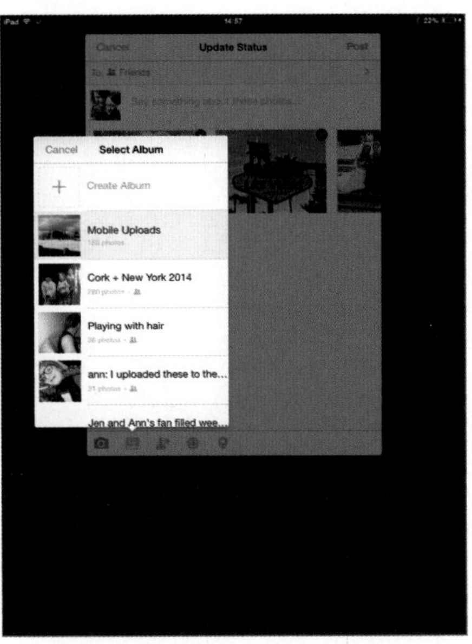

05 Share images

Tap on Photos at the top. You will have to allow photo access. Tap on the photos and tap Done. At the bottom you can add to albums and tag friends to your post. When done tap Post.

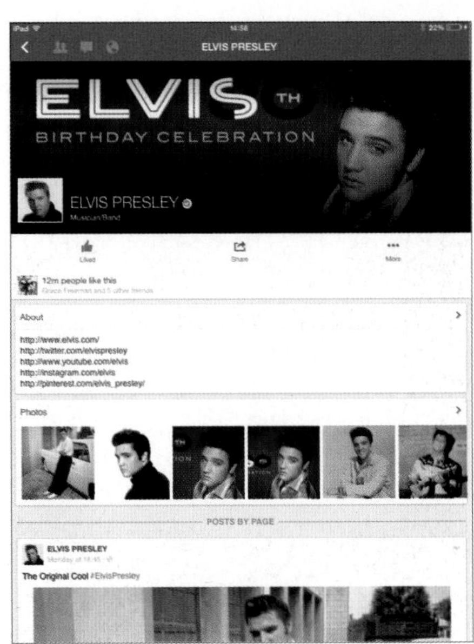

06 Keep up with your interests

Search for your interests in the top bar and you will be given the options. Tap on the name of the page to go to it, then tap on the Like thumb beneath their user picture to like the page.

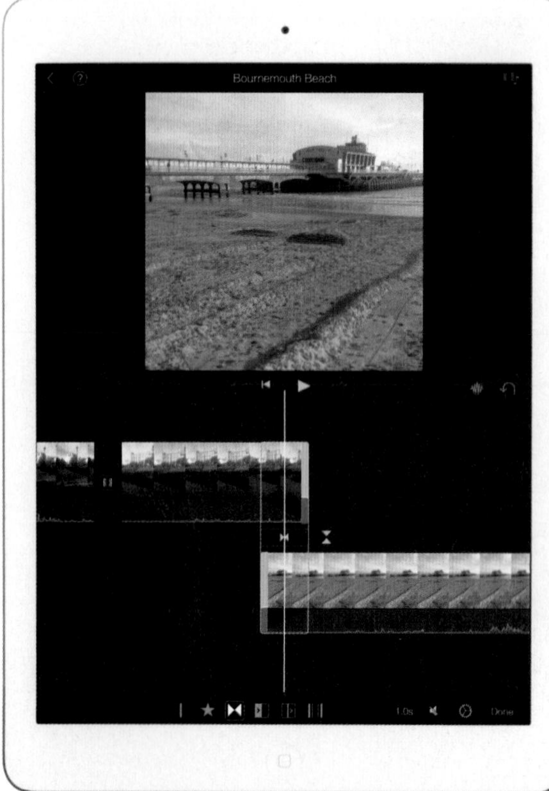

Edit a movie in iMovie

You can edit iMovie content as many times as you like and the results will always look professional

Touch is the key word when it comes to editing projects in iMovie on your iPad. You can swipe a clip up to the top of the screen to delete it, pull a bar to lengthen it or hold it to choose more subtle options. Apple has done an exceptional job of ensuring that the system works as naturally as possible. It is likely that every movie project will require some tweaking, so take some time to view what you have put together before converting it to a movie. The conversion process can take a while to complete, so be patient to be sure your project looks right first time.

If you want to create professional-looking movies with minimal editing, the app's trailer function is worth checking out because it ensures your clips flow well, with lots of hints along the way. This tutorial covers the basics, but remember: the trick to creating professional content is to remove the need for editing as much as possible. However, iMovie lets you edit every part your movie and the process is as natural as can be.

"Apple has done an exceptional job of ensuring that the system works as naturally as possible"

iMovie Edit iMovie projects

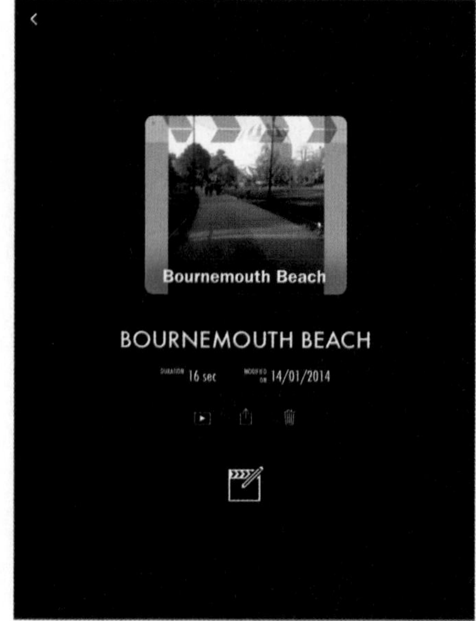

01 Tap to edit

All of the projects you create in iMovie will be shown in a list on the front screen. Simply tap one to bring up a title screen for the project. Tap again to start the editing process.

02 Delete clips

If you need to delete specific clips in a project after you have viewed the movie, simply hold it with your finger and swipe it up the screen. It will disappear immediately from the project.

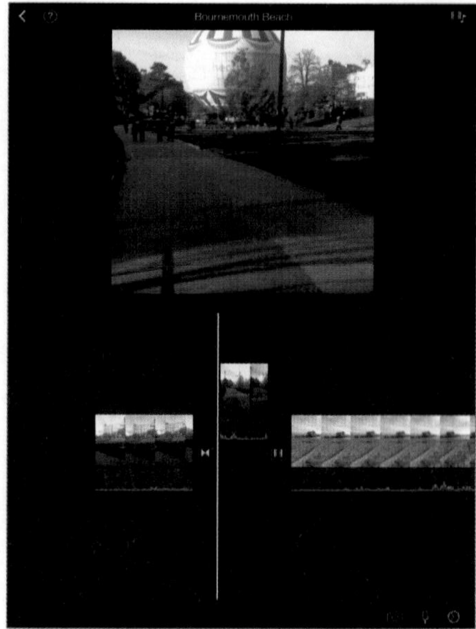

03 Move clips

To move clips within the project you need to hold your finger down on one and then drag it to the desired place within the timeline. You will use this technique often as you get more experienced.

All the tools you need

Multiple utilities in one screen

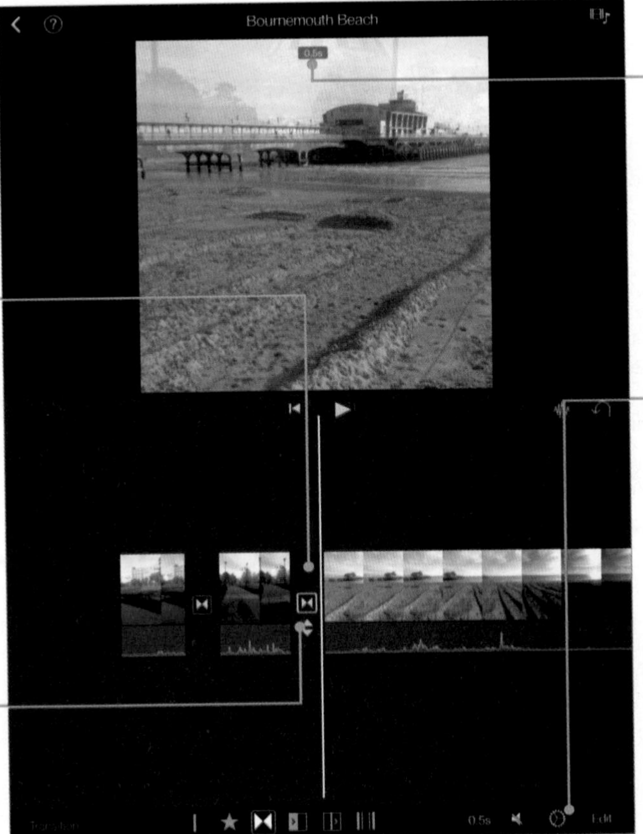

Detailed information
Information is shown on screen as you make adjustments so that you can be sure that everything will flow as you want it to. It's the perfect balance between simplicity and complexity

Clip timings
You can adjust the length of each individual clip by moving the yellow bars left and right. Tapping each clip will make them available and they are easy to manage

Total changes
With this icon you can change the entire theme of your movie as well as the start and end transitions. Try each one to see which works the best for the content you have included

Clever transitions
Tapping the bow tie icon between each clip lets you change the transitions to fade in and fade out as you prefer. You can choose different transitions for each clip to add variety

Movies and projects
As you edit projects you need to be aware that this will not change the movies you have already exported. They are saved files which will stay the same until you delete them. Each edited project needs to be converted again to create a new movie.

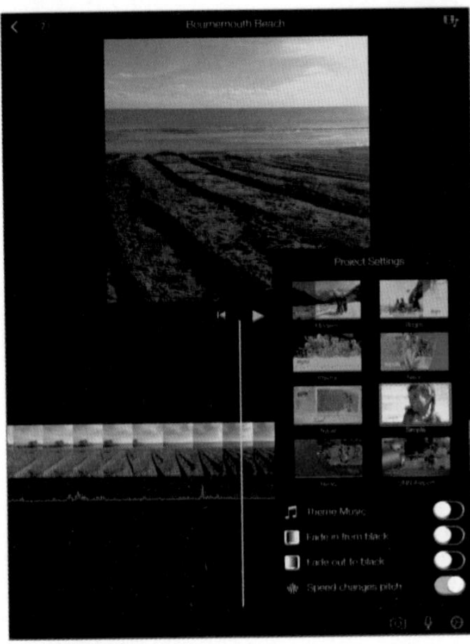

04 Project settings

Video clips that are used within a project will need to be managed. Hit the cog icon in the bottom-right to select an appropriate theme or choose to fade in or out.

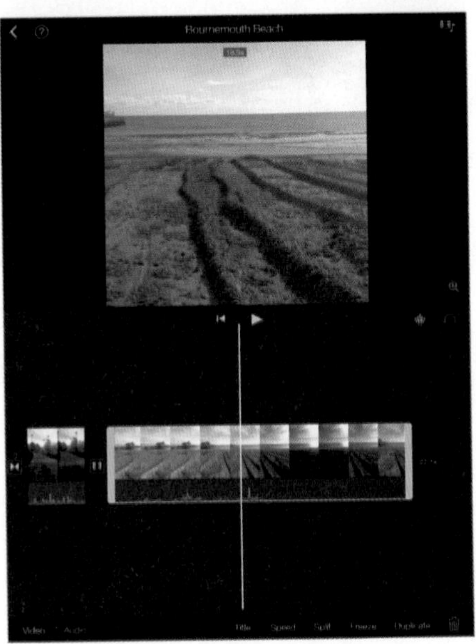

05 Different trimming types

Trim selections by dragging the yellow bars accordingly. Trimming a photo in iMovie changes the amount of time it is displayed, but video trimming will cut out some of the selected clip.

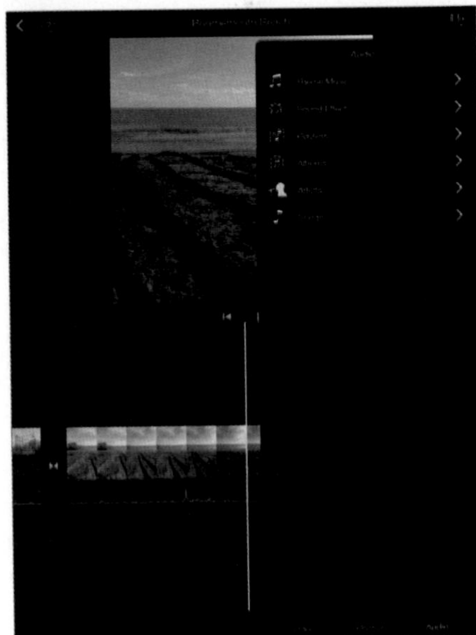

06 Sync the audio

Once you've chosen your subscription and entered your password, the latest issue will become available in the magazine's library. Tap it to download and start reading.

Inserting and arranging clips in iMovie

Learn the basics of adding clips to timelines and find out what other insert options there are

With iMovie on your iPad you are no longer limited to adding your clips in a linear order to build your movie. With the various insert options you can now create cutaways, add images side by side each other and quickly edit your clips before adding them to your timeline. The more time you can spend shortening your clips from the clip library, the easier it will be for you to edit your movie in the timeline. Rather than dumping your entire clip into a timeline, you can shorten it to roughly the length you want it to be, and then insert it.

By doing this you're effectively building an assembly cut of your edit, which can then be refined as necessary. Follow these steps to learn how best to place your clips in iMovie.

> "With the various insert options you can now create cutaways, add images side by side each other and quickly edit your clips"

Create a timeline Adding and arranging clips

01 Browsing footage

In the footage bin tap Video to display all video clips on your iPad. iMovie will display all clips by default. Tap the Back icon to view clips in dated folders. This can also be done with photos.

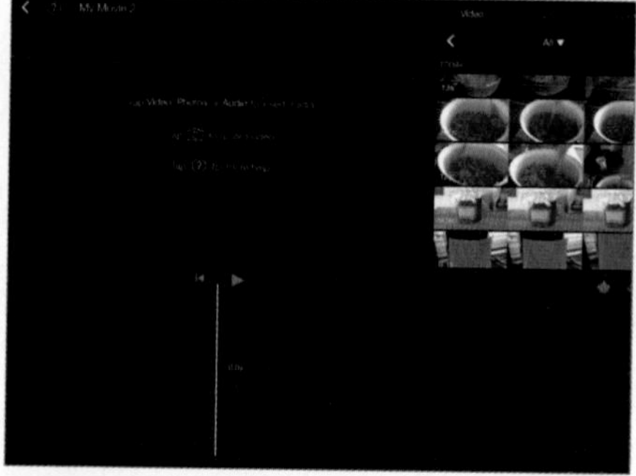

02 Selecting footage

Your clips will appear in a column of thumbnails. Tap on one to select it in its entirety. A yellow band will appear around the clip. Tap and drag upward to scroll through your clips.

03 Preview and edit

Tap the Play icon to preview a clip. Press and drag on the yellow band at the beginning or end of a clip to shorten it. If you deselect the clip you'll have to repeat this process.

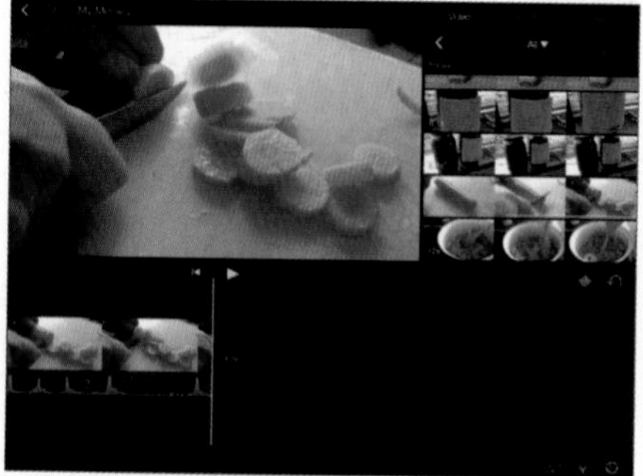

04 Insert your clip

Once you've shortened your clip, tap the down-facing arrow to add it to the timeline. It's easier to edit clips down before adding them to a timeline rather than afterward.

05 The Insert toolbar

With a new clip selected in your clip bin, tap on the More options icon to view all the alternative methods by which clips can be added to your main timeline to build up the story.

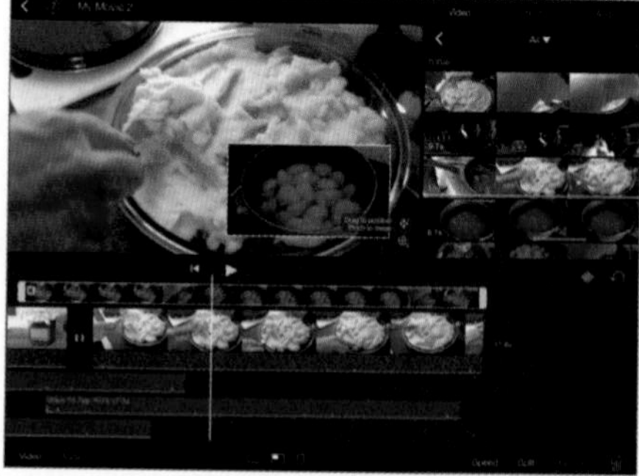

06 Insert options

Adding a clip as a cutaway will place it on a new layer above other clips in the timeline. Use the picture-in-picture tool to insert a clip over another one in a smaller box.

Editing clips in iMovie

There are various ways to edit and insert clips in iMovie…

Precision Editor
The Precision Editor can be used to adjust the starting and ending points of clips more accurately. Tap on a transition between two clips, then tap on the yellow arrows below the transition icon. This will open the Precision Editor in your timeline, where you can then determine the exact starting and ending frame of a clip.

Side by Side
The Side by Side option enables you to create a split-screen effect so you can see two clips at the same time within the timeline

Import audio
Tap here to import the audio from a clip into the timeline. The audio will be placed at whatever point the Playhead cursor is within the timeline

Editing in timeline
Tap on a clip in the timeline then press and drag on the yellow band to shorten it. Tap the Split button in the bottom toolbar to cut the clip in two

Arranging clips
To place a clip in between two others in the timeline, move the Playhead cursor to that point and then insert it

Insert tools

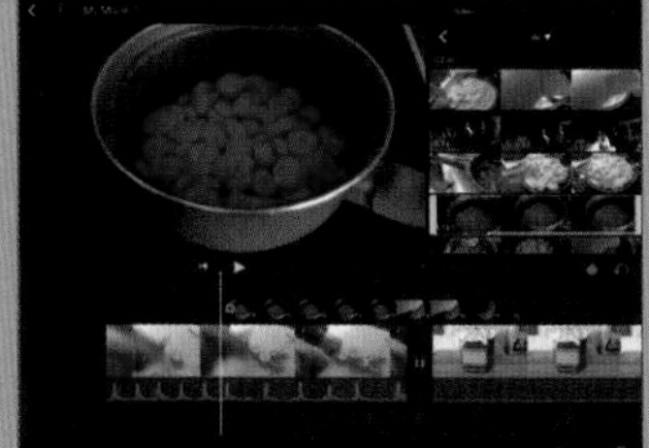

Cutaways
Cutaways add variation to keep the story dynamic and interesting. As soon as the Playhead cursor reaches a cutaway shot, your movie will cut to it. Cutaway shots can be split into multiple halves and moved around to any point in your movie.

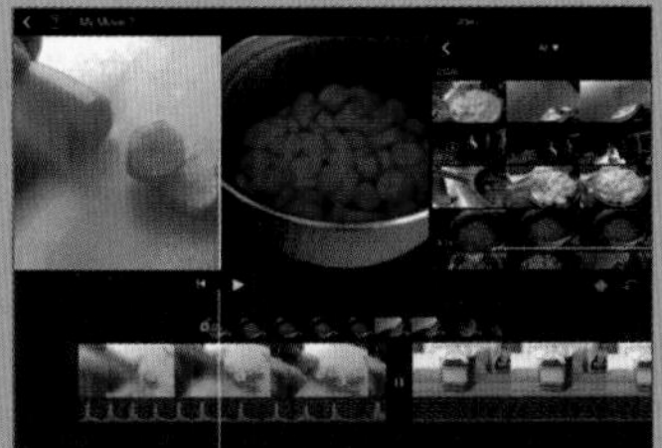

Side by side
Use the Side by side mode to view two sections of video simultaneously. Press and drag on either clip in Side by side mode to reposition it. You can also pinch either of the clips to zoom in and out. This option works for any clip in iMovie.

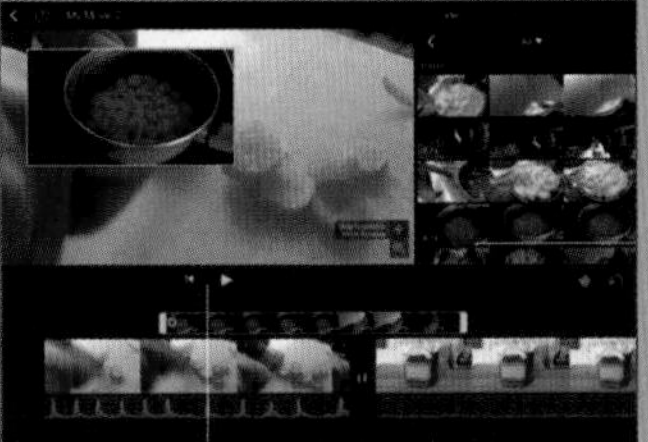

Picture in Picture
Creating a similar effect to Side by side, this mode keeps a primary clip. With a Picture in Picture clip selected, tap the four-way arrow icon in the viewer window to reposition and resize it. Use the zoom tool to reposition the clip within its box.

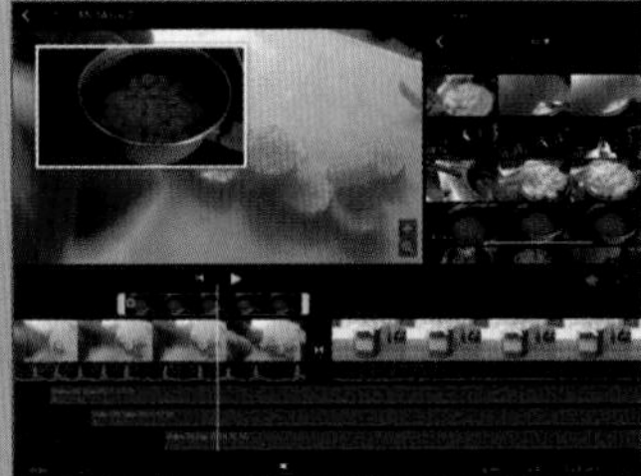

Audio tracks
You can add a single or even multiple audio tracks to add character and atmosphere to the timeline. These can be imported independent of the video clip they are linked to. You can also record audio with your iPad's microphone within iMovie.

Make music in GarageBand

Apple's GarageBand app is an easy-to-use mobile recording studio that you can use to craft your own brand of music. Here we show you how to get started

By far the best thing about GarageBand is its overall accessibility. No prior musical know-how is needed to start using Apple's music-making app because all of the tools that you need are made instantly available, right down to the actual instruments.

When you first create a new song, you can choose from a wide range of built-in 'smart' instruments that you can play on-screen using a variety of touch gestures. You can strum the chords of an acoustic guitar or lash out individual notes on an electric, pound out the rhythm on an on-screen drum kit and even add some orchestral strings into the mix. Whatever you choose to play, you can effortlessly record and view each track on a mixing desk, trimming excess flab, looping or adding effects to make sure you get the perfect sound.

Better still, if you own an instrument like an electric guitar then with the right adaptor (such as an iRig), you can plug in directly to your iPad and play for real. And if your own amp isn't great there are a stack of virtual ones included to help you obtain the sound you desire. Finished songs are then automatically saved to your iCloud so you can continue working on them on a different device later, and exporting your tracks to social media or your own iTunes library couldn't be more simple. Here we show you how to start recording and making simple edits to your tracks.

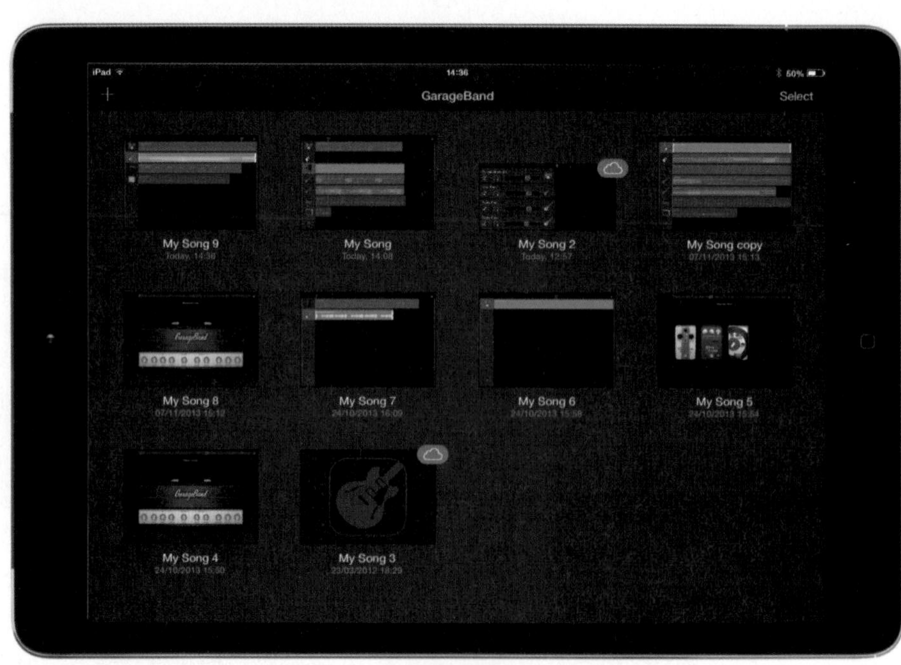

"When you first create a new song, you can choose from a wide range of built-in 'smart' instruments that you can play on-screen using a variety of touch gestures"

GarageBand Start making sweet music

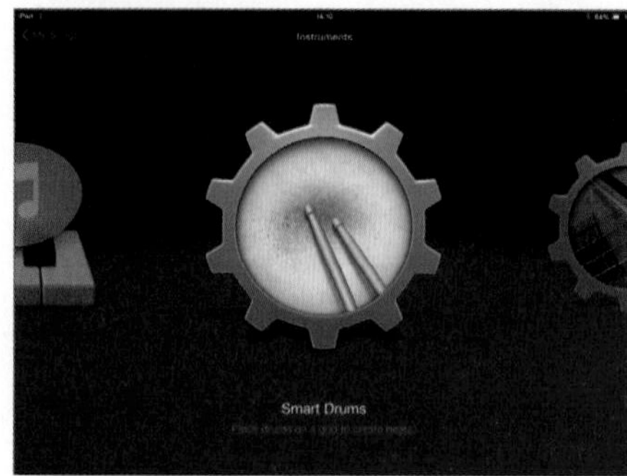

01 New project

When you launch GarageBand, tap the '+' icon in the top-left corner of the screen and then scroll through the various instruments on offer. Tap on an instrument to go to its playing interface.

02 Start recording

Hit the record button and start using your on-screen instrument. When you've recorded a few bars, stop recording and tap the tracks icon to the left of the playback controls.

03 Trim your track

Tap the track and move the handles on either side to trim the segment. Tap it again to display options, including Loop, which you can use to extend and continue a trimmed track.

The GarageBand interface

Create sweet music in no time with these simple controls

Your tracks
Any tracks that you record using the various instruments will be listed on the tracks screen. You can switch between the track and instrument screen using these icons. While on the track screen you can trim, and loop your tracks

Settings
Tapping the spanner icon will bring up the general settings that include the option to include a metronome to help with your beat and timing and a count in to help you get started. You can also adjust the tempo, key and time signature

Edit tracks
Tap on a track to 'frame' it and then drag the edges of the frame to trim. You can then tap on it to display various options including Trim, Split, Loop and Edit. Tap the levels icon to mute tracks or adjust the sound levels in the mix

Adding instruments
Tap this icon to add more instruments into the mix. You can choose from a variety of smart instruments that you can play on-screen or plug in your own and add a wide range of cool effects to your sonic arsenal

Export your songs
When you have finished recording and mixing your song, tap 'My Songs' and it will save to iCloud and you'll be taken back to your projects screen. From there, tap the Select option in the top-right corner, tap on a song and then tap the share icon. You will find options to share it to social media sites or to your iTunes library.

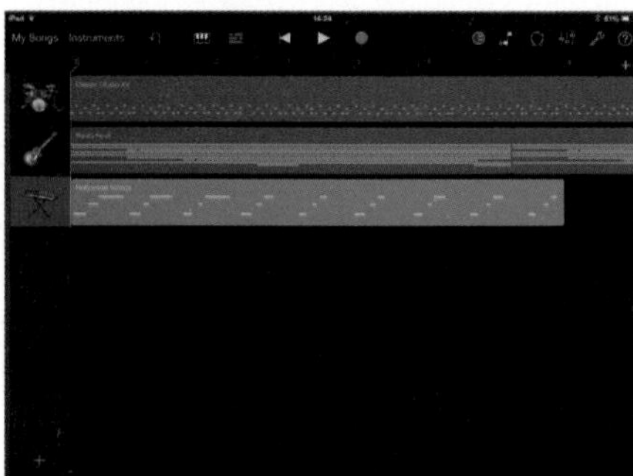

04 Add more instruments

While in track view, hit the '+' icon in the lower-left corner and choose another instrument to add. Record additional tracks as before and they will stack up on the track screen.

05 Record real instruments

If you own the appropriate adaptor you can connect real instruments to your iOS device and play with a range of effects. Tap the plug in the top-left corner and slide on Monitor to hear it.

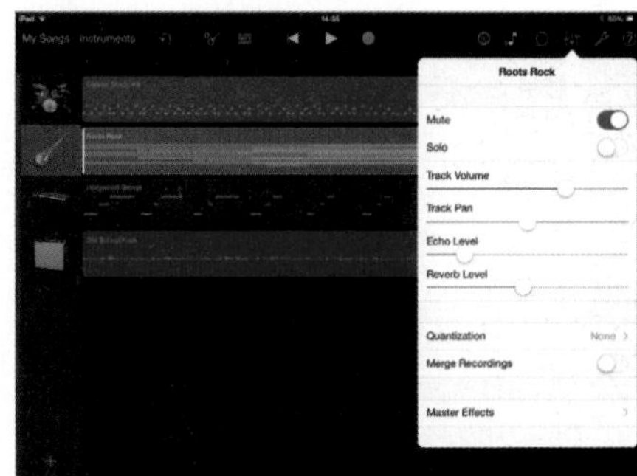

06 Mute tracks

If you wish to mute certain tracks to help with the editing process then select the track, tap the levels icon in the top-right corner and slide the Mute switch to the On position.

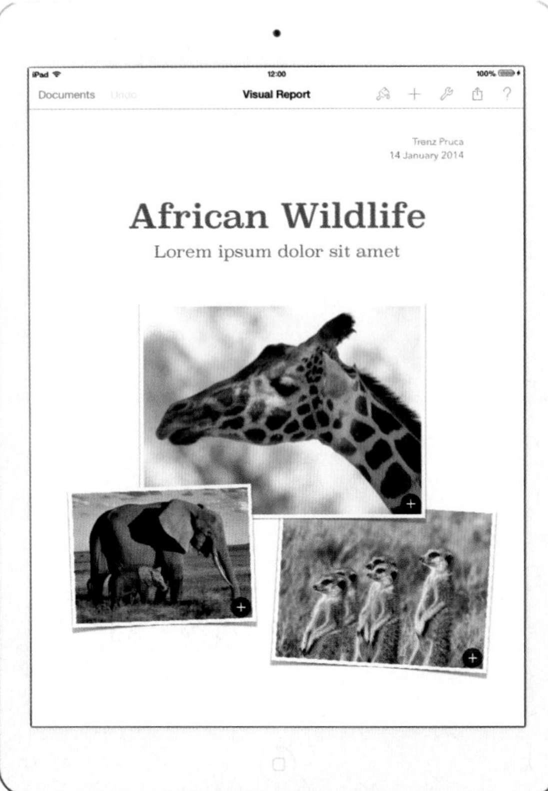

Design documents in the Pages app

Apple's Pages takes the mobile word-processing experience to a whole new level

Pages is not like most word processors – it combines the most used features in an interface that includes very few icons. Getting to know the app is not difficult, although it does help to understand where the main functions reside in order to get you started, and doing so will open up the power within.

Despite its rather sparse interface, the Pages app is packed with formatting options and clever little tricks that make previously tiresome manoeuvres a thing of the past. For example, you can move an embedded image around an article and the words will automatically reposition themselves around it. All the included templates are also completely customisable, which enables you to get creating in no time at all.

However, not all specific needs are catered for in this word processing app, such as a word count, but Apple has done a good job of defining the most commonly used functions that people need, including being able to share your creations without touching a desktop - which is another great advantage. You can even decide which format to save these documents in and, best of all, if you have iCloud enabled then you can sync your pages wirelessly between devices. This means you can start a new layout on your iPad and finish it later on your iPhone or Mac. In this tutorial we guide you through the basics of this incredibly versatile app.

Pages Create stunning documents on the move

01 Grab the app

Search for Pages in the App Store. If your iPad came with iOS 7 or above then it is completely free. The first time you visit the App Store with iOS 7 or above you will be prompted to get it.

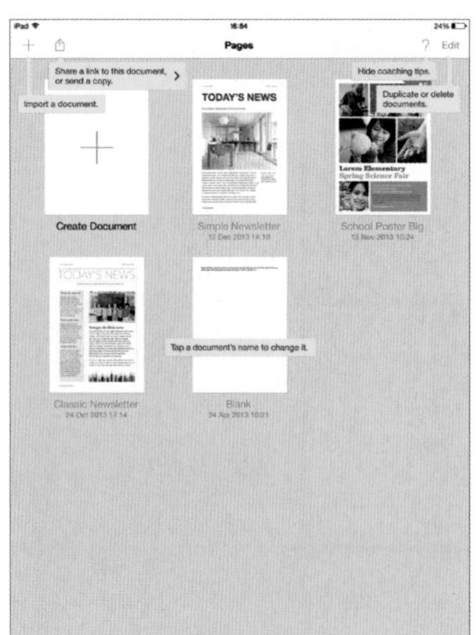

02 Have a look around

Pages is so visual that you could just wander around the icons and start typing, but the best place to start is the pre-loaded tips, accessible by tapping the question mark in the top right.

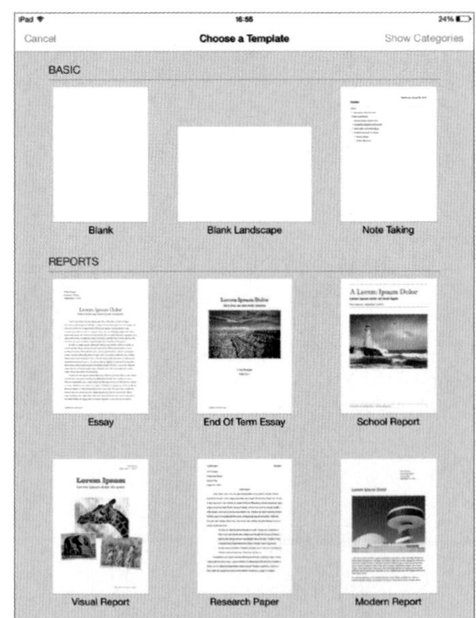

03 Create your first document

In the first screen, tap the '+' icon at the top and then tap New document. This will bring up a screen with templates on. You can choose anything from a blank page to a party invitation.

Making the most of Pages

Learn all the tricks of the Pages trade

Extra formatting
Simply tap the brush icon to access extra formatting features such as bullet points, subtitles and headings. The options automatically change if you have an image highlighted

Document handling
Your completed documents are never far away. A tap of the 'My Documents' icon will bring up a page showing all of your saved work. Each document is saved automatically after every change

All the standards
All of the standard formatting options such as bold, italics and underline are easily accessible from the top bar. Highlight a word and click an icon for the desired effect

Easy image manipulation
Once inserted, images can be resized, moved and even twisted to the position you need. The words will automatically move to around them and into the right position

Work with templates
Templates can make the process of creating eye-catching documents incredibly easy and Pages includes a variety of styles. Once you create a new document using a template you can change the images and all of the background text to your needs. You can also create your own templates for future use.

04 Test the options

Type a few words and then check the formatting options at the top. Select words by tapping and holding, at which point you can use the icons to format the text. Clicking 'i' gives further options.

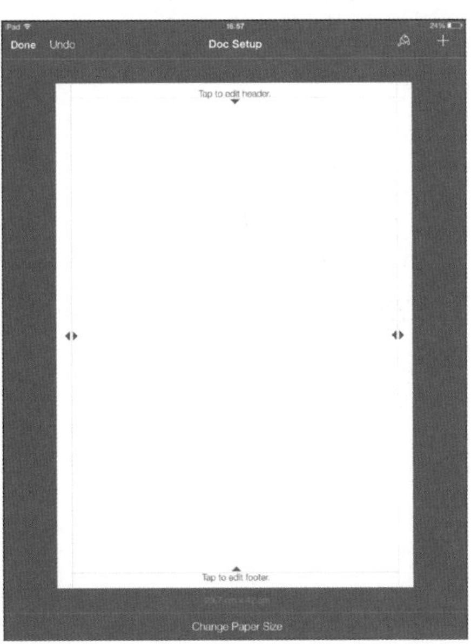

05 Delve deeper

Other options include a document setup wizard, defined by the top-right spanner icon and a quick tap of the picture icon lets you insert an image into your document.

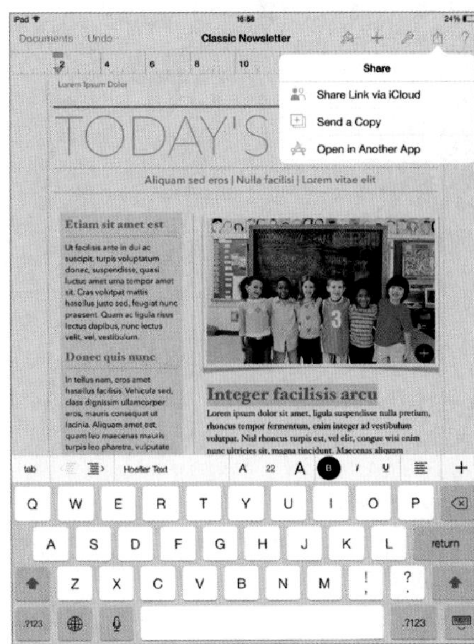

06 Share your work

You never need to save your work because Pages does it whenever a change is made, but you can export it to PDF, Pages or Word format and send by email with the tap of one icon.

Make spreadsheets with Numbers

Use Numbers to create business or personal spreadsheets to suit all tastes

Spreadsheets are a part of everyone's lives these days and have taken on multiple roles in business and at home. Most spreadsheet programs tend to focus on the business side because this is where they are mainly used, but spreadsheets have myriad other uses that aren't often explored.

Numbers puts multiple uses front and centre with special templates built in, which brings a new way of working to the mobile user. The process of creating the spreadsheet you want becomes much quicker, which suits the on-the-go nature of devices like the iPad.

However, the interface and function locations may feel alien to those who have used Excel for a long time, therefore a short introduction will help you to get to grips with the app quickly. There are a lot of functions built in to Numbers and some of these are not obvious, so take a look at these simple steps to start number-crunching straight away.

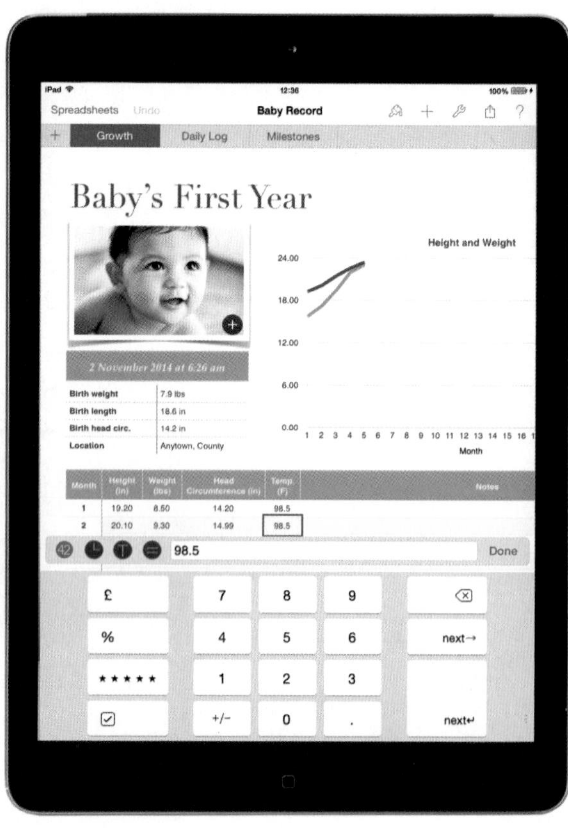

"Most spreadsheet programs tend to focus on the business side, but spreadsheets have myriad uses"

Numbers Explore the power of this spreadsheet app

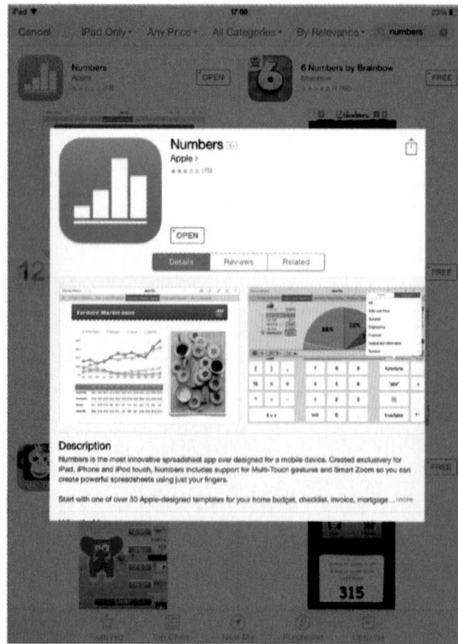

01 Grab the app

If your iPad came with iOS 7 or above, Numbers is available for you to download for free from the App Store. It's well worth taking time to grab it, even if you only need spreadsheets occasionally, so head to the App Store and download.

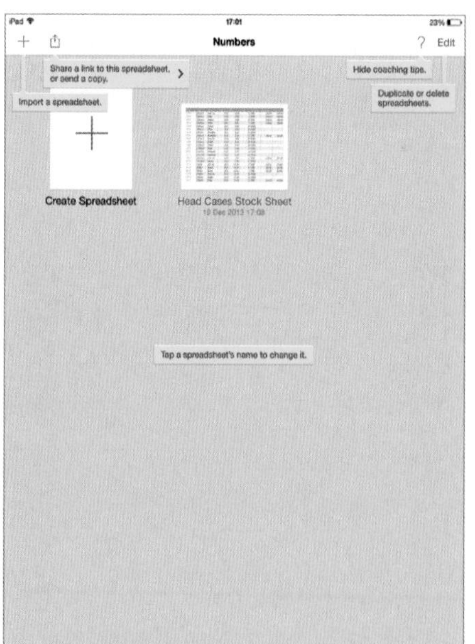

02 View coaching tips

To get to grips with the Numbers interface, tap the question mark icon in the top right-hand corner of the app to bring up some handy tips that will explain some of the basic functions. This should help you get to know the essentials quite well.

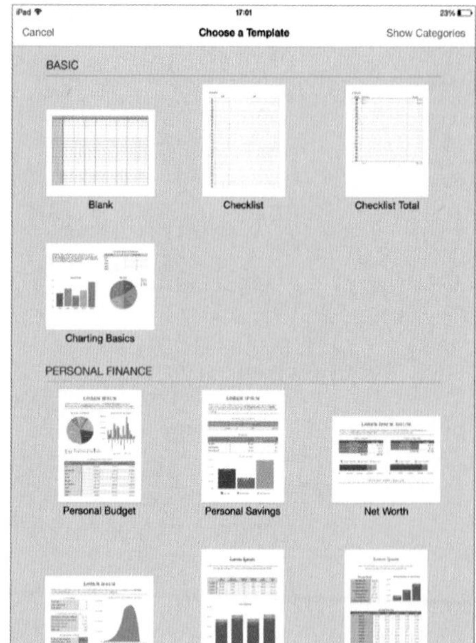

03 Your first spreadsheet

Tap the screen to create a new spreadsheet. You'll now be offered a choice of templates, which include everything from a blank sheet to a mortgage calculator. Each template can be amended to suit your needs.

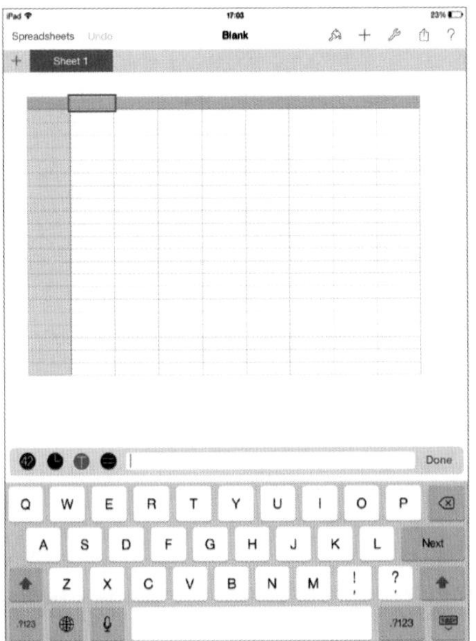

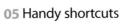

04 Add data
Choose the blank template option in the top-left corner and double-tap an empty cell. This brings up a dialog with four icons for numbers, date/time, text and formulas. This should help you avoid formatting issues when you input some data.

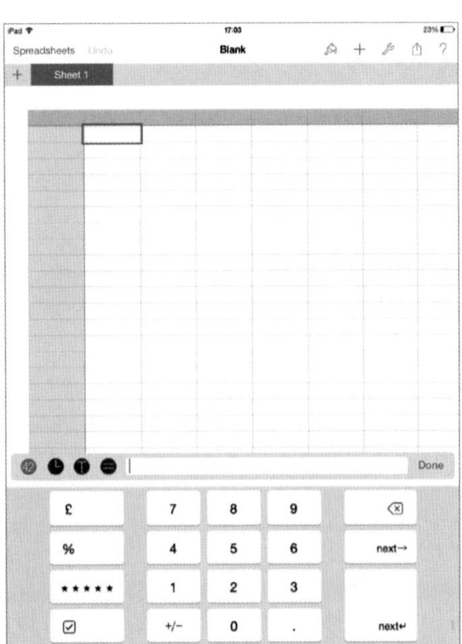

05 Handy shortcuts
Tapping any of the icons brings up a dialog with shortcuts which may be relevant to the data you want to input. For example, the number icon will bring up a number pad plus a percentage button and more.

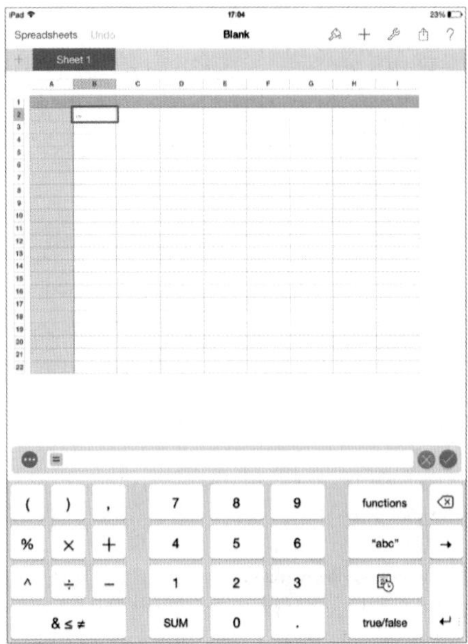

06 Use the data
Once you've understood where each function resides you can now do something with your content. Tap the '=' icon and you can choose from a wide range of simple functions that will pop up to start creating formulae.

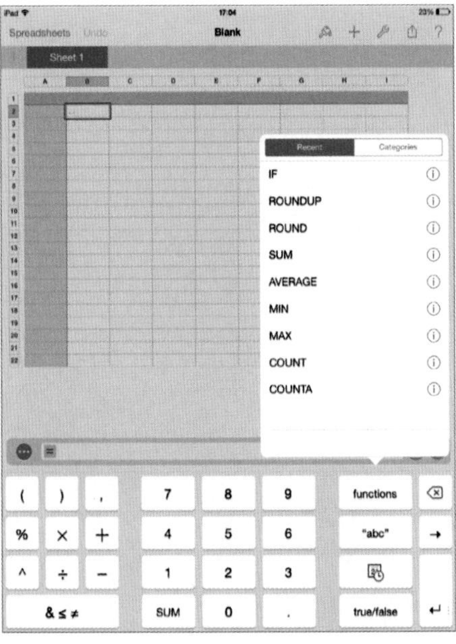

07 Advanced functions
Once you have created your spreadsheet, you should get to know the functions button, which is a window to some serious capability. This includes categories of advanced functions such as Trigonometric, Engineering and Statistical.

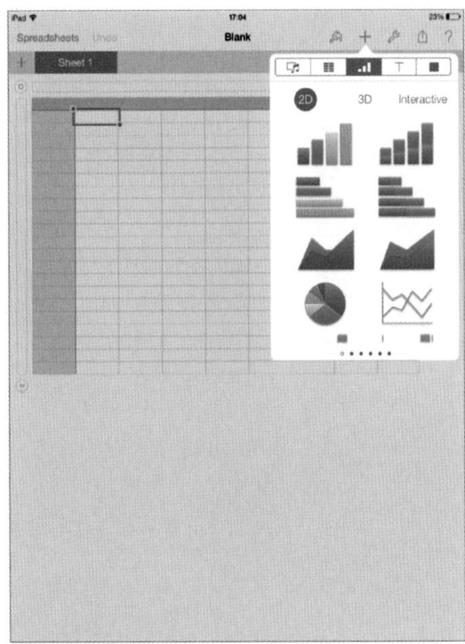

08 Add some media
Once you have your basic data built into your spreadsheet, you can tap the plus icon in the top-right and insert photos, tables and shapes which will help to make the data more visual. The graphs could help you see your data more clearly.

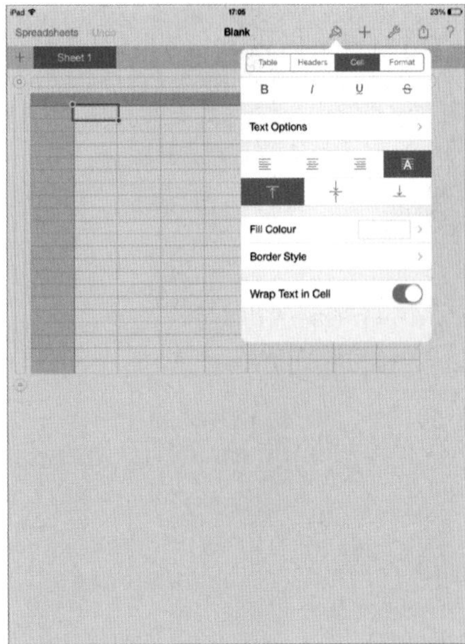

09 Practise your touch
Numbers is touch-only and this is likely to present certain problems at first, but the more you practise the more natural the user experience begins to feel. The interface looks simple, but it hides a huge range of options, so get experimenting!

Make a holiday slideshow in Keynote

Turn your summer holiday snaps into a beautiful slideshow with Keynote

How many times have you gone on holiday, taken hundreds of photos, and then done absolutely nothing with them? Because the iPhone has such a brilliant camera that's always to hand in your pocket, all too often people will snap dozens of photos on a trip. More often than not, these brilliant shots are allowed gather dust in an iPhone, Mac or camera, left unseen except when you're scrolling through a packed iPhoto library. So it's time to do something about it.

Keynote might not seem the first port of call for a photo slideshow, but the tools it offers actually make it more than suited to creating a fantastic finished slideshow to share with your family and friends. Before you know it, your daytrip snaps will be primed for sharing in a way that doesn't bore the viewer! So let's make the most of your holiday shots in nine simple steps.

> "Before you know it, your daytrip snaps will be primed for sharing in a way that doesn't bore the viewer!"

Animating your slideshow

Quickly create dynamic effects with Keynote's animations and transitions

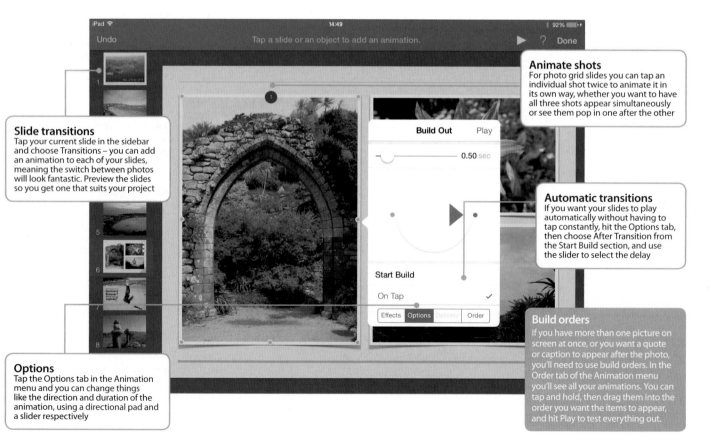

Animate shots
For photo grid slides you can tap an individual shot twice to animate it in its own way, whether you want to have all three shots appear simultaneously or see them pop in one after the other

Slide transitions
Tap your current slide in the sidebar and choose Transitions – you can add an animation to each of your slides, meaning the switch between photos will look fantastic. Preview the slides so you get one that suits your project

Automatic transitions
If you want your slides to play automatically without having to tap constantly, hit the Options tab, then choose After Transition from the Start Build section, and use the slider to select the delay

Build orders
If you have more than one picture on screen at once, or you want a quote or caption to appear after the photo, you'll need to use build orders. In the Order tab of the Animation menu you'll see all your animations. You can tap and hold, then drag them into the order you want the items to appear, and hit Play to test everything out.

Options
Tap the Options tab in the Animation menu and you can change things like the direction and duration of the animation, using a directional pad and a slider respectively

Create a slideshow Animate your holiday snaps

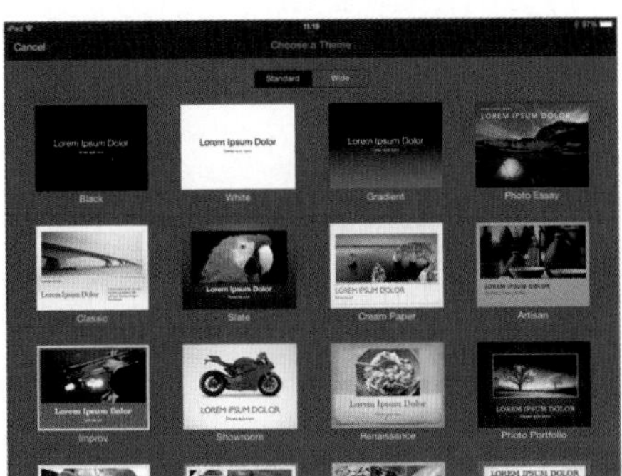

01 Pick a theme

Every theme in Keynote contains options for full-screen photos and grids of snaps, so you can just choose one that suits a selection of holiday snaps, like Cream Paper.

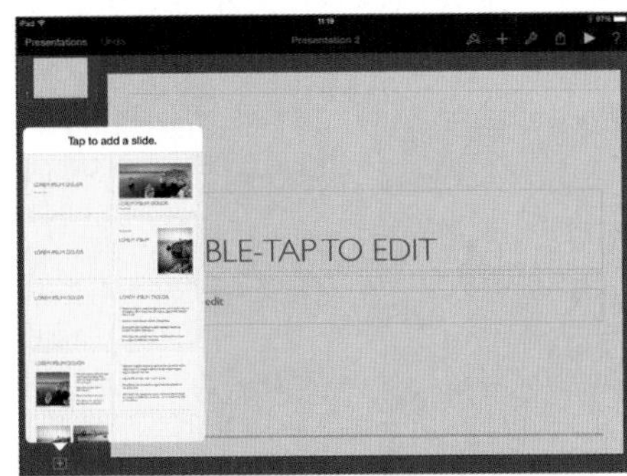

02 Add a photo slide

The default slide will be for text, so tap the + icon in the bottom-left of the screen to see the other slide options. Tap the full-screen photo slide to add it to your slideshow.

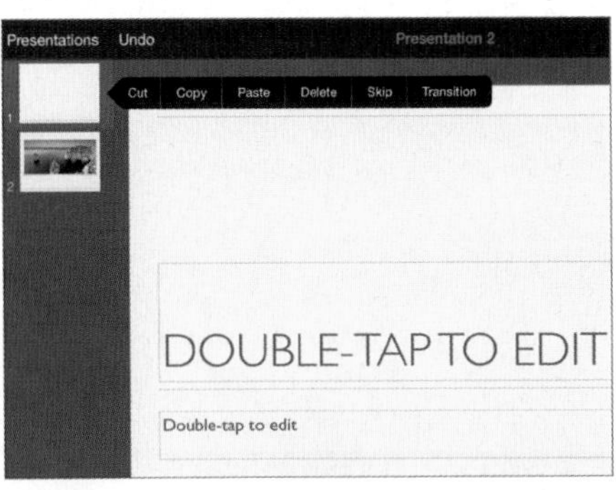

03 Delete unwanted slides

There are better ways to open your slideshow than a blank slide with text, so tap twice on the first slide to bring up the context menu and tap Delete to remove it.

04 Add more slides

Before you start adding photos, you can start adding multiple slides to speed things up later. Try to include a grid of pictures every now and then to add some variety.

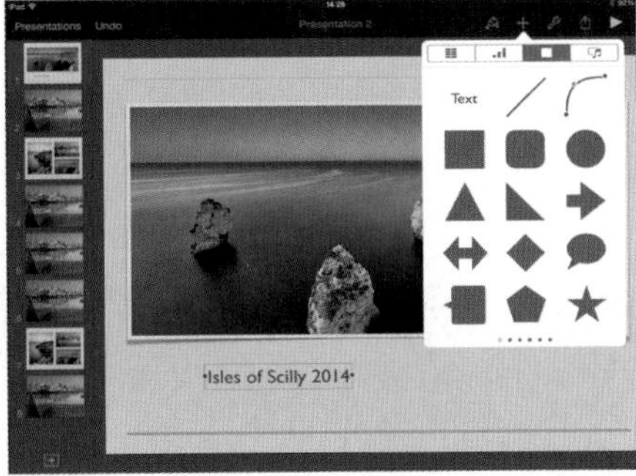

05 Give it a title

On your first slide, tap the + icon at the top of the screen and choose the Text option in the Shapes tab. Into this box, type in the title you want to give to your slideshow.

06 Edit mask

If you've chosen an opening slide with a smaller photo, double-tap it to open the masking controls. Drag the frame out so it takes up almost the entire slide so it commands attention.

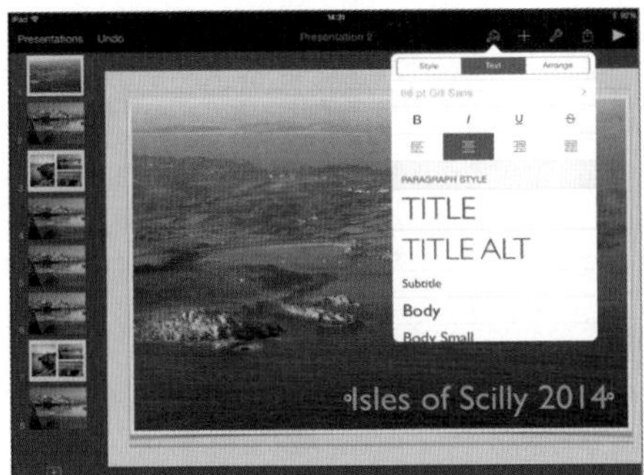

07 Edit text

Now you can edit the text. Double-tap to select it, then choose the Format button and change the font, size and colour so that it stands out against the photo it's on.

08 Replace images

Now you can go through your slideshow and replace all the images. Tap the + icon in the bottom-right of each photo and pick your desired shot from the library.

09 Captions and quotes

Don't feel you have to stick to the template completely. Adding text boxes to your photos with quotes or captions can create a bit of character or humour to your slideshow.

Perform presentations in Keynote

Keynote for iPad brings the Apple ethos of keeping things simple to the world of presentations

Creating presentations in PowerPoint has caused as much scratching of heads over the years as almost any other software solution. Despite this, it has been widely used in the corporate world and still dominates the presentation software market. Keynote for iPad brings the advantages of being mobile and incredibly easy to use.

Since the iPad is finger-driven, Apple has had to do away with the preciseness this type of software normally requires and has managed to make the entire process finger-friendly and much quicker than the competition. It will still take some time to get used to, though, because the commands are different and at times it feels almost too easy. In this guide we will show you how to create your first presentation and how to make the most of the features and the fact that you can create wherever you are without the need for wires.

"Apple has managed to make the entire presentation process finger-friendly and much quicker"

Using Keynote

Make your presentations look professional without needing to touch your desktop PC or Mac

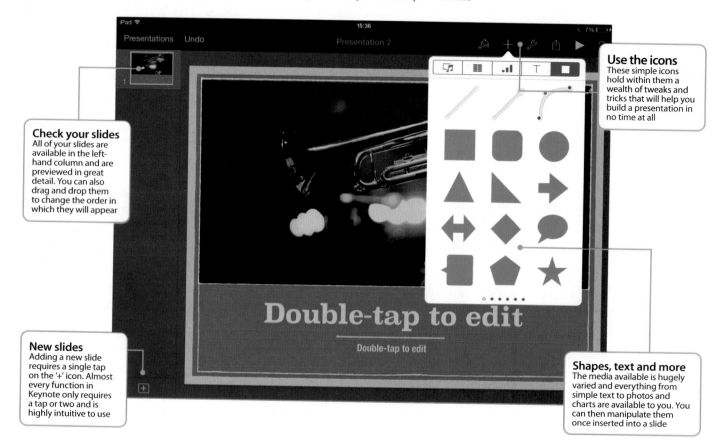

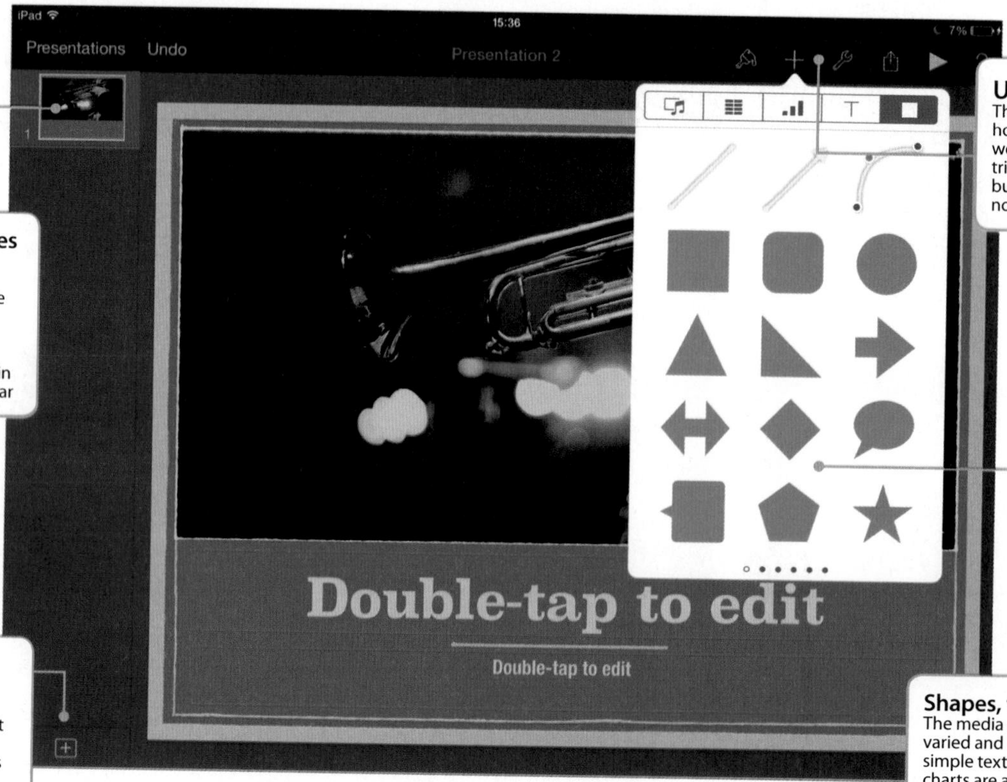

Use the icons
These simple icons hold within them a wealth of tweaks and tricks that will help you build a presentation in no time at all

Check your slides
All of your slides are available in the left-hand column and are previewed in great detail. You can also drag and drop them to change the order in which they will appear

New slides
Adding a new slide requires a single tap on the '+' icon. Almost every function in Keynote only requires a tap or two and is highly intuitive to use

Shapes, text and more
The media available is hugely varied and everything from simple text to photos and charts are available to you. You can then manipulate them once inserted into a slide

Keynote Build a Keynote presentation

01 Get Keynote

Keynote is now available on the iTunes App Store and is part of the iWork for iPad solution. All you need to do is download it and install it on your iPad as normal.

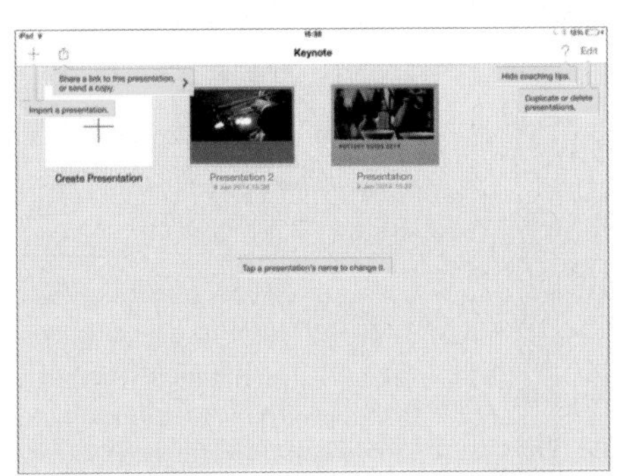

02 Open it up

Once you've opened Keynote up, it's worth pressing the question mark icon in the top-right corner to bring up the coaching tips that explain the app's key functions.

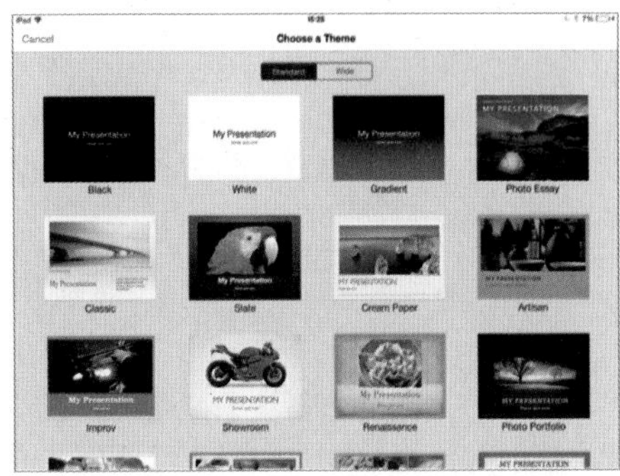

03 Create your first presentation

Click the '+' icon and then select Create Presentation. You can choose from 30 themes, covering a variety of appearances and styles, from Parchment to Leather Book.

04 Build your first slide

On the first slide, tap the default image and a bar with several options, such as delete or copy, will pop up. Tapping the small plus icon on a default image allows you to replace it with your own.

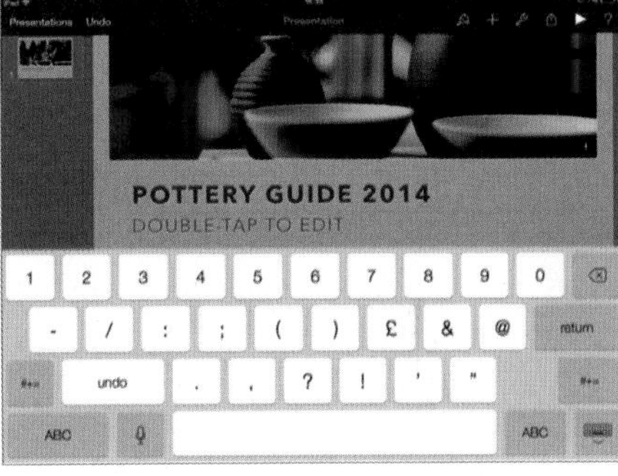

05 Use words

Double-tap the text and add your own words. When done, tap on the words and tap the brush icon. This will bring up a selection of styles and colours for the text.

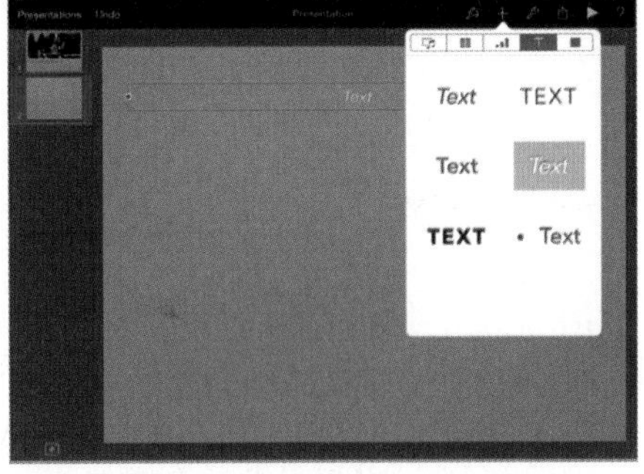

06 The important second slide

Tap the '+' icon on the bottom-left to create a second slide. Tap the '+' icon on the top bar and then choose the 'T' tab. Choose one of the options to insert a new text box.

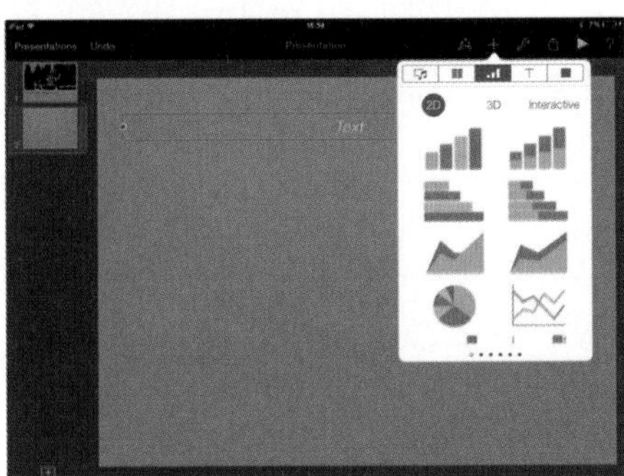

07 Add media

You will have noticed from the previous step that you are able to insert photographs, tables, charts and a variety of different shapes through the '+' command.

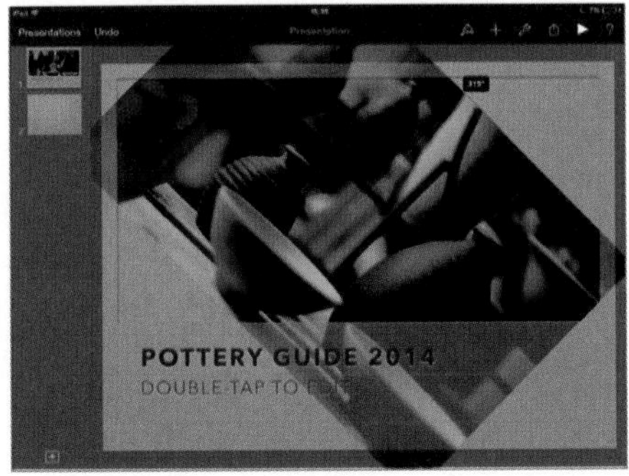

08 Time for tweaks

You can manipulate your media easily within Keynote. Tap a photograph and then hold two fingers on it – you can now spin it round to any angle you like.

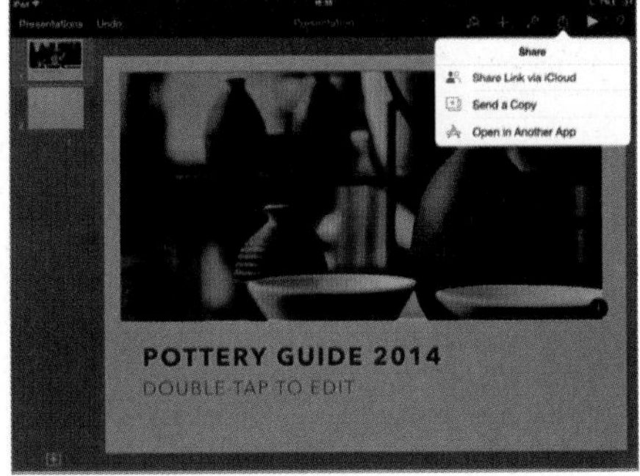

09 Share your work

Once you have finished, you are able to share your work by tapping the share icon along the top bar. You can also print by pressing the spanner icon and selecting the Print option.

Send your files with AirDrop

AirDrop can help you to share and receive files with anyone who happens to be in the vicinity

AirDrop is designed to let you send and receive files to any compatible phone or tablet that is within close proximity to you. This means that you can share files in a couple of seconds with anyone who is happy to receive it and, of course, it works the other way around too. We will show you how to use AirDrop, the process really is extremely simple, and – more importantly – very reliable. Multiple file types are supported and you can share many files at the same time, and even large files are supported within the technology. The idea is that no real set up is required and that the process feels almost invisible in use. You may not use it often, but when you need it everything will work seamlessly and without any fuss at all. It is very secure and you always have control over which files you are dealing with. Permission has to be given to receive files and enough information is available so that you know who you are sharing with and what it is they are sending or you are sending them. Let's get started with AirDrop.

"Multiple file types are supported and you can share many files at the same time – even large files are supported"

AirDrop Share files with AirDrop

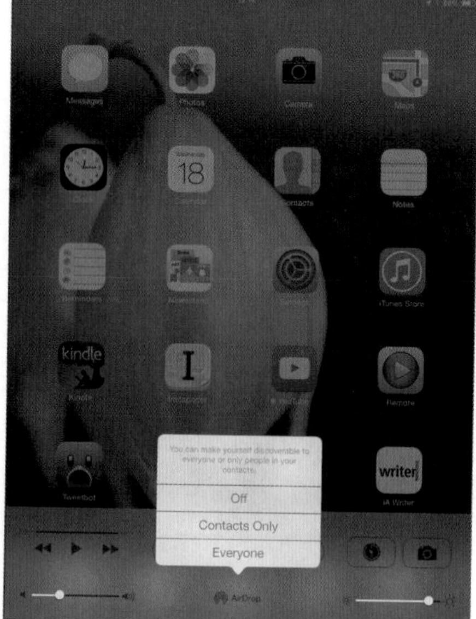

01 Turn it on

Pull up the Control Centre and then tap the small AirDrop icon. A menu shall appear and you will be offered a choice of options. Choose 'Everyone' to get started.

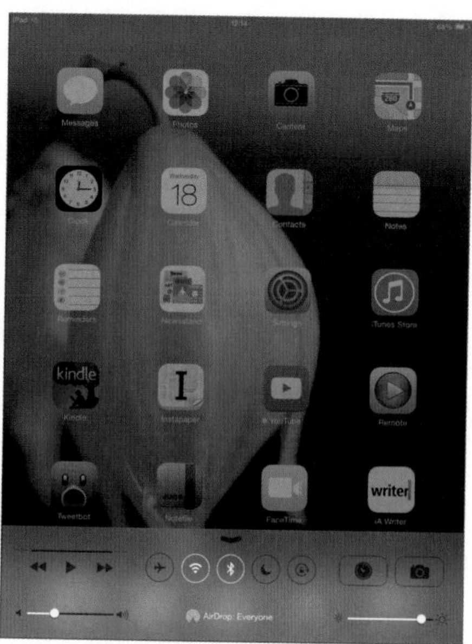

02 Small changes

The icon will turn white which means that AirDrop is now activated and available to send and receive files to your device, provided someone else is close to you.

03 Choose a file

Choose a file to send, such as a photo, and then tap the share icon bottom-left. You should see an icon showing who is near. Select the person you would like to send your files to.

The AirDrop interface

Share files with one tap

File types
Many different file types are supported in AirDrop. Some will open automatically and others will offer choices for which app to use

A large space
The sharing space allocated to AirDrop is generous. Tap anywhere to send a file or to see warning message if something goes wrong

Make your choice
You can choose how you want to use AirDrop here. Turn it on and off or send to specific contacts or anyone in range

A visual indicator
If someone is within range and has AirDrop activated you will see a different icon replace the AirDrop one. Simply tap to send

The important details
To use AirDrop on an iPad, Wi-Fi and Bluetooth must be switched on which applies to both the sender and receiver devices. It is at this stage only compatible with the latest Apple devices, but multiple files can be sent at the same time to one recipient.

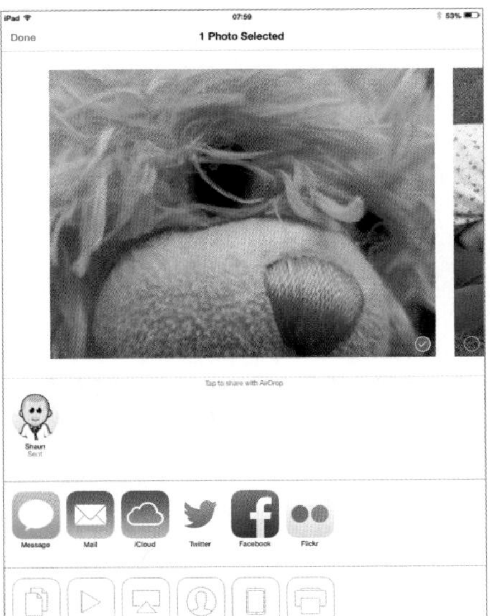

04 It's now sent

Once the recipient has accepted the file and it has been sent through, you will be able to see the status of the file beneath the sender's name. The file is then 'sent'.

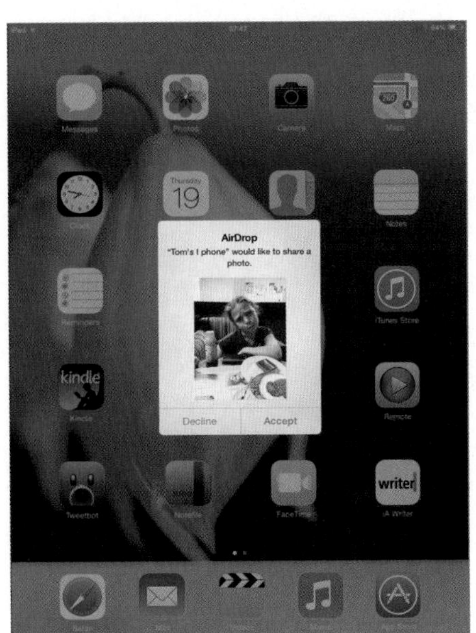

05 Receiving files

If someone attempts to send you a file, a notification will pop up no matter what you are currently doing on the iPad. Tap 'Accept' in order to receive these files.

06 The correct apps

Depending on the type of file received, it may open automatically in the correct app. Photos for example will open immediately in the Photo app.

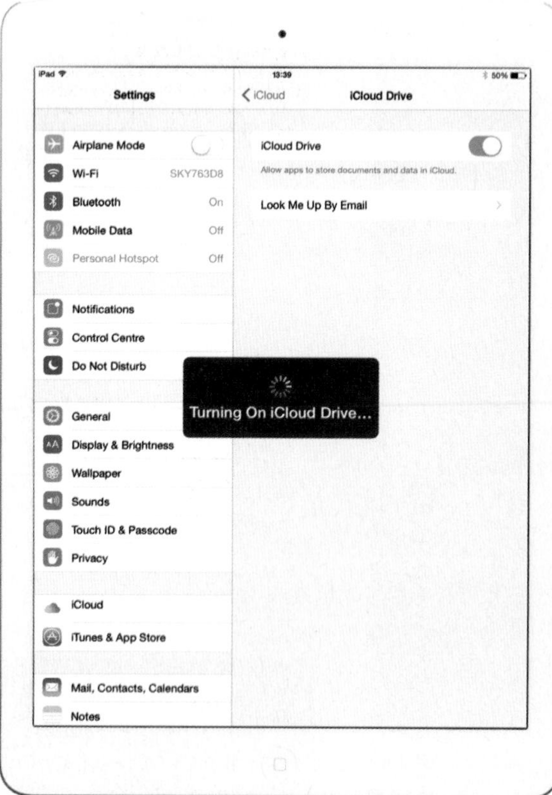

Get more from iCloud Drive

Automatically save files on an iOS 8 device and access files from a PC or Yosemite-enabled Mac

Apple's new competitor to the likes of Dropbox and Google Drive lets you sync files across multiple iOS devices and computers. It goes beyond the regular iCloud service since it not only allows you to create and save documents in Pages on your iPhone and then open them in Pages on a Mac. For instance, it also allows other apps to easily access those files. Files created by one app are no longer restricted to that app alone. This means you could start creating a drawing in one app, finish it in another and then use it in a presentation. Before, you would have to save it to the Camera Roll, import it, and save it again as a separate image. Now one file is needed that is automatically updated when changes are made, vastly improving your workflow. Before you upgrade, though, it's important to note that iCloud Drive is only compatible with iDevices running iOS 8, Macs with Yosemite installed and Windows 7, 7.1 or 8 PCs. If you need to sync with any other or older devices, then it's best that you don't upgrade to Drive just yet.

"You can start creating a drawing in one app, finish it in another and then use it in a presentation"

iCloud Drive Save files to iCloud

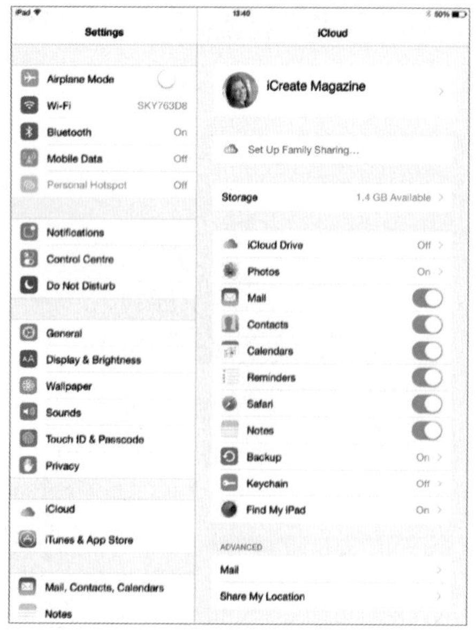

01 Activate iCloud Drive

If you skipped over the option to activate iCloud Drive when you installed iOS 8, then head over to Settings >iCloud and tap iCloud Drive to activate the service.

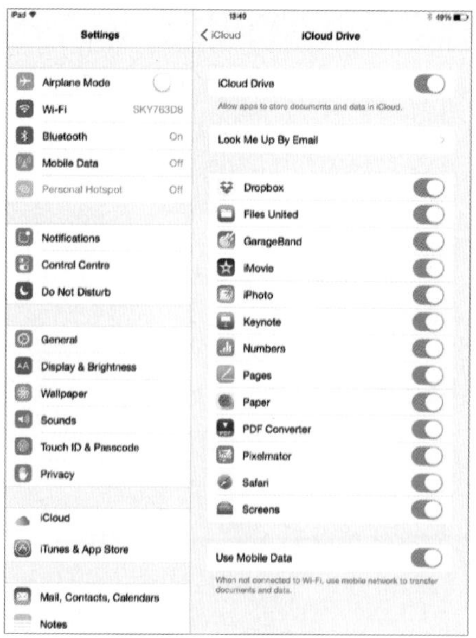

02 See compatible apps

Any apps that are using Drive are listed in iCloud Drive settings. You can turn off access to specific apps if you wish, otherwise the apps will automatically upload files.

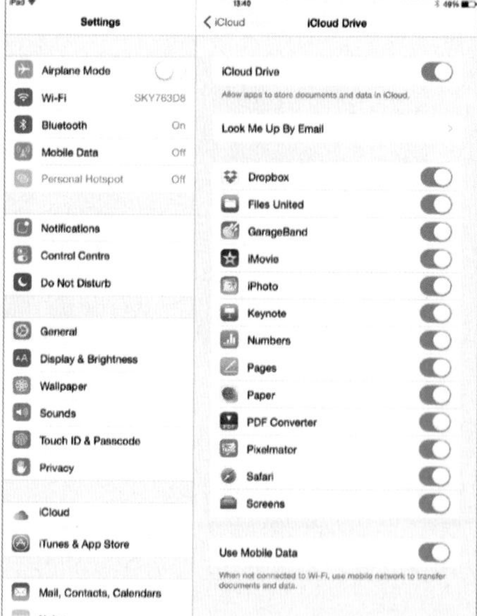

03 Use Cellular Data

At the bottom of the iCloud Drive settings page you'll see the option to Use Cellular Data, which allows data to transfer to iCloud Drive using your mobile phone plan.

iCloud Drive's file structure

Looking at where items are saved

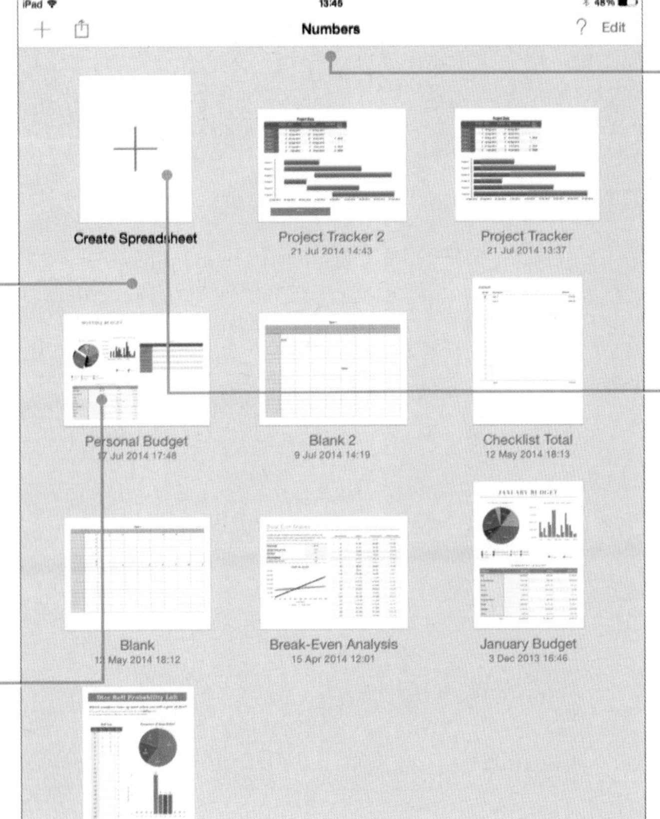

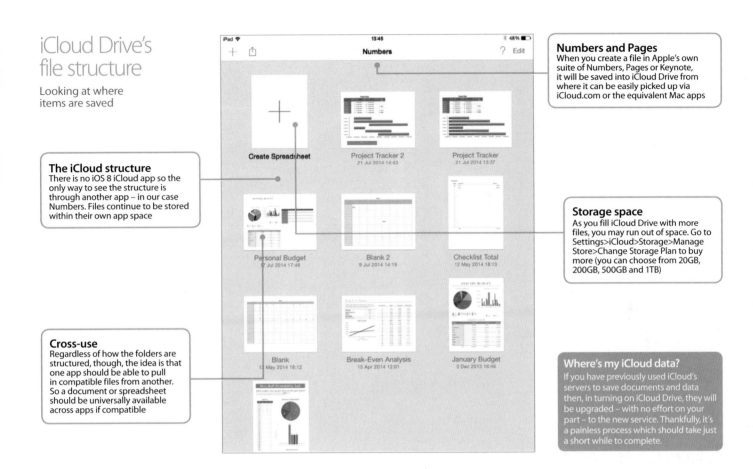

Numbers and Pages
When you create a file in Apple's own suite of Numbers, Pages or Keynote, it will be saved into iCloud Drive from where it can be easily picked up via iCloud.com or the equivalent Mac apps

The iCloud structure
There is no iOS 8 iCloud app so the only way to see the structure is through another app – in our case Numbers. Files continue to be stored within their own app space

Storage space
As you fill iCloud Drive with more files, you may run out of space. Go to Settings>iCloud>Storage>Manage Store>Change Storage Plan to buy more (you can choose from 20GB, 200GB, 500GB and 1TB)

Cross-use
Regardless of how the folders are structured, though, the idea is that one app should be able to pull in compatible files from another. So a document or spreadsheet should be universally available across apps if compatible

Where's my iCloud data?

If you have previously used iCloud's servers to save documents and data then, in turning on iCloud Drive, they will be upgraded – with no effort on your part – to the new service. Thankfully, it's a painless process which should take just a short while to complete.

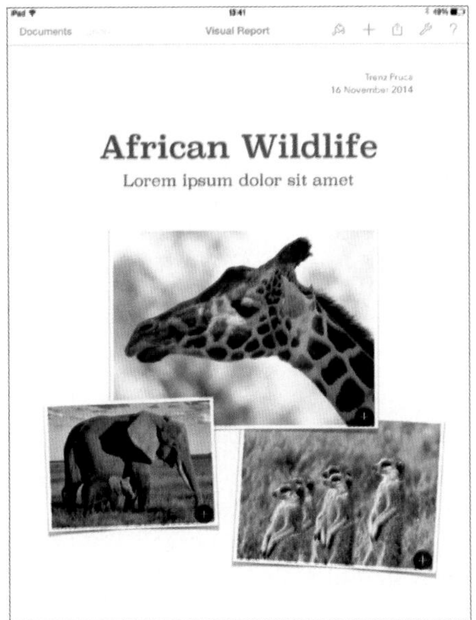

04 Saving from Drive

There's no standalone iOS 8 iCloud Drive app. Instead, to use the service you must create a file within an iCloud Drive-enabled app for it to automatically save.

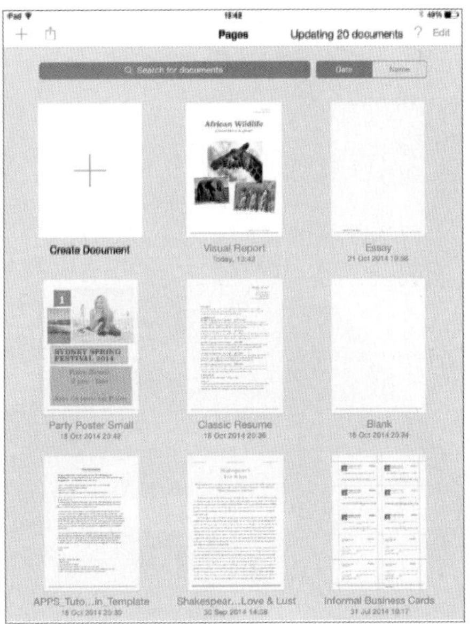

05 Finding saved files

When browsing files, any that are stored in iCloud Drive which aren't downloaded yet have a downward arrow. Tap the arrow to open and store on your iPhone.

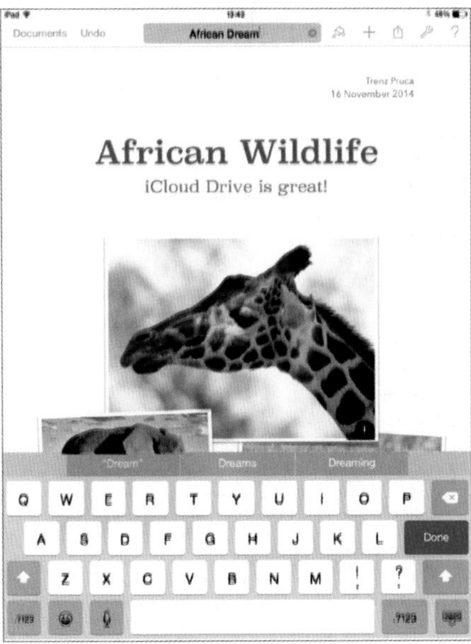

06 Make changes

Any changes you make to a document will now be replicated in iCloud Drive, so you no longer need to make numerous copies of a single file to keep everything up to date.

Essential
iPad
apps
Our list of the very best apps you need to download onto your iPad right now
NETFLIX
HD
W
Calendar
Clock
FaceTime
Contacts

The iPad is nothing without apps. They are at the very core of Apple's tablet experience, and if you buy an iPad without installing any extra apps on it, you're really missing out on what makes the iPad so special.

With that in mind, we have worked hard to put together a list of the very best apps available for the brilliant tablet. These are all available from the built-in App Store, and the vast majority are available completely for free, without you needing to pay a penny.

No matter what you want to use your iPad for, there is bound to be an app you will find fun or useful in the App Store. You can complete all kinds of tasks with just a few taps of your finger. In this feature, we've rounded up the very best apps available today, in every category, so you're bound to find something in here that suits your needs perfectly.

And we really have covered every base, whether you want to relax with the best new games, perfectly organise your emails, or even just watch your favourite films on the go, you'll find the app designed to complete that task in the next few pages.

Of course, we haven't just listed dozens of apps, we've also explained what it is that makes them so good, and in many cases shown you how you can use the apps to get the most from your device.

So get your iPad and your Apple ID at the ready and prepare to download the essential apps that every iPad user should own. In no time at all you'll understand exactly why the iPad is so special.

Power up your email

Mailbox

Price: Free

When it comes to email, sometimes the iPad's built in Mail client just isn't good enough. While it doesn't do anything particularly wrong, Mailbox is a big step up in both functionality and design.

The clean and simple look is just the start; the biggest advantage comes in the form of gestures that help you quickly sort your mail. Whether you need to deal with a message later, archive or delete it, it's just a slide away in Mailbox. It's incredibly customisable, too. The main focus, though, is getting your Inbox to zero. Move and delete your messages and you'll achieve Mailbox zen in no time at all.

"Mailbox is a big step up in functionality and design"

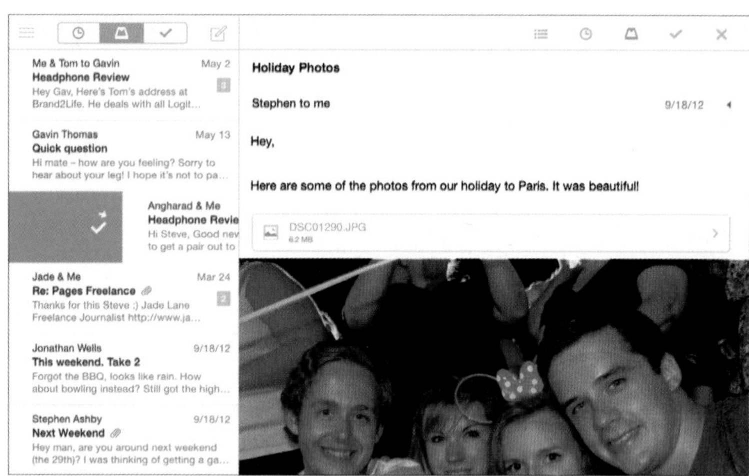

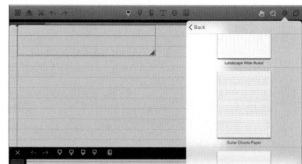

1: Gesture based
Swiping left and right on your messages at the side of the screen will compelte different actions, and move your messages into your own custom folders, or quickly delete them.

2: Get to zero
The main goal of Mailbox is to help you to an empty inbox. Delete unwanted messages, save those you do need and defer others until later to completely clear out your email inbox.

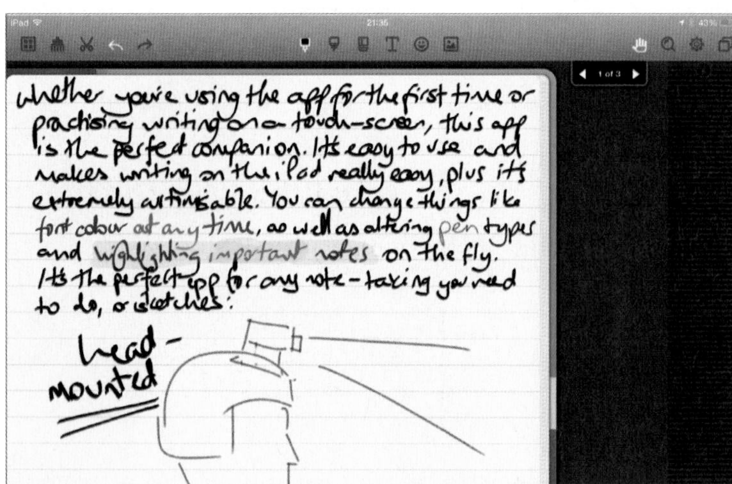

Make vital notes on iPad

Noteshelf

Price: £4.49/$5.99

When it comes to making notes, there's few things better than an iPad. While a pen and paper may always have a place in people's hearts, on an iPad you can hold hundreds of thousands of notes in one place, tag them and organise them, and correct mistakes without messing up your page. And with Noteshelf, things are even easier. Not only can you organise your notes with tags and notebooks, you can also use the handwriting feature to quickly take neat, hand-written notes. The app uses a zoomed-in section at the bottom of the screen, which allows you to write at a comfortable size, and see your notes appear smaller at the top. It's perfect to keep all your notes in one place on your device.

1: Set up your page
The app offers plenty of customisation options for your page. From paper type to pen colour and note size, you can make each notebook your own. Customise the level of zoom for the handwriting section to your needs so you're ready to go.

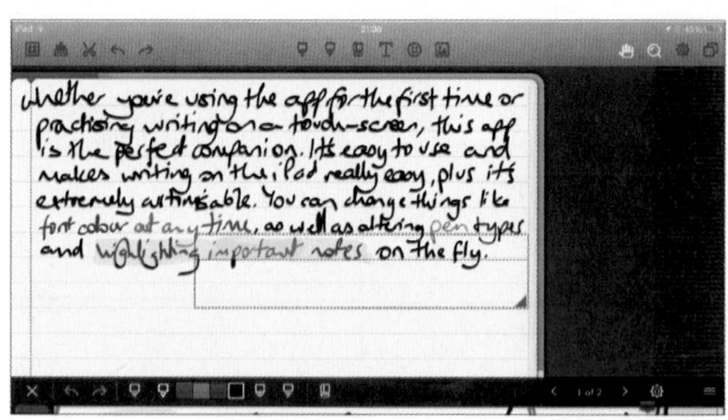

2: Start scribbling by hand
You can then write in the lines at the bottom of the screen and have your words transferred up to the section above. When you reach the section on the right of the box the whole thing will shift sideways to help you carry on writing unhindered.

Take notes and projects with you

Evernote

Price: Free

Notes
Every note you make is synced to your Evernote account, so they're accessible everywhere

Sync
Click the sync button at the top to instantly update Evernote on all your devices

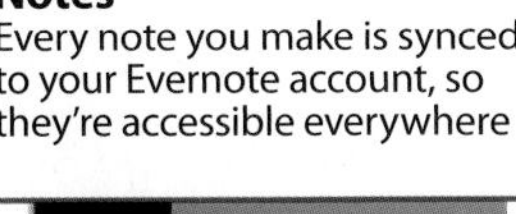

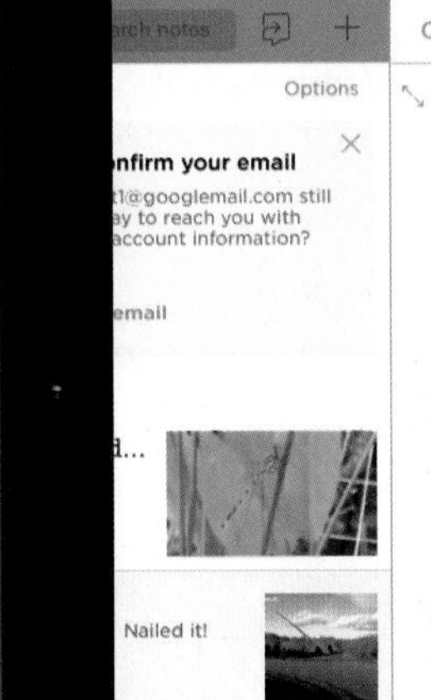

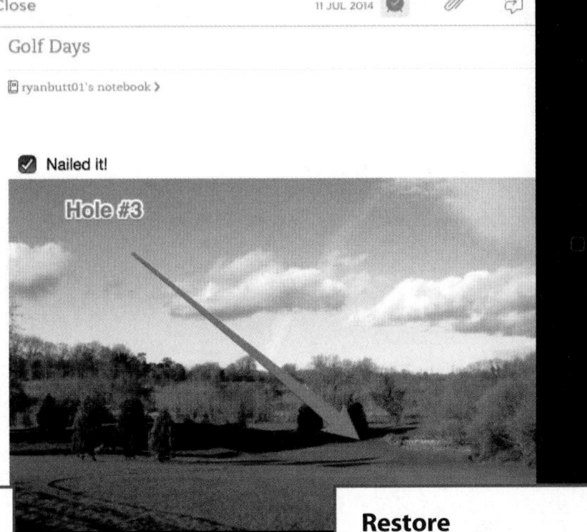

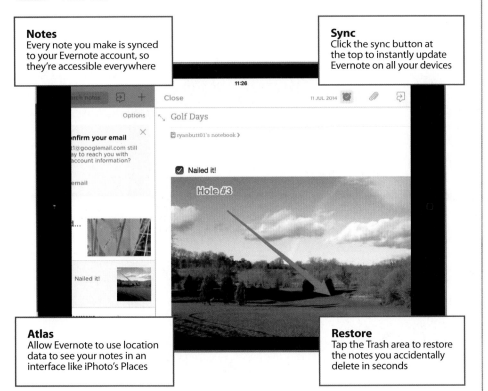

Atlas
Allow Evernote to use location data to see your notes in an interface like iPhoto's Places

Restore
Tap the Trash area to restore the notes you accidentally delete in seconds

Bookmark webpages to read later

Pocket

Price: Free

Pocket's cross-platform bookmarking utility and minimal interface for reading your saved articles make it a firm favourite for iPad users. You can even tag articles as you save them.

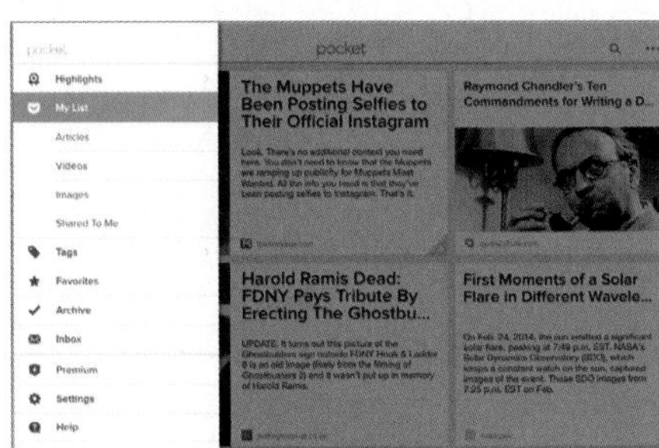

1: Save articles on the iPad
Open Pocket on your iOS device and tap Help at the bottom of the main menu. Tap How to Save, scroll down to From Mobile Safari and tap the all-important Install button.

2: Read your articles
All your articles are saved to your account, and will be synced between all devices using the app. You can see all your saved articles and read them with a tap via the slick interface.

Type with confidence

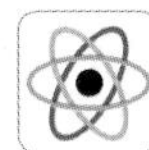

Letterspace

Price: Free

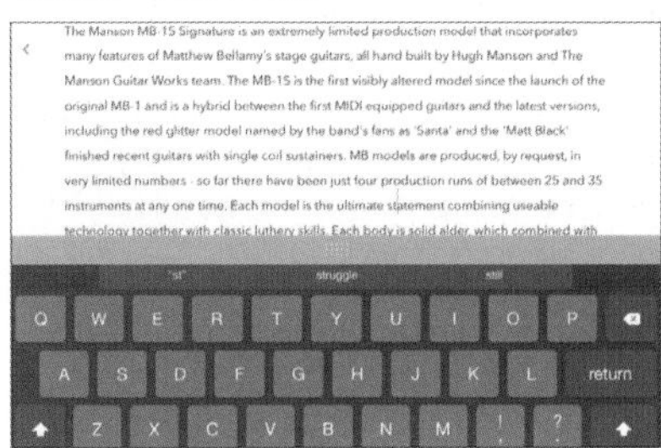

Not only does this app allow you to create quick and easy notes that can be synced to the cloud and made accessible on other devices, it also boasts an excellent leyboard interface. A bar above the keyboard lets you move the cursor around, so you no longer have to rely on your fat fingers jabbing at the words on screen in order to make precise edits. Expect to see this in an iOS soon.

Stay up to date with events

Sunrise Calendar

Price: Free

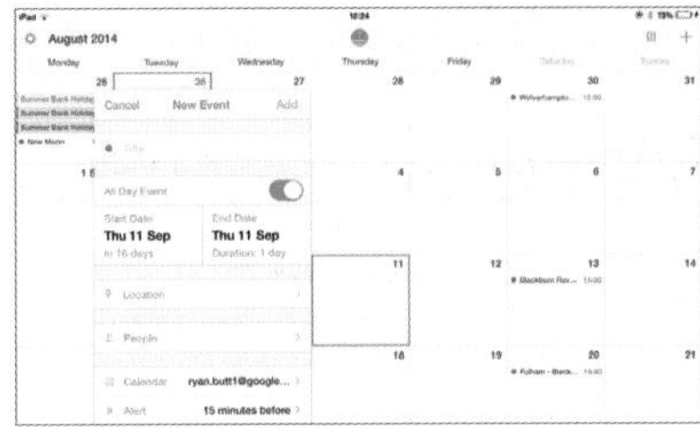

The iPad's built-in Calendar app is okay for managing a small number of events, but if you really want to take control of your life, Google's Sunrise Calendar is the app to do it. You can create events and appointments quickly and easily and even import a wide range of calendars from the initial set-up, including the fixtures of your favourite teams.

Watch your shows wherever you are

Netflix

Price: Requires subscription; £5.99/$7.99 per month

Search
Tap the search bar in the top-right to quickly find content you're looking for on the Netflix service

Personalise
To get recommendations, and to improve the quality of current ratings, rate as many items as possible

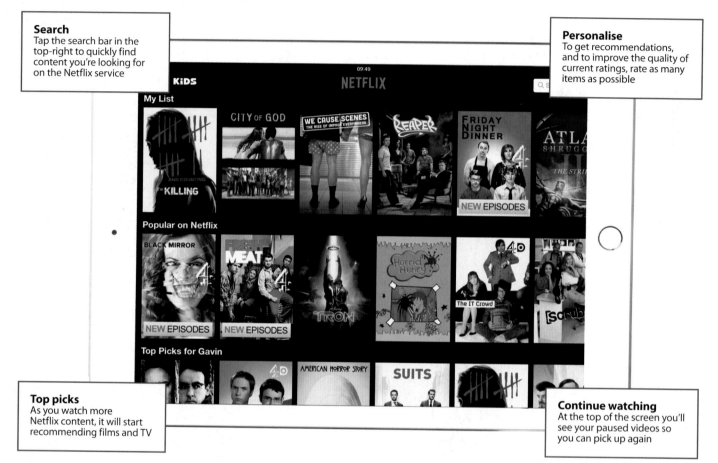

Top picks
As you watch more Netflix content, it will start recommending films and TV

Continue watching
At the top of the screen you'll see your paused videos so you can pick up again

Listen to your radio

Spotify Music

Price: Free

One of the biggest names in audio streaming, Spotify is an on-demand music service. Thanks to apps for Mac, PC, Android and iOS, you can create playlists anywhere and have instant access to them on your iPad. While the service used to be paid for use on iPhone and iPad, you can now listen to your favourite tracks for free if you can put up with the ads. Of course, if you want to subscribe for a paid account, you'll have the added benefit of being able to download tracks to listen to offline, remove the adds, and much more.

1: Create a playlist
Click New Playlist in the left-hand sidebar, and give it a name. Either select from the app's featured tracks, or search for your favourites and drag them to your new playlist.

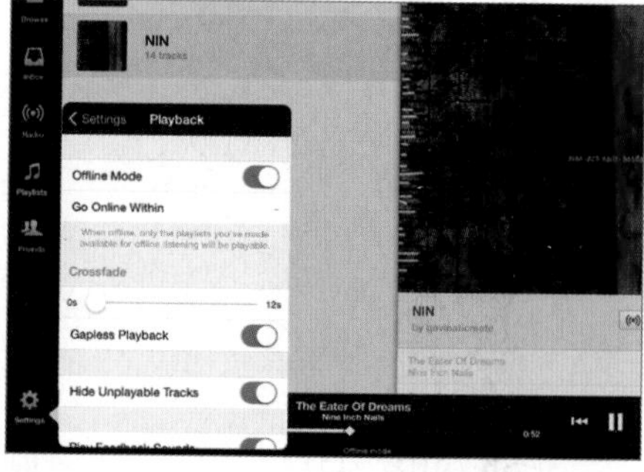

2: Personalise your music
Tap Settings and you'll see a number of options. You can adjust things like Gapless Playback, or activate Offline Mode if you have a paid account, so you can listen anywhere.

Supercharge your web browser

Chrome

Price: Free

Sometimes, Safari just isn't enough. If you have a Google Account and like to keep everything in sync, Chrome is the perfect app to grab for your iPad. A free add-on to your tablet, you'll be able to log in with your Google email and password and have favourites and open tabs synced between your Mac or PC and your iPad's browser.

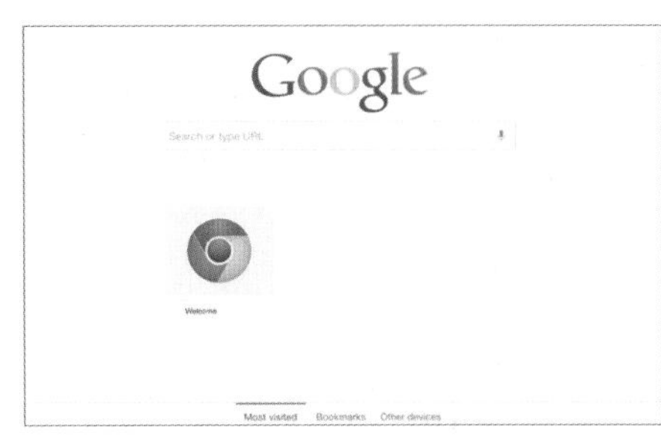

Video chat from any device...

Skype

Price: Free

Skype has been around since 2003, and these days not only supports video chats but also messaging, with full emoticon and photo support within the app. All this is free, so it's a great option for video chats with friends and family who aren't using FaceTime. You can make audio calls for free over Wi-Fi or 4G, too, saving you credit. Not only that, you can add Skype credit to your account and use it to make audio calls to landlines, effectively replacing your FaceTime and Phone apps. You can log into your Skype account (once created) on any device, whether it's running iOS, Android, Windows or OS X.

"Make audio calls for free over Wi-Fi or 4G"

Control your Mac from your iPad device

Screens VNC

Price: £14.99/$29.99

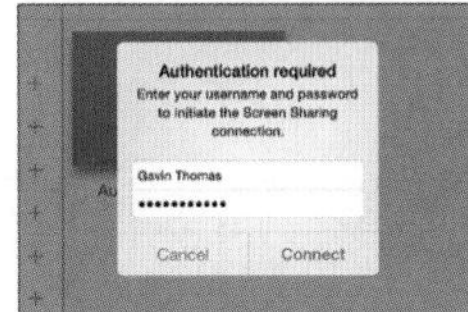

1: Connect locally
Open Screens in iOS and tap your Mac, then Save. Tap the new thumbnail and input your Mac login details – you need to be on the same Wi-Fi network.

2: Connect from afar
To use Screens at long range, head to edovia.com/screens and download Screens Remote for your Mac (free). Install it, create a Screens ID and sign in.

Control your home media

Remote

Price: Free

Remote is a very useful app if you wish to control your iTunes library from anywhere in the house. For example, if you have Airplay speakers then you can instantly stream music from your library using this app as the go-between. You can also browse your entire iTunes library on your iPad and use the app to contreol Apple TV. Using Apple TV you can stream your library to the device and play your music through your TV and connected sound system. Using this app to search for items on Apple TV is also a great time saver as you have the full iPad keyboard to use instead of selecting one letter at a time, as per the standard Apple TV remote.

Adobe Creative Apps

Previously available to purchase individually or as part of the Creative Suite package, Adobe's apps are now only available with Creative Cloud (CC) membership. So, rather than pay once to keep the apps, you must instead take out a regular subscription. Full details of the pricing plans are available to browse at **adobe.com/uk/products/creativecloud/buying-guide-at-a-glance.html**.

Subscribing to Adobe Creative Cloud

One CC app:	All CC apps:	All CC apps:
£17.15/$19.99	**£45.73/$49.99**	**£68.60/$74.99**
per month (annual commitment)	per month (annual commitment)	per month (month-to-month)

Enhance and organise photos

Lightroom

Lightroom for iPad requires you to have Lightroom 5 for Mac or PC, and you'll need to sign in with your Adobe CC account to get even basic use. But once you've signed in, any edits you make will be automatically synced between your Apple devices to allow you to work on later. The editing tools are surprisingly powerful, too. You'll be able to edit your iPad's own photos to RAW images taken on professional DSLRs, and the app is also great for sharing your snaps from your iPad to your Lightroom library.

Turn your photos into art

Photoshop Touch iOS

It's a little expensive, but this powerful editing suite offers extra controls that you don't find in apps. Alongside the standard editing options like Contrast and Brightness controls, Photoshop Touch offers full layer controls. Whether you want to edit a photo or create a drawing of your own using your finger or a stylus, Photoshop Touch gives you all the tools you need, wrapped up in an easy-to-understand interface. Well worth a look for those looking to dabble in image editing while on the go.

Create vector illustrations

Adobe Ideas

Much like Photoshop Touch, you can use Adobe Ideas without a CC account. However, sign in and you unlock the ability to sync your creations with Illustrator CC, so you can turn your quick iPad sketches into fully realised vector artwork on your desktop. The key advantage here is that with Adobe Ideas on iPad, you have support for the biggest styluses – the Adonit Jot Touch 4 and Jot Script, Wacom Intuos Creative and the Pogo Connect – which means you can draw digitally by hand on the go.

Stream your media to iPad at home

Plex for iPad & Plex Media Server

Price: £3.99/$4.99

We particularly like Plex for streaming movies and TV episodes. There's a little more to set up than the other apps we're looking at here, as you'll need an app for your Mac or PC as well as the iOS counterpart, but once you're up and running you'll be able to keep all your media on your main Mac and stream to your other devices, no matter where you are. Plex is also great because it automatically gives media beautiful artwork, information and descriptions, even if they aren't included in the original files. It's a great way to watch movies and TV shows on your touch-screen.

1: Plex Media Server
Click on Plex Media Server's menubar icon and choose the Media Manager. Use the '+' button to add folders on your Mac or PC.

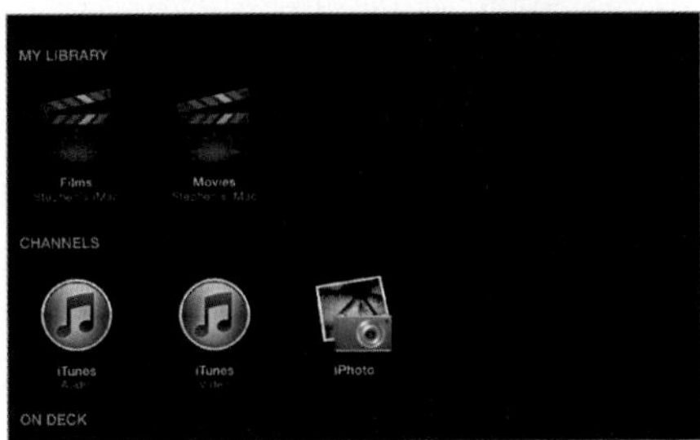

2: Set up the Sync
Put Plex on your iPad and connect to your server (Media Manager needs to be running). You'll now have access to all the media on your computer.

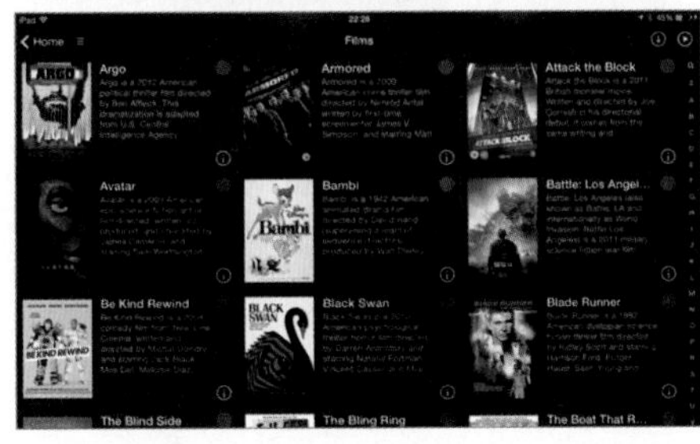

3: Beautiful media
Plex will retrieve artwork for your movies and music to create a beautiful library view. Tap one and it'll stream from your Mac or PC instantly.

Put a library in your pocket

Kindle

Price: Free

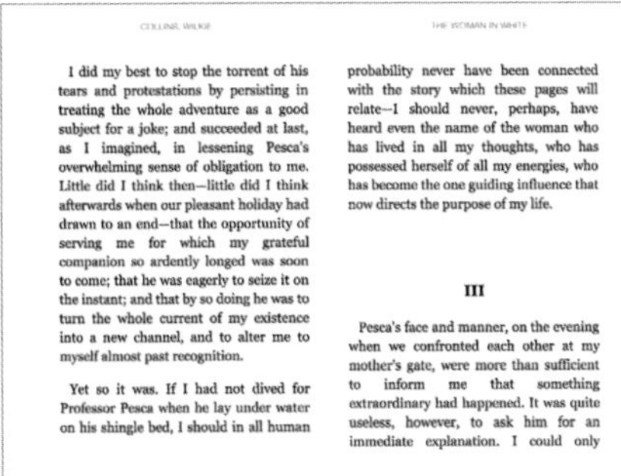

I did my best to stop the torrent of his tears and protestations by persisting in treating the whole adventure as a good subject for a joke; and succeeded at last, as I imagined, in lessening Pesca's overwhelming sense of obligation to me. Little did I think then—little did I think afterwards when our pleasant holiday had drawn to an end—that the opportunity of serving me for which my grateful companion so ardently longed was soon to come; that he was eagerly to seize it on the instant; and that by so doing he was to turn the whole current of my existence into a new channel, and to alter me to myself almost past recognition.

Yet so it was. If I had not dived for Professor Pesca when he lay under water on his shingle bed, I should in all human probability never have been connected with the story which these pages will relate--I should never, perhaps, have heard even the name of the woman who has lived in all my thoughts, who has possessed herself of all my energies, who has become the one guiding influence that now directs the purpose of my life.

III

Pesca's face and manner, on the evening when we confronted each other at my mother's gate, were more than sufficient to inform me that something extraordinary had happened. It was quite useless, however, to ask him for an immediate explanation. I could only

Grab the free app from the App Store and you can read all your favourite ebooks on the go. You'll need an Amazon account, but all your bought books will sync automatically.

Kobo

Price: Free

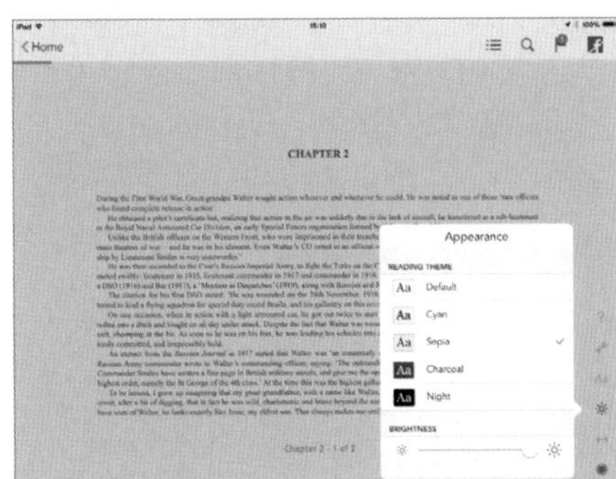

You can also get hold of a huge range of books and magazines via Kobo. Just buy what you want from the Kobo store online and then everything will sync to this handy reading app.

Sync all your files and folders

Dropbox

Price: Free

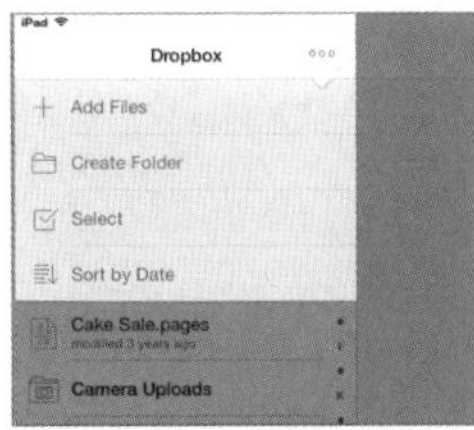

1: Create folders
Tap the elipsis button in the top of the Dropbox sidebar, then select Create Folder from the menu to add a folder inside the one you're viewing now.

2: Add photos
Tap the elipsis button again and select Add Files from the top of the menu. Tap the images you want to add to your dropbox, then tap Upload above.

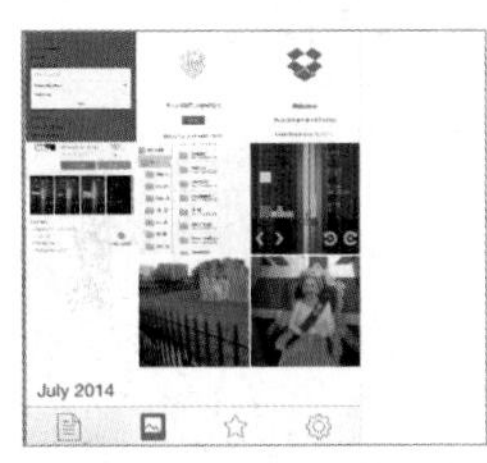

3: Photos View
Tap the Photos tab at the bottom of the sidebar to see all of your uploaded shots in a grid. Tap on any one for a full-size preview on the right of the screen.

4: Favourites
When you're viewing a large preview of the file you like, tap the Star icon in the top-right of the entire screen to add it to your favourites so it's easier to find.

5: Open files in selected apps
Some files, such as PDFs and Microsoft Word documents, can be opened in other apps for proper viewing or editing. Tap the Share button and tap Open In…

Essential apps

Take Gmail with you

Gmail

Price: Free

If you are one of the millions of people who use Gmail as their primary email service, the iPad app is sure to please. All your mailboxes and contacts from your gmail account will be synced across to your iPad automatically, and you'll get the same easy-to-understand interface across all of Google's services. Other apps may require complex setup to get your Gmail mailboxes to sync properly, but with the official Gmail app you'll be ready in no time at all. Grab the Gmail app and take true control of your emails, whether you're on your computer or your iPad.

> "Mailboxes and contacts will be synced across to your iPad automatically"

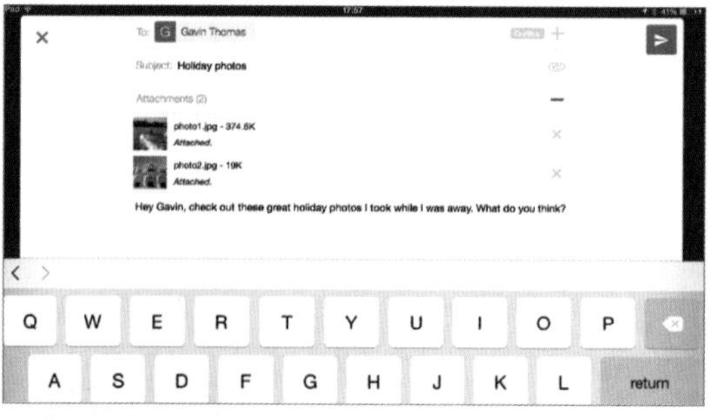

1: Writing messages
Tap the red Compose button at the top of the message list to open up a new message. Here you can attach photos, add contacts from your iPad Contacts, and tap send in the top-right.

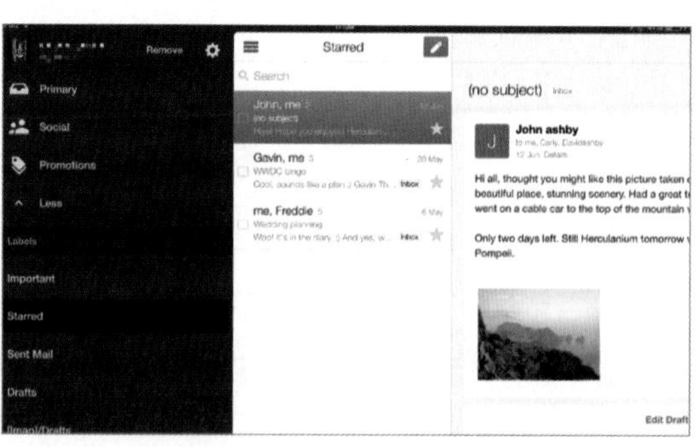

2: Sorting and starring
If you want to be able to find certain messages quickly, just tap the Star icon next to the message in the sidebar to favourite a message, then you can choose the Starred section to see them all together.

Discover what's around you

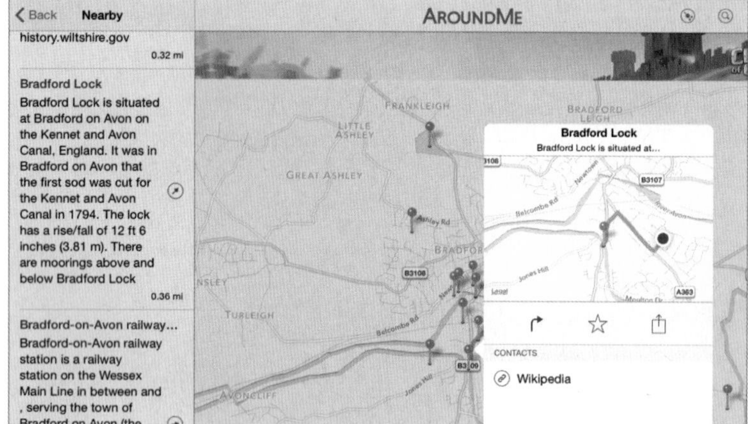

AroundMe

Price: Free

This app can come in very useful to discover what's in your local area. For example, if you are enjoying a weekend away then you can use this app in your hotel room to see what places are there to be checked out nearby. Simply choose a category from the list to the left, that includes bars, coffee shops, concerts, movie theatres and many more, and then all of the corresponding places will be presented in a handy list for you to scrol down through and check out reviews and ratings. All of the places are also displayed on the map in the main window, so you can see where everything is in relation to your current location. You can also save places as favourites so that you can return to the em again and share them with other people via social networks. Go on, see what's around you!

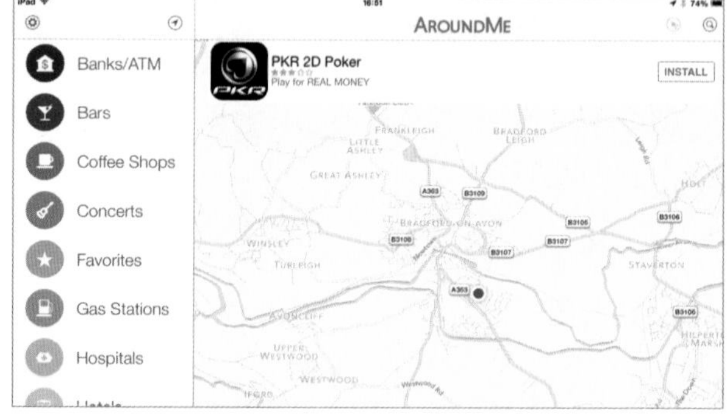

1: Select a category
Grant the app permission to use your current location and then tap on one of the place categories in the left-hand column. All of the places nearby that fit the description will then be listed.

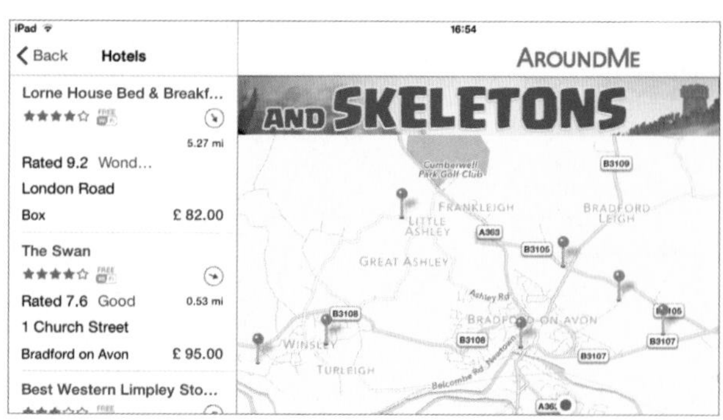

2: Find the place
As well as in the list to the left, all of the places will also be indicated as pins on the map. So if you simply want the nearest, you can instantly see which in is closest to your current position.

Never get lost again

Google Maps

Price: Free

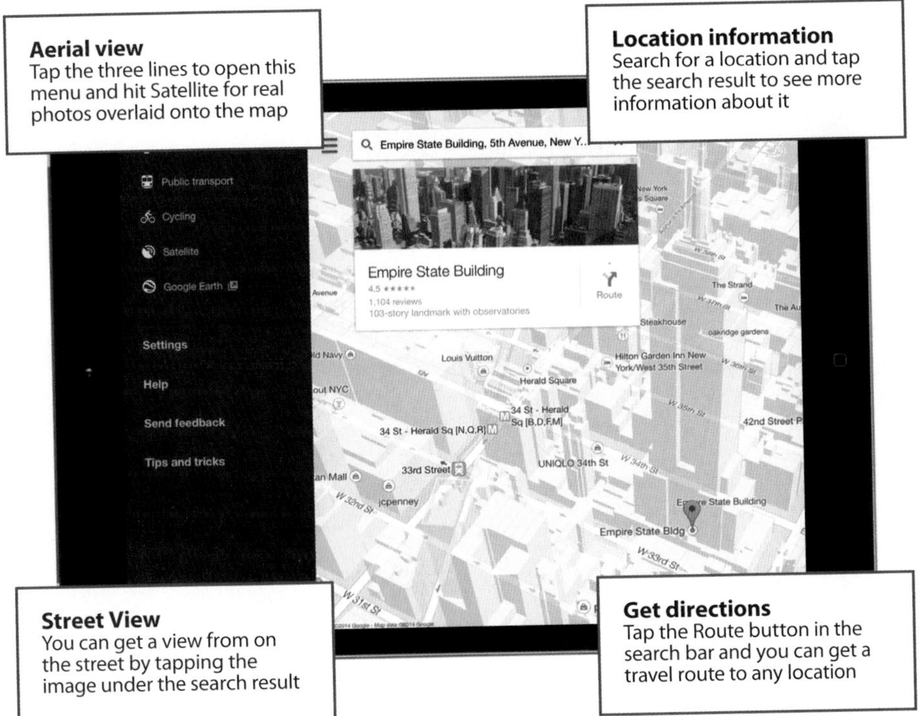

Aerial view
Tap the three lines to open this menu and hit Satellite for real photos overlaid onto the map

Location information
Search for a location and tap the search result to see more information about it

Street View
You can get a view from on the street by tapping the image under the search result

Get directions
Tap the Route button in the search bar and you can get a travel route to any location

Share your photos with the world

Instagram

Price: Free

Although Instagram, strangely, doesn't yet have its own iPad app, you can download the iPhone version that works just fine on the bigger screen. Here we show you how to start following folk…

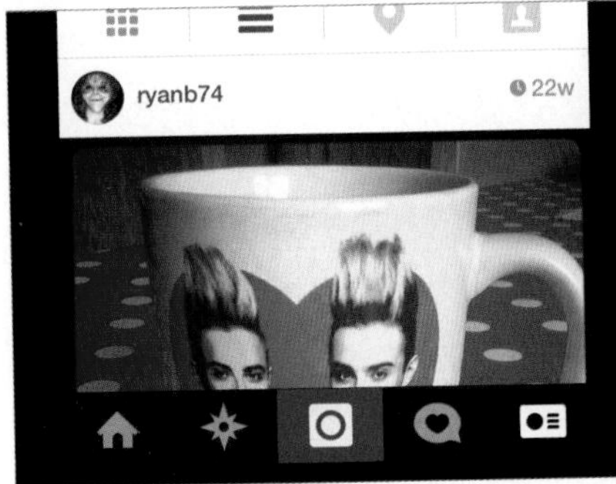

1: Go to your profile
Tap on the far-right icon at the bottom of the interface followed by the cog icon in the top-right corner. Now select 'Find People to Follow'.

2: Connect and follow
Use the Connect to Facebook and Connect Contacts options to find your friends on the service or scroll down for suggestions and trends.

Shop for goods on your iPad

Amazon

Price: Free

This app makes it easy to buy a selection of items in one go thanks to the range and diversty of items on offer. Anything from totem poles to a box canvas print of Paul Ross are within searching distance and you can buy your items with a single click to make the whole buying process dangerously easy. You can also add items you find to your personal wish list and send items as gifts for other people.

Gather inspiration

Pinterest

Price: Free

Pinterest is like a handy online scrapbook into which you can gather the things that interest you from around the web. This is ideal if you are planning to redecorate your house, getting married or simply want to compile a host of styles and images that inspire you. Or perhaps you want a new tattoo; here you can collect designs on which to base yours. Whatever the theme, Pinterest lets you gather ideas easily. Your collections will also helpfully sync across devices.

Get organised and share tasks

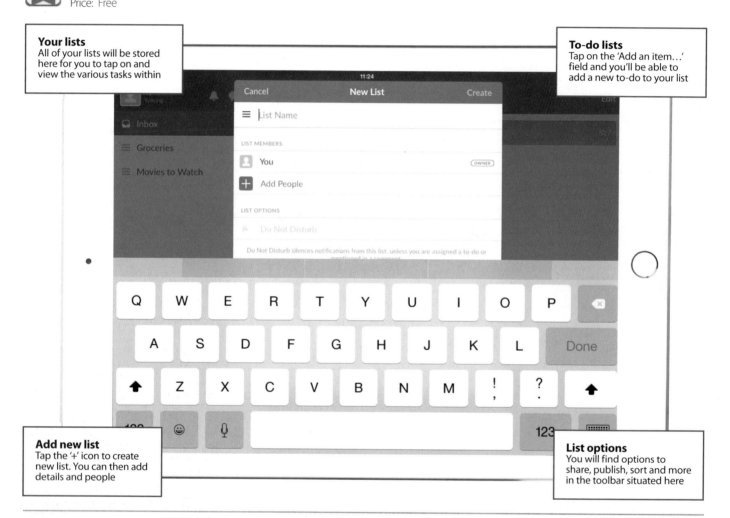

Wunderlist: To-Do Lists & Tasks

Price: Free

Your lists
All of your lists will be stored here for you to tap on and view the various tasks within

To-do lists
Tap on the 'Add an item…' field and you'll be able to add a new to-do to your list

Add new list
Tap the '+' icon to create new list. You can then add details and people

List options
You will find options to share, publish, sort and more in the toolbar situated here

Watch live TV

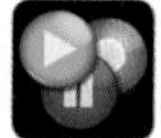

TV Catchup

Price: Free

The iPad is perfect for watching your favourite shows. Plug in a pair of headphones and you have a personal and portable TV as thin as a notebook. TV Catchup is a brilliant service that allows you to watch live Freeview TV channels through a wireless connection no matter where you are. Now you never need to miss your favourite show again – simply open up TV Catchup and select a channel to start watching live.

1: Choose a channel
Tap a channel from the bar on the left-hand side and you'll see a preview of what's on now, and what's coming on soon. Tap the top choice to play the TV show live.

2: Select the settings
Tap the cog in the top-right and you can adjust the settings within the app. Pick your television region, and choose whether your iPad can use the app via your mobile network.

Share any file to iPad wirelessly

Files United

Price: £3.99/$4.99

The iPad is great for viewing all your media, from movies to photos, but sometimes getting your stuff onto your tablet can prove more difficult than it should be. While you can sync files through iTunes, syncing can take a long time, and when you just want to add a few photos, it's barely worth the effort.

That's where Files United comes in. Grab the app on both iPad and Mac, and you can simply drag and drop the files you want on your iPad into the app on your Mac. It all happens instantly over your local Wi-Fi connection, making the transfer process considerably more painless than a time-consuming iTunes sync. Soon you'll have universal access to all your favourite media.

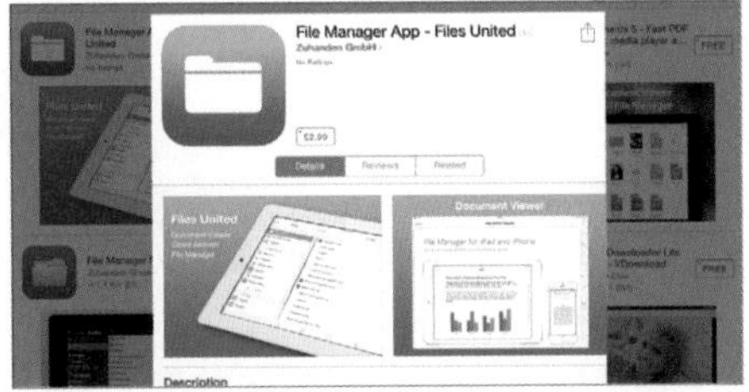

1: Get both apps
If you want to sync your files between your devices, you'll need the app on both Mac and iPad. Alternatively, just grab the iPad app for the file management tools.

"It happens instantly over your Wi-Fi"

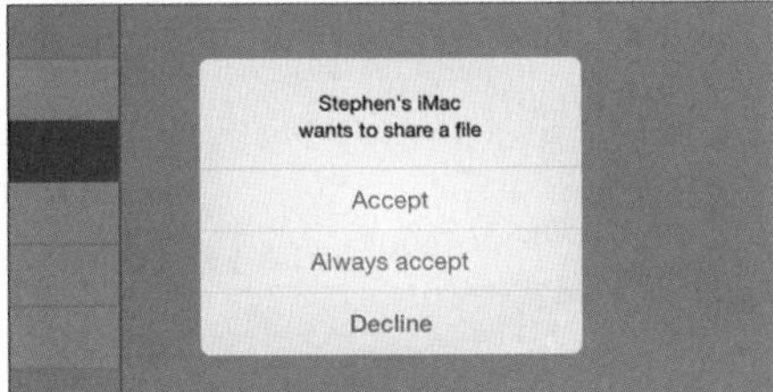

2: Transfer wirelessly
With both apps open, drag a file onto the app on your Mac and wait for a confirmation to appear on your iPad. Tap accept and your files will be added instantly.

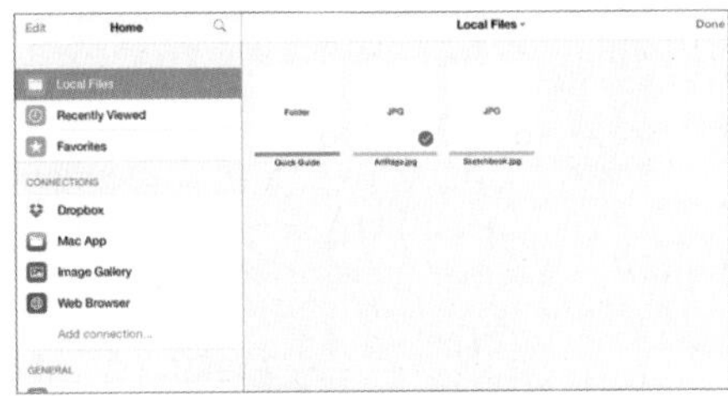

3: Manage your files
Once you have transferred your files onto your iPad, you can open them with a specific app, or tap Edit in the top-right and tap a file to see your sorting options.

Create incredible photo edits

Snapseed

Price: Free

This editing app gives you loads of powerful tools, from basic controls, like cropping and straightening, to more advanced options like vintage effects or HDR controls.

Pixlr Express

Price: Free

Pixlr Express offers a number of editing controls, as well as creative effects, overlays, borders, text and even stickers. If you want to give your photos a new twist, it's perfect.

Record shows remotely

Sky+

Price: Free

1: Sign in
When you first open the app, you'll be prompted to login with your Sky ID, the one that is linked to your Sky+ box. You can also create a new ID in-app if you don't have one or use the app without signing in.

2: Browse the TV guide
Tap on the TV Guide option at the main menu and you'll be able to see the live Sky TV listings, swipe to the left to advance through the hours of the day.

3: Record TV shows
Tap on a programme within the TV listings to bring up an info box. From here you can tap on the Record button to save the show to your SKY+ box when it is aired.

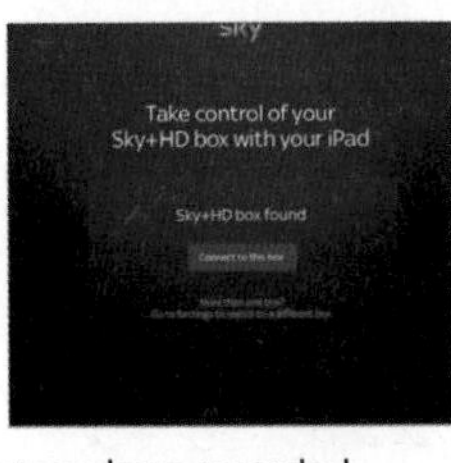

4: Connect to Sky+ box
From the main menu, tap on the Planner option and you will be prompted to connect to your Sky+ DH box. Do so and you will be able to see what you have recorded.

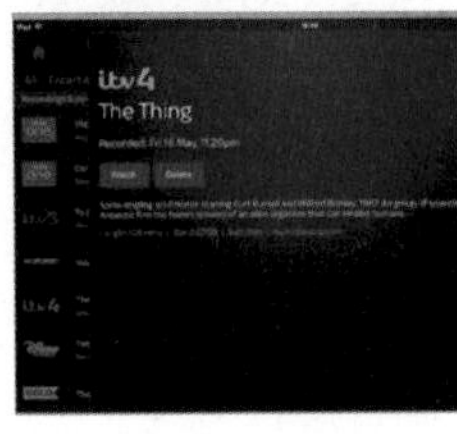

5: Control your Sky+ box
Tap on an item in the planner and you'll be able to delete it from your planner or use your iPad as a remote control to command your Sky+ box to play the item.

Microsoft Office for iPad

Apple's own Office-like apps – Pages, Numbers and Keynote – offer iPad users access to powerful document tools for free, but for those who want the tools that they're familiar with may prefer Microsoft's new Office apps for iPad. They offer plenty of functionality for free, and those with an Office365 subscription will get even more out of them, with cloud storage for your files.

Subscribing to Microsoft Office 365

Office 365 Home:	Office 365 Personal:	Office iPad apps:
£7.99/$9.99 per month (No annual contract)	**£5.99/$6.99** per month	**Free** Extra features with Office 365 account

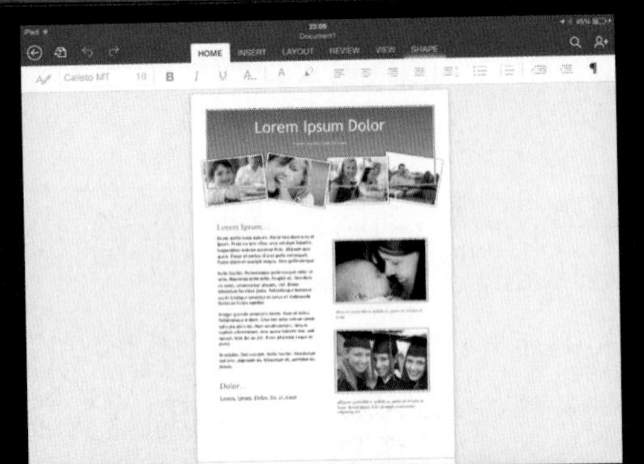

Create incredible documents

Microsoft Word for iPad

Microsoft Word has become synonymous with word processing over the last 20 years, and now that it is finally available on iPad you'll carry all its power while you're on the move. The iPad version offers plenty in the way of document control, so you can set up your page however you like. There is also a selection of pre-made themes to start your document, and a huge number of formatting options for your text. All of this is wrapped up in an interface that's very easy to understand and familiar to anyone with a modern version of Word. A fantastic way to work on your iPad.

Design powerful spreadsheets

Microsoft Excel for iPad

Who said you can't use the iPad for serious work? Microsoft's Excel app is perfect whether you want to put together a holiday planner and budget, or whether you need to create serious spreadsheets for your business. The chart options are as detailed as you would expect, with powerful formulas just a few taps away and graphs that look great and are very simple to create. The touch screen really breathes new life in to what is often referred to as a 'boring' app, which is a great bonus.

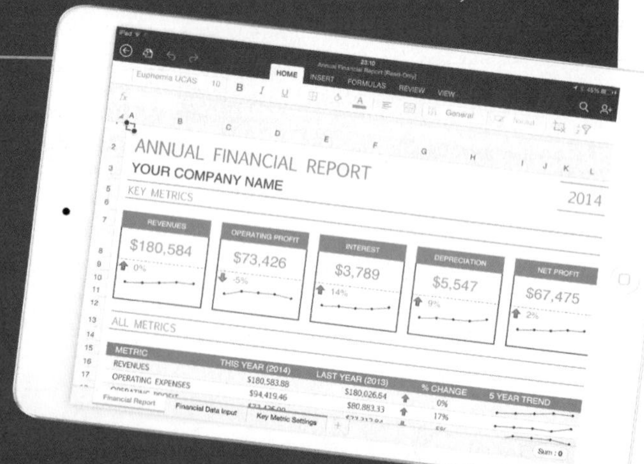

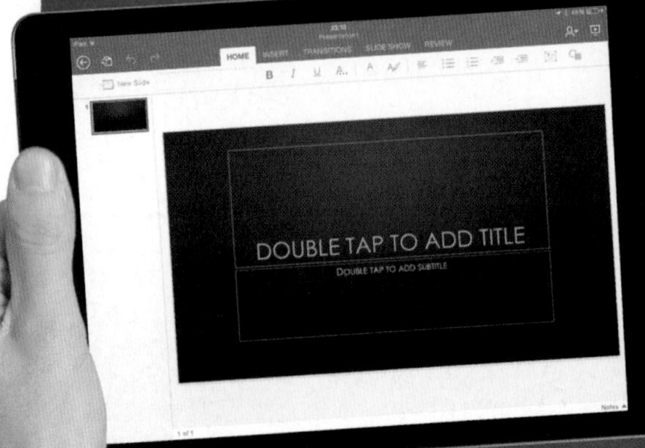

Give amazing presentations

Microsoft PowerPoint for iPad

Previously, adding animations and tapping the spacebar on a PC was enough to wow in a presentation, but now there is nothing cooler than swiping across a tablet as you present. PowerPoint brings all the brilliant transitions and object animations that you remember from the PC version of the app to the iPad, along with a whole new interface that you'll get to grips with in just a few seconds. It's an incredibly powerful tool.

Take amazing photos on the iPad

Camera+ for iPad

Price: £2.49/$2.99

The built-in Camera app on the iPad is great, but there are some options that it just doesn't offer, including timed shots, stabilisation options, and a burst mode than can be activated to take multiple shots in quick succession. Camera+ does all this and more, offering powerful editing options that you can apply straight after you take a shot.

Watch your favourite shows

BBC iPlayer

Price: Free

The BBC offers hundreds of TV shows, and often a few films, completely free as long as you pay a TV licence in the UK. And the iPad app is the perfect way to watch these shows, wherever you are. The app uses a scrolling carousel to show you recent shows, popular options, and featured programs. Tap any one and you can watch it, ad-free, right away.

What makes the app brilliant is the sheer number of excellent programs available to watch. From big-name blockblusters like Sherlock and Doctor Who, to films that have recently aired on a BBC channel, there's plenty of choice. And with an easy-to-use interface and great options to subscribe to a series you love or download shows, it's an essential app.

"What makes it brilliant is the sheer number of shows available to watch"

Read amazing comics digitally on your iPad

Marvel Comics

Price: Free

1: Download your favourites
Use the tabs at the bottom of the interface to search for comics, purchase them in-app and then download them to your device.

2: Viewing options
When you've got an issue you want to read, you can swipe between pages as you would expect, or double-tap a single panel so it fills the whole screen.

Create your own digital magazine

Flipboard

Price: Free

Flipboard is a digital platform that allows you to create your own magazine based on the topics and websites you love. When you first start with the app, you can add your own Facebook and Twitter feeds if you wish, and then choose topics that interest you so they can be added to your account. From here you'll see a grid of your chosen subjects, and you can tap one to be taken to the big stories in that topic. From here, tap the '+' button in the bottom-right to create your own personalised magazine, which will be laid out beautifully for you to catch up with later or read immediately as you wish. It's the exact content you want, presented perfectly.

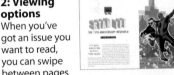

Essential apps

Burn some rubber

Asphalt 8

Price: Free

When it comes to gaming on the iPad, few titles manage the same high-octane, high-speed thrills that Asphalt 8 manages. Pick one of the 56 licenced cars and leap into a race, either as part of the offline career, or online against your friends, family or even strangers.

The latest in the Asphalt series adds aerial action to the racing, allowing you to pop 360-degree turns or barrel rolls as you work towards getting into first place. You can control your cars either by tilting the iPad, or with customisable touch-screen controls. Either way, this is an action-packed thrill ride.

"Few titles manage the same high-octane, high-speed thrills"

1: Car choices
There are 56 cars that you are able to buy within the game, including impressive powerhouses from names like Lamborghini and Ferrari. You'll have to work hard to unlock them, however.

2: Ready, Set, GO
The race is incredibly intense once it starts; you'll be bumping opponents left and right, boosting whenever you've managed to build up enough, and pulling off some huge stunts whenever you come to a ramp.

A beautiful and taxing puzzler

Monument Valley

Price: £2.99/$3.99

This brilliant and beautiful puzzle title takes its inspiration from the 'impossible' optical illusions you may have seen before. Each level gives you the goal of guiding a silent princess to the exit by revealing hidden pathways, unfolding optical illusions to make them into safe passageways, and outsmarting the enigmatic crow people. The game looks incredible, offering colourful worlds and a stunning art style. While most puzzle titles will have you assessing each level when it first appears, Monument Valley will have you scratching your head every time. The first levels are easy, but the difficulty ramps up later and solving each level is a real achievement.

It's hard to explain what makes Monument Valley so special, but the design alone is worth its price tag.

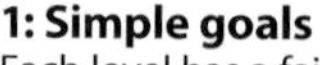

1: Simple goals
Each level has a fairly obvious end-point – usually a door or a plinth on which to place a special item. But they are all in completely unreachable locations for any normal platforming title. You need to reshape the whole landscape of the level if you want to succeed, using spinning handles or draggable sections. Just don't get a headache!

2: Mind-bending solutions
Each level comes with sections which you can grab to rotate. Sometimes you'll need to spin the whole thing around to change the angle, and doing so will transform impassable gaps into straightforward paths. Other times the path will be just that little bit more obvious, but getting to it will require a little more thought than simply tapping the exit.

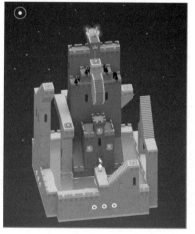

A new twist on a classic genre

Hitman GO

Price: £3.99/$4.99

Board games
The whole game is designed as a board game, with each character a piece in the game

Sneaky sneaky
You must sneak past guards and other obstacles to reach your target or goal

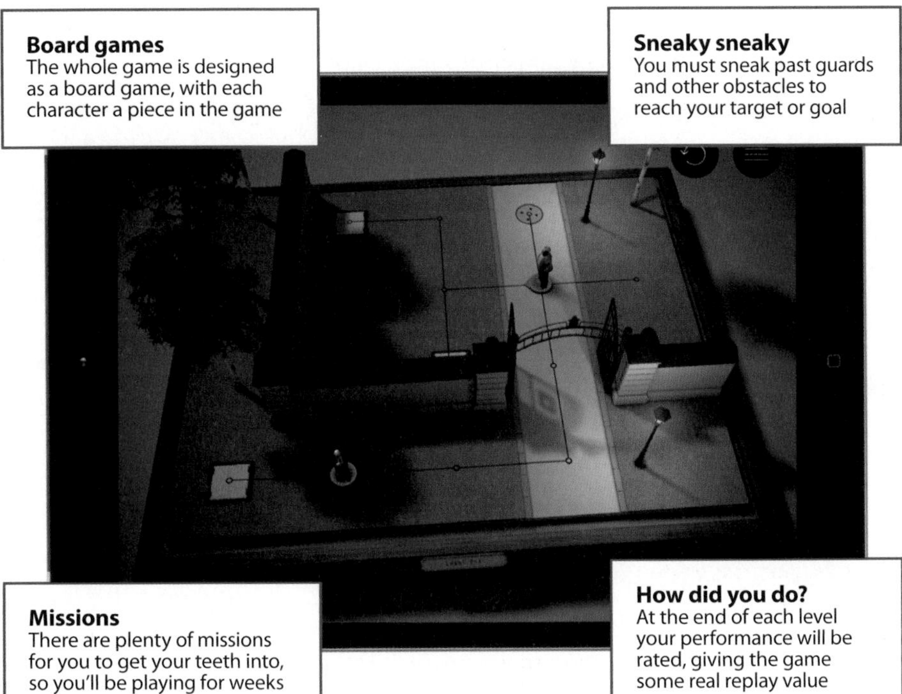

Missions
There are plenty of missions for you to get your teeth into, so you'll be playing for weeks

How did you do?
At the end of each level your performance will be rated, giving the game some real replay value

Projectile puzzling at its finest

Angry Birds HD

Price: Free/$0.99

Angry Birds HD has been an iOS stalwart for years and comes rammed full of challenging levels. Just in case you have been living on a different planet, here's how the gameplay works…

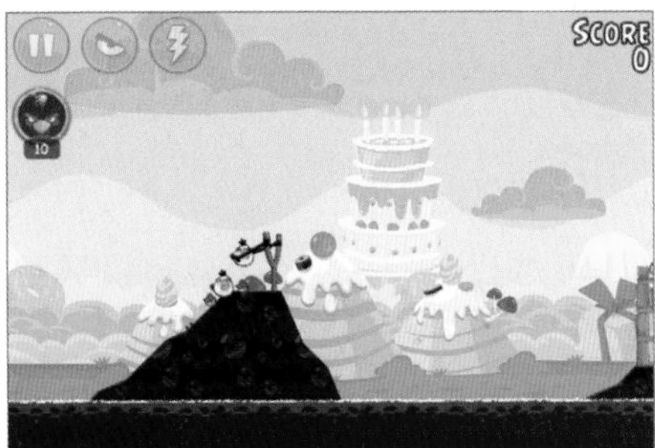

1: Pick a level
Choose a level pack and then use the catapult to launch the arsenal of birds at the pig-populated structures over to the right. Different birds have different abilities.

2: Ramp up those points
The aim is to get three stars on every level and the amount of stars you get relates to how many points you score. Clear the level with as few birds as possible to earn the big points.

Escape the system

République

Price: Free

République is a tense stealth game in which you help a young woman escape her captors. You watch the action through a series of CCTV cameras, distracting guards and picking up evidence as you go. The story is engrossing and you'll find yourself exploring levels just to find the extra newspaper and notes that give the plot some background.

Connecting the dots

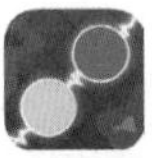

Two Dots

Price: Free

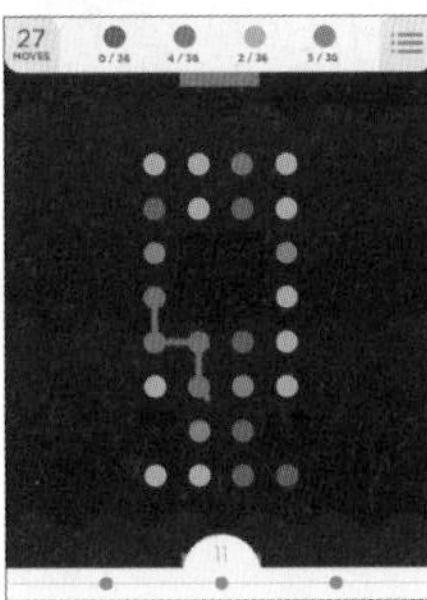

This simple game challenges you to clear a certain amount of coloured dots from the screen within a limited amount of moves (and time if you are going for the big scores). You clear dots by drawing straight lines through them (no diagonals) and drawing squares clears the screen of an entire colour. It's tricky as you have to plan moves in advance, but it's hopelessly addictive and is sure to keep you amused.

Your iPad glossary

What does it all mean? We guide you through the common features and terms that you're likely to encounter while using your iPad

Apple ID
This is the name and password you use to log in to the various Apple services, such as iTunes, the App Store and iCloud.

Application (app)
An application, or app, is a software program designed to perform one or more functions. Apps can be downloaded from the App Store.

App Store
The App Store is a digital distribution platform for Apple users. Users are able to browse, purchase and download iPad and iPhone apps from the App Store to run on their device.

Dock
The Dock on your iPad is a row of icons that can be set to appear at the bottom of your home screen in the faded block. The Dock is ever-present as you scroll through screens and allows you to access your favourite, most-used apps easily. You can add and remove apps by pressing and holding on an icon until it starts to shake and then dragging it into position.

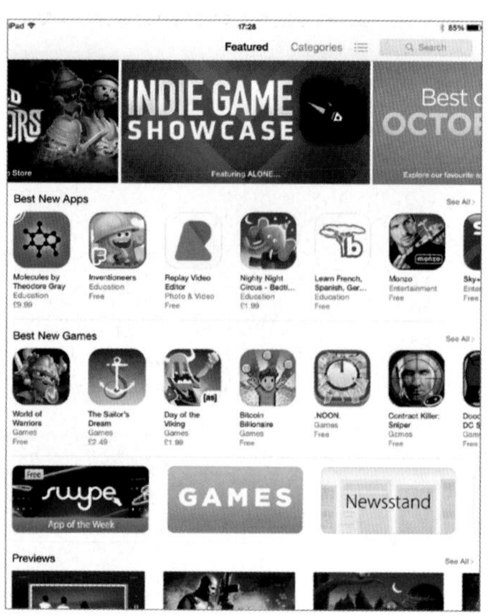

■ You can shop and browse apps by popularity and category at the App Store

Game Center
Apple's gaming portal where you can shop for new games, find friends and play against them online or compare high scores.

Gestures
These refer to the finger commands that you perform on your iPad's touch screen to carry out various functions. Multitasking Gestures were added to iOS 5 and later, that let you use five fingers to pinch to reveal your Home screen or swipe up, left or right to reveal your multitasking bar or cycle between open apps.

Gestures jargon:
- **TAP**

This is the most common and basic gesture to perform on your iPad; it involves tapping the screen with your finger.

- **DOUBLE-TAP**

This involves tapping an object twice in succession. You use this gesture mainly for zooming or highlighting text.

- **TAP, HOLD & DRAG**

Some functions, such as highlighting text, copying and pasting require that you tap and hold down on the screen and then drag your finger to select what you want.

- **PINCH**

To zoom in or to open something, place your thumb and index finger, pinched together, on screen and spread them apart. To zoom out, perform the reverse.

- **SWIPE**

Swiping is one of your primary navigational tools. You perform a left or right swiping motion with your index finger to move through app pages or images in the Photos app, for instance.

Home Button
This is the large circular button on the front of your iPad that you use to quit apps and return to your iPad's home screen.

Home Screen
This is essentially the desktop of your iPad that you see when you boot up or unlock your device. From your Home screen, you can launch apps and access your Settings.

iCloud
iCloud is a free cloud storage and syncing service available with iOS 5 and above. With iCloud you can share data, files, music and photographs between devices without the need for manual connecting, syncing and transferring.

iCloud jargon:
- **ITUNES IN THE CLOUD**

With iCloud, the music you purchase from iTunes appears automatically on all of your devices. You can also download past purchases where you want, when you want.

- **PHOTO STREAM**

With iCloud, when you take a photo on one device, it automatically appears on all of your devices. Photos transferred from a digital camera connected to your Mac will also be pushed to your mobile devices.

- **DOCUMENTS IN THE CLOUD**

If you have the same iCloud-enabled apps on more than one device, iCloud automatically keeps your documents up to date across all devices.

iOS
Whereas Macs run on an operating system called OS X, your mobile devices – iPhone, iPad and iPod touch – use iOS. A large number of changes were made with the iOS 8 update, including the introduction of iCloud Drive.

iTunes
This is Apple's flagship digital distribution centre that lets users browse, purchase and download a wide range of digital media, including music, books,

movies and TV shows. Using an Apple ID, users log in and store payment details to make downloading media quick and easy.

iTunes jargon:

FEATURED

All of the latest, most notable music, movies and TV shows will be showcased under this tab at the front of their respective store windows.

● TOP CHARTS

See what's hot and popular on the iTunes Store by tapping on this tab.

● GENIUS

This is a feature that recommends new music, films

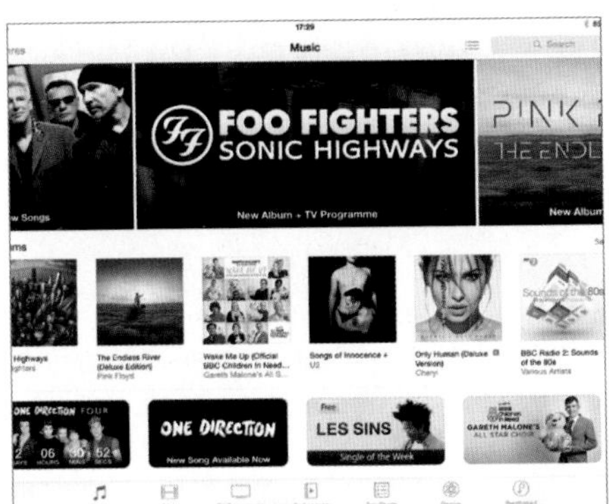

■ iTunes is the ultimate digital marketplace for buying and downloading new music and entertainment for your iPad

and shows based on what is currently in your library. Genius can also create playlists for you.

● ITUNES U

iTunes is also a great source of educational materials, and you'll find a wide range of digital books, videos and podcasts by tapping on the 'iTunes U' link.

● REDEEM

Occasionally you may be gifted a product from iTunes in the form of a code. Click on the 'Redeem' link and input the code to download the product.

Newsstand

This app comes free with iOS 7 and above, and is a place where all of your digital magazines and newspapers are stored and can be accessed.

Safari

This is Apple's premier web browsing app that comes as standard with all iPad operating systems. The app boasts a wealth of new enhancements to make surfing the web a quick and easy experience.

Settings

Accessible from the Dock or home screen, Settings is where you can tweak all aspects of your iPad as well as the apps and utilities that make it tick.

Side Switch

This is the small switch on the edge of the iPad that you can assign, via Settings, to act as a mute button or to lock your screen rotation.

Sleep/Wake Button

This is the lozenge-shaped button on top of the iPad that you use to turn your device on and off.

Wi-Fi

Wi-Fi refers to a wireless networking system that allows you to connect to the internet without any cables. You will need access to a wireless router for this to work with your iPad.

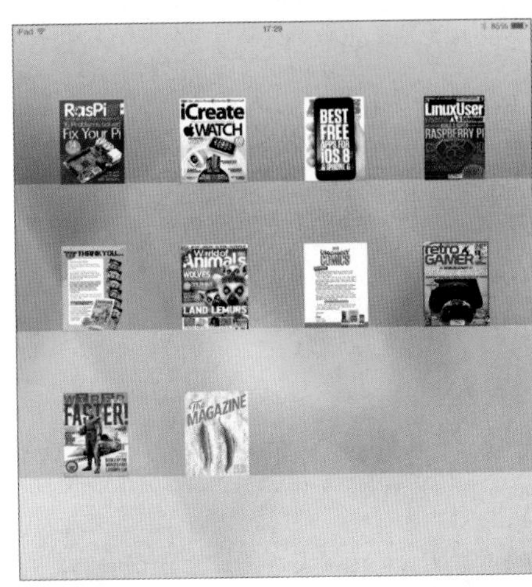

■ The Newsstand app is where all of your digital magazines and newspapers are safely stored